MY LIFE AND TIMES
OCTAVE SEVEN:
1931-1938

BY COMPTON MACKENZIE

Novels and Romances

SINISTER STREET
SYLVIA SCARLETT
GUY AND PAULINE
CARNIVAL
FIGURE OF EIGHT
CORAL
THE VANITY GIRL
ROGUES AND VAGABONDS
THE ALTAR STEPS
THE PARSON'S PROGRESS
THE HEAVENLY LADDER
HUNTING THE FAIRIES
WHISKY GALORE
KEEP THE HOME GUARD TURNING
THE MONARCH OF THE GLEN
THE RIVAL MONSTER
BEN NEVIS GOES EAST
THE RED TAPEWORM
PAPER LIVES
ROCKETS GALORE
THE STOLEN SOPRANO
THE LUNATIC REPUBLIC
POOR RELATIONS
APRIL FOOLS
RICH RELATIVES
BUTTERCUPS AND DAISIES
WATER ON THE BRAIN
VESTAL FIRE
EXTRAORDINARY WOMEN
THIN ICE
EXTREMES MEET
THE THREE COURIERS
OUR STREET
THE DARKENING GREEN
THE PASSIONATE ELOPEMENT
FAIRY GOLD
THE SEVEN AGES OF WOMAN
PARADISE FOR SALE
MEZZOTINT
THE FOUR WINDS OF LOVE:
    THE EAST WIND
    THE SOUTH WIND
    THE WEST WIND
    THE NORTH WIND

Play

THE LOST CAUSE

Verse

POEMS 1907
KENSINGTON RHYMES

History and Biography

EASTERN EPIC. VOL. I

ALL OVER THE PLACE
GALLIPOLI MEMORIES
ATHENIAN MEMORIES
GREEK MEMORIES
AEGEAN MEMORIES
WIND OF FREEDOM
MR ROOSEVELT
DR BENES
PRINCE CHARLIE
PRINCE CHARLIE AND HIS LADIES
CATHOLICISM AND SCOTLAND
MARATHON AND SALAMIS
PERICLES
THE WINDSOR TAPESTRY
THE VITAL FLAME
I TOOK A JOURNEY
COALPORT
REALMS OF SILVER
THE QUEEN'S HOUSE
MY RECORD OF MUSIC
SUBLIME TOBACCO
GREECE IN MY LIFE
CATS' COMPANY
CATMINT
LOOK-AT CATS

Essays and Criticism

ECHOES
A MUSICAL CHAIR
UNCONSIDERED TRIFLES
REAPED AND BOUND
LITERATURE IN MY TIME
ON MORAL COURAGE

Children's Stories

LITTLE CAT LOST
SANTA CLAUS IN SUMMER
TOLD
MABEL IN QUEER STREET
THE UNPLEASANT VISITORS
THE CONCEITED DOLL
THE ENCHANTED BLANKET
THE DINING-ROOM BATTLE
THE ADVENTURES OF TWO CHAIRS
THE ENCHANTED ISLAND
THE NAUGHTYMOBILE
THE FAIRY IN THE WINDOW BOX
THE STAIRS THAT KEPT ON GOING
    DOWN

Autobiography

MY LIFE AND TIMES: OCTAVE ONE;
OCTAVE TWO; OCTAVE THREE;
OCTAVE FOUR; OCTAVE FIVE;
OCTAVE SIX

MY LIFE AND TIMES

OCTAVE SEVEN

1931-1938

Compton Mackenzie

1968

CHATTO & WINDUS

LONDON

Published by
Chatto & Windus Ltd
42 William IV Street
London, W.C.2

Clarke, Irwin & Co. Ltd
Toronto

137251

Printed in Great Britain by
T. & A. Constable Ltd
Hopetoun Street, Edinburgh

To
Frasers and Maxwells galore

CONTENTS

*

ACKNOWLEDGMENTS

My grateful thanks for permission to quote letters are due to the following: The Hon. Sir Harold Nicolson, K.C.V.O., Mr Desmond Flower and Mr George Malcolm Thomson, and to Sir Rupert Hart-Davis for Hugh Walpole, the Literary Executor for W. Somerset Maugham, and the Trustees of the Letters of T. E. Lawrence for T. E. Lawrence.

I would like to offer my apologies to those literary heirs whom I have been unable to trace. I hope they will accept this general acknowledgment for material I have quoted.

C.M.

PLATES

*

FORTY-EIGHT YEARS OLD: 1931

"THE Earl of Moray gave them the full run of Darnaway Forest, where they built their 'forest hut' of moss beside the Findhorn, and during this period they continued protestants, for, dressed as always in full Highland garb, they attended the presbyterian worship in the parish kirks. But from their settling in 1838 on Eilean Aigas, a lovely islet in the river Beauly, where Lord Lovat built them an antique shooting lodge, they seem to have been devoted catholics. Eskadale, where they are buried, is two miles above their islet, and every Sunday they used to be rowed up to mass, with a banner flying, which was carried before them from the riverside to the church door."

Thus writes the *Dictionary of National Biography* of John Sobieski Stolberg Stuart (1795-1872) and Charles Edward Stuart (1799?-1880), the two brothers who claimed to be descended from Prince Charles Edward Stuart and to be the legitimist heirs to the Crown of Great Britain and Ireland.

"The brothers were courteous and accomplished gentlemen. But apart from their Stuart likeness, the sole strength of their pretentions would appear to reside in the credence and countenance accorded them by men of rank and intelligence, such as the tenth Earl of Moray, the twelfth Lord Lovat, the late Marquis of Bute, Sir Thomas Dick-Lauder, and Dr Robert Chambers."

Thus concludes the article on the Sobieski Stuarts in the *Dictionary of National Biography*, and today nobody supposes that the claim of these two brothers to be the grandsons of Prince Charles Edward Stuart through his daughter the "bonny lass of Albany" is anything but a fantasy, as much of a fantasy indeed as the imaginary tartans they invented for Scottish clans, which nevertheless are today accepted as genuine by many of those clans; I recall in particular the black and yellow of the Dress Macleod. Cunninghame Graham knew the younger of the brothers and told me that his likeness to King Charles the First was extraordinary. Nevertheless, he could not accept their claim to royal ancestry.

Undoubtedly the two brothers believed the facts for which their imagination was alone responsible and Eilean Aigas offered an encouragement to such dreams, however fantastic.

The carriage drive up to the house was on the other side of a bridge under which the Beauly came foaming and leaping from the gorge that separated Eilean Aigas on one side from the mainland. Once it had emerged from that gorge between sheer cliffs it flowed round the other side of the island as gently as sweet Afton itself. There the woodland with its undergrowth of rhododendrons and azaleas sloped down to a level green bank whitened with lilies-of-the-valley in their season. At the narrowing northerly end the river flowed in from the torrential gorge as placidly as a pool and it was shallow enough to wade in and search for the mussels in which one sometimes had the luck to find a sizable pearl. That woodland at the top of the island was magical. I have never seen nobler larches anywhere. As one wandered through it one caught a glimpse of the white scut of a roedeer or the red eye of a capercailzie. Crossbills were busy about their foraging. Brown squirrels were plentiful. And once I had the enviable sight of a woodhen carrying her chicks to what she thought was a safer place. So rare was this sight that at one time its existence used to be argued over by ornithologists. I doubt if anybody who saw those two chicks clinging to their mother's breast could bring himself to shoot another woodcock.

The house itself was still haunted by those strange brothers, not by their ghosts but by relics of them like the powder-boxes and snuff-boxes and the gothic chairs they had themselves made. My books were still on Jethou and I did not feel justified in moving them north until I had found a house of my own in the Highlands or Islands. So I acquired a billiards-table for what had been the brothers' library and used for my working room a cosy den beyond, with a kind of large cupboard at the end of it in which I wrote. I did not acquire a barge to be rowed to Mass at Eskadale Church, but I did rejoice in the magnificent comfort of the Sobieski Stuart pew as big as a parlour with thick red velvet cushions on which to kneel in a luxury of devoutness; I have never been able to enjoy such luxurious reverence since. The Lovat pew was in the gallery above, and the sensible sermons of Father Aeneas Geddes proved that brevity was as much the soul of piety as of wit.

Since I wrote of moving from Jethou to Eilean Aigas in order to pursue with ardour that passionate obsession with Scottish Nationalism I have been faintly shocked to discover among my letters and papers the evidence of what must have seemed to others an alarming, an almost unnatural confidence in my financial future. My overdraft at the Westminster Bank was £8,000 and I was pledged to reduce this annually by £1,000. I had to find over £900 a year for my endowment and life policies with the Sun Life Assurance of Canada. And by coming to Scotland I was now subject to income tax.

I was doing a certain amount of broadcasting but the fees paid then were still very low. I find a letter protesting that 15 guineas was an inadequate reward for a debate with Stephen Gwynn about the comparative merits of Irish and Highland scenery lasting for half an hour. In the reply it was explained that the recognized fee now was a guinea a minute and that the half hour would be split between Stephen Gwynn and myself, and then another letter from the producer to say that after a hard wrestle he had managed to extract 17½ guineas from the authorities.

The proofs of *First Athenian Memories* arrived during that January but I had contracted to sell outright each volume of my war memories to Cassell's for £500 a volume, and I knew I must somehow get two novels published this year. I had started a novel called *Buttercups and Daisies* in Herm, but had put it aside after an opening chapter. Newman Flower offered to publish this book in May if I could finish it before the end of February. So I got to work at once and should have managed to do so if I had not been laid up in the last week with an attack of neuritis. As it was I did not finish it till March 10th, at 4 a.m. I find noted. I then undertook to finish another novel in time for autumn publication.

I realized that however hard I worked there was no chance of my reducing the overdraft of £8,000 unless I sold my lease of Jethou for which I hoped to obtain £3,000. So after a preliminary article in one of the Sunday papers about the joys of life on a small island I advertised my willingness to sell the lease of Jethou subject to the Treasury's approval of the purchaser as a tenant of the Crown.

To advertise a small island for sale is to invite a number of enquiries from dreamers of various kinds, all of them dreaming of an idyllic life on a small island and most of them without any means to support such life. One letter has survived from the waste-paper basket and I think it is worth preserving as an illustration of what must have been that despair of so many Germans in 1931 which drove them to imagine that the witches' broth brewed by Hitler was a healthy tonic.

The letter came from Aachen:

Most respectable Mr Mackenzie,

Recently in an information published in a newspaper of here, you intend to farm out the Isle of Yarhou (Norman Isle) which belongs to you.

In consequence, I beg to draw your attention to my life-work which consists in helping people thrown into misery owing to undeserved distress. I want to give to these people a dwelling on their own soil, if they are willing to live according to God's Commandments.

Therefore, most respectable Mr Mackenzie, I beg to address myself to you with my request, asking you to help me in my work which serves the general welfare of men, in letting me the said isle, in such a way that time of lease and rent do begin only when the economy and cultivation of the isle (Agricultural and breeding cattle) produce corresponding profits.

I am obliged to be favored with such advantage, as those who I want to settle there, have no money now to enable me to pay the lease immediately. Please, do hand the isle over to me to hold it in trust for you, and in case I should not act up to my engagements, you only withdraw your aid from me.

I intend to create a new home to those who owing to want of work populate the country roads, and who in honestly looking round for work, are constantly in danger of hopeless sinking in abyss, to what bad, at least shortsighted laws do contribute.

For, what a torment is it not, to be driven to begging by hunger, to be arrested for the first time, to be robbed of man's honour, to be thrown into prison together with rabble sunk lower and lower since long, and then, perhaps, during a sole winter, poor of work, to be obliged to rove restless about, with bitterness in the heart against God and man, and loosing all sense of shame, and having no other comforter than the alcohol, so that at last the desire of being saved does no longer rise from the tired breast of people in such distress.

To prevent this, that is my life object, and that is why I appeal to all those who can help according to the words of our Lord Jesus Christ:

That thou hast done in my Name to the
most humble thou hast done it to Me

Therefore, most respectable Mr Mackenzie, please help me to perform my plan. Let me make on the isle the beginning of a great social work. Help me to build up a colony. Where the hope may be nourished that many of those who now already fail against God and man, sinking more and more into the morast (sic) of vagabondage, and being obliged to seek night's shelter in asylums, whatever rank they might have been and of whatever nationality they may be,—may again step on the way to hope of life and hapiness (sic) instead of alms, the great benefit will be conferred upon them of eating bread they earned they themselves. To help here is but our bounded (sic) duty to man and to God who has given us the Command:

Thou shallst love they fellow Creature like thyself.

Here is a field to exercise charity,—a better one can never be thought of, and on which, I hope, many 'Volunteers' will step on, who, it is true, have no money, but good sense, love and charity for their fellow creatures.

Therefore, most respectable Mr Mackenzie, I beg you to examine my plan with the most benevolent sentiments, and to let me know as soon as possible, how you take it up, suggesting the way which will be satisfactory for both parties.

In this expectation, I remain,
Most Respectable Gentleman,
Yours very truly,
X— Y—

How I must have hated writing to shatter that dream in Aachen, for the passionate sincerity of the dreamer was so clearly evident.

My own dream of finding somebody to take over the Crown lease and pay the premium of £3,000 I was asking for it was equally fragile. The weeks went by without that somebody's materializing. Toward the end of the summer I brought up Macdonald and his wife and also Keegan and his wife to live in the two cottages on the other side of the bridge where the Eilean Aigas garden was. The Macdonalds had never been out of the Channel Islands, and when they arrived I asked them what in England and Scotland had most impressed them, expecting to be told of their first experience of a railway train or the noise and size of London. Not at all. What had most impressed them was the sight of cows grazing loose. In Alderney, and for that matter in Guernsey too, all cows were tethered by a rope long enough for them to chew the cud of the day's ration of grass.

I put Kemp, my boatman, in charge of the island, little thinking that two years would pass before I should manage to find somebody of whom their Lordships of the Treasury would approve to take over my lease.

I have written in *Cats' Company* of the arrival of Sylvia with her four sons. The Thailanders, as they became in Scotland, were shocked by their first meeting with a horse and even more shocked by encountering in their own drive a flock of sheep which had stampeded across the bridge. On the other hand, motor-cars, thanks to their familiarity with an electric installation on Jethou, left them unconcerned. Finally, Stumps killed a polecat nearly as big as himself and recovered from being teased by me about the fright that the first horse had given him.

In spite of the tiresome problems of money that were incessant for the whole of the time I was living at Eilean Aigas I look back to that time as one of the golden ages I have enjoyed in my life. For this the Frasers and Maxwells galore to whom this Octave is dedicated were primarily responsible. Beaufort Castle, Farlie House, Moniack Castle . . . I lay down my pen, wondering how I shall bring you to life upon the printed page.

Simon, the 14th Lord Lovat, was one of that memorable decade of the 'nineties at Magdalen. He had created the famous Lovat Scouts for service in the South African War. They would later become one of the regiments in the Highland Mounted Brigade which Simon Lovat commanded in Gallipoli, France and Flanders. At this date he owned nearly 200,000 acres of Inverness-shire and was interested as Chairman of the Overseas Settlement Committee in a great scheme for developing land in Brazil. He had been Parliamentary Under Secretary of the Dominions Office for a year or two in the last government. Apart from his military, political and other interests he was Convener of the Inverness-shire County Council, the best they ever had, and his devotion as a Highland laird was exemplary.

I think it was this January that another Magdalen man of the 'nineties was staying at Beaufort. This was Francis Lindley[1] who had just been appointed Ambassador at Tokyo after Lisbon. One evening after dinner at Beaufort Simon Lovat, Lindley and I were talking of old days at Magdalen and were recalling famous rags of the past.

The Master of Lovat, who was then nineteen and would be going

[1] The late Rt. Hon. Sir Francis Lindley, G.C.M.G.

back to Magdalen after the Christmas vac., evidently made up his mind that contemporary Magdalen must hold its own at ragging and there was a heavy bill to pay for his demonstration.

I hear now Laura Lovat saying to me:

"It was entirely your fault, Monty, for making Simon and Frank Lindley talk about their rags of forty years ago. Poor Shimi felt he had to hold his own".

Laura Lovat was a daughter of that superb figure of what a nobleman ought to look like, Lord Ribblesdale, and a granddaughter of Sir Charles Tennant. Her brother Charles Lister had been in the Naval Division and had been killed at Gallipoli. He had been a great friend of Ronnie Knox[1] and one of so many who had they lived might have helped to build a truly great Britain after "the great war for civilization".

It had been Ronnie Knox who as I told in Octave 6 had introduced me to Laura Lovat. She was about ten years younger than myself but she always seemed to belong to my generation. She had been hostess for her father when she was only seventeen and had married Simon Lovat in 1910 before she was twenty. She was very tall and very slim, full of music and poetry. She and Faith used to play Bach and Handel duets, but the musical moment at Beaufort which returns most vividly to my memory is sitting with Laura on either side of the big fireplace in the music-room while Veronica with two candles to light the music in the fading dusk played one of Mozart's early sonatas. I went back to Eilean Aigas that evening and wrote a sonnet in an attempt to preserve that echo of the young Mozart himself, but a few days later, when I intended to make a copy of it, in a moment of aberration I flung it into the fire. So the sonnet perished and the room would one day also perish in the great fire at Beaufort. Laura herself has left us and that beloved child just ten years old is now a grandmother.[2]

Six days after myself in that January of 1931 Hugh Fraser[3] had his thirteenth birthday.

"Oh dear," Veronica sighed to me, "isn't Hugh lucky?"

"Well, he's only two days further away from Christmas than you are the other way round. Yes, January 23rd is a bit too close for a birthday as I learned when I was your age."

"It's not that," she said. "He's lucky because he was born before the Armistice and I wasn't born till two years after it. Almost two years and a month," she sighed.

Veronica's cousin, Irene Stirling, came from Keir to stay at Beaufort and I had the fortune to be considered good company by those two little girls with whom I used to wander round the island. I recall one walk

[1] The late Rt. Rev. Mgr. Ronald Knox.
[2] The Hon. Lady Maclean.
[3] The Rt. Hon. Hugh Fraser, M.P.

when we decided to cut our initials on the trunk of a tree to commemorate it. Among the crossbills and tree-creepers we carved away with my *sgian dubh* with such determination that the point of it was broken. I never look at that blunted *sgian dubh* without conjuring the scene of long ago.

I have a relic of those island walks in two letters from those little girls when I was laid out with one of my goes of neuritis. They must have been dictated to Chrissie and typed by her:

Eilean Aigas
Beauly

Dear Monty;
  I really regret about your hypochondriac illness.

Yours very sincerely

Katherine, Mary, Veronica,
Nell Fraser.

E. M. Compton Mackenzie, Esq.,
Dear Sir,
  You have my deepest sympathy. We entered into your beautiful mansion half an hour ago and since then we have been waiting in breathless suspension till we receive the news that your gracious leg is better, then we will mount the stairs and walk into your Majesty's room.

Your humble servant

Irene Katherine Teresa Stirling.

At the time of the Coronation Irene Stirling was helping in the office of the Duke of Norfolk and I was told a story which I feel sure is true.

The telephone rang and was answered by Irene Stirling.

"This is Somerset Herald," said a grave voice.

"The Earl Marshal cannot accept any calls from the Press," said Irene.

"This is Somerset Herald," the grave voice repeated with the hint of a rebuke in it.

"I don't care if it's the *Daily Express*," said Irene and rang off.

Veronica had inherited music from her mother. To Magdalen Fraser[1] had come her mother's appreciation of colour and form. She was now just seventeen, taller than her mother, as tall indeed as Mary Queen of Scots. She was at Les Oiseaux, a convent school at Westgate-on-Sea in Kent, and was under the impression that she had a vocation for the convent. Simon Lovat had refused to accept this vocation as immediately urgent and, as I remember, had ruled that any discussion of it must be postponed for at least six months. I suggested that Magdalen should do some little headline illustrations for *The Gramophone* and she did these with such attractive skill that I promised to persuade Newman Flower

[1] The Countess of Eldon.

B

to let her illustrate the head of each chapter in the novel I was proposing to write after *Buttercups and Daisies*. Magdalen's vocation like the vocation of so many schoolgirls at her age would fade away to leave one of the most beautiful young women I have known.

In a letter to me I find Laura Lovat saying that Magdalen's drawing had a Du Maurier touch surprising for someone of her generation. It was not so surprising really because Laura herself had preserved in a fragrant pot-pourri the flowers of the past. She loved Morris wall-papers and readers of my Third Octave will realize what it must have meant to me to see in the dining-room of Eilean Aigas that daisy pattern again. And like myself she found Medici prints of Botticelli upon the walls more grateful to the eye than the cult of ugliness for the sake of ugliness which by this date was already attracting the youthful eye. She, like myself, had a too literally extravagant passion for flowers. Her herbaceous border at Beaufort was a marvel of exquisite and prodigal arrangement. When I look back at those groups of *Lilium auratum* growing profusely at intervals of a few yards for about a hundred yards even I am faintly awed by the thought of the nurseryman's bill.

The two most constant visitors at Beaufort were Maurice Baring and Ronnie Knox. I was a little distressed that the children found 'Uncle Maurice' rather heavy going but I had to admit to myself that the bewitching humour of twenty years earlier seemed to have left him. I suppose he was already in the grip of that infernal Parkinson's disease which made the end of his life a slow agony. When Laura Lovat came to live at Eilean Aigas herself Maurice Baring was there until he died in 1945.

I had known Ronnie Knox since he was at Eton and with him I had much good conversation during my time at Eilean Aigas. Among his many gifts was an ability to do *The Times* crossword puzzle, a recent innovation, faster than anybody I have ever met. In those days *The Times* crossword required twice as much of the back page as it does today. I hope that the strip-tease act of the new *Times* will not lead to a fresh contraction of its allotted space.

At Farlie House a mile or so away was Bernard Constable Maxwell[1] whose wife Alice was a sister of Simon Lovat. He was 83 and had only recently given up hunting to become a formidable croquet player. I had supposed I was a fairly good hand with a mallet but I was always severely defeated by him on the Farlie lawn. I used to excuse myself to myself by supposing that 'Elsie' Maxwell's lilies which grew beside the croquet lawn distracted my attention from the game. Her speciality was white martagons but she knew a great deal about all lilies and one day would write the best handbook to lily growing that can be read; she was over eighty when she wrote it.

[1] The late Hon. Bernard Constable Maxwell.

In her late eighties Mrs Constable Maxwell would write a long book called *Avenue of Ancestors* for which I was honoured by the family in being asked to write a Foreword. This completely absorbing chronicle of Frasers, Maxwells, Welds, Howards and others can safely be called the most remarkable literary achievement ever accomplished by a woman of her age, the mother of twelve children, or indeed ever likely to be accomplished in the future. I salute her memory and as I write these words I am still sitting beside her on that big sofa in Moray Place, Edinburgh, as she adjusts her hearing aid to listen to what I am saying and to reply with winged words of charity and wisdom.

There had been a great gathering of Maxwells in the December when we arrived at Eilean Aigas for the marriage of her fourth daughter Joan to Henry Bridgeman.[1] There were two daughters left at Farlie after that wedding—Betty and Ursula[2] and the youngest son Michael aged fourteen.

At Moniack Castle was Simon Lovat's younger brother Alastair with his wife Lady Sybil. Ancient Moniack Castle was inclined to be a rather chilly residence in winter, but it never seemed cold, warmed as it was by the gaiety and boisterous energy of another delightful family of children.

In that February I was asked by representatives of the Glasgow University Nationalist Association if I would accept an invitation to stand as their candidate for the Rectorship when the election was held next October. I hesitated because I felt that if I made a much poorer show than Cunninghame Graham's triumphant second to Stanley Baldwin in 1928 such a sad anti-climax might be a political setback to the Nationalist cause. Then I was the guest of the Institute of Journalists at a dinner in Edinburgh. In the course of my speech I said, "if the journalists of Scotland choose to see that their country with a Parliament of its own again has a part to play in the future of Europe, and if they feel that profoundly, not as a journalistic stunt but with faith and fervour, then the journalists of Scotland have the future of Scotland in their keeping."

After my speech I was astonished when Sir George Waters, the editor of the *Scotsman*, told me that, although he did not agree with my political views and thought that Home Rule would be a disaster for Scotland, my speech had sent a thrill down his back and would I look him up next time I was in Edinburgh and talk it all over. To have been able to thrill that stern editor who was a dour son of Caithness made me wonder if I should be over timorous by not accepting that invitation to stand for the Rectorship.

Two evenings later there was a debate on Nationalism at the Scottish

[1] Lt.-Col. the Hon. H. G. O. Bridgeman, D.S.O., M.C.
[2] Mrs Chalmers Davidson.

Arts Club when dear Bob Boothby said that I evidently supposed the tree was dying and that we should cut off a branch and replant it to survive. He added with that lovable indiscretion for which he has been so long renowned,

"I sometimes wonder in the present muddle we are in whether he may not be right."

That indiscreet remark was flared across one of the Scottish newspapers next morning.

In the course of the debate Professor Grierson[1] observed that he was worried by the Roman Catholic and Communist influence in the National Party. I said I was shocked to find the Professor of Rhetoric at the University of Edinburgh apparently under the impression that Catholicism was a distinction without a difference from Communism.

In a letter I wrote at the time about that debate I find:

The Advocate-Depute, young Cameron[2] made a very strong speech in favour of complete independence but I cannot see him as a possible Labour candidate for an Edinburgh constituency, which I am told he is considering. I'm glad I managed to drive Will Y. Darling[3] into being more definite than he ever has been so far.

Those two or three days in Edinburgh decided me to accept the invitation to stand as a candidate for the Rectorship if it was formally offered to me; on March 3rd it came to Eilean Aigas.

The Committee of the Glasgow University Scottish Nationalist Association met this afternoon and decided unanimously to invite you to be our candidate for the Rectorial Election of October 1931. We hope that you will see your way to accept this invitation. We have very good hopes of success, and wish to start the fight immediately.

If you are in a position to accept, we intend that John MacCormick should announce your candidature at a mid-day meeting in the Union before the end of term. We are all enthusiastic about having you as Nationalist Candidate.

Four days later the President of the G.U.S.N.A. wrote:

Your candidature was announced to-day at a meeting of about four hundred students in the Union. The meeting began noisily, but Mr MacCormick kept it well in hand and made all his points.

The main point was my promise to be a working Rector if I was elected. For many years now the Rectors of Scottish Universities with the exception of St Andrews had been prominent politicians. The Glasgow students had made an exception when they elected Poincaré as Rector during the First World War, but they then reverted to political figures whose Rectorial duties were considered fulfilled by delivering a

[1] The late Sir Herbert Grierson, Litt.D., LL.D.
[2] The Hon. Lord Cameron, D.S.C.
[3] The late Sir William Y. Darling, C.B.E.

Rectorial Address. The Rector was Chairman of the University Court but attendance at that was delegated to the Assessor he nominated. I pledged myself to attend the monthly sessions of the University Court and devote myself to the interests of the students I represented. The Rectors of Scottish universities are survivals of the mediaeval administrators of the European universities on whose model they were founded. Oxford, Cambridge and Durham are Masters' Universities. The undergraduate even when he has taken his B.A. has no status. Technically a B.A. of Oxford is still liable to be summoned before the Proctor for appearing in the streets after 9 p.m. without his gown.

John MacCormick had been the inspiring influence in persuading his fellow students to shake the whole of Scotland by nearly getting Cunninghame Graham elected as Rector. It had then been my job to announce his candidature to a mid-day meeting in the University Union. I knew what it meant when such a meeting began noisily. John Mac-Cormick himself would be elected Rector of Glasgow University twenty years hence.

Undoubtedly the two students who did most to make the campaign for my election as Rector a success were Harold Collier and Archie Lee. The latter, an Orcadian, is now one of the key figures of the B.B.C. in Glasgow; Harold Collier was to die a year or two later. He was Jewish and already afflicted with that exophthalmic goitre which for its victims doubles the pace of time and makes them impatient of what they think is the slowness of other people. The service rendered to my candidature was his brilliant editorship of the *Glasgow University Nationalist*, the five numbers of which that came out at intervals from May until the eve of the election in October were incomparably superior to the magazines published by the Tories for Sir Robert Horne, the Liberals for Professor Gilbert Murray, the Labour people for Tom Johnston, and the New Party for Sir Oswald Mosley. Moreover, no Rectorial magazines that I have seen during the last thirty-five years has produced as much forceful wit and as many brilliant cartoons.

Harold Collier and Archie Lee came up to spend a night or two at Eilean Aigas in the Easter recess, and after that visit Harold Collier wrote a five-page presentation of me which was a model of what such a brief biography should be. It wound up:

"It is the darkest hour before the dawn. The monotonous rush of the surrounding river has lulled all life to sleep. From the grey house amid the green trees come faintly the exquisite strains of Mozart played by the master hand of Kreisler. As the last echoes fade into the night, in a lamp-lit room, suffused with the glow of a peat fire, a human being lays down his pen. He brings his mind back from that world where paper is flesh and ink is blood. Slowly he extinguishes the light. And so to bed."

That first number of the *Glasgow University Nationalist* would appear in

May. In it Collier reprinted an article I had written for the *G.U.N.* in 1928 when Cunninghame Graham was the Nationalist candidate. It was entitled "The Thistle and the Donkeys" and it expresses so much what I was still feeling in 1931 and much of what I am still feeling in 1966 that I reprint it in this Octave.

"I have heard it called romanticism, this National movement which is stirring all over Scotland. Nothing would be less accurate as a label for what is an almost totally practical creed. If you want the fragrant air of lost causes and impossible loyalties the Liberals will have to provide it when they dream their dreams in a melancholy twilight, those phantasmal figures in frock coats who haunt the farther bank of that wide river of war, and who are as unlikely ever to be ferried across into the present as King Arthur is to rule again in Avalon. Ghosts! Ghosts! We hear rumours of a revival of Liberalism, but the evidence for it is as unsatisfactory as for most spiritualistic experiments. So many dishonest mediums that will raise and describe the leaders of the Liberal Party! And yet, were I a young man, I should prefer to go spirit-rapping with Mr Lloyd George than to lie down weakly in front of the Tory glacier and allow myself to be crushed into commonplace extinction. There is something profoundly disturbing in the thought of anyone's being ready to surrender himself to that ponderous aggregation of ice and rubbish; it implies a devitalization that is just a little too discouraging. However, the conventional young men and women who have made up their minds, or rather who have had their minds made up for them, to vote for Mr Baldwin, are not subjects for argument, because such people are slaves, and it is hardly decent for a free man to taunt a poor devil of a slave about his fetters.

"Fabre once tried an experiment with the caterpillar of the pine-moth, which travels in a procession of myriads and does as much damage to the pines in the south-west of France as the Tory Party has done to Europe since the entry of Disraeli into politics. Fabre set these processional caterpillars to walk round and round a flower-pot in an eternal circle, and the silly fellows did it. That is the state of the Tory Party. They are not actually despoiling pine-trees at present; but for the last four years they have been following one another round a flower-pot. And Mr Baldwin asks the electorate of Scotland, Wales and England to send him back and lead a long trail of caterpillars round a flower-pot.

"The Labour candidate, Mr Rosslyn Mitchell, is another proposition. He, so far as I have been able to understand from the expounding of the Labour policy by various Labour friends, believes earnestly in what he calls Home Rule for Scotland. If Home Rule is to be the affair of milk with a lot of water added from the parish pump which is what is called Home Rule in Northern Ireland and what the Labour Party calls Home Rule, better it should be postponed indefinitely.

"The Nationalist Association believes that nothing matters except the state of the country, and it refuses absolutely to recognize the right of any political party to use the Rectorial Election as a drying-ground for the dirty linen of party politics.

"The students of this ancient University have in this year of grace a chance to do something that within the range of my reading and experience I cannot recall was ever offered to students before. It will not matter half-a-column in a daily newspaper whether Mr Baldwin or Sir Herbert Samuel or Mr Rosslyn Mitchell be elected Rector. The only fire that will kindle will be in the kitchen-grate next morning. But if the students of Glasgow University elect Mr Cunninghame Graham they will set a nation on fire, and do more to influence the future of Scottish history (and for that matter Imperial history) than any students ever did before them. Incidentally, they will provide the world with the pleasure of reading a Rectorial Address by a master of prose.

"Style is the man, and Mr Cunninghame Graham's style is more definitely so than any I know, for it is fine and supple and sharp and well-tempered as a Toledo blade. It was fashioned in no library; it was hammered out upon the anvil of a long and chivalrous life. Look back through the social progress of sixty years, and you will always find him in his ideas a decade or more ahead of most of his contemporaries. He was fighting—literally fighting on that day in Trafalgar Square—for the cause of Labour twenty years before the students who are thinking of voting for Mr Rosslyn Mitchell as the representative of progress were born. Now after a life of variety and accomplishments, after travelling the world round and upholding the tradition which once kept this country more closely in touch with European civilization than the intellectually more isolated English, after an intimate knowledge of the culture in Europe as much akin to the genius of Scotland as it is remote from that of England, Mr Cunninghame Graham has decided that the only thing which matters to him now is the preservation of his country's life.

"To ask students to vote for Mr Cunninghame Graham because he is a good writer or fighter is to insult their intelligence and his, but I could not resist the opportunity of paying him homage as an artist of life and letters. It is the cause as well as the man which counts in this Rectorial. If Lord Birkenhead were to declare himself a Nationalist I would vote for him; I do not believe that I could withhold my support even from that comic Savonarola, Sir William Joynson-Hicks, in such a case. Let Glasgow University lead the country. It would be a glorious achievement to upset the political apple-cart; Glasgow University can do it. *Nemo me impune lacessit*. Shall political donkeys devour that thistle, ay, and thrive and grow fat on the diet?"

I did not suppose for a moment that I had the slightest chance of being elected Rector, and when it was announced that Gilbert Murray would be the Liberal candidate I felt that the best I could hope for was third place. However, I had so many other things to occupy my mind that beyond suggesting the names of some people who might be willing to give Harold Collier testimonials to use for his magazine, I was in fact beginning to regret I had accepted the invitation to stand, when correspondence with my supporters in Glasgow was added to my already uncomfortably heavy correspondence.

Three gardening talks I did for the B.B.C., that discussion with Stephen Gwynn about the comparative beauty of Irish and Scottish scenery, and finally a discussion about Gallipoli with Sir Ian Hamilton on the sixteenth anniversary all added to my correspondence. I was dictating to Nellie Boyte and Chrissie MacSween nearly 200 letters a week. All my life I have tried to answer letters. If somebody has taken the trouble to write an encouraging letter to me I am always grateful. When one or two of my contemporaries have boasted that they ignored 'fan' letters I have always rebuked them. A novelist who seeks to earn his living by persuading the public to read his books is as much a servant of the public as an actor, and I have little patience with novelists who imagine that like poets they are living in an intellectual sanctuary.

After the Gallipoli broadcast Sir Ian Hamilton wrote from Kilbryde Castle, Dunblane:

Dear C.M.

Clearly we have made quite a scoop! Every one here is excited. I might have won a great victory—and so you feel too no doubt.

As to the libel actions they have not yet begun to get a move on.

Yours
Ian Hamilton

I find a carbon copy of the letter I wrote in reply:

Yes, everybody seems to have enjoyed the discussion except General X who wrote a furious letter to the B.B.C. An astonishing thing that he should still be seeking to justify himself to himself. You may remember I had a letter from him about Gallipoli Memories.

Did you see Sidney Moseley's sneer in the Daily Herald, *asking what you would have done in a discussion with Ashmead Bartlett? By a strange coincidence poor Ashmead Bartlett died the following day.*

I have been having a vile go of the sciatica, so forgive a typewritten letter. My duty to Lady Hamilton . . . I need hardly tell you what a great pleasure and privilege it was for me on the night of April 25th.

That February British International Pictures had announced definitely their intention to make a film of *Carnival*. I told in my previous Octave of the amount of time I wasted in discussing a proposed film about Oxford life. I cannot remember what they were going to pay me for that, but whatever small sum it was the same was offered for the film rights of *Carnival*. Matheson Lang had the impudence to announce that *Carnival* was his title and that he was going to make a film of the play for which he had stolen the title from my book.

I extract a sentence from a letter which was printed in the *Daily Film Renter*:

"I can easily accept Mr Matheson Lang's assurance that he had never heard of my book *Carnival*, for I know from a long personal experience in what an atmosphere of remoteness from contemporary literature the average actor-manager lives."

At the end of February I received a letter from the Scenario Director of British International Pictures:

"At the moment I am not so much concerned about the question of the title as I am delighted—as I feel you will be—that this subject is going to be handled by a young director of such talent as Anthony Asquith. I may say, in strict confidence, that I have been rather sitting on this subject until a director came along who one knew would really 'feel' your story: this Asquith does."

I was naturally delighted by this news and when Puffin came up to Eilean Aigas to discuss the film I felt all would be well. Alas for my hopes, the film people surrendered to Matheson Lang and decided to call *Carnival* by some idiotic film studio name "Dance, Little Something or Other". Was it 'lady'? On top of that the casting was all too often badly misjudged. I saw some rushes at Elstree and came away resolved to avoid exasperating myself by ever seeing the completed film. It was not Puffin's fault. As a young director he was not yet in a position to dictate to the fossilized remains of the silent film industry. I recall walking round the island with him and prophesying that—the title comes back to me *Dance Little Lady*—would not be a success, let alone a great success.

In contrast to the disappointment of the film version of *Carnival* I was cheered that Spring by the French translation of the book published by the Revue Française in a series of translations called *Les Grands Étrangers*. This translation was made by Mademoiselle M. Canavaggia and could not have been better.

In my last Octave I mentioned an article I wrote for the *Sunday Pictorial*, advocating the equalization of freight charges by the railways in accord with post office practice with letters and parcels. Correspondence on this subject was heavy but I had too many other things to occupy me this winter to lead a crusade. Reading through some of those letters today I am convinced that equalization of freight charges would do more to justify British Railways than raising fares and freight charges. So long as these preposterous fares and freight charges continue the great wen of London will swell and swell. Presumably those who brought about the nationalization of our railways supposed that it was for the benefit of the country's economy. Why then do they make no attempt to use them for that purpose?

In my Second Octave I wrote a brief and inaccurate paragraph about my choice of West Bromwich Albion as a signpost to my own fortune. A history of West Bromwich Albion by Peter Morris helps me to correct that paragraph. It was in 1891, when I first went to Colet Court, that I began to back West Bromwich Albion, partly because a schoolfellow whom I did not like was backing Aston Villa and partly because I felt that Aston Villa was having it too much its own way.

In 1892 I had the pleasure of having backed the winner of the Cup when West Bromwich Albion beat Aston Villa at the Oval. Three years later Aston Villa would beat West Bromwich Albion at the Crystal Palace and five long years of school lay before me. West Bromwich emerged from the Second Division in the year I went up to Oxford and went down again at the end of the 1904-5 season, when I spent the saddest months of my life. West Bromwich Albion remained in the Second Division until 1911, the year in which my first novel was published, and were runners-up for the Cup in 1912 when *Carnival* was published. In 1927 they went down into the Second Division and I had that desperate money struggle.

Now in this year 1931 West Bromwich Albion not only went up into the First Division but won the Cup as well. As a result I began to hope that perhaps after all I might be second in the Rectorial, and with somewhat excessive optimism that Jethou would be sold and my financial stress relieved.

I recall telling Gilbert Harding about this mascot of mine when I met him at one of Mrs Roebuck's super-ceilidhs. Christina MacPherson Roebuck was a Skye woman who was the cordon ultramarine of Edinburgh cooks. She had been many years in the U.S.A. where she had married but was now separated and she had a hospitable flat at the top of 1 South Charlotte Street with a young daughter and Moray McLaren as a lodger. More of Christina Roebuck later. It was David Cleghorn Thomson who told me that a young schoolmaster was anxious to meet me.

"You can just be kind to him for a minute or two," I was coached by David.

I have as a souvenir of that meeting a letter from St Andrew's Priory, Canaan Lane, Edinburgh dated May 16th 1931:

Dear Mr Mackenzie,

I do hope you have not forgotten that you once (or rather twice) asked me to come and see you in your island. I felt at the time that they were not merely empty invita-

tions and I have been looking forward ever since to being able to come and see you. And my desire has been whetted just lately by an orgy of reading all your books. I've just finished Fairy Gold *for the second time. I first read it at Truro—four years ago.*

You were expected in Edinburgh last week end. I was hoping to see you but you didn't come.

I don't see much of David these days—he dislikes me. I always find it terribly hard to forgive people who do that—and harder still to go on liking them.

We've been having a hellish time lately with our school. The Abbot has been making an Abbatical visit and we are waging a losing battle with the Education Authorities. I'm very tired of it.

So I write to you—I told you once you were my literary hero—perhaps that depressed you—I hope not.

May I come and see you one week end?—and when?

My depression will vanish as I cross the Forth Bridge.

I hope you get this soon and that I shall hear from you—

Yours v. sincerely
Gilbert Harding

I have a notion that Gilbert Harding left Edinburgh that autumn, for he never came to Eilean Aigas. I lost sight of him for many years and met him again when he was managing a B.B.C. broadcast from the Cambridge Union. I had first seen him at the Cambridge Union when he spoke in the debate I wrote of in my last Octave. Our friendship was unbroken until his death. I am glad to think that he and I are back to back in a gramophone record of *Face to Face*.

At the end of June we had the agreeable excitement of a visit by the Prince of Wales to Beaufort. He was to arrive in his Puss Moth before tea-time on a stretch of meadowland beside the Beaufort woods.

Faith and I had to go to Strathpeffer that afternoon to open a cake and sweet sale in aid of the Mòd at Dingwall, but we were on the landing-field by four o'clock, waiting with other people for the plane's arrival. A message came to say the Prince had been delayed and would not arrive before half-past seven. So we all sat down at a huge table piled with cakes of every kind. After tea Simon Lovat suggested some of us should go along to watch the salmon-netting which he had arranged for the Prince's entertainment. We had hardly arrived at the netting when the Prince's scarlet Puss Moth was sighted. Simon Lovat and Lochiel[1] dashed into a car to drive off at full speed to the landing-ground. Mackintosh[2] offered Faith and me a lift in his pre-war Daimler, as spacious as an Edwardian boudoir, and incidentally the model for Ben Nevis's pre-war Daimler in *The Monarch of the Glen*.

---

[1] The late Col. Sir Donald Cameron of Lochiel, K.T.
[2] The late Col. A. D. Mackintosh of Mackintosh, C.B.E.

"I told Simon it was a mistake to bring us up here," said Bernard Constable Maxwell, shaking his head as he got into the Daimler.

"Just like him, just like him," said Mackintosh. "I doubt if he and Lochiel will get there in time to receive the Prince."

The Chief of Clan Chattan was celebrating his eightieth birthday and was not going to let that Daimler behave like Simon Lovat's car. I recall Mrs Mackintosh's saying,

"I hope the Prince won't do what his father did once."

We asked what that was.

"Why, when King George came to Moy for the Twelfth he refused to let the women of the party join him at lunch because he said my cape would scare the grouse."

She pointed to a black and orange check tweed cape hanging up in the car.

We arrived at the landing-ground just as the Prince was walking along with his Cairn terrier to a waiting car and we drove on after him to Beaufort. The Prince had gone to change. Presently he appeared in a kilt of the Rothesay tartan which had been specially woven for him in hard tack, a combination of wool with linen that was the regular material for a laird's kilt once upon a time. I wonder if such material is being woven anywhere today. I ventured to admire his kilt when I was talking to him after being presented.

"And I rather like those brogues you are wearing," he said. "Would you mind giving me the name of your bootmaker and would you mind if I had them copied?"

I said quickly that the Captain of Dunstaffnage was the designer of the brogues I was wearing, which were made by Sinclair of Nile Street, Glasgow, and I was sure Dunstaffnage would be flattered.

In due course those brogues were copied and worn by the younger members of the Royal Family instead of the over-embossed brogues of older members. Years later at a small gathering to meet the Duke of Windsor in Upper Brook Street I was wearing a pair of those brogues in black leather, and the Duke whom I had not met since this time at Beaufort said to me,

"I see you're still wearing those excellent brogues of yours."

In that June of 1931 I was working from dusk to dawn to finish my novel *Our Street* by the beginning of July in order that Cassell's could publish it in the autumn. In March *First Athenian Memories* had been published and the reviews had been friendly. I had been grateful for a letter from Eric Holt-Wilson[1] who as one of the heads of M.I.5 had reported so generously on my work in Athens after he returned to London that we got all I had asked for. I told about his visit in Octave Five.

---

[1] The late Brigadier Sir Eric Holt-Wilson, C.M.G., D.S.O.

"War Office
Whitehall
S.W.1.
5th May 1931

"Dear Mackenzie,

"I have just read with great interest your *First Athenian Memories*, and much enjoyed your vivid pictures of those days.

"You may remember that early in 1916 I was sent out to Egypt, and then on to you, to see how things were shaping in the 'I' World, after the Dardanelles collapse.

"The first impressions of Egypt in February 1916 were that there were scores of under-employed Generals, surrounded by a dense cloud of Intelligence Officers, mostly sleuthing each other, and owing allegiance to about a dozen different chiefs!

"I heard little of your lone outpost, until I got an urgent cable from K[1] saying that C[2] would like me to run over and look you up. I remember being much impressed by your unusual grip of your task; and you probably remember that I was able subsequently to get a good many of your difficulties straightened out by old C. on my return.

"The E.M.S.I.B.[3] as an agreed condensation of 'I' forces took shape in March 1916, as a result of reports I drew up for Egypt to send to London. I do not think the Malta conference had much to do with it, except to take note of its foundation.

"If you are writing up any further Athenian Memories and would care for any facts and dates to be checked on matters outside Greece, I have old records here, and should be only too glad to read any of your MSS for you, so far as it concerns the E.M.S.I.B. or the London end of your work of those days.

"What do you make of B.T.'s[4] book on the subject? He seems to have made a dead set against your French colleague, de R.,[5] and I presume you may have something to say on this in your next essay!

"Let me know if I can be of any assistance to you.

Yours sincerely
Eric Holt-Wilson"

I wrote back to thank Eric Holt-Wilson but said I did not think I should have to consult his files because I had triplicate copies of what I thought was important. We shall hear more of this letter next year.

Then suddenly just after that visit of the Prince of Wales I received a

[1] The late Maj.-Gen. Sir Vernon Kell, K.B.E., C.B.
[2] The late Captain Sir Mansfield Cumming, K.C.M.G., C.B., R.N.
[3] Eastern Mediterranean Special Intelligence Bureau.
[4] The late Sir Basil Thomson, K.C.B.
[5] The late Count de Roquefeuil.

letter from T. F. R. McDonnell to say that he had been grossly libelled by me on page 187.

It was a memory of the Stop the War meeting in Trafalgar Square on a Sunday afternoon in September 1899.

"There have been many famous gatherings in Trafalgar Square, but I should doubt if there was ever a larger number of stupid people gathered together in it than on that September afternoon. Not a single one of the orators who were haranguing the crowd from the pedestals of the lions had a chance of making his voice heard above the roaring of *Rule Britannia* by the crowd. . . . I caught sight of McDonnell whose tumbled red hair had nearly as much eloquence as his own elegant tongue. McDonnell was an elder brother of Sir Michael McDonnell, who is now Chief Justice of the Supreme Court of Palestine, a classmate and a friend of mine at St Paul's . . . (he) was standing there between the paws of one of the lions and shaking his fist like the good Irish patriot he was at the beery exhalation of *Rule Britannia* by the mob."

Newman Flower, like all publishers, dreaded a libel action, and finally it was arranged with McDonnell's lawyers that the page should be re-written and a footnote of apology added. On August 2nd I was writing to Newman Flower:

Of course you will charge up the expenses of this tiresome business to me. I must say I resent the blighter's getting away with it; but obviously it's a matter of my word against his and a jury would be bound to accept his. I can still see him being helped down from the plinth by a couple of policemen and led away out of reach of the angry crowd. I could actually swear which lion he was standing by and moreover could add that he was wearing a dark suit and no hat.

I am sending off by this post the first fifty galleys of Our Street. Will you give me the latest possible date for Magdalen Fraser to do the drawings. The young lady has been away in France and I have just got in touch with her again.

About eight years later when I was looking through some old numbers of *The Pauline* in the island of Barra I read in the December number of 1899 a report of the forty-sixth Anniversary meeting of the Union on October 26th at which several honorary members were present. Among these was Mr T. F. R. McDonnell, St John's College, Cambridge, ex-President of the Cambridge Union. The subject for debate was "That this House strongly disapproves of the African policy of Mr Cecil Rhodes".

"Mr McDonnell talked mainly off the point about many things; he spoke of the Transvaal, Machiavelli, the woes of Ireland and Trafalgar Square. He told the House a story of what he did there last month, and of what two policemen did to him."

I must say I do regret that I was never able to see the expression on Mr McDonnell's face when my counsel in cross-examination asked him how he accounted for that speech if, as he claimed, he had never attended a meeting in Trafalgar Square in his life.

T. F. R. McDonnell was in the Malay Civil Service and had written to me that his position in the service had been damaged by what I had written in *First Athenian Memories*. That seems a poor excuse for what he must have known was a lie.

With typical generosity Newman Flower insisted that Cassell's would pay the £200 which that corrected page and note of apology cost. Magdalen Fraser's delicious illustrations for *Our Street* were gathered in and the book was published late that autumn. By an agreeable coincidence on the morning of the day I wrote these last words I received a letter from a French publishing firm to say that they were sending me the schoolbook in which the Second Class in English would be tackling the extract from *Our Street* I had authorized them to use.

At the end of that July there seemed at last good hope of finding somebody to take over the Crown lease of Jethou. Faith went down to make arrangements about furniture, books and gramophone records. I had been offered £2,500 but I was holding out for £3,000. Finally Walter Martin of Guernsey, the man who introduced Panatellas to the British smoker, after going to £2,750 offered to toss Faith for the remaining £250. She won and I was immensely relieved early in August to have her telegram to say that Jethou had been sold. Unfortunately, after waiting nearly four months to give or withhold their consent, their Lordships of the Treasury refused to accept Martin as a Crown tenant.

My practice has always been to lighten a financial blow by indulging in some extravagance. While reading André Maurois' enthralling life of Balzac, so admirably translated by my old friend Norman Denny, I was encouraged to find that the Colossus of the novel always did the same.

In *First Athenian Memories* I had paid a tribute to the Sunbeam car which had carried me safely through various exciting experiences in 1916. The Sunbeam people wrote to ask leave to print my testimonial in a leaflet they intended to distribute about the Sunbeam. I asked them if they would be willing to let me have a Sunbeam by paying for it in three years without any preliminary payment. They agreed, and Cecil Pollard with his brother drove it up from London. Faith had learnt to drive but while I was perfectly willing for her to drive me in our second-hand Austin I felt the Sunbeam was too big an undertaking. So the Austin was sold and I secured a green Wolseley Hornet for Faith.

While she was still in Jethou Bob Boothby came for a night to Eilean Aigas on his way to shoot up in Caithness with Sir Archibald Sinclair[1] before going the rounds of his East Aberdeenshire constituency which he loved as dearly as his constituents loved him.

---

[1] The Rt. Hon. Viscount Thurso, K.T.

"Anything exciting going on behind the political scenes, Bob?" I asked.

"Nothing at all."

"Well," I said as we took our lamps up to our bedrooms, "you'll be enjoying a jolly vacation away from the humbug of Westminster."

Next morning when Bob Boothby left for Caithness in his Humber Snipe I drove with him as far as Bonar Bridge, with Ashie Macrae, our chauffeur, following in the Austin to take me back; the Sunbeam had not yet arrived.

At Bonar Bridge I bade Bob farewell.

"I may look in on you again before I go south at the end of next month," he said.

"Unless you're fetched back by some political crisis. From what I can make out in the papers the financial situation is getting tricky."

"That'll settle itself," said Bob comfortably. "Ramsay MacDonald has gone to Lossiemouth. All looks quite peaceful at the moment."

And Bob drove on northward in a serene holiday mood, unaware that the Bank of England was in the position of one of its own clients called upon to pay off an overdraft.

I quote from *The Windsor Tapestry*:

"On August 9th the Old Lady of Threadneedle Street flung herself on her back in the traditional style of hysterical matrons, drummed with her legs on the pavement, and howled for Mr Ramsay MacDonald to come down from Lossiemouth and restore her. Mr MacDonald drenched the Old Lady with sal volatile from the Finance Committee, but to no purpose. When the Cabinet met, the opinion was expressed that the hysterics were being prolonged with the intention behind most female hysterics of having her own way. It was even suggested, though of course not in so many words, that the Old Lady of Threadneedle Street had been carrying on with Mr Baldwin and Sir Herbert Samuel as well as with Mr MacDonald and that as a result she bore in her womb the embryo of a three-headed bulldog whose name—National Government —had already been chosen. And the Cabinet resented Mr MacDonald's attempt to saddle them with the responsibility of procuring an abortion by doing what the Old Lady wanted. In the end the King travelled down to London from Balmoral by the night train on Saturday August 22nd and according to popular gossip let loose so much Admiral's language at Mr MacDonald that he frightened him into accepting the paternity of the National Government of which the Old Lady of Thread-needle Street was safely delivered on August 25th.

"The alacrity with which Mr Baldwin entered one of those destructive Coalition Governments he had so much deprecated in 1920 is a remark-able instance of his self-sacrificing patriotism, and the modesty with

which he consented to serve under Mr MacDonald is an equally remarkable instance of his political skill."

My own finances did not allow me to waste any emotion on the
finances of the Old Lady of Threadneedle Street and the other banks.
When the Treasury refused to accept Walter Martin as a Crown tenant
of Jethou I knew that there was no chance of finding another applicant
before next Spring. Nevertheless, I did not worry. I suppose that if one
is called upon to fight pain as much as I was one is so deeply preoccupied
with the effort that one has no time to worry about anything and when
one is free of pain one's mind is occupied by making up for lost time
with the work of the moment. Release from violent pain is such a mental
relief that one feels capable of settling any problem financial or otherwise.
I am fortunate, too, in my friendship with cats. Dogs are too sympathetic;
they encourage their owners to worry. The cats who own people dis-
courage them from worrying about anything except their own comfort
and well-being.

In spite of the enthusiastic belief of my supporters in the Rectorial
campaign I did not think I had a chance of being elected in October.
The Distributists were anxious to put up G. K. Chesterton again. He
had stood as a Liberal in 1925 and had run fairly close to Austen
Chamberlain. G. K. had refused to stand again and speaking at the
Union to a Distributist gathering he had advised them to vote for me.
This enabled the anti-Nationalists to argue that the Distributist support
of my candidature was a Popish plot in disguise.

In spite of endless quarrels among themselves due to mutual jealousies
the Nationalist paper under Harold Collier's skilful editing continued to
appear. One of the quarrels was about who had lost the testimonial
Frank Swinnerton had kindly provided for me.

They were jugginses to go and lose it, he wrote, *and I was sorry that (having
as old J. M. Dent used to say done it 'con amore') I had no copy to send them
when they let out a final prayer.*

Francis Brett Young wrote a more than generous testimonial, too
generous for me to quote.

What I cannot resist quoting is a beguiling story about Francis and
Jessica Brett Young that came in a letter from Frank Swinnerton:

*Charlie Evans, of Heinemanns, found Francis in a suit of plus fours, with a pair
of perfectly marvellous stockings (details unknown to me). He said: "Good God,
Francis! What stupendous stockings!" Francis said: "Jessie made them". Jessie
said: "Do you really like them? I'll make you a pair just the same." Charlie Evans
expressed his gratification.*

*A few days later, he received a letter from Jessie which said, "I am sorry that
I can't get any of the same kind of wool; but rather than disappoint you I have been*

C

*looking through Francis's old stockings, and am sending you a pair of them. You
will be interested to know that it was in these stockings that Francis wrote 'Mr and
Mrs Pennington'." Did you know that tale? I do hope not.*

I told in Octave Three of my first meeting with Ronald Knox in my
brother-in-law's house at Eton when he was Captain of the school. In
a testimonial he sent to the *G.U.N.* paper he wrote:

"Why I appreciate Compton Mackenzie, and recommend him to the
appreciation of others, is that he remains so young, the sort of man
professors shake their heads over. In point of years he is, I am glad to say,
my senior; but what a difference in essential youthfulness! I have found
myself before now, almost patting him on the head. I first met him, I
suppose, a round quarter of a century ago; he was the first man I had
ever seen wearing a soft shirt with evening dress, and I envied him as my
own starched breastplate crackled and crumpled and asphyxiated me;
here I felt was a Liberator."

The uncertainty about the sale of the Jethou lease and the financial
situation were lightened when on August 19th William McWhirter,
Editor-in-Chief at Northcliffe House, wrote:

"I am extremely anxious to have some first-class book reviewing done
in the *Daily Mail* and remembering as I do the excellent gramophone
comments you did for me in the *Sunday Pictorial*, it occurs to me that you
are the very man. . . .

"I am willing to pay you at the rate of £750 a year for the first three
months, and if the feature is a success I will give you a contract for a
further year at £1,000 per annum."

It had been a blow when earlier in the year the *Sunday Pictorial* had
decided to give up my weekly gramophone article which I had been
writing for five years, and I was much relieved by the prospect opened
by that letter. At the same time, I knew that the reviewing of books
would occupy much more of my time than the reviewing of gramophone
records and when I went down to London to talk it over with McWhirter
I pointed this out. On August 24th he wrote:

"Confirming our conversation of yesterday, I hereby offer you the
position of Book Critic and Reviewer to the *Daily Mail* for a period of
three months at a salary of Twenty Pounds (£20) per week, the first
article to appear on Tuesday, September 8.

"It is understood that if the feature is a success the fee will be increased
at the end of those months to a sum not less than that paid by the
Evening News for a similar feature, the second engagement to be for one
year."

So on September 8th began my weekly reviewing for the *Daily Mail*
which with missing only two or three weeks would continue for five years.
For this I was paid £1,500 a year. The *Mail's* reviews for some time

before that September had been done by Douglas West, and well done too. Some men would have resented giving place to an outsider from Fleet Street. Not so Douglas West. He did everything he could to oil the wheels of my job and would become a dear and intimate friend. He was an Old Pauline, much junior to myself of course, and was married to a kinswoman of mine, Kitty Leaf, a granddaughter of John Addington Symonds, and daughter of that great Greek scholar, who was also chairman of the Westminster Bank, Walter Leaf.

Douglas West came up to Eilean Aigas in that October and wrote from Northcliffe House on his return:

I found on my return that McWhirter has gone away for a few weeks. This very possibly means that he is being frozen out in the typical Daily Mail *way. I see no reason why it should affect you. Everyone in the saddle at the moment considers your article a highly successful feature, and I gather that the decision to invite you to become a contributor was by no means wholly McWhirter's. My own stock just now stands moderately high: so do not hesitate to make use of me as a channel for suggestions—or even protests. There is a welcome air of internal stability about the office this week which offers some hope that no startling changes are contemplated. One of the books you must certainly write one day is the inner history of the* Daily Mail *since Northcliffe's death.*

I so much enjoyed my visit. My one regret is that I did not claim a guest's privilege to induce you to go on talking after 4 a.m. But, after all, you must sleep sometime when your waking hours are haunted by that horrible fungus of new books. It was tremendous fun, and I was extremely sorry to leave.

Douglas West continued to do everything possible to lighten the strain of that weekly task and later on he went into publishing on his own account. Alas, he is no longer with us.

Of books that came out in that autumn of 1931 I shall recall one or two of my reviews.

"A great deal of nonsense has been written about D. H. Lawrence since his death, and now in D. H. Lawrence's posthumous work *The Man Who Died* (Secker) we have a great deal of nonsense written by D. H. Lawrence about Our Lord.

"No contemporary of my own has been able to take the English language as Lawrence has done and make of it not merely such a perfectly beautiful, but also such a perfectly serviceable vessel to contain his own ideas. Yet in admiring the beauty and serviceableness of the vessel we should beware of supposing that it contains more ideas than it really does.

"There were moments in reading *The Man Who Died* when I could have fancied that I was embarked upon one of the late Marie Corelli's theological adventures, had I not been continually reminded by the writer's mastery over his material that this was the work of a great artist.

We have on top of that some of Lawrence's typical sensationalism about Mary Magdalen, whom he has called Madeleine. The story of Mary Magdalen and Our Lord as told in the Holy Gospels is so sacred a story, so intimate a revelation of the Divine Mind, that I confess I was nauseated by the corrupt scent with which she is here bespattered.

"Yet the landscape in the second part is as lovely as any that even Lawrence has given us. He can enshrine the whole Mediterranean in one charmed sentence; but though he will almost make the very pages tremble with the wind in the stone-pines that he conjures, he cannot infuse with the breath of life one solitary human figure of those he tries so arrogantly and so ineffectually to create. Lawrence understood flowers, birds and animals, even to the extent of someone we read of in a fairy-story to whom had been granted the ability to understand their veritable speech; but some bad fairy saw to it that he must nearly always *mis*understand human beings as soon as their mental processes were complicated by what we call civilization.

"Unfortunately he lacked humility. Thus to him was denied the vision which was given to Blake. He saw the visible world as a savage sees it but not as an innocent child. He was near enough to primitive man to long for Eden, and indeed often he seemed to remember Eden as if he himself had sojourned therein; but there is always a suggestion that his dignity had been hurt by the Angel who drove him forth."

Should I modify that expression of opinion today? No.

A fortnight later broke *The Waves* by Virginia Woolf (The Hogarth Press).

"I feel as if I were setting out at dawn to capture a fairy. The magic of the poetess has led me on over hill and over dale, on and on by haunted moorland waters, down through forest and through fernbrake, to come out at last on yellow sands.

"But like everybody else who has the experience of being pixy-led I can but declare at the end of it that the experience is incommunicable.

"As I start sentence after sentence, each one gets more hopelessly ink-logged than the last, and I know I shall never succeed in finding words for the rapture into which this book carried me. I do know, however (and how rich that knowledge is seeming!), that I have not actually begun to enjoy the book at a first reading. I know that I shall be able to read it again and again, and should fancy every time that I had never really read it before.

"With the arrogance of the lover who supposes that no lover ever loved so deeply and so wildly before himself, the reader of an authentically great book is always inclined to suppose that he in all the world must appreciate that book a little more intimately than anybody else. Jealousy not snobbery may be the reason why we so often resent popularity for the books we love best.

"While I try to express my delight in *The Waves* I am feeling confident that no reader of the *Daily Mail* can possibly enjoy this book as much as I have. As for other critics, for the moment I laugh at them from a remote privacy of genuine appreciation. No doubt I shall read next week a review of *The Waves* which will say successfully what I am trying to say, and in reading it I shall be suitably mortified. Never mind, I shall soon be happy again in the thought that analysts, geographers and reviewers are not required to tell the world of time and space about a timeless, spaceless fairyland.

"This book is Prospero's island. It will never be charted by critics."

When one reaches the forties one does not expect to get the kind of thrill Keats got when he first read Chapman's version of the *Iliad*. Yet that was the kind of thrill I got from *The Waves*. For me it was a sign that English poetry must one day emerge again from the bad prose which the contemporary poetic fashion was encouraging. I fear I was too optimistic. The influence of the group-mind grows stronger all the time. Humanity seems to be marching resolutely onward along the evolutionary path taken once upon a time by ants. The magic of words is already beginning to seem like an old-fashioned conjuring trick to the nurselings of English Literature being crammed with the tinned milk of literature for a degree.

When the *Daily Mail* took me on as their literary critic I was working hard at a broadcast play about Prince Charles Edward Stuart in which I was proposing to use as far as possible nothing but recorded historical material that could be verified. I was not prepared to encourage romantic twaddle about his relations with Flora MacDonald or commercial inventions about secret recipes for liqueurs. Work on *The Lost Cause* was pleasantly interrupted by the Dingwall Mòd.

Lady Elspeth Campbell escorted by the Captain of Dunstaffnage were our guests at Eilean Aigas. Angus Dunstaffnage was devoted to Lady Elspeth; he was less devoted to Gaelic. I remember his trying to argue with me that the origin of Campbell was the Italian Campo Bello not the Caimbeul or 'crooked mouth' of the Gaelic. There was a fashion in the early nineteenth century for lairds of high degree to claim a Norman or Italian origin for their names. This was in fact justifiable for the Frasers, the Chisholms and the Gordons. The Mackenzies discovered they were really Giraldini, which may have been true of the Fitzgeralds but was certainly not true of the Mackenzies. Yet we must not feel too superior about the romantic aspirations of lairds in the early nineteenth century. They are just as romantic today. There are only three 'The's' in Scotland—The Chisholm, The Pope and The Devil. Today definite articles in front of the names of the Chiefs of Clans are as plentiful as the chamber-pots which in the prim nineteenth century were politely alluded to as 'articles'.

Susan Duchess of Somerset had a house-party at Coul near Strath-peffer and we went to lunch with her.

"Oh dear," said Lady Elspeth, "I know Susan Somerset will ask me to sit next her at the grand concert tonight. When she does you must tell her that I must sit next to you because we are bringing out these Gaelic records to encourage people to learn Gaelic."

I demurred to this,

"I think the excuse will come better from you."

Sure enough the Duchess did say from one end of the crowded lunch-table,

"I do hope I will be sitting next you, Elspeth, at the concert tonight so that you can tell me what the songs are about."

"No, no, I'm afraid that's not possible," said Lady Elspeth firmly. "Mr Mackenzie and I have to sit together because we have to make notes for our gramophone records. But you're coming to the ceilidh afterwards at Eilean Aigas and I'll be able to tell you then anything you didn't understand."

The poor Duchess shook her head.

"Yes, I was afraid you wouldn't want to sit with me, Elspeth," she sighed.

One of the pictures at Coul was of two young Mackenzies at the beginning of the last century wearing trews with a tartan of square-inch checks of pale green and french-grey. I was much struck by this because I wondered if it afforded a clue to the lost Mackenzie tartan. The accepted Mackenzie tartan of today is really the military tartan used at this date by the old Seaforth Highlanders and Highland Light Infantry. The tartans of the Highland regiments are really the tartan of the Black Watch to which red and white was added for the Seaforths and yellow for the Gordons. The tartan of the Cameron Highlanders was a combination of the tartans of Cameron of Erracht and MacDonell of Keppoch. The Argyll and Sutherland Highlanders' tartan is Campbell.

Veronica went off to Keir immediately after the Mòd and soon a letter gave me her news:

Darling Monty

Today things have not been going very well with me. First I felt naughty at lessons so I began to whistle 'O! me darling Clementine.' Of course I was sent next door (Irene's room) and told to stay there till I felt sorry. Well, I did not feel sorry and so I spent an agreeable half hour in Irene's room throwing bits of paper as far as I could out of the window by way of amusement till suddenly I thought that perhaps I might be made to do all that I missed in free-time, so I went back to the school room and for the rest of the morning was as good as gold.

In the afternoon I did not know my history. Before tea I discovered a trick. I put a handkerchief under my jersey and then I drew my dirk and stuck it into the hankie

through my jersey. It looked very real and Irene got quite a fright when she came
back and saw me dead on the sofa but unhappily Zelle saw through it. Besides that
Miss Vickers reprimanded me for making a huge hole in my jersey (Miss Vickers
is Aunt P's maid). Isn't this a long letter? Please write again.

Tons of love from Veronica

Irene gives her love.

Faith's book about Christina of Sweden called *The Sibyl of the North*
was published by Cassell's that September. Earlier in the year a collection
of her short stories called *Mandolinata* in a beautiful limited edition had
appeared; this had been supervised by Colin Summerford when Sandys
Wason bought an almost extinct firm of publishers called Cope and
Fenwick. The reviewers praised both works and I could feel that she
would now carry on with her writing and at last express fully the artist
that was in her. She went down to London early in October to enjoy
her success; I went to Glasgow for rehearsals of *The Lost Cause.*

In those days the headquarters of the B.B.C. in Glasgow were in
Blythswood Square on the opposite side from the house in which once
upon a time Madeleine Smith played in a drama more tragic than any
broadcast drama.

Andrew Stewart, the present head of the Scottish B.B.C., played
Charles Edward Stuart. I read the narrative that linked the scenes and
I also played O'Neill, the Prince's friend who came with him to South
Uist. All the Highland parts were played by Highlanders, and we were
much amused by the notice next morning in the Glasgow *Daily Record*
when it expressed surprise that Mr Compton Mackenzie of all people
should have allowed the Highland parts to be played by Irishmen. How
a Glaswegian critic of all people came to make such a howler was
inexplicable. There were over fifty letters from enthusiastic Jacobites,
and *The Lost Cause* was published later by Oliver and Boyd.

By now the Rectorial campaign was in full swing and I tactfully
withdrew from Glasgow to Edinburgh. My supporters were full of optimism and I began to think I might possibly pull off second place in the
voting. Harold Collier was cheerful because the new president of the
G.U.S.N.A. had been kidnapped by the Tories and only released when
he gave his word not to take any further active part in the campaign.

"Which will be a great advantage to us," said Collier.

In the fourth number of the paper he wrote:

WHAT WE STAND FOR

In view of the campaign of calumny and gross misrepresentation which
has been carried on against us, we are proud to enunciate clearly the
principles on which Mr Compton Mackenzie's nomination for the
Rectorship is based.

That the Rectorship is not a nominal post, not merely an honour but an obligation, an office of trust and responsibility.

———————

That Compton Mackenzie has promised that, if elected, as is now more than likely, he will attend every single one of the meetings of the University Court, and that his counsel and aid will be available at any time to each individual student of the University.

———————

That Compton Mackenzie is the representative of a movement which is striving for the regeneration of Scotland as a vital force in European culture.

———————

That Compton Mackenzie is the representative of a movement, the members of which genuinely believe that the cause of disarmament and world peace would be enhanced by a delegate from Scotland in the League of Nations.

———————

That Compton Mackenzie is the representative of a movement which stands definitely for self-government for all nations in general and Scotland in particular.

———————

That Compton Mackenzie is one whose outlook is not that of the party politician but rather that of the artist, and, above all, one who is a writer and a personality of world-wide distinction.

On the opposite page under a photograph of myself was "I have a great admiration for Compton Mackenzie. James M. Barrie."

Of the twenty-eight distinguished men and women who generously sent tributes to the editor of the *Glasgow University Nationalist* only seven are still alive.

Just before I went down to Edinburgh I had a letter from Veronica at Keir.

Darling Monty

Thank you very much for your long letter. Last Saturday I went to Edinburgh to see the dentist. I had my teeth exerade! It was rather fun. After that we went to the Mikado. I loved it.

There is a Princess who has got plucked eyebrows and red finger nails. She is a Russian. Isn't it a pity my skian-doo is confiscated So I can't kill Irene, what a world (!) (Exclamation of sympathy).

There's nothing much more to say except that I have been as naughty lately and grunted when Zelle told me to go out of the room.

Tons of love
from
Veronica

A day or two after that letter from Veronica I had driven down to Edinburgh with Ashie Macrae and was staying at the Tartan Hotel kept by the outstanding Gaelic tenor, Kenneth Macrae, when the result of the Rectorial election was announced on Saturday October 29th. To my amazement I was rung up by Harold Collier and told that I had beaten Sir Robert Horne, the Tory candidate, by 87 votes. Would I come over to the Central Hotel as soon as possible?

Ashie Macrae was so much excited by the news that on our way out of Edinburgh he got the Sunbeam into a mix-up with the regulations of a traffic roundabout.

"Where are you going?" a stern Edinburgh constable demanded.

"Glasgow," Ashie answered in his broadest Inverness-shire accent.

"Ach! I thought so," said the constable, his countenance softening to a kind of compassionate contempt.

Edinburgh waved Glasgow on. What could an Edinburgh constable expect from a Glasgow driver except stupidity was asked by that constable's gesture.

I hesitate to put an exact figure on the time Ashie took to reach Glasgow, but it was certainly much the fastest time in which I have driven from Edinburgh to Glasgow. As the Sunbeam was held up by the traffic lights just before we reached the Central Hotel a little man on the pavement popped his head in at the window.

"It's Mr Compton Mackenzie?"

"It is," I agreed.

"Will you do something for me, Mr Mackenzie? I'm a camera-man. Will you stand for a press photo with Mr Baldwin?"

"Of course, but is Mr Baldwin in Glasgow?"

"Ay, he's here for the big meeting tonight to open the election campaign. All the papers have been asked to send their best camera-men because the outgoing Lord Rector and the new Lord Rector would both be on the platform together."

"Sir Robert Horne may be there but I'm afraid the new Lord Rector won't be there."

"No, that's why I'm hoping Mr Baldwin will let me take a photo of you and him together. It'll be a grand scoop for me."

Unfortunately for that little camera-man's hope of earning some useful guineas Mr Baldwin declined to be photographed with me, and his refusal was quickly circulated. Later on I was told by members of the Nationalist Committee that there was a huge crowd of students gathered in the Central Station to welcome me and that I must come out and make a speech.

As I walked slowly down the wide staircase of the Central Hotel into the entrance hall Mr Baldwin was waiting by the reception desk with Sir Henry Mechan, his Assessor, and one or two others, waiting for the car that was to drive them to St Andrew's Hall for the opening meeting of that disastrous General Election which would return the National Government to power.

Just as I reached the entrance hall the doors on the right leading directly into the Central Station burst open and half a dozen students shouted at Mr Baldwin to shake hands with me. The porters rushed to drive the students back into the station; Mr Baldwin and his escort hastily went through the swing doors on the opposite side to get into their car.

To my regret I never did meet Lord Baldwin, but some ten years later during the war he came to stay with Francis Brett Young at his beautiful house in Worcestershire, and caught sight of my name in the visitors' book at an earlier week-end.

"Now there's a fellow I've always wanted to meet," he declared.

I was amused by a somersault turned by Sir Robert Bruce in the *Glasgow Herald*. On the morning of the Rectorial election there was a leader reminding me that I was standing as a political candidate and would receive from Scottish youth the answer that my ridiculous advocacy of Home Rule deserved. On the following morning there was a leader to warn me against supposing that my election had the faintest political significance. My election was due to the support of the Irish Catholic vote.

On Guy Fawkes day David Anderson, the editor of the *Daily Record*, wrote to me:

You will see in the Glasgow Observer *that the credit is given there just as it was given in the* Glasgow Herald *to the Roman Catholic vote for your return as Lord Rector.*

Since then, the 'vote' feeling has become very definite. From my point of view it is a tremendous pity that this religious red herring has been drawn across the whole issue, and threatens to destroy the merits of your victory.

Already, allegations are being thrown out that you will appoint a Catholic Assessor of some prominence. In order to dissipate all the rumours and the fears, would it not be a great gesture if you were to nominate a Protestant Assessor? By so doing you would probably wipe out the impression that religion had anything to do with your triumph.

Anderson went on to suggest one or two Protestant names. I set his mind at rest by letting him know that Sir Iain Colquhoun[1] had agreed to be my Assessor.

That religious red herring kept on being dragged across the issue until it stank. But enough of it for the time. I print in Appendix A a sane estimate of that Rectorial election.

A couple of days after the election I was dining in Edinburgh with a sports club of which Iain Colquhoun was president and asked him if he would allow himself to be nominated as my Assessor. To my deep gratification he kindly agreed, and when the Students' Representative Council had expressed their enthusiastic approval of my choice that most lovable of men, Iain Colquhoun, whose loss to the country is still felt, accepted the Assessorship.

I had over 300 letters and telegrams of congratulation. One telegram gave me particular pleasure. It was from Robert Rait,[2] Vice-Chancellor and Principal of the University.

On behalf of the University I welcome you warmly as our Lord Rector.

I had not yet met him but that telegram was the beginning of an unbroken friendship.

The temptation to quote from many of those letters is strong but I resist it and restrict myself to three. The first is from George Gordon, the President of Magdalen:

I am sure that the College would wish me to congratulate you on your triumphant election as Lord Rector of Glasgow University. A College as such has no literary taste, and no organ for expressing it. It is therefore possible (I don't know) that previous triumphs of yours outside the academic world have drawn no voice from Magdalen. But we all understand being elected Lord Rector.

I do so more particularly, being a graduate of Glasgow and having narrowly escaped a night in the police-station at Lord Rosebery's election in 1899.

Another letter was from Norman Sturrock at 14 Howe Street, Edinburgh, a bank-manager whose dry wit was one of the delights of the Scottish Arts Club.

Hearty congratulations on your latest venture. I don't know much about Scottish Nationalism and I don't think I like it. But I do think a Scottish University has chosen a Rector as will be a Rector and I look forward to your Address impatiently. How to greet you now is my difficulty. I've met very few Lords but David (Cleghorn Thomson) will coach me. He knows. I did not get the news until the evening—at dinner with friends. I gave a squeal of joy, and then thought the orthodox dressed cutlet of these occasions had turned to ice pudding. I saw a gloomy face being shaken from side to side and I heard a sepulchral voice muttering about Catholics battening at our vitals or sucking our hearts' blood or something. I said in my

[1] The late Sir Iain Colquhoun Bt. of Luss, K.T.
[2] The late Sir Robert Rait, C.M.G.

brightest manner "What a very unpleasant thought in the midst of such a delightful meal as our hostess has provided." More pin-dropping silence broken by the tactful host who said it was a sign of the times when the wife of an S.S.C. had the audacity to speak to the wife of a W.S. on the strength of meeting in a Hydro in August—and it occurred in Princes Street! God bless my host, but I spent the rest of the evening silently cheering you.

Please don't give up Edinburgh for that cesspool called Glasgow.

The last letter I shall quote was from Hugh Walpole whose father was Bishop of Edinburgh.

Brackenburn Park
Keswick.
Oct. 25th '31

My dear Monty

I must send you a line of congratulation. When I heard the news on the wireless I was delighted and afterwards drank the health of the Old Firm. For we are the old Firm, you know, bound together by nearly mutual scorn and hatred!

Honestly I am delighted. Will see you King of Scotland ere now!

Your old friend
Hugh Walpole

I had laughed at two of Walpole's novels—*Fortitude* and *The Duchess of Wrexe*—because I thought (and still think) they were unintentionally comic novels. I had laughed, too, at Hugh Walpole himself, but I never laugh at people I dislike. Gradually Walpole came to realize that my laughter was completely devoid of malice or jealousy. I think what brought this home to him more clearly than anything else was *Cakes and Ale*, which had been published in the previous year. The portrait of Hugh Walpole is a bad caricature, and so for that matter is the supposed portrait of Thomas Hardy. When a new edition of *Cakes and Ale* was published after Walpole's death Maugham foolishly admitted that Alroy Kear was in fact a portrait of Hugh Walpole. I say 'foolishly' because he misjudged the result if he thought that in Alroy Kear he had painted a good portrait. Maugham wrote as if he had always laughed at Hugh Walpole.

"I could think of no one among my contemporaries who had achieved so considerable a position on so little talent." Yet sometime in the early 'twenties Maugham once reproached me because I was not taking literature as seriously as Hugh.

"That is because I have a sense of humour," I replied, "which you and Hugh Walpole are without."

A month after getting that letter from Hugh Walpole I took the risk of his assuming that a criticism of the Book Society, of which Hugh was one of the founders and chief judges, was a personal attack on Hugh himself.

"Since reading *Festival* by Struthers Burt (Peter Davies) I have been wondering what qualities in this pretentious novel persuaded the judges of the Book Society to make it their choice of the month. . . .

"It is definitely a bad book, and not the least exasperating part about the badness is that the author seems to share with the judges of the Book Society an impression that he has written a good book. . . .

"After 350 wearisome pages of costive prose, Mr William Dorn Griffiths becomes American Ambassador to Italy, chiefly through his wife's desire that he should be doing something again. After his soliloquies I must confess to sympathizing with the wife, though I felt a little sorry for the Italians.

"The judges of the Book Society commend the wit and wisdom of Mr Burt.

"Here is a specimen of the wit:

" 'Towards the end of the voyage elderly gentlemen complained of pains in their stomachs, and were nursed by their wives who, being women, were more used to pains in their stomachs'. . . .

"It is a pity Mr Burt did not take the trouble to find out more about the Romans, especially as his hero was going to be inflicted on them as an ambassador. At what date, I wonder, was Rome 'Augustinian'? But perhaps because Augustinian is a longer word than Augustan, Mr Burt thought it was a better word. Yes, that must be it, for a few lines further down the same page we read of 'Sardanapalusian luxury'. Sardanapalian was too short for Mr Burt, though long enough for other writers.

"However, an evident ignorance of Latin does not prevent his using long Latin adjectives. On the first page of his book we are told that 'silver spider-webs frosted the implacable green'. People who use long Latin words should look up in a dictionary what they mean, and even with the help of an English dictionary it is more prudent not to use them unless one has learnt to use a Latin dictionary in youth. . . .

"Mr Hugh Walpole has declared that this story catches you by the ear; in saying that I think he was assuming that some of us have longer ears than we hope we have. In conclusion I may mention that *Festival* has for six months headed the list of best sellers in the United States. I do not find this surprising."

That summer Peter Davies, the original Peter Pan, a personality of quiet charm and an artist among publishers, had asked me to suggest a subject for one of the volumes in the series of brief biographies he was setting out to publish. I had suggested Frederick of Hohenstauffen, Stupor Mundi, and had rashly proposed to finish it by the end of the year. By June I had changed that to the end of January next year. "It is not the writing but the reading that will take the time, because it means reading a good deal of mediaeval Latin."

On September 4th Peter Davies was writing:

"I should like to take this opportunity of congratulating the *Daily Mail* on your forthcoming debut as its Literary Critic. This seems to me a most admirable move, out of which much good will arise, and of course great benefit to publishers who find it more and more difficult to get the kind of notice which really interests people in books. Arnold Bennett used to have more effect than anyone else. But you with the enormous *Daily Mail* at your back will work wonders."

I realized fairly soon that I was being absurdly optimistic in my proposal to write about Stupor Mundi and I asked Peter Davies if he would mind my doing Charles Edward Stuart instead. In writing the broadcast play for October I should have read all there was to read about him. On September 15th Peter Davies wrote:

"Curiously enough, your letter was forwarded to me in Guernsey where I was staying with the Ruthvens and reached me on the evening of an expedition to your island, which seemed to me so delightful a place that I can hardly understand your ever leaving it.

"The crucial sentence in your letter is that the life of Charles Edward is a book which you passionately want to write. This being so, I am obviously bound to say yes, write it. My first feeling, I admit, was that he is not nearly an important enough figure historically for inclusion so early in the series, but on consideration I do recognize that so romantic a figure might well have a large appeal to the public. . . . In many ways he must be an ideal figure for a short book of this kind . . . and I know you will make a significant book. Let us regard Frederick and Pericles as future possibilities."

Not long after this Peter Davies would be marrying one of those fascinating Ruthven twins. What an ideal letter that was to get from a publisher! As I look back I realize how lucky I have been in my relations with publishers. The early death of Peter Davies was a blow to British publishing. When I wrote to him at the beginning of January to say that the combination of the *Daily Mail*, the Rectorship and a month of bed during the last two months meant that I would not be able to finish Charles Edward by the end of January and when soon after this I asked him to give me until next July before I wrote Charles Edward he agreed without a grumble. Nor, incidentally, did he complain of the slating I gave to that American best-seller he published. I salute his memory.

I expected my first appearance as Chairman of the University Court would be an ordeal. I knew that a good deal of academic opinion in the University had been fancying that the Wild Man of Borneo had been inflicted upon them. Thanks to the goodwill of Robert Rait, the Principal and Vice-Chancellor, that ordeal was a most pleasant experience and with him beside me to prompt I successfully avoided any breach of academic decorum. Luckily there was no controversial matter on the agenda. When I look back to those monthly meetings of the University

Court the argument that remains most vividly in my mind is the question of whether two extra lavatories should be provided for Queen Margaret's and if so where and when. A committee was nominated to decide the latter after the Court had voted unanimously in favour of giving to Queen Emmas two new lavatories. As I remember the committee over-weighted by those two lavatories appointed a sub-committee to deal with the problem of when and where they were to be installed.

Robert Rait was nine years older than myself who after a successful scholastic career at Aberdeen University had gone to New College, Oxford, of which after a First in History and winning the Stanhope Prize he had become a Fellow and Tutor just before I went up in 1901. He had written various historical works which had been highly esteemed. He was a firm supporter of the Union and our views of Scottish history were almost diametrically opposite to one another. Nevertheless, we agreed to differ and the generous hospitality of the Principal's Lodging was always given to me. Mrs Rait, as she still was, never let me feel that I was trespassing on that hospitality and always made me believe that the Raits enjoyed having me as their guest. Ruth and Margaret, their two daughters in their late 'teens, were as kind to me as their parents.

It was the usual custom for a Rector to give his address to the students in the second year of his holding office, but there was no rule about this and I asked Rait if there was any objection to my giving mine as early as January next year.

"I want to get it written as soon as possible so that I can concentrate on the books I have to write."

It was settled that I should deliver my Rectorial address on January 29th 1932.

I attended the University Court again in December and with sixteen of my supporters occupied seventeen stalls at the Alhambra Theatre to see my sister Fay play Dick Whittington with that great comedian Harry Gordon. The pantomime was a tremendous success. I doubt if any future Rector of Glasgow will have a sister playing principal boy in a pantomime during his term of office. A year or two after this Fay played *Dick Whittington* at Drury Lane. I remember saying to my mother,

"I see Fay is to play *Dick Whittington* this year at Drury Lane."

"Yes," said my mother who was then past eighty. "And I have no doubt she will give a more virile performance of *Dick Whittington* than Ivor Novello next week of *Henry V.*"

There was a dinner that week of the Dumbarton Education Authority at the Grosvenor Restaurant at which Iain Colquhoun and I were guests.

"My family are going to the pantomime while I'm at this dinner," said Colquhoun. "I've told them I'll join them in the box at ten. Our dinner ought to be over by then."

"It ought to be over," I agreed, "because we are sitting down at half-past six. Nevertheless, I think you're being optimistic in hoping to join your family by ten."

I was right. The speeches began at half-past eight when the Church of Scotland minister spoke for half an hour to be followed by the Catholic priest for another half hour and for another half hour still the Episcopalian canon before either Colquhoun or I were called upon for our speeches. Iain Colquhoun did not see much of *Dick Whittington*.

I had to attend a number of other dinners that December at all of which I had to make speeches and I was glad to get back to Eilean Aigas and the Christmastide enjoyed with Frasers and Maxwells galore. On January 2nd Faith was writing to my mother:

We had a children's party which was a roaring success. It went with a roar from start to finish, and the child who enjoyed it most was the Lord Rector. He will have told you how lovely he thought Fay was in the Panto. . . . This is going to be a terrific month. M. has much more work than it's possible for any human being to do."

FORTY-NINE YEARS OLD: 1932

I TOLD in my last Octave of my first meeting with Rosamond Lehmann when she had a cold in the head which was the heaviest in my experience until it was beaten this January by Jamie Hamilton. He was then on the verge of launching the successful publishing business of Hamish Hamilton and, as I remember, came up to Eilean Aigas to find out if there was any prospect of my becoming one of his authors. He had donned his kilt for the journey from London; it was a rash if patriotic gesture. Jamie's cold in the head remains the heaviest cold in the head I have seen (and heard) and has been surpassed by nobody since. Two long and dearly cherished friendships have been founded upon colds in the head.

Laura Lovat had promised to arrange some tableaux for a concert at Beauly. I have a notion that Magdalen Fraser was Mary Queen of Scots. What I do know is that I played George Staunton to the Effie Deans of Veronica.

With my usual bubbling rashness I had promised to write a play about Walter Scott for production in Edinburgh at the celebration of his centenary in this year 1932. At the moment, however, I had to get down to composing my Rectorial Address for January 29th, which was the hardest task I ever faced with a pen. When it was finished I sent it to Robert Rait who wrote to me on January 20th:

My dear Mackenzie,

I have read the Address with very great interest and admiration, if not, as you know, always with entire agreement with its standpoint. No one can fail to appreciate the grace and dignity of your exposition of a creed which is only at times political in any real sense, or to feel stirred by the force of an eloquence which is almost austere in its simplicity and therefore makes an appeal which does much more than gratify the ears (though it does that also). Nor can anyone do other than recognize the weight and sincerity of your argument or the thought, as well as the imagination which had been devoted to the elucidation of fresh aspects and points of view.

Will you forgive me if I venture to press one consideration upon you? It has been the invariable rule in Rectorial addresses that no Lord Rector remind his audience that they include a victorious party and a defeated party (or parties) in the contest which resulted in his own election. To that rule I attribute in large measure the cessation of the bad tradition which denied a hearing to Lord Rectors. In Glasgow that tradition is almost extinct, though the recent experience of Mr Churchill in

D

Edinburgh shows that it can still exist elsewhere.[1] *You will remember that you are speaking to an audience of hot-headed and excited youths, to most of whom the recent Rectorial contest represented their first experience of political controversy, and that those who lost the fight have had their first experience of losing. They are therefore much more sensitive than old campaigners, and a very little irritation leads youth to seek relief in the chance of a row. There are only a few sentences which seem to me unwise in the circumstances. I have noted specially on p. 2 of the typescript the remark about its being expedient that a defender of Nationalism should affirm his creed and that this creed has been endorsed by an expression of youthful opinion; remarks which though in themselves reasonable and, indeed, undeniable, might— I think would—be interpreted as a challenge and give the entirely false impression that the Address which followed was to be a piece of party propaganda. Then on p. 3 the reference to the walls of Jericho would be resented, and the remark on p. 28 about re-creating a State (about the precise significance of which I am myself not quite clear) might have a similar effect.*

You will understand that I am not trying either to do anything so absurd as to flatter you or to underrate the significance of the victory of the Nationalist Party when I say that your eminence as a man of letters ("known and read of all men" as the Apostle aptly says) was a fact in your election and that some of your supporters were non-political. You have put so much of yourself into your books that no one can separate you from them and the vision which inspires your Address would alone be sufficient evidence that no mere politician was elected in October. As a man of letters you will retain—what you have, since this election, secured—the allegiance of the whole body of students, of all parties, and of no party. Please do not misunderstand me when I venture to suggest that the Address should be free from any possible suspicion of political propaganda, as free in detail and in wording as it already is in essence. Your position as a leader of the Nationalist Party is understood and recognized, just as Mr Baldwin's position as a Unionist leader was understood and recognized, and nobody will misinterpret the absence of political references. Their presence may be misinterpreted.

The typescript goes to the printer to-day and I have asked him to post a galley proof to you on Friday. My suggestions do not imply much change, and if we can have the proof back by Tuesday morning it will be in time for Friday, the 29th.

I want to tell you of a graceful intention, which, unfortunately cannot be carried out. Sir Robert Horne was in Glasgow on Monday and he asked Sir Robert Bruce why no invitation for the 29th had been sent to him as member of the constituency in which the University stands. Bruce replied "For an obvious reason," and Horne said "Well, they are quite wrong. Compton Mackenzie is a good fellow and I should like to support him on the platform, and will accept invitations both to the Address and to the luncheons." Bruce telephoned to me and I sent invitations yester-

---

[1] In fact both Austen Chamberlain and Stanley Baldwin had been given noisy hearings in Glasgow.

day but in the interval, Horne has telegraphed from London that he finds it is impossible to get away on the 29th.

Do forgive me for these suggestions.

Ever yours

Robert S. Rait

My wife and I will take Mrs Mackenzie here on the 28th while you proceed by torchlight from the station.

I find a carbon copy of the letter I wrote back on January 22nd:

I am greatly indebted to you for your suggestions, and shall certainly act upon them. As you know, the harder one works on anything the more difficult it becomes at the end to criticize one's own work, and a phrase like that about the walls of Jericho gets altered so many times from the right order of the words that one is apt to lose sight of implications.

The Address is being broadcast from Daventry as well as Scottish stations, and I am most anxious to avoid any suggestion of Party propaganda. I had at first intended not to say anything about Nationalism at all, and to take an entirely different subject. However, after a great deal of heart searching I decided that the entire avoidance of the subject would savour of cowardice.

If, after I have been through the galleys, you still think there is anything it would be wiser not to say, it could easily be cut from the spoken speech, even though it were printed.

I much appreciated Sir Robert Horne's expression of good will, and am only sorry he cannot be present after all.

Mr MacSporran rang me up to-day to hope I would attend the dance in the Union on the evening of the 28th. I was out at the time, but I am writing him that I shall be very glad to attend after your dinner-party. I unfortunately set rather a high standard of Rectorial activity by dancing till two o'clock at the Ossianic centenary.

Just after I finished writing that letter I was seized by as vicious a *grippe* as ever seized me. My temperature went up to 104 and Dr Mackay told me there was no chance of my being fit to travel on the 28th.

"Somehow I have got to travel," I told him. "The invitations have all gone out. The complicated arrangements have all been made. I *must* get down on Thursday. I cannot upset them at the last minute. Somehow you *must* reduce the fever."

Dr Mackay performed wonders but my temperature in being got down to normal perversely sank below normal. This was countered by pills in which there was enough strychnine to quicken things up. On Thursday, January 28th, Faith and I travelled down from Inverness. At Buchanan Street station were Principal Rait and Mrs Rait, my beloved Assessor Iain Colquhoun, and the representatives of the S.R.C. Faith with a bouquet was taken off by the Raits. Iain Colquhoun took me along to the unhorsed carriage in which he and I would be drawn to the University by Blues accompanied by a torchlight procession of students. As it happened the 'Wild Men of the Clyde' were having a processional demonstration that evening and there was some anxiety about the two processions meeting. Luckily that was avoided and about seven o'clock I reached the Principal's Lodging where before going in to change for dinner I had to make a speech to a tight throng of students. After the dinner-party at which there were mercifully no speeches I managed to fulfil the promise to appear at the eve of the Rectorial ball in the Union and somehow to dance until two a.m.

I had a delightful reminder of that ball a quarter of a century later when I was giving away the prizes at a fashionable Convent school. The Reverend Mother —— said to me,

"You don't remember when we first met?"

I shook my head.

"I danced two dances with you at the ball in the Union on the night before your Rectorial Address."

One of my problems had been sartorial. My Nationalist supporters were sure that I ought to appear beneath the black and gold Rectorial robe in the kilt. I insisted that this would be an unsuitable combination, and most unwillingly they ceased to argue. I wore instead a black suit which alone of my wardrobe had escaped being destroyed when my house was shot to pieces and sacked in December 1916. Apart from an invisibly mended bullet-hole, it was as good as it was when Forster's of Grafton Street made it for me in 1912. A year hence I should wear that suit again in the dock at the Old Bailey.

The proceedings next day started with my being capped and gowned as an honorary LL.D. After that the academic procession moved on to the platform at St Andrew's Hall, when I had to doff my scarlet gown to be robed in black and gold with a heavy golden-tasselled cap.

There was a tempest of shouting while this was going on and cries from various parts of the huge hall of "Whaur's your kilt?" However, to my surprise and acute relief the moment I started my Address there was silence and for the next hour there was hardly an interjection from the audience. Indeed, I remember only one. I asked "Is there anybody here who believes that a universal man like Göethe could exist today?" A voice from the front row commented "Not even Archie Lamont?" "No," I looked down to say. "Not even Archie Lamont." He had been on the Nationalist Committee.

I probably read the Address too quickly. Each time the strychnine constricted my throat I had a sudden dread it would suddenly constrict it so tightly that I should dry up. On top of that I was nervous that I should be cut off by the B.B.C. for overrunning my time.

A letter from my sister Fay to my mother has survived from which I quote:

It was all tremendously thrilling—and utterly unlike what I had expected. I had thought everything would be most quiet and full of decorum. On the contrary, as I came into the Hall, there was the sound of loud singing from hundreds of throats: the students were beguiling the time, waiting for the Professors and the Lord Rector, by singing their songs—and a very pleasant sound it was accompanied by the organ at the other end of the Hall. Below the organ in tiers were sitting the Professors, etc., in their scarlet gowns. That made a beautiful picture.

I was up in the gallery, just above them; and saw and heard everything perfectly. Eventually a set of Professors came in from one side of the Platform, and Faith with them. At the sight of Faith, with great difficulty I refrained from bursting into tears!

There were songs being sung, while they came in. Then Monty came in, in his scarlet robes—and only the thought of my eye-black trickling down my face stopped the tears this time! . . .

A lot of ceremonies took place—none of which I heard at all, as the students were all shouting, talking, singing, whistling and cat-calling during it all. This began to give me a very bad attack of stage-fright for Monty, as I thought "How is this unfortunate man going to speak—far less read—an address?" I was relieved in a way that you were not sitting next to me, as I think it might have worried you a great deal more than I care to have you worried.

The next ceremony was changing Monty's scarlet robe to the black and gold robes of the Lord Rector. Bless his heart, he was dead white and obviously very nervous, which had the effect of making him look about twenty-five, and when he gave us his charming smile, he looked about nineteen! . . .

It is a most remarkable tribute to him, that during the long reading of his address, the students were practically silent—there were just a few harmless interruptions. I understand from the Principal of the University that this is simply incredible: the unfortunate Baldwin was not allowed to be heard at all—and Curzon they treated in an even rougher way. They just broke the benches while he was speaking, and threw them about! Dear little things, aren't they? There was such cheering and enthusiasm at the end of the address, and I felt tremendously proud, and again very near to tears.

At the lunch afterwards all was very pleasant and peaceful. I sat between an ex-Lord Provost and a Professor of Theology—which frightened me at first, until I found how very easy and kind both were to talk to. They were most charming about Monty. He had to get up and make another speech—the most modest and delightful one—it won all their hearts. Altogether a most thrilling day.

I received a lot of letters and telegrams from people who had 'listened in' as they called it in those days to the broadcast of my Rectorial. None gave me greater pleasure than one from J. M. Barrie, who himself had delivered a famous Rectorial Address at St Andrews some years previously:

Congratulations on address and all good wishes. Barrie.

After that fairly tough ordeal I was the guest of the Senate at luncheon when Principal Rait in the Chair proposed my health, after which I had to propose the University replied to by W. G. Cowan, the President of the Students Representative Council. After this Iain Colquhoun proposed the City of Glasgow to which the Lord Provost, Sir Thomas Kelly, replied.

During the afternoon my Assessor and I had to visit one or two hostels, which at this date all too easily became a controversial topic. So Colquhoun and I had to be tactful in our remarks. From the hostels we went on to take tea with the Queen Emmas at Queen Margaret's. Another speech! And that confounded strychnine catching again at my throat.

Finally there was the big House dinner at the Union with G. R. Roxburgh, the President of the Union, in the Chair. I looked at the long menu with some doubts of my ability to do justice to it, but I looked at the toast list with a momentary emotion of despair. Twelve speeches!

The first was of course brief. The Chairman called upon us to be up and standing to drink the health of His Majesty the King, followed by that gratefully received permission to smoke.

The next toast was Alma Mater which was to be given by Rosslyn Mitchell. Under the names of the various toasters were relevant quotations. Under my name was:

> "Ye maun a' learn the Gaelic
> Don the red gown and the kilt."
> Folk Song.

Under Rosslyn Mitchell was a quotation from the G.U.M. when he became President of the S.R.C. in 1901.

> "Mr Mitchell was the man of the hour."

Rosslyn Mitchell proceeded to live up to that quotation by speaking for fifty-five minutes. As M.P. for Paisley he had had a success in the House of Commons with a speech he made against any changes in the Book of Common Prayer and such was his Presbyterian eloquence that the House rejected the Bill. That success went to his tongue and at this date he was engaged in writing a book called *Ladies and Gentlemen: The Craft of Public Speaking* which was published a year later.

I was sitting between the Chairman and the Principal. I hear now Rait muttering, "He's giving us the Rectorial Address he would have delivered if he had been elected by the Labour students in 1928."

On and on went Rosslyn Mitchell with excellent elocution, but only one gesture, the right and left hand jerking down alternately throughout. . . . Rait turned across behind me to remind the Chairman that I had presently to make the chief speech of the evening. The Chairman called on the Secretary of the Union to remind Mr Rosslyn Mitchell of this but the Secretary did not feel he could tell an ex-M.P. to shut up and sit down. By the time Rosslyn Mitchell had finished we were fifty minutes behind time with that toast list. Professor Currie who had to reply to the toast of Alma Mater took hardly more than two minutes. Then the Chairman rose to propose the health of the Lord Rector. He, too, was as brief as possible. When I rose to propose The Union there were still seven or eight speeches to come and it was already after half-past ten.

"Gentlemen," I said, "trains and trams like time and tide wait for no man and there is really nothing for me to add to Mr Rosslyn Mitchell's eloquent speech except to thank you once again for the honour you have done me," and after a few more words I sat down, grateful in a way to Rosslyn Mitchell for giving me an excuse not to make a long speech because by now I was beginning to feel rather exhausted by my day.

The last speech was made by Hector McNeil[1] to propose the health of the Chairman. Hector McNeil was the President of the Socialist students who had supported Tom Johnston in the Rectorial contest. I had been much attracted to his personality and had prophesied a great career for him in politics. His early death in 1955 was a severe loss to his party.

I had to leave Glasgow next day to fulfil an engagement to speak to some literary club in Newcastle where I stayed with Angus Watson of Skipper sardines. His son had gone into partnership in the publishing firm of Ivor Nicholson and Watson. My financial affairs were getting into more of a tangle all the time, and as I remember I put up to Angus Watson the suggestion of paying me a large sum down for a series of historical novels of which I could guarantee to deliver one a year. I went back from Newcastle with a second seizure by *la grippe* which was followed by bronchitis and then by an infernal bout of sciatic neuritis. However, somehow or other I started dictating to Chrissie MacSween my third volume of war memories, having got Peter Davies's consent to postpone my life of Prince Charlie till the end of July. I managed also to read a book a night for the *Daily Mail*. Among the books I read in that month of almost incessant pain of one kind or another was *The Fountain* by Charles Morgan of which I wrote:

"It is hardly reasonable to expect a critic in the course of the week's usual work to deliver a completely confident valuation of a novel like *The Fountain* by Charles Morgan (Macmillan). The book is a long one, hardly less than 175,000 words; the author has devoted much loving care to the prose; he has obviously been profoundly conscious that he was attempting to produce a genuine work of art; he has left nothing undone which might suggest to the critic that a masterpiece had been born.

"However, I lack the courage which has emboldened some of my

[1] The late Rt. Hon. Hector McNeil, M.P.

confrères to guarantee space on the immortal shelves of the future to Mr Morgan's book. *The Fountain* may be a rightful heir to the ages, or it may be just a beautiful Perkin Warbeck of a book, for being taken in by the claims of which a critic who is compelled to give his verdict within a week of publication may be readily excused. Over many pages of *The Fountain* I was reminded again and again of *John Inglesant*. Shorthouse's romance shall be the criterion for Mr Morgan's romance, and judging it by that criterion I have no hesitation in deciding that *The Fountain* is the inferior book.

"The theme of *John Inglesant* is a nobler theme than Mr Morgan's, and the treatment of it is more dignified. Indeed, it is not unfair to say of *The Fountain* that after we have dispelled the flattering mists of Platonism and Quietism, by wrapping his personages in which Mr Morgan seems to suggest that he is removing them from the chains of a commonplace morality, there remains little but that eternal and much battered triangle, the rust on which it will take more than what are apt to sound somewhat pretentious allusions to Bossuet and St John of the Cross to remove.

"The fact is that the husband, the wife, and the lover, in spite of the half hours they have spent with the mystics and in spite of so much beautiful, if perhaps excessively grandiloquent abnegation, all three surrender to the flesh.

"You may search Plato from end to end but you will find no instruction there how to eat your cake and have it, and the attempt to do so is really the theme of *The Fountain*. It is a pity that after the study of Socrates Mr Morgan did not study the mediaeval ascetics more intelligently. He would not then have fallen into the old error of attributing to them Manichean beliefs which they did not hold.

"Those trappings which must seem so impressive to the critic who is less familiar than Mr Morgan or myself with the mystical writings of the 17th century are likely to stifle the book when it sets out upon the march to immortality.

"What an admirable exemplar of the dangers inseparable from the rule of life advocated by Molinos the Jesuits would have found in Lewis Alison, whose weaknesses are occasionally reflected in Mr Morgan's prose, particularly when, as Schubert often did, he writes in an exhausted key.

"However, Mr Morgan must be too well aware of what good prose is to let himself be affected by the laudation of critics who know very little about it. . . .

" 'Here, indeed, the hours went by in untroubled calm, there being in old books, as in a country churchyard, so deep and natural an acceptance of mortality, that to handle them and observe their brief passion, their urgent persuasion now dissipated, now silent, is to perceive that the pressure of time is itself a vanity, a delusion in the great leisure of the spirit.'

"That looks at first like a really good piece of architectural prose; but when it is read aloud, a monotony of cadence and assonance reveals itself, the lack of nicely varied broad vowels becomes apparent, and the superfluity of sibilants irritates.

"However, if we lower the standard and do not claim too much for *The Fountain* prematurely, for what a fine and distinguished piece of work we can thank him, and how much self-denial is involved in resisting the temptation to overpraise it!

"My personal enjoyment of the book was intense. Grudging though this criticism of it may seem, it is only grudging because I respect Mr Morgan too much to deck him with bays culled from Chelsea shrubberies."

Many years later I was asked to reply for Literature at a lunch in the Guildhall to celebrate something to do with the library. I asked to be excused from replying to the toast because I could not be sure of being able to attend the lunch. In fact I was able to be present and found that dear Charles Morgan had been booked to reply. He was a handsome figure as he stood up.

"I do not know why I have been chosen to reply to this august toast," he said gravely. "I look round and I see others more worthy than myself to respond at such a solemn moment. I see, for instance, Mr Compton Mackenzie who I recall once rebuked me for my failure to appreciate the importance of varying my broad vowels, for the monotony of my cadence, for my indulgence in assonance . . ."

I see now the puzzled expression on the faces of the Lord Mayor and Sheriffs. . . .

". . . for my excessive use of sibilants, yes, my Lord Mayor, and warned me against bays culled in Chelsea shrubberies."

By this time the Lord Mayor and Sheriffs were looking completely bewildered.

After lunch I told Charles I was sorry my critical observations had annoyed him and excused myself by recalling that they were written at a time when I was ill and in a big financial jam.

"You have nothing to reproach yourself for, Monty. Your criticism was just; I paid attention to it," Charles assured me.

I was without the company of Veronica and Irene that March to brighten what little leisure I had.

A letter from them both at Keir is still a joy to me:

Dear Monty,

Thank you terskumtively for your lovely long letter. I am sorry that you were in bed all that time.

The Hall-boy here has got measles. Miss Vickers would not tell us what the first simtons where so we (Irene and me) looked in a Girl Guide book and found them. So G— G— do serve for something. Irene has got an obvious temperature and will soon have a rash.

At this point Irene took up the letter:

I am well, you are well, we are well, who isn't well? Answer. Ask your Granny. Arn't we clever!!! at least Veronica and I are.

Tomy wrot. Chah! pshaw! Tosh!

Thank Cryiessea for her letter and tell her I might write to her this year, next year, sometimes, never.

What do you think we are doing. Writing a letter to you. Ain't we brainy poets.

> *Tons of love*
> *From*
> *Veronica and Irene*
> *XXXXX*

Veronica added:

Irene is a son of a wrotten egg of a bamboo-stick but all the same she was intelligent enough to have a birthday on March 9th which gave us a 'He' oliday.

On March 3rd I received a letter from Newman Flower in his own handwriting:

When you said something to me last year about doing an historical novel I frankly did not realize that you were so keen on the idea as you appear to be. . . .

But believe me, dear Monty, if you are set on writing any book do it, so far as we are concerned. I do believe in every author writing what he is keen on at the moment . . . and I regret I did not realize at the time that you were so keen on the historical book.

As I told Ralph Pinker . . . it would be a bad blow to Cassell's prestige if you wandered from us even for a single novel. Especially if you went to the sundial firm! You are the star in the Cassell firmament, and your departure would be a sad affair for me. Our relations have been so cordial all along that your going simply cannot happen, and that's all there is to it!

So I hope you will consider yourself free with your agreements with us to write just what you want to write. It's sure to be first class whatever it is, and there are damned few authors one can say that to!

I was naturally moved by that generous letter and wrote immediately:

Your letter gave me more pleasure than any letter I have had for a long time. As a matter of fact, I am not proposing to do the historical novel next. . . .

I shall be doing a short biography of Prince Charlie for Peter Davies, but at the moment I am wrestling with a play about Scott which the Masque Theatre people have commissioned for production in June. . . .

I've been ill ever since the Rectorial, and got up only yesterday for the first time.

I have been rattled about finances and not wanting to be always drawing on you in advance of books and thinking that the idea of historical novels did not appeal to you, I suggested when I was approached by Nicholson and Watson that if they put down a largish sum within the next month or two you might not want these novels.

The financial trouble has been that after having disposed of Jethou for £3,000 and having been paid the 10% deposit early last September the Treasury in December refused to transfer the lease to the proposed tenant though they could easily have said 'no' at once. The result was that I had to pay back the deposit and Jethou is still on my hands. . . .

The Daily Mail *reviewing has held up my getting on as I should have with* Second Athenian Memories *and being late with them was worrying me on your account. I have engaged to go on with the* Daily Mail *till next December, but I don't think I can go on after that, invaluable though the money has been every month for running expenses. Still, if I can judge from my correspondence I have done myself quite a bit of good with this reviewing, and I find a tendency, which I know will please you, for people to say that I have taken the place of Arnold Bennett as a guide to books. Of course, my criticisms are entirely different from his, but I think people feel they are equally sincere and independent. The trouble is the appalling sea of books in which I have to splash about, and I make a rule of not reviewing any book of which I have not read every word.*

I now decided to make one book of *Second* and *Last Athenian Memories* and to call it *Greek Memories*. All through that March I was wading among the papers I had kept and dictating to Chrissie at the rate of nearly 5,000 words a day.

On April 1st Newman Flower wrote:

I am very pleased to hear the book is going so well. I like the title better than Last Athenian Memories. *I should think we can probably get 8s. 6d. for it. I am not quite sure how far it is wise to raise the price, but I will go into the whole question. If you can let me have it at the end of May, I think the best time to publish would be the end of September.*

To this I replied next day:

I am glad you approve of Greek Memories. *The price is entirely a matter for you to decide, as the book is already paid for. . . .*

I have got a hell of a good scheme for a long novel, not a costume one by the way, but I won't worry you with the details of that at present.

I have just agreed to surrender all my Insurance policies to lower my overdraft.

On June 20th I wrote to Newman Flower:

As far as I can work it out Greek Memories *will run to 175,000 words, but the last chapter is now being typed. Each chapter occupies a month, and is subdivided into sections. It is a genuinely important historical contribution, and three-quarters of the book is taken up with facts which have never been published hitherto; some of these facts are known only to myself and two or three other people, and some even to myself alone.*

What do you think of The Four Winds of Love *as a title for a novel? It is what I am proposing to call my next novel.*

On June 29th Newman Flower wrote:

The length of Greek Memories *does not appal me—in fact I think it is rather a point in its favour.*

I hope you are going to make the novel a long one. It is time we had a long serious novel from you. When I say this, I don't cast reflection on the lighter books which, as you know, I like very much, but I think you have also a serious public which now needs a little attention.

On July 3rd I wrote:

I sent off the first eight chapters of Greek Memories *on Friday, and the rest will go off on Monday morning. The actual narrative can be estimated at 175,000 words, and the appendices will make another 10,000 words.*

The Four Winds of Love is intended to be a very long novel, and will consist of four love stories and four philosophies of love and four decades of a man's life. The problem will be how to finance myself while it is being written, because if I write a novel of probably more than 200,000 words, I don't see how it can be ready for you to publish before next Spring.

On August 31st Newman Flower wrote:

Now that I am back from holiday I have had a chance to read Greek Memories. *I do want to say what a delightful book I think it is—easily the best book of the series. I think it ought to raise a lot of controversy also and be a good winner at the same time.*

On September 3rd I wrote:

I am most delighted that you find Greek Memories *all right. Ought we not to include a map which could be used again in* Aegean Memories?

I am leaving here for Poland on Tuesday and shall see you, I hope, when I get back to London on the 19th.

I was glad to dig out those letters of 1932 because I had forgotten that the conception of *The Four Winds of Love* came to me in that year. As circumstances would rule *The East Wind of Love* would not be published until 1937 and *The North Wind of Love* would not blow until 1945. The long novel of 200,000 words would become a rather longer novel of nearly a million words.

I have run ahead and must go back to the Spring when Newman

Flower wrote me that heartening letter. I received another heartening letter from a little girl who lived at 10 Cholmondeley Road, Pendleton, Salford. In the corner was a picture of Mother Hubbard going to the cupboard:

Dear Mr Mackenzie,

I have just been reading your book entitled Santa Claus in Summer, *and I think it is lovely. Mummy got it out of* The Times Book Club Library *for me. I think it is wonderful for you to think of such a thing, but what has happened to Simple Simon and Old King Cole? I have a big book of Nursery Rhymes with nearly every Nursery Rhyme and Riddle in it, yet there are only about two in your book I have not heard of. I have a lot of good books such as the Doolittle ones, and I think Santa Claus is so nice I must have it for my own. I am saving my money up to buy it, but until I have enough I am going to ask Mummy if she will keep getting it out of the Library every few weeks.*

Mummy says you have got a little island all to your self, and I do envy you, because I like little islands. Daddy takes The Gramophone *and as we do not know any other address we have asked* The Gramophone *office to send this to you. I love Daddy to put records on such as the Drinking Song from* Othello, *The French Marseillaise, the Clock Symphony, The Ride of the Valkiries, Nursery Rhymes and Songs from when we were very young.*

Love
From

Margaret McFarlane Crawford
aged 8

Dear little girl who wrote me that fairy tale letter once upon a time, you are now aged 42. I am sure I wrote at the time to thank you for it, but let me thank you for it again now.

In that April I was at last able to keep a speaking engagement in Aberdeen under the auspices of the University Celtic Society and Nationalist Association, when in the Debating Hall of Marischal College I addressed what the *Aberdeen Free Press* in a two-column report described as a "large and enthusiastic audience" on "The Future of Scotland in Europe". The audience was so encouraging that my speech lasted for an hour and a quarter.

I extract a few sentences from the report of that speech:

"He had to face the fact of Nationalism in Scotland and see how it affected the great world movement going on to-day. He did not attach the slightest importance to whether we should run our own trams or 'buses, county councils and burghs, even our own Parliament, unless we were to do something worth doing with that power when we had got it.

"We had a superb and magnificent affair called the British Empire, made very largely by Scotsmen. If Scotland could take the lead with that Empire, he believed it could still continue to endure, but as it was not enduring at the present time because it had the wrong background. He was not an anti-Imperialist, but he was very much against running the British Empire as a suburb of London. . . .

"To take one point of division between Scotland and England alone, take the question of law. Scottish law was based on and linked with Roman law, while English law was an improvised law, full of legal fictions, without logic. Yet we were trying to run the Empire against a background of English common law. . . .

"He did not believe for one moment that if we had Home Rule—and he hated the words for they implied mere parochialism—that things would get along easier. On the contrary we would have what we might describe as Hell for say ten years, but if there was in the youth of this nation a belief in the future, if there was real vigour and real vision, it would be glad to live through this purgatory in order to achieve the paradise beyond; but it had to be lived through first. . . .

"Was all that had been fought for in the war to go for nothing, because at this moment it suited the financial heads of Europe to say that small nations were now a nuisance again?

"Those calling themselves Nationalists put themselves on the one hand against the Capitalist idea in which everything was to be managed to suit the big banking groups of Europe, but on the other hand, against the Communist idea, which was that individually man was not much good but, lumped together, could be made splendid. . . .

"The British Empire was heading for ruin. . . . He did not say that the British Empire was any worse than any other large conglomeration of States, but the only way to perfect the whole was the perfection of its individual component parts, and that, he submitted, was the value of nationalism, a determination not to be swept into this miserable accumulation and aggregation of nonentities. . . .

"He did not say that Home Rule would bring immediate benefit, but he believed that out of it, by the pulling of the country together and the responsibility cast upon young people—the chance they would have to make something of themselves—we could make something of our nation again, and by making something of our nation we could lead Europe and the world as once upon a time the Romans did."

That Aberdeen audience was one of the most responsive of all the many audiences I have addressed in my life. There is a strange idea that Aberdeen is the most hard-headed and materialistic of our Scottish cities. On the contrary, it is and always has been the most romantic. It was not Edinburgh or Glasgow or Dundee which gave most to the Stuart cause; it was Aberdeen.

In spite of the responsiveness of that audience I was a little shocked to find when I sat down that I had been talking for an hour and a quarter. So I was relieved to get the following letter from the Secretary of the

A.U.S.N.A. which as I write these words is still by far the most alive of the University Nationalist Associations:

"Your meeting was a great success and has aroused a lot of interest not only among the students but also among the general public. The manner in which you held the audience was amazing, and many who, to my knowledge, came to scoff were struck dumb by the intensity of the attention you forced them to give you. Thank goodness literature and the histrionic art are not mutually exclusive: you have made the best of both worlds—a difficult and unusual accomplishment."

On the 25th of that April was published the second volume of the *Official History of the Gallipoli Campaign* by Brigadier-General Cecil Aspinall-Oglander. Cecil Aspinall of whom I had written in *Gallipoli Memories* had married the heiress of an ancient Isle of Wight family and added her name to his own. I was glad when the Editor of the *Daily Mail* allowed me to give that official history a long notice on the day of publication.

"During the last year or so we have had at least two excellent stories of Gallipoli written by people who were not there. There was a recurrence of the belief that with another General than Ian Hamilton the campaign would have gone better. I disagree.

"For many years the Dardanelles Expedition has been regarded as a foolish and reckless project of Mr Winston Churchill's, foolishly and recklessly carried out by Sir Ian Hamilton. It is good to think that both of them have lived to see themselves vindicated in the eyes of all un-prejudiced men. That both made mistakes is evident; but the mistakes they made were not those attributed to them by common report.

"Another, too, is vindicated in these volumes, and that is the goddess Fortune. We can no longer say that luck was against us. She distributed her favours and her frowns equitably to both sides, and at the moment when most sorely of all her favour was needed she bestowed it upon ourselves. It will not detract from the astonishing feat of that triple evacuation to say that without Fortune's good-will the end of the Dardanelles Expedition would have been more bitter and more bloody than that of the Syracusan Expedition almost exactly 2,300 years before. Nor was it Fortune's malice that ruined the Suvla landing. The landing failed for a variety of reasons, in every one of which human fallibility is conspicuous.

"The tale is told. Jealousy, intrigue, faith, hope, fear, valour, fortitude, ambition, suffering, and regret, all are quiet now upon the printed page, quiet as the dead who lie out there upon this April morning, the song of many larks filling the sky above their graves, the first poppies breaking scarlet upon the slopes of Achi Baba beyond, and the blue Aegean lapping those beaches as gently as it lapped them on that April morning seventeen years ago."

In February the announcement had been made that Iain Colquhoun was to be Lord High Commissioner. I telegraphed my congratulations and he wrote:

It was kind of you to send good wishes and by gosh I need them. I am slowly recovering from the shock and I hope to be able to summon up a wan smile by the time I take up residence at Holyrood.

In May I attended the formal dinner at Holyroodhouse, the first Catholic to attend such an occasion since the birth of the Church of Scotland. I was to have sat next to Lady Oxford but she had a ferocious cold in the head that almost matched the colds of Rosamond Lehmann and Hamish Hamilton, and asked if I could go to her room after dinner. I like to think that when I drank to the toast of the Church of Scotland I was closer in touch with the spirit of today than the spirit of over thirty years ago.

I had met Lady Oxford last at that dance in Devonshire House of which I wrote in Octave Five. That long talk in her room after the dinner was the beginning of a much cherished friendship. When at the end of our talk I said I ought to be joining the company downstairs she insisted on coming out in her dressing-gown and showing me the way. I protested against exposing that cold of hers to draughts.

"Nonsense. You'll never find your way down without my help," she said.

And she was right. I should have been discovered wandering like the ghost of Riccio but for the guidance of Margot Oxford through corridor after corridor to the right staircase. She wrote me a letter next day when on her way to stay with the Crewes which, alas, has not survived.

On the way back to Eilean Aigas the steering gear of the Sunbeam locked as we were taking a sharp turn under a railway bridge some miles before Pitlochry. As a result the Sunbeam went into and over a low wall. I managed to hire a car in Pitlochry but Ashie Macrae had a deuce of a time getting the Sunbeam to a garage for repairs which cost over £50, on top of which I had to pay for the repair to the wall. According to Ashie Macrae all I said as we crashed over the wall was "Damn! I'll be late now with those *Daily Mail* reviews."

Somehow I managed to finish *Greek Memories* and send off the 850 pages of typescript by the beginning of July, but Chrissie was laid out for a week after taking down about 5,000 words of dictation a day and Nellie Boyte was almost laid out by typing the revised fair copy.

One morning I woke from dreaming that a shell had burst close by me to find that the larger part of the ceiling in my bedroom had fallen down. Luckily the extent of it did not come further than the edge of my chin, but except above my head there was no ceiling left, and I had to shout for help before I could extricate myself from the weight of plaster a testimony to the builders of earlier years.

In June I had to go down to a graduation in Glasgow. The most memorable honorary degree awarded that year was the LL.D. to Helen Keller. Her speech of thanks at the luncheon was delivered as clearly as a bell and like a bell on one note. She was sitting next to me and when I rose to pay my tribute and saw my poor words being tapped out upon her hand by Miss Anne Sullivan, the devoted teacher who brought her into life from blindness, deafness and dumbness, it was all I could do to go on speaking, so close was I to tears.

It may have been during that visit to Glasgow that one of the professors asked me to dine and meet the Archbishop of York.[1]

"The last time I saw you was when you were playing Phidippides in *The Clouds*. My goodness, that's about thirty years ago," said the Archbishop.

"Ah, but I remember Your Grace over forty years ago," I said. "A fat boy in Etons at Colet Court, known as Temple Secundus."

The Archbishop gave what can only be called a thunderous guffaw.

"I correspond with Temple Primus in India. He's a great supporter of my paper *The Gramophone*."

"Dear old Richard! Yes, I know he's mad on music."

I wrote soon after this to Richard Temple, and at the end of a long letter about records that were urgently needed by the faithful, he wound up *I'm glad you've seen fat William again.*

A day or two later I went to Stirling to take part in the annual commemoration of Bannockburn by the National Party. Cunninghame Graham and I were in his ancient car driving up the hill at the tail of the procession. It may have been the emotional effect of that speech I had heard at the Glasgow graduation, for which I had been called upon with Principal Rait to pay our tribute to that wonderful woman, that made my speech at Bannockburn more emotional than I usually allowed myself to be. I wound it up with the words Hugh MacDiarmid used in his lyric about the little wild rose of Scotland. That lyric has been perhaps the best loved of all he wrote. In the first edition it was printed (with acknowledgments to Compton Mackenzie).

When the speeches were over Wendy Wood led a party of enthusiastic young Nationalists to Stirling Castle where they forced their way through some Argyll and Sutherland Highlanders of the garrison and pulled down the Union Jack flying over the Castle.

I had already been irritated by the way some members of the National Council were protesting that the movement for Home Rule was merely a demand for a Parliament to deal with domestic affairs and refused to demand as much independence as had been granted to the Irish Free

[1] The late Archbishop of Canterbury.

State. I still saw no value for a Parliament that would merely be a glorified County Council. I was beginning to distrust the way some members of the National Council were preoccupied with nursing constituencies they were hoping to contest at the first opportunity. When one after another of them disowned Wendy Wood's action in press criticisms and when finally it was proposed to censure her officially I wrote a private letter to J. B. MacCormick:

> Eilean Aigas.
>
> 28th June, 1932.

I hope that no formal and official censure will be moved on Wendy Wood. I could not identify myself with such a motion and it will involve me in resignation from the Council into which I do not want to be driven. I write to you privately so that you know in advance what my attitude would be and so that with your capacity for diplomacy you can use this knowledge in handling the situation.

On the same day Wendy Wood wrote to me:

Your kind letter has roused my spirits—not that I was downhearted, because, so far from being a sudden impulse, my campaign is the result in a way of eighteen years' work for our common end. . . .

I thank you in deep sincerity for your backing, the more so that I know that nothing would deter you from hanging me if you thought my action bad for the Cause.

Today Wendy Wood is still fighting for the Cause and three or four years ago I gave myself the pleasure of dedicating to her a book I wrote on moral courage of which she remains a conspicuous example.

In spite of lowering my overdraft with the Westminster Bank by surrendering my endowment policies, finance was still a problem. I realized that Eilean Aigas was going to be too expensive an establishment to maintain and resolved to sub-let it if possible and find a smaller house. Faith had gone to Dryden Chambers and was working with *The Gramophone*. That was becoming a bit of a problem owing to the financial squeeze which was affecting the sale of books and records. With astonishing courage Edward Lewis[1] had acquired Decca and after losing thousands of pounds was slowly building it up to become the Decca of today. Nevertheless, advertising of records was being cut down.

We had some nibbles at Jethou this Summer and Faith went down there in July to do her best to display the island to advantage.

I heard of a manse in Stoer, a remote township in the Stoer peninsula on the north-west coast of Sutherland. So Ursula Maxwell, Chrissie and I set out in the Maxwell Chrysler to investigate that manse. How Ursula drove that large car over the road on which we travelled is a marvel in

---

[1] Sir Edward Lewis.

remembrance. We stayed at the Inchnadamph inn at the head of Loch Assynt on the way back, because I was going to spend a night with Hector and Christobel Munro-Ferguson just beyond Evanton on the north side of the Cromarty Firth. In the post office at Stoer I sent a telegram to give the time of my arrival next day. I wrote it out and was just going to read it aloud when the old lady of over eighty who was taking the telegram said:

"Och, I've read it. I know fine who you are."

People have complained with reason of the illegibility of my hand-writing; how that old lady of eighty was able to read that handwriting of mine upside down seemed miraculous.

Ursula and Chrissie left me at Assynt, as the Ross-shire house of the Munro-Fergusons was called; they had an incredibly remote lodge in Assynt itself which could only be reached by nearly a mile of moist walking over the moor.

Christobel Munro-Ferguson was a remarkable woman who had per-formed deeds of derring-do in that freezing retreat over the mountains of Albania to the Adriatic when the nurses had to leave Nish before the advancing enemy. Hector Munro-Ferguson was always stimulating company. He made a major contribution to my future physical comfort when he introduced me to a closet-pan six inches lower than the stock pans that sanitary firms provide. I followed his advice and shall deserve the gratitude of those who are wise enough to take it.

It was on that visit that I met for the first time Lady Londonderry. When I was leaving with Ashie Macrae next morning she said to me suddenly in that rich voice of hers:

"I think Ramsay MacDonald ought to meet you. I must arrange a meeting."

I wondered vaguely if she was serious about this; as it would turn out she was.

Soon after this Chrissie and I set out for Barra where I should have to work hard at my life of Prince Charlie for Peter Davies. We were to stay with Ruairidh MacNeil and his wife at Northbay on the other side of the bay from Father John Macmillan's house and the church. Owing to the recurrent surnames in the Islands almost everybody has a nick-name. John Macpherson, the outstanding character in Northbay, was the Coddie; Ruairidh was the Crookle. I say that the Coddie was the outstanding character but when I look back at them all the characters in Barra were outstanding in one way or another.

The Crookle had been a merchant seaman and had been caught with his ship in Smyrna when the Turks went to war with us in 1914. So he had spent the whole war as an internee in Smyrna. He was a great reader and I recall the eagerness with which he used to read the proofs of *Greek Memories* when they arrived. Bean Crookle, his wife, was a Macdonald, and with them lived her father, a saintly old man in his eighties whose charity was boundless and faith unquestioning; one thing only slightly perturbed him and that was when the Crookle and I went off on Sunday evening to play auction bridge with Father John and Neil Sinclair, the schoolmaster of Northbay, always known as the Sgoileir Ruadh—the red scholar—to distinguish him from another great character John Johnston, the Sgoileir Bàn or fair scholar who was the schoolmaster at Greian.

This faint disapproval of playing cards on Sunday was a survival of the Jansenist tendencies of the Catholic islands in the eighteenth century; the Scots College in Paris was always held by the Jesuits to be tainted with Jansenism. I remember old Mr Macdonald's telling me a story of how as a young man he had seen fairies making boats of the iris flags that lined the banks of one of the lochs and sailing away across the loch in those tiny green boats. It never occurred to me for an instant when I was listening to this tale that it did not happen exactly as he described the incident. More and more, as I have grown older, I have come to believe that there really are more things in heaven and earth than were dreamt of by Horatio. I believe that human beings have passed out of the stage when they were in communication with what we call fairies. Similarly so-called civilized humanity has lost much of its sense of smell, touch and sight.

I happened to read that July a thriller by C. P. Snow called *Death Under Sail*. I wrote in the *Daily Mail*:

"The publishers seem much impressed by the fact that Dr Snow is a don of Christ's College, Cambridge, engaged in vitamin research, and that he wrote *Death Under Sail* while taking a holiday on the Norfolk Broads. Their testimonial reminds me of Dr Johnson's testimonial to a woman's preaching. It was, he said, like a dog walking on its hind legs. It was not well done, but it was surprising to see it done at all.

"Dr Snow is a distinguished authority on vitamins, but he has not yet discovered how to put vitamins into his characters. The only live person is the Harley Street specialist, and he is murdered on p. 32. However, *Death Under Sail* is a good specimen of the chess-problem thriller and incidentally offers a suggestive peep into the schoolgirl naïvety of the scientific mind on holiday."

Lord Snow would have been still in his twenties when he wrote that thriller and that engaging naïvety of the scientific mind on holiday is still perceptible. He would not be able to see fairies making tiny boats of flag irises. Yet the scientist's vision of the future is for them fairyland.

That summer I had another example of schoolgirl naïvety in *Down the Garden Path*.

"Mr Beverley Nichols has bought a cottage in Huntingdonshire, and this eclogue in prose is the result. It is always entertaining, for Mr

Beverley Nichols, even when he is weeping in a close-up like a cinema star, can hardly help being entertaining, and though I find his coyness a little out of keeping with Cowper's landscape, who am I to ask the leopard to change its spots or the kitten to cease chasing its tail?

"Mr Beverley Nichols is not oppressively reliable as a horticultural adviser. *Sternbergia lutea* will need more sun in summer than we have been having lately if he wants to be sure of its October gold in Huntingdon-shire. He will stand a better chance with *Schizostylis coccinea* (the Kaffir lily), which will give him what he has not yet secured for his winter garden—a blazing crimson in November."

I remember saying as I finished dictating that review:

"This book *Down the Garden Path* ought to be called *Colney Thatch* or *A Tile Off.*"

Before the end of July, I managed to write 45,000 words of *Prince Charlie* and then cut 15,000 out of the biography in order to bring it into line with the series. I also had to read the proofs of *Greek Memories* which was quite a job.

The hard work was rewarded by the news that Magdalen, Veronica and Hugh Fraser with Betty Maxwell were going to spend a week with me in the Crookle's cottage.

That week at the end of July with Betty, Magdalen, Veronica and Hugh, all of whom somehow or other we managed to pack into that cottage, comes back in memory on waves of laughter which echo in my mind like the Atlantic waves upon that island of the blest. Hugh, who was now fourteen and a half, had acquired a movie camera, and to his impatience the weather decided to be obstinately calm at first. Luckily, just before the end of that week the waves behaved themselves. We all went up to Faire na h'Abh and Hugh was able to get some good pictures of real breakers. Later on at Beaufort there was a party to see Hugh's presentation of his skill with a movie camera. The screen was set up; the lights were dimmed; we heard the click of the camera. And Hugh suddenly rushed out of the room in despair; he had put the film on upside down.

The end of that week came. We all went over to Pollochar with the Coddie in his boat and spent the day in South Uist before our beloved visitors had to take the boat at Lochboisdale that evening. We drove in two cars to the Creagorry Inn beside what used to be called the South Ford to Benbecula; there is a bridge over it today. I see what appears in memory as hundreds of swans swimming lazily upon the silvery blue of Loch Bee. I see lochan after lochan almost completely covered by water-lilies. I see the Coddie get out of his car and beckon mysteriously to the Crookle and the two drivers.

"Going to look at the water-lilies," says the Coddie, as the four of them vanish for a minute or two behind a protective bump in the flat moorland.

"I think they've gone to look at the whisky-lilies," says eleven-year-old Veronica to me.

At the Creagorry Inn the Coddie persuaded the hostess to serve us with the lobsters that were intended for the lunch of the Colonels when they came back from their fishing. So the Colonels had to wait for their lunch. Those fishing Colonels became a joke throughout lunch. Finally Hugh and Veronica could not resist going into the drawing-room as the 'lounge' of today was still called.

"Do you mind not jumping about?" said one of the Colonels crossly. "Can't you see that I'm trying to extract a hook from my friend's thumb?"

How that Colonel was hooked in the drawing-room we never knew, but for the rest of their lunch which we were eating in the dining-room we kept finding one more hilarious explanation than the last.

It was only a week, but in memory that week seems a month of delight. Magdalen wrote from Stronelairg Lodge, Whitebridge:

Dearest Monty,

Thank you so very much for the quite lovely days at Barra.

I can't tell you how much I enjoyed every moment.

I do hope you aren't too weary. You were so wonderfully well when we arrived. I'm afraid we rather wore you out.

We had a pretty stiff crossing. Betty was defeated by it and we all felt somewhat squeamish.

We had a hectic week-end at Morar, Veronica succeeding in making Ibbie[1] green with jealousy. Every day her stories grew better.

There were two balls on Monday, one at Mallaig, another at Morar but they weren't nearly as much fun as the Luadh.[2]

Here is the £1 that you lent us—we succeeded in travelling 1st on steerage tickets so didn't need it. . . .

I do hope you'll soon come back to Eilean Aigas.

With best love
Magdalen

When I showed that letter to Betty Maxwell thirty-four years later she told me that her defeat was due to Magdalen's making her drink Worcester sauce as a certain cure for sea-sickness.

The address above that letter reminds me of a visit to the shooting-lodge in a remote part of the moors when Father D'Arcy, S.J. was staying at Beaufort. The wind blew shrewdly and Laura Lovat insisted on lending Father D'Arcy one of Simon's greatcoats which swept the floor round Father D'Arcy's feet.

[1] A Moniack Fraser.
[2] A *luadh* or waulking of the tweed in the parish hall at Northbay.

Veronica wrote from Glenmar Cross Farm, Arisaig:

Darling Monty,
    I am awfully sorry for not having written before to thank you terrifically for my visit to Barra, etc, etc. I did so love it, etc, etc, etc.
    I am having great fun here and would love to write you a longer letter if Ibby and Ian weren't busily removing me down to the beach.
                        Tons of love and kisses
                                        from
                                        Veronica
P.S. Irene is coming to-day. Thank Chrissie for my clothes and give her, Crookle, Peggy, Coddy my love.

During that August the wretched Kensitites had been pestering Bernard Walke and desecrating his church down in Cornwall. I was delighted to see letters from that saintly man George Lansbury and A. J. Munnings[1] in *The Times.*

From the latter's letter of August 23rd I quote:

"I would like to take this opportunity, though late, of thanking Mr Lansbury for all he has said in his letter to *The Times* about the Rector of St Hilary, who in this time of trial has the sympathies of many, myself included.

"It seems incredible that such a miserably petty outburst can have happened in our world of to-day. I know the Reverend Bernard Walke as a friend. A true Christian and a lover of humanity, he is loved and trusted by his parish. I see the old Rectory at St Hilary plainly in mind as I write, with its large garden, planted here and there with rare plants and shrubs given him by Compton Mackenzie when he lived there long ago."

What a grand chap Alfred Munnings was!

Somehow the proofs of *Greek Memories* and the revision of *Prince Charlie* were dealt with that August in time for me to go to Poland early in September with what was variously described as a cultural mission and a deputation of the Scottish National Party but what was in fact as jolly an excursion party as ever sailed.

The party had been arranged by Francis Czarnomski, the cultural attaché at the Polish Embassy in London, and consisted of David Cleghorn Thomson, Moray McLaren, Guy Warrack, Robins Miller, Eric Maschwitz, Philip Jordan and myself. We sailed from London for Gdynia in the S.S. *Lwow.* The day before we were to sail I received a letter from Lord Beaverbrook, asking me to lunch at Stornoway House four or five days later. He was at this date launching the *Scottish Daily Express.* Gladstone Murray who was the liaison between the B.B.C. and

---

[1] The late Sir A. J. Munnings, P.R.A.

the Press urged me to put off Poland for such an occasion; as arrangements had already been made for me to be received by the Rector of
Warsaw University and address the students as Rector of Glasgow
University I did not feel that I could accept Lord Beaverbrook's invitation.

We had a riotous voyage to Gdynia. I expected to be sea-sick but a
Polish liqueur made from blackberries was so fortifying that none of us
was sea-sick.

At Kiel in the Canal Cleghorn Thomson was met on the wharf by his
former governess with four of her offspring and we watched them click
heels one after another and bow to their mother's former pupil. I refused
to go ashore, not wishing to break a resolve made in childhood never to
set foot in Germany.

From Gdynia, an attractive brand new town, we went on by train to
Warsaw. The train happened to pull up just before we reached Danzig
station beside the squalid outskirts of the city. On a tumbledown fence I
saw a swastika either tarred or painted and was filled with an awareness
of utter evil. The black swastika on that decayed fence with the degraded
dwellings beyond seemed as much alive as a tarantula, venomous and
malevolent.

Czarnomski had insisted that those of us with kilts should wear them
when we arrived at Warsaw station for the benefit of the Press photo-
graphers. As soon as we reached the Europeyski Hotel Moray McLaren
and I got into trousers, but Cleghorn Thomson's enormous trunk had
gone astray and he was unable to change.

I found waiting for me a telegram from Beaverbrook:

Charter plane and come to lunch on . . . whatever day of the week it was.

This was accompanied by a telegram from Gladstone Murray urging
me to do so. I replied that I had academic and other engagements in
Warsaw and so regretfully could not attend the lunch.

I heard the sequel from Bill Murray when I returned to England.
Beaverbrook had tossed my telegram across the table to Murray with
these words,

"Does this fellow think Warsaw is of more importance to him than I
am?"

For some years my name was always cut out from any reference to it
in the *Daily Express*. I recall sitting next Tom Driberg, the original
William Hickey, at a Foyle's lunch and his saying to me he could have
had three paragraphs out of our chat but that my name was not allowed
at the moment. The ban was raised in due course and for thirty years
the *Daily Express* has been kind to me.

Once upon a time Alfred Harmsworth could damage a reputation as
when the *Daily Mail* always reported the cases lost by Marshall Hall at
length but his successes in a few lines. Marshall Hall's income was

reduced for a while. The power of the *Daily Mail* once upon a time has never been attained by any other newspaper.

After we had changed, Moray and I set out for a stroll round Warsaw before we went to lunch. Suddenly we caught sight of David Cleghorn Thomson followed by a crowd of about two hundred youthful Poles. We dived into a church to escape. Mass was going on, and as the priest turned to say 'Dominus vobiscum' we saw an expression of incredulous amazement on his face as two vergers hurried toward the west door to turn David away. They thought he was a woman who had come in without a hat on her head.

After Mass Moray and I walked cautiously along and then again catching sight of kilted Cleghorn Thomson followed by an even larger crowd we dived into a restaurant, and ordered lunch.

A minute or two later we saw everybody in the restaurant standing up. It was the sight of kilted David in the doorway. Moray and I prayed he would not come into the restaurant and to our ineffable relief David passed on.

That evening I was due to address a gathering of students, male and female, with the courteous Rector of the University in the chair. The address was followed by a jolly and informal meal after which Moray and I suggested that some of us should go and dance in a night club. I recall that over the doorway of that night club there was a lighted picture of the Blessed Virgin with the Holy Infant in her arms. We danced into the small hours. Fortified by that Polish liqueur we had enjoyed on the *Lwow* Moray and I danced a terrific polka mazurka to encouraging applause.

Next morning I was visited in my mid-Victorian room at the Europeyski by the leading nurseryman of Warsaw called by a name like Maclowski. He had no English and I had no Polish. So we conversed in French. He told me that he was descended from a Macleod of Skye who had come to Poland in the seventeenth century and asked me to take back to Scotland an album bound in red morocco leather which he desired to present to the Clan Macleod Society. Inside was his line of descent and beautifully illuminated coats of arms of various Skye lairds from whom he traced his descent. That album is now in the possession of the Clan Macleod Society. I was moved by this encounter. We have been privileged in Scotland to offer a second home for Poles who fought by our side in the last war. It was returning Polish hospitality as far back as the fifteenth century when so many Scots went to Poland that there was a Scottish ghetto in Warsaw to accommodate them.

I cannot recall in detail our lavish entertainment in Warsaw. There was a P.E.N. Club gathering which was exactly like any P.E.N. Club gathering wherever it gathers. Mr Zalewski, the Polish Foreign Minister, gave us a lunch and I had the privilege of an hour's talk with him afterwards in the garden of the Ministry. He spoke perfect English and was sympathetic with my aspirations for Scottish autonomy. I went to our Embassy and found the Rt. Hon. Sir William Erskine, G.C.M.G. just the same as the Willie Erskine of Athens and Rome. I had not seen that lovable man and smiled with him over human absurdity for twelve years.

We visited the Palace where we had to discalce ourselves to walk across the exquisite floor of the great hall. I suppose the Palace was destroyed by the Germans. There was a small room off the hall in which was a solitary full-length picture of a man dressed in a costume, half Elizabethan, half eighteenth century. This man had a countenance which fascinated me. When I consulted the guide to find who he was I learnt to my gratified astonishment that it was Gustavus III of Sweden whose biography I had often planned to write. He was not only a King but a playwright of poetic power who was assassinated during the bitter strife between the Hats and the Caps. What endeared me to him was his kindness to Charles Edward Stuart in the days of his adversity. The bitter 'ifs' of history! If those two royal personages had been given their chance democracy might have come to Europe much sooner and without the miseries that darkened its coming.

One last memory of Warsaw and that is of the vodka into which had been dipped blades of grass from the hay harvest, which made it taste like the scent of hay.

Some of the party had to go back home after Warsaw but when Francis Czarnomski suggested a visit to Cracow and Zagopani Moray McLaren, Philip Jordan and I stayed on for another week.

Even as a schoolboy I had felt as much distressed by the two Partitions of Poland as by the failure of the '15 and '45 rebellions. I was deeply affected by that too brief visit to the ancient capital of Poland.

"The old palace of the kings on the Wawer used by the Austrians as barracks less perhaps from any desire deliberately to abase yet further Polish nationhood than from that Teutonic insensitiveness which despises defeat, was still eloquent of past greatness, and that mound, that hill indeed, raised by Poles with bags of earth brought from all over the world to make a site for the statue of the patriot Kosciuszko, heaved up from this teeming plain of central Europe to forbid despair." One morning I left the crowded sunlit market-place for the "glowing twilight of St Mary's Church. A late Mass was being said at a side altar by the south door, and I passed through the group to sit and meditate in one of the isolated carved pews of the Renaissance in the body of the church which was empty except for a few devotees kneeling before the gleaming jewelled caverns of saintly shrines. The outside of the church, mellowed though its red bricks and steep-pitched copper roof might be by the sun and snow and wind of seven hundred years, did not prepare the visitor for the wonder of colour within. The absence of a great west window as in most of the Gothic churches of France and England intensified the solemnity of the twilight stained with rays from the high windows of honey and emerald and that warm gules which Keats recorded thrown upon the breast of Madeline, that rose-bloom which fell upon her clasped hands. The vaulted roof was blue as night and gilded with a multitude of stars, and above the high altar the sublime triptych of Veit Stoss, the nearest that mortal artist has ever come to portraying the Assumption, was of live gold and azure, carved with such boldness of relief that the angels bearing the body of the Virgin aloft seemed to float away with the Queen of Heaven and hang suspended between earth and sky above the altar. The narrowness of the nave appeared extreme compared with the height, but that accentuated the soaring quality of the interior, the very architectural design being itself an Assumption."

When I came out of the church the stillness of a hot September afternoon was over the square. "The market women were nodding under their coloured parasols, and business was for a while at a standstill. Suddenly, above the cooing of a myriad pigeons, the trumpeter's horary tune was heard from his room under the eight small spires of the taller of the two towers of St Mary's Church. That tune had been blown halfway through the thirteenth century to warn the city that the Tartar hordes were at hand. An arrow had pierced the watchman's throat before the tune was finished, and ever since, without missing an hour of the day or night, trumpeter after trumpeter had blown that same tune from the four windows of that room at the top of the church tower and ever since had ended on the same wavering note, the last note blown by the watchman before the Tartar arrow pierced his throat. Eastward the trumpeters had blown defiance to the Tartar, and southward they had blown defiance to the Turk. To the west they had proclaimed that Poland was the guardian of Europe against Mahomet and to the north they had given warning that she stood firm against Luther."

Those words above in inverted commas would be written four years later in *The East Wind of Love*, unaware that four years later still a fouler horde than Tartars or Turks would ravish Cracow and carry away that sublime triptych to Germany. I believe that the triptych has been restored but I do not know if the trumpeter still blows his horary defiance.

In *The East Wind of Love* I described the fantastic salt-mine of Wisliczka which we visited before we went on to the agreeable highland spa of Zagopani. I regret I did not make more of that experience in *The East Wind of Love*. Writing about it now thirty-four years later it is difficult to recall it exactly. What I recall most vividly is a ten-mile gradual ascent into the Tatra mountains and an open fair Mass attended by hikers of various nationalities amid a lofty and wide prospect of

mountains. On the ten-mile descent my confounded sciatic nerve mis-
behaved itself and each mile was more painful.

A day or two later Philip Jordan and I were in a boat bound for Hull.
I had run out of Veganin and the passage through the Kiel Canal was
infernally unpleasant. The only relief from pain was a glorious 'literally'
in *The Times*; their racing correspondent when summing up the chances
of various horses for the St Leger said that the claims of —— who had
literally run away with the Two Thousand Guineas must not be overlooked. I cannot give the name of the three-year-old who performed that
feat because the new style *Annual Register* of 1932 does not mention any
sporting events. One of the tragedies of this century is the progressive
decline in the value of the *Annual Register* to the social historian. Recorded
for September in the paltry Chronicle is this pathetic and worthless piece
of information:

"The World's Fastest Train, the Cheltenham Flier, completed the
journey between Swindon and Paddington (G.W.R.) in 65 minutes,
being an average speed of 71·3 miles an hour."

I went from Hull to Bradford where as the President this year of the
English Society I had to deliver an address on Sir Walter Scott. In the
effort to get *Greek Memories* written I had had to give up the play I had
agreed to write about him and I was glad to pay my tribute to him in
this centenary year. I had reviewed two biographies of Scott which I
could not entirely commend. Of *The Laird of Abbotsford* by Dame Una
Pope-Hennessy I wrote:

"Her book is readable, but her manner of an arch hostess explaining
to some dull guests the whims and foibles of a great writer is to me an
exasperation. I am thankful that so great a man as Scott could have his
weaknesses; but I owe no thanks at all to the patronizing biographer
who assumes the right of a valet to call no man he serves a hero.

"We are none of us above gossiping about the petty weaknesses of the
great; but let us keep such gossip for the nuts and wine or the drawing-
room fireside and not give it the quasi-veracity of print. It is an old plea
of such biographers that they desire to present the victim as a human
being; do they suppose in their self-conceit that the man presented by
Lockhart was not a human being?"

Of *Sir Walter Scott* by John Buchan which I commended more warmly
I wrote:

"I am curious to know what Mr Buchan means by this sentence: 'The
kilt, the former garb of servants, was assumed to be the Scottish national
dress, since it had been worn by the King.' One can sympathize with
Mr Buchan as a Borderer over those mock tartans which were foisted
on the great Border families by Edinburgh haberdashers; but he should
be above writing such nonsense about the kilt, for the right to wear which
men had been ready to die, not so long before Sir Walter Scott was born.

It might astonish Mr Buchan to know that there is no word for 'servants' in Gaelic, except a modern adaptation from the English."

One of the pleasures of that visit to Bradford was meeting Father John O'Connor, the original of G. K. Chesterton's Father Brown, who proposed my health at an early dinner at the Midland Hotel before the address.

"Don't eat much," my host warned me. "We'll be having supper afterwards."

That kind host was Alderman Illingworth, and that supper given by him and his charming wife was a remarkable meal; we stayed up talking till the small hours.

I had a splendid audience in the Eastbrook Hall, because one or two Scottish societies in Bradford had joined up with the English Society for the occasion. The Yorkshire papers were all very good to me.

I was sorry to have to leave Bradford next day. Perhaps because I was born in the north of England I always felt refreshed by visits to northern cities as once upon a time Antaeus by Mother Earth.

On October 3rd I was writing to Faith in Dryden Chambers from Eilean Aigas to say how disappointing it was to hear she had bronchial 'flu and might not be able to come to Glasgow for the conferment of honorary degrees on the Duke and Duchess of York.

I made what was apparently an electrifying five minutes' speech in the Usher Hall at Edinburgh on Friday in which I denounced Devolution and Compromise. The whole audience of 1,000 rose to its feet and cheered for three minutes and as I hurried from the platform to catch the train to Inverness the firemen rushed forward to pat my back. Even the Daily Record, *sponsor of moderate home-rule, said I raised myself and the audience to heights of patriotic enthusiasm.*

To-day I lunched with the Munro-Fergusons, where was Lady Londonderry who eloped with the Prime Minister. Something is afoot. She was ringing the Prime Minister on the 'phone and told me that he said specially how sorry he was he could not be at lunch. She then suggested bringing him over to Eilean Aigas to see me or possibly taking him to the Mòd at Fort William one day. I can't make out what's going on. But it is all to be very secret.

In the end it was arranged that I should meet the Prime Minister at the Spean Bridge Hotel, on his road to the Mòd from which I should be coming away.

Looking back at that Fort William Mòd, I think I enjoyed it more than any Mòd at which I have been. One reason for that has nothing to do with Gaelic; it was at this Mòd that I met for the first time Eric Linklater, and from the moment we shook hands we were intimate friends. I remember on that first night that the rain gave a downpour notable even for Lochaber. Eric and I were at the Highland Hotel where the venerable fathers of the Mòd were staying. We sat up together in the smoke-room. It must have been around midnight when above the swish of the rain without I heard the deep and solemn tones of Eric Linklater.

"You can always charm the Celt with a song."

"Oh, that's very interesting, Mr Linklater," observed one of the venerable fathers turning to another. "Did you hear what Mr Linklater said, Mr Macleod? You can always charm the Celt with a song."

"Yes," Eric went on. "I remember in the war when I was with the Black Watch my section was getting rattled by the heavy shelling. 'Who do you think you are?' I said. 'The Black Watch or the f---ing windy Sussex?' You can always charm the Celt with a song."

The expression on the faces of the venerable fathers is still in my mind's eye.

The next day I stopped at the Spean Bridge Hotel, on the way back to Eilean Aigas, to await the arrival of Ramsay MacDonald. A quarter of an hour later he arrived with his secretary and immediately went to the telephone box in the entrance hall, where he put through a call to the Foreign Office. He did not close the door of the box and anybody in the hall could hear "This is the Prime Minister speaking. I shall be travelling back to London tomorrow by the night train. If I am needed urgently I shall be at Fort William till then." Then he turned to greet me, and we had a talk lasting about twenty minutes about Home Rule of which he had been a fervid supporter in the old days. When he got up to go the manageress of the hotel asked if Mr Ramsay MacDonald and I would put our names in the visitors' book.

I was just telling her that the Prime Minister was at the moment incognito when he broke in.

"Certainly, we'll write our names in the visitors' book."

And if that visitors' book still exists the name of Compton Mackenzie under the name of Ramsay MacDonald can be seen on an early October day in 1932.

Before he got into the car to drive on to Fort William Ramsay MacDonald said to me,

"Now don't forget that Alastair has a father, and come and see me at Hampstead."

Alastair, his elder son, was a friend of mine; I had not yet met Malcolm. Then as he was stepping into the car the Prime Minister looked round and said over his shoulder,

"Tell Lady Londonderry we have had this talk, and I shall get a good mark."

There was something endearingly ingenuous about Ramsay Mac-Donald. Those years of premiership cannot have been too happy.

A few days later I went down to Glasgow to attend the conferment of honorary degrees on their Royal Highnesses, the Duke and Duchess of

York. I recall the Vice-Chancellor's anxiety over the ability of the Chancellor's[1] health to stand the strain of the proceedings.

"He's determined to come up from Argyll, I only hope his heart will behave itself. I'm putting a tiny flask of brandy in my pocket and you'd better do the same."

The Duke and Duchess were received on their arrival at the University by the Principal and myself. The Duchess was wearing a frock of pale blue velvet. I am always warned by women friends to avoid trying to describe female attire. So I shall not attempt to say more about that pale blue velvet frock except that the wearer of it looked enchanting.

The Vice-Chancellor's anxiety about the Chancellor's heart was needless. As we marched downstairs and upstairs preceded by the Bedell, Mr Ramsay, with his heavy mace, Sir Donald Macalister's steps never faltered once.

After the ceremony of conferring the honorary degrees we adjourned for lunch at which the Chancellor was in the chair at the high table. The Duke sat on his right with the Vice-Chancellor on his other side: the Duchess sat on his left with myself on her other side.

My gratification may be imagined when the Duchess told me that she had listened to my Rectorial Address on the wireless and had agreed with all I said. Then she added quickly:

"But I think you and Mr Cunninghame Graham sometimes go too far in your speeches. You seem to support the idea of a republic for Scotland."

"I assure you, ma'am, that neither of us has any belief in a republic. We simply want to dissolve the Parliamentary Union, but preserve the Crown."

The Duchess asked me what I thought was the feeling in the country about royalty. I could reply with sincerity that I thought the last part of Great Britain that would turn against royalty would be Scotland.

"Still, it would be wonderful, ma'am, if Princess Margaret Rose could be educated in Scotland, learn Gaelic, and become one day Princess of Scotland with Holyroodhouse brought to life again."

At the end of lunch Sir Donald Macalister rose to propose the health of their Royal Highnesses in an excellent speech, to which the Duke of York replied. He said how grateful he and the Duchess were for the honour conferred upon them by this ancient University and he wished to express their particular thanks to Sir Donald Mac . . . and then he paused. The Duchess was tapping the menu card and murmuring 'Macalister, Macalister, Macalister'. The academic wives at the tables down below were sitting in what they hoped were respectful attitudes of bright-eyed attention. And then after some seconds the Duke said 'Macalister' and went on to make his speech without a trace of that

[1] The late Sir Donald Macalister, Bt., K.C.B.

occasional impediment which he had conquered with such determination.

On our way to the Principal's Lodging after lunch where a car was to come and take the Duke and Duchess to perform some of those endless functions royalty is called upon to endure, the Duke asked me why a certain window was where it was.

"It offends my notion of symmetry," he said and went on to suggest an architectural improvement.

I was able to say without the slightest suggestion of courtiership that his Royal Highness knew much more about architecture than I did.

In spite of the weather which after a mercifully fine morning had turned to rain the tour of Glasgow made by the royal pair was enthusiastically welcomed, and I felt that the Duchess would be able to feel quite happy about Scotland's affection for royalty.

I had a crowded few days after this. I find in a letter:

On Wednesday evening I have to go to the big Glasgow Trades dinner. On Thursday I am broadcasting and attending the Catholic men students' smoker and on Friday I have to go to Kilmarnock to deliver the Scott oration.

I break off to recall an old gentleman's coming up to me afterwards and asking me if I would like to see the house in which my father used to lunch every Sunday with the Provost in 1875. That was when as a very young man he was playing at Kilmarnock in stock as repertory used to be called. The only difference is that he would have had to learn and play at least three dozen parts in three or four months, which would be quite beyond any actor in a repertory company today. So next morning I was taken by the old gentleman to look at a pleasant house beside the river. I resume the letter:

Back on Saturday. Then on October 24 I lecture to the University on the Novel, on October 25 I address the Ministers' Fraternal in the morning and foregather with the Catholic girl students at Notre Dame Convent in the evening. On October 26 I speak at Paisley and Johnstone. On October 27 I address the Students International Club. On October 28 I speak at the great Nationalist rally in St Andrew's Hall, going on from Glasgow to Dublin where I have to talk in Trinity College.

I went on with my programme for the rest of the year; circumstances would prevent my fulfilling that programme.

Greek Memories was published a week or two later. There was a long and encouraging notice in *The Times Literary Supplement*, but J. B. Priestley found them dull and disappointing and made some rather rude remarks. Newman Flower wrote:

Thus your friend J. B. Priestley in the Evening Standard *to-night*, and stuck the review underneath, adding some much ruder remarks about J. B. Priestley.

C.M. with the Duke and Duchess of York and Sir Robert Rait
(Principal of Glasgow University) at the time of Lord Rectorship

Faith, Captain of Dunstaffnage and Lady
Elspeth Campbell at Dingwall

C.M. and Eric Linklater

I wrote to say he must not be too angry with J. B. P. because in a review I had pulled his leg about a novel called *Faraway* by saying I was sometimes under the impression that we were crossing the Pacific with Mr Priestley, not in a ship but in a char-à-banc.

I was to address the students at the International Club on the evening of the day that indignant note came from Newman Flower. As I went into the crowded hall I saw a stuffed peacock hanging in a frame. I had told in *Greek Memories* of the peacocks sent to me by the Mayor of Sparta and of their ill omen which warned me of the sacking of my house in Athens. The sight of that stuffed peacock disquieted me and as I went to the platform I tried to avert the evil eye with the southern Italian gesture of the two out-thrust fingers.

The evil eye was not averted. When I sat down after talking for some three-quarters of an hour the Chairman asked if I would go to the telephone. My secretary at the Central Hotel had rung up while I was in the middle of my speech and had been asked to ring again later. I went to the telephone and Chrissie's voice sounding worried told me that Ralph Pinker had rung up to say that the authorities had warned Cassell's that the Government might take legal action and that meanwhile it would be wise for the publishers to withdraw *Greek Memories* at once.

I got in touch with Ralph Pinker who thought it would be prudent if I came down to London immediately. I said I was booked to speak in Dublin on November 4th but would return like a second Guy Fawkes to London next day.

The Historical Society of Trinity College, Dublin was a venerable institution which had been founded by Edmund Burke. It was the custom for the Auditor (as the President was called) of the year to read a paper to the Society and invite four guests to make their observations, two of them proposing and seconding a vote of thanks, the other two a motion that the Auditor's speech should be printed.

It was a full dress occasion with the 'ascendancy' in full force as an audience. The Auditor for 1932 was Terence de Vere White, a remarkable youth of about eighteen who had already taken his degree and would presently be a full-fledged solicitor. In his invitation he had said he was going to read a paper on Communism. Maurice Dobb, a Cambridge don, and that old Liberal stalwart H. N. Brailsford would be kind to Communism; G. K. Chesterton had agreed to be unkind. Would I join with him?

Then one or two clerical busybodies in Dublin had suggested to G. K. that Trinity College was an unsuitable background for a Catholic writer and G. K. had weakly cancelled his acceptance. His place was taken by Desmond Fitzgerald who had been Minister of External Affairs in the Free State Government but had been out of office since the February

F

election when Fianna Fail and Mr de Valera had ousted the Cosgrave government.

As usual I had a grand week in Dublin, staying at Corbawn with Hilda and William Nolan. Young Terence White was perfect company and at that first meeting a friendship began which is still one of the pleasures of my life thirty-four years later. Desmond Fitzgerald was an interesting figure. He had been exiled as a boy in the south of England and still spoke with the genteel accent which today has become characteristic of dwellers in the Home Counties. I would use his background to some extent for my young Irishman in *The Four Winds of Love*, though Edward Fitzgerald is in no way even a partial portrait of Desmond Fitzgerald. I was amused when driving to dinner with him that week; as the car drove up to his house it was stopped by three or four armed men demanding to know who I was. At this date all the members of the previous government were afforded protection by the new government.

I met Mr de Valera for the first time this week. The contrast between the Eamonn de Valera of 1932, with the wise Eamonn de Valera out of office in 1950, and even more with the benignant and completely easeful President de Valera of 1963 is vivid in my memory. In 1932 he was still self-conscious with the self-assertion of somebody who is not quite clear what his position is.

I asked him what would be his attitude to an autonomous Scotland. He did not think there was any likelihood of that.

"Ten years ago there was no likelihood of your being where you are today. If the unlikely happens in Scotland, would a free Ireland work in economic concord with us?"

"What can you give Ireland that we have not got?"

"Coal for one thing."

"We have coal."

"Oh, come, come, Mr President. All you have in Eire is some rather inferior lignite. And what about wheat?"

"We have enough wheat in Munster. Should there be any scarcity we can always import Canadian wheat."

"But if you dissociate yourselves from this so-called Commonwealth of ours will you be able to obtain Canadian wheat? Won't you have to get your wheat from the United States and pay accordingly?"

By this time I could see that the President of the Executive Council was getting tired of Scotland; I could not resist adding,

"And of course, Mr President, we might manage an exchange of populations—the Scots planted in Ulster to be uprooted and returned to Scotland and the Irish in Glasgow and elsewhere to go back to Eire."

In the middle of that week the British Press announced that I was to be prosecuted under the Official Secrets Act and I received an anxious telegram from Ralph Pinker begging me to return at once. I telegraphed back to say I should be arriving at Euston from Holyhead on Guy Fawkes Day.

Several of the Fianna Fail T.D.'s rang me up to say that if I did not want to return to Britain they were sure the Irish Government would refuse to extradite me. I thanked them but said I was quite willing to stand trial.

Terence White's paper was a great success, and in the battle with Dobb and Brailsford Desmond Fitzgerald and I felt we were the winners. I think Communism presented itself to me that evening as an assault upon the freedom of the Press[1] and I was as indignant as my Pauline predecessor John Milton, with a sympathetic audience to accompany me with gratifying laughter and applause.

I was met on my arrival at Euston early in the morning by a crowd of camera-men and reporters and after a rough night in the Irish Sea I looked a bigger villain in those press photographs than any figure the writers of popular thrillers could conjure up on the jackets of their books. The reporters were anxious to know if I had received the summons yet. I told them that so far I had had no official intimation of any proceedings but that no doubt it would arrive at Dryden Chambers in the course of the day.

I was relieved to find Faith much better. It was just as well, because the telephone continued to ring almost incessantly for the next two days to enquire about that summons; no summons arrived. Ralph Pinker had suggested Lewis and Lewis of Ely Place to act as my solicitors, and I appealed to Sir Reginald Lane Poole,[2] the head of the firm, to protect me against the telephone by persuading the authorities to serve that evasive summons. So Sir Reginald rang up the Old Jewry to find out what the City Police could do about it.

"Ah, is that you, Inspector S—? This is Sir Reginald Poole. I believe you have a summons for Mr Compton Mackenzie. Can you let me know when it is likely to be served? As soon as possible? Yes, but Mr Mackenzie is being pestered day and night by the Press to know if the summons has been served. Oh, the Chief Constable of Inverness wanted to serve it? Well, Mr Mackenzie won't be back at Eilean Aigas yet. You'll be getting the summons returned by the day after tomorrow? Well, Mr Mackenzie will be lunching with me in Cumberland Place. I suggest you come along about half-past two and serve it then. That'll be all right for you? Capital."

So at the time appointed Inspector S— arrived in Cumberland Place and I took an immediate liking to him which I felt was reciprocated. He seemed to me youngish for an inspector, a fair man with eyes that

[1] The freedom of the Press for which Milton fought was freedom of the printing-press not merely newspapers.

[2] The late Sir Reginald Lane Poole, K.C.V.O.

expressed such candour and kindness as almost to mask the intelligence behind them.

"Well, sir," he said to me, "this is one of those times when one wishes one had stuck to one's original job instead of going in for the law."

"What was your original job, Inspector?"

"I was in publishing."

"Indeed? What firm were you with?"

"I was a packer at Macmillan's before I gave it up and went in for the law. Yes, it's often a sad and disagreeable business. But I've had a number of interesting gentlemen pass through my hands. Lord Terrington, Lord Kylsant, and last but by no means least, Mr Clarence Hatry, one of the nicest gentlemen I ever met. We all liked him very much at the Old Jewry. He could have caused us a lot of trouble but he was always helpful and saved us no end of time in going through the mass of papers. Yes, sir, we were really grateful to Mr Hatry at the Old Jewry and when Mr Justice Avory gave him fourteen years we thought the sentence very harsh. We didn't like it at all at the Old Jewry. Well, really, we resented it, as you might say. I'm sorry you've had all this bother from the telephone. I'll be seeing you at the Guildhall. The date and time are in the summons. And I wish you the very best of luck."

I have not often shaken hands with such a warmth of cordiality; when the Inspector was gone I read the summons:

"That in July 1932, having in your possession information which you had obtained owing to your position as a person who held office under His Majesty, to wit, as holding a commission as a lieutenant, and subsequently as a captain, in His Majesty's Royal Marines, unlawfully did communicate the said information to persons, to wit, to Cassell and Company Limited, and to persons in the employment of the said company, the said persons not being persons to whom you, the said Compton Mackenzie, were then authorized to communicate the said information, contrary to the Official Secrets Act, 1911-20."

Now came the question of counsel. I insisted that my old friend and contemporary at Magdalen, St John Hutchinson, should be the junior; the leader I left to Sir Reginald's judgment. He decided on Sir Henry Curtis-Bennett, K.C. as the best for an Old Bailey jury. Somehow I had not imagined myself at the Old Bailey and as I had been collecting for many years Old Bailey Sessions Papers back to the beginning of the eighteenth century I was rather tickled by the prospect.

Sir Reginald rebuked me.

"You are taking this too lightly. It's very serious. I understand the Government intend to make an example of you if they can, in order to warn Lloyd George and Winston Churchill that they can go too far in using information they could only have acquired in office."

Four or five years later Winston Churchill told me that when my trial came on he did burn a lot of papers he afterwards regretted burning.

My own feeling was that M.I.1(C) and M.I.5 had been upset by the way I had brought out the comic side of their activities. Presently Simon Lovat told me that there had been a Cabinet meeting at which the Attorney-General had announced I had destroyed the whole Secret Service with my book *Greek Memories* and that it was going to cost the country at least two million pounds to undo the harm I had done.

I was urged to take advantage of that meeting with the Prime Minister to enlist his interest but I have never been able to run the risk of embarrassing people by buttonholing them in the corridors of power in search of favours. I did, however, feel I was entitled to give an opportunity for the Opposition to do some embarrassing, and talked to Arthur Henderson[1] and other prominent Labour politicians. They were sympathetic but did not feel they could do anything.

"You see, we might want to use the Act ourselves when we get back into power," Arthur Henderson told me.

I must still have seemed to be making a joke of the whole business. Anyway Jack Hutchinson like Sir Reginald Lane Poole warned me not to take it too lightly.

"These devils are out for your blood," he assured me. "They're determined to have a state trial with a red Judge and the Attorney-General."

Nevertheless as November 16th drew near the only thing that really did worry me was the problem of reaching the Guildhall punctual to the second. The traffic between Oxford Street and the City in the morning made that a tough problem. I was glad I had fussed about the traffic because Eustace Fulton,[2] the Crown Prosecutor at the Central Criminal Court, who was opening the case got off to a bad start at the first hearing by arriving at the Guildhall ten minutes late. Alderman Sir George Truscott, who in his blue fur-trimmed robes reminded me of Alderman Fitzwarren in the stock opening of how many Dick Whittington pantomimes, did not accept Mr Fulton's apologies with the best of grace.

"The traffic may be a problem," he said, "but Crown Counsel are making a habit of being late. They should take proper steps to avoid the traffic problem," he added severely.

I had insisted that Jack Hutchinson should raise an objection to my being tried in England in that I was domiciled in Scotland and that the offending book had been written in Scotland. This plea was rejected by the Alderman presiding, as of course we knew it would be. If the book had been published in Edinburgh, could the Crown still have insisted on the Guildhall and the Old Bailey?

I was invited to take my seat on a comfortably padded chair in front

---

[1] The late Rt. Hon. Arthur Henderson, M.P.

[2] The late Eustace Fulton, K.C., Chairman of County of London Sessions.

of the table at which Counsel were sitting. The Crown Prosecutor rose to outline the case against me, which was that, while occupying an official position during the war, I had become aware of various facts through occupying such a position and that in spite of my having pledged myself never to communicate such facts either in speech or in writing to others I had done so. Jack Hutchinson intervened to assure his learned friend that I had never been asked to give such a pledge, which in fact was never asked for at the date I had been seconded to the Foreign Office. Mr Fulton accepted his learned friend's correction, but pointed out that I had committed an offence under the Official Secrets Act without regard to any pledge I had or had not given. However, he was willing to withdraw at once the allegation that I had given any such pledge. He then went on to call a witness from the Foreign Office who testified that I had in my book paraphrased telegrams passing between London and Athens in 1916. The poor young clerk from the F.O. library nearly collapsed in the witness-box when Jack Hutchinson in cross-examination asked him if he thought any harm had been done by the publication of those telegrams; he looked appealingly at Eustace Fulton, who came to his rescue by asking Sir George Truscott to say that this witness was not required to answer such a question. This Sir George endorsed, and the young clerk left the box with a sigh of relief.

Now the Crown Prosecutor rose and in grave tones requested that the next part of the case should be heard *in camera*; the Court was then cleared of spectators and reporters. He went on to enumerate a list of more than a dozen names I had mentioned in my book of people connected with the Secret Service sixteen years ago and declared that this was a most dangerous disclosure because it might be necessary to use them again in the event of another war. I was staggered when I heard that list of names. Even I with all my first-hand experience of incompetence should have hesitated to impute such stupidity to the Intelligence pundits who had drawn up that list. Then followed other reasons to explain why the damage I had done had led to these proceedings. I had revealed, for instance, that the Passport Departments in our various Embassies were a cover for Intelligence work.

The first hearing ended, Simon Lovat, wearing a well-worn covert coat, came forward to ask the Alderman if he wanted bail. Sir George shook his head, and Simon Lovat walked quickly out of the Court. He probably had a luncheon engagement.

When the Alderman had departed and the Court was empty, one of the Guildhall ushers in a blue and gold livery offered me a cigarette.

"Can we smoke here?" I asked, eyeing the figure of Justice above the Bench.

"It's the same as any other place when the Court has adjourned," I was assured.

So I lit up and at that moment Inspector S— approached.

"Good morning, sir," he said with a benevolent smile. "I want to introduce you to Inspector J— of the Metropolitan Police. J— and I would be very happy if you would come down King Street and have a drink with us."

We walked along King Street until we came to a very small bar on the left-hand side behind which was a late Victorian barmaid with a yacht's fender of fair hair piled on top of her head.

"Now, sir, what's yours?" Inspector S— asked.

"I think a pink gin at this moment would be a good idea."

"What's yours, J—?"

"A pink gin for me too," said the colleague of Inspector S—.

"Three pink gins, miss."

I can see now those three pink gins set out in a neat row in the exact centre of the bar hardly four feet wide. When we had picked them up Inspector S—, holding his glass in his hand, addressed his colleague.

"You represent the Metropolitan Police and I represent the Old Jewry, and I know I'm speaking both for the Metropolitan Police and for the Old Jewry when I say we do not consider this a prosecution but a malicious persecution. Here's to you, sir."

With this we drained our glasses. I wanted to stand the next round but the right to do this was claimed by the Metropolitan Police, after which the two inspectors insisted on getting hold of a taxi for me.

Even at the Guildhall that morning when I had asked the way to the Court the policeman directing me had murmured, "Good luck, sir."

What was the secret of this warmth of goodwill from the police?

In my preface to *Greek Memories* I had impugned Sir Basil Thomson's[1] veracity. He had been an Assistant Commissioner of the Metropolitan Police and as such he had had the job at Scotland Yard of handling the spy cases produced by M.I.5 during the First World War. In that capacity he described himself as Director of Intelligence. Later he had been involved in a Hyde Park indiscretion and when charged he had accused the police of framing him and of perjury. His accusation had not been accepted by the magistrate and his official career was finished. He was paid to write *The Allied Secret Service in Greece* out of funds available to the exiled Greek Royal Family for propaganda. When I condemned that scurrilous and mendacious book, the police felt that I had exposed Sir Basil Thomson's accusation of perjury against the police as the word of a man who himself had no regard for the truth.

Ella Cook whose splendid work under me in Greece I had praised in *Greek Memories* wrote to ask if she could come and see me. When the Aegean Intelligence Service was broken up in 1917 she had been taken on by C. and was now working with M.I.5.

[1] The late Sir Basil Thomson, K.C.B.

"You're looking very scared, Ella."

"I was afraid they might see me coming to Dryden Mansions."

I laughed.

"It's nothing to laugh at," she protested. "Don't you realize that they're hoping to get you put in prison? I wanted to warn you that they really are out for your blood."

"It's no use, Ella. I cannot take these cloak and dagger buffoons seriously."

"You must, you must," she urged. "And I *had* to warn you."

To my relief Hope-Johnstone now arrived on the scene and we worked hard on preparing a deadly cross-examination for Jack Hutchinson when the names on that list of 'secret servants' eligible for the next war should be presented by the Prosecution.

I was getting innumerable letters, not merely from personal friends but also from unknown friends among my readers. Some of these letters I still have; one from Lady Oxford was very welcome:

I only want you to let me know how things go and if I can do anything for you, for as you know, I am a most genuine article, and don't forget your visit to me when I was so ill in Edinburgh.

Don't let this get on your nerves. You are like me very sensitive. Look at it as part of the great adventure of life, and to live it all you must live dangerously.

Yours ever

Margot Oxford

I went to see that superlative woman at 22 Bedford Square and I hear and see her now as she says with passionate conviction:

"I think you ought to go to prison if you possibly can. No one alive could write such a wonderful book about life in prison."

"I doubt it," I replied. "Didn't Shakespeare say, 'Art is tongue-tied by authority'? I should be as bored as I used to be toward the end of my time at school."

"Yes," she agreed pensively, "it might be rather boring."

Chrissie sent me two letters she had received from Barra.

The Coddie wrote to her:

I am rather in the dumps on hearing that my friend is in difficulties. So early this morning I was in church, kneeling before 12 lit candles, praying hard that God would keep him against his enemies who are very numerous. I have every confidence that my appeal will be attended to; seldom if ever I failed in cases I prayed hard for. . . . I have not got under the circumstances a proper appetite to read the life of Prince Charlie.

The Crookle wrote to her:

I may tell you I have been very downhearted since I read in the paper about Mr Mackenzie. All in the house were the same and you may be sure there has been plenty of praying which I am sure and I also hope in God that he will come off top. . . .

The second hearing at Guildhall on November 24th opened with a touch of farce. The Crown had forgotten to have anybody called to identify me as the Compton Mackenzie who had served in the Secret Service, so poor Fulton had to admit the oversight to Sir George Truscott and ask him to have me formally identified forthwith. Into the witness-box went Percy Sykes,[1] an old friend of mine at 2 Whitehall Court, who had had the tough job of handling Secret Service finances.

"Do you say that this is Edward Montague Compton Mackenzie?"

"I do."

And then we both laughed aloud until I saw Sir Reginald Poole's forefinger wagging at me to stop our merriment.

"I do wish you wouldn't keep looking amused," he said afterwards. "You'll prejudice the Judge if you do that at the Old Bailey. I do wish you would be more serious."

If I had known then what the case was going to cost me I should have looked as serious as any judge myself.

After I had been identified the Crown Prosecutor addressed the Alderman in a low awe-struck voice.

"I am now going to call as a witness a present member of the Secret Service. And although we are *in camera*, Sir George, I am going to ask you if he may keep his name secret and that he be alluded to as Major X?"

Sir George Truscott agreed to this blanket of anonymity being flung over Major X who then went into the witness-box. The fatuity of those responsible for this feeble attempt at melodrama may be gauged by the fact that at the next hearing when the Court was *not* 'in camera' the full name and regiment of Major X could be read in the leaflets scattered about the Court in which were recorded the names of those who had figured at the previous hearing. This may seem incredible, but it is true. I who had never seen Major X till he entered the witness-box could now reveal his name and regiment, but he cut such a pathetically ridiculous figure in the witness-box that I feel it would not be fair to tell his name, and I shall let him remain Major X.

After his examination by Crown Counsel St John Hutchinson rose to cross-examine Major X, armed with all the information supplied by Hope-Johnstone and myself about the dozen or so alleged ex-members of the Secret Service whose future careers I was supposed to have imperilled.

"Major X, you have told my learned friend that by publishing in his book the names of these gentlemen who worked on Intelligence duties in the war Mr Mackenzie has jeopardized their future. Why?"

[1] Commander P. S. Sykes, C.M.G., O.B.E., R.N.V.R.

"Because when war comes . . ."

"When war comes? Are we to feel indebted to our Intelligence Service for knowing when war will come?"

"I meant if another war comes."

"Ah! Please go on, Major X."

"If another war comes we may want to call upon their services again."

"I see. So that you must know where all these gentlemen are and what they are doing now?"

Major X hesitated for a moment or two before answering and gulped at the large tumblerful of water beside him.

"I have no doubt we know, yes," he replied at last.

"Then shall we go through the list? The first name is Mr C. E. Heathcote-Smith.[1] Do you know where he is now?"

"I don't myself know but I've no doubt that it is known."

"Perhaps you don't know that he is now His Britannic Majesty's Consul-General in Alexandria?"

"I hear you say so."

"You can trust your ears, Major X. Have you read Mr Mackenzie's two previous volumes of war memories?"

"I have, and if I may say so with very much pleasure."

"I'm sure Mr Mackenzie and his publishers will appreciate that unsolicited testimonial."

Major X was unfortunately placed in the witness-box because he had to answer Jack Hutchinson's questions across me, and when he had answered this last question he had had to give me what might almost be called a propitiatory smile.

"Then don't you remember, Major X, that in *Gallipoli Memories* he wrote at some length of Mr Heathcote-Smith's Intelligence work when he was Vice-Consul at Mytilene. And perhaps you are not aware, Major X, that in the entry in *Who's Who* under his name Mr Heathcote-Smith says that he was working in Intelligence from 1915 to 1916?"

Major X took a gulp of water.

"I hear you say so."

"You can take it from me, Major X, that *I* am not indulging in fantasy."

The last observation was edged with sarcastic contempt.

"Well, so much for the Consul-General of Alexandria. Let us take the next name on the list. Mr A. J. B. Wace. Do you know where Mr Wace is now?"

"I do not know myself."

"Then perhaps you do not know that he is the Deputy-Keeper of the Victoria and Albert Museum?"

"I hear you say so."

[1] The late Sir C. E. Heathcote-Smith, K.C.M.G., O.B.E.

"Perhaps you do not know that Mr Wace was never in the Secret Service?"

There was no answer, and then one by one Jack Hutchinson made the miserable and embarrassed Major X, who had been supplied with a third large tumblerful of water, admit to complete ignorance about the names with which he had been supplied for the purpose of illustrating to the Court the damage I had done with my book to that future of Intelligence.

"And now, Major X, this last name on your list? Captain Christmas."

The Major drained his fourth tumbler and was given a fifth. Then he waited for the blow.

"Surely, Major X, the page in Mr Mackenzie's book about Captain Christmas shows that Captain Christmas was nothing more than a figure of fun?"

"Well, as a matter of fact, Mr Hutchinson, we do not wish to press that name."

"No? Why not?"

"Because we have found out that Captain Christmas is dead."

"Indeed? When did he die?"

"I believe it was about ten years ago."

"*Indeed!* So that not even the Secret Service will be able to call upon Captain Christmas when war comes—I should say if another war comes. Thank you, Major X. I have nothing more to ask you."

Jack Hutchinson turned to his learned friend with a compassionate smile, but Mr Fulton was not going to risk looking as ridiculous as Major X by re-examining. The present member of the Secret Service whose testimony the Crown Prosecutor had announced so portentously hurried from the witness-box and out of the Guildhall as fast as Mr Winkle after his examination by Serjeant Buzfuz.

The last of the preliminary hearings was held in the old Court of the Guildhall which for some years had hardly ever been used except as an adjunct to City banquets where the wine would be uncorked. It presented a very different appearance from the Court generally used, and before the proceedings opened I was looking at a kind of box inscribed 'Waiting Attorneys' when the Clerk of the Court, a distinguished and ceremonious figure, said to me,

"As a writer, Mr Mackenzie, you will be interested to know that the Court in which your case is being heard this morning is quite unchanged since the days when Mr Charles Dickens used it as the setting for the famous case of Bardell *versus* Pickwick."

"Did he, by Jove?" I exclaimed, looking up at the lantern in the roof at which Sam Weller had stared when the Judge asked him if he could see his father anywhere in Court. "Bardell and Pickwick, eh? Well, I suppose this case must be the most ludicrous case heard in it since."

I was wishing that Major X had made his Winkle-like exit from this Court when Alderman Sir George Truscott came in and we all stood respectfully until he had climbed to the Bench once occupied by Mr Justice Stareleigh.

The proceedings were short. My Counsel rose to argue that the Crown had failed to produce any kind of a case which warranted Sir George Truscott's committing his client for trial at the next Sessions of the Central Criminal Court. Sir George was obviously inclined to agree with Mr St John Hutchinson, and the Clerk of the Court jumped up nervously to murmur something to him.

"I can't hear you, Mr Richards," said Sir George fretfully. He was used to having the Clerk at his elbow, but he was now a good ten feet away from him.

"The Attorney-General has issued his Fiat," the Clerk of the Court said more loudly.

"Ah, yes, yes, precisely. No, I'm afraid I've no option but to send this case to the Old Bailey."

"Very good, Sir George," said my Counsel. "Do you wish securities for bail?"

"No, no, I am quite content to accept Mr Mackenzie in his own recognizances."

With this the dear old gentleman rose and bowed to me with a charming courtesy.

By now I was in communication with various former members of the Military Control Office in Athens and the Aegean Intelligence Service in Syra. I was anxious to find out how many of the names produced by Major X were still in fact engaged in Intelligence work. I find the rough draft of a letter of mine to my old Number Two, Charles Tucker, asking him if he was still buying oranges and I have his reply saying that he had not bought any oranges since 1919. In other words he had been doing no Intelligence work for more than twelve years. This was equally true of all the others mentioned except Arthur Whittall whose taking over of the island of Cerigo while still in his 'teens I narrated in Octave 5. Arthur Whittall was now in charge of the Passport Department of the British Embassy in Turkey. The Passport Department of every Embassy whatever its nationality all over the world was now the cover for Intelligence work. Besides old friends in Greece I had promises from old friends in France and Yugoslavia who were prepared to testify. At this moment in Athens, a Monarchist paper and a Republican paper were publishing translations of *Greek Memories* with photographs of many of the characters I had mentioned. I felt confident that the Prosecution was in for a disagreeable surprise at the Old Bailey next month.

The next time I saw Sir Reginald Lane Poole he said reproachfully and severely,

"You never told me you had been warned."

"Warned about what?"

"About publishing your book."

"I never was warned."

"Weren't you? What will you say when the Attorney-General produces a letter from you acknowledging the warning?"

I thought hard.

"I wonder if that letter I had last year from Holt-Wilson was supposed to be a warning."

"Have you got that letter?"

"It'll be up at Eilean Aigas. I'm going there in a day or two and I'll hand it to you with a copy of my reply."

We had a terrific hunt for that letter which was printed in the last chapter; mercifully we found it at last. The copy of my reply has not survived in my files. Probably I never got it back from Lewis and Lewis.

In spite of the prospect of the Old Bailey three weeks hence Christmas at Eilean Aigas was as merry as ever with Frasers and Maxwells galore. I was back at Dryden Chambers by the new year.

FIFTY YEARS OLD: 1933

AT the last conference held in Jack Hutchinson's chambers in Plowden Buildings, Middle Temple (those conferences cost sixty guineas a time) Curtis-Bennett told me that I must plead guilty at the Old Bailey on January 12th.

"I will not plead guilty. You don't think I ought to plead guilty, Jack?"

Etiquette forbade Jack Hutchinson to express an opinion in front of his leader; it was Sir Reginald Poole who told me I must listen to Sir Henry's advice.

"If you plead not guilty, you can call those witnesses from Athens and Constantinople and the case could go on for two or three weeks and cost you £15,000 or more, and at the end of it the Judge will tell the jury that it is not their business to say whether any harm was done by your book but merely to say whether or not you had used information in it which you could only have obtained in the position you occupied officially. Well, you don't dispute that. The evidence from the Foreign Office was sufficient. And then the Judge might send you to Wormwood Scrubbs for nine months—not a pleasant experience—and the public would think that you must have done something dreadful to get such a sentence. And as the case will be heard *in camera* you won't be able to tell the public about it because it is contempt of court to say what happened *in camera*."

"The Star Chamber all over again," I observed.

"Yes, but listen. I showed the Attorney-General that letter which the other side claims was a warning and which you acknowledged in the letter he was shown by M.I.5. He said at once that he had been misinformed, and added that the warning was more like an encouragement to go on. So I've arranged with the Attorney-General who has arranged with the Judge that it will only be a fine not exceeding £500 and £500 costs."

I gasped.

"Well, you've destroyed almost my last illusion. I hadn't many left. But I did believe that the judicature in this country was incapable of being influenced by the executive. Influenced? I could say corrupted."

"Oh, don't say that, don't say that," Sir Reginald broke in. "In some ways Hawke is rather a weak judge."

"The fact remains that a deal is to be made which will get these comedians in M.I.5 out of a sticky spot. Oh, well, I really do feel such a genuine contempt of court at this moment that I'll contemptuously pay the fine."

Yes, that sounded all right I reflected as I walked along into the Strand where the young crescent moon in the winter sky was shining westward, but where was the £1,000 coming from? My legal expenses would be well over that. I would have to refund Cassell's the £500 I had been paid for the book and on top of that reimburse them for the cost of publication. But perhaps *Greek Memories* could be revised with cuts and after such an advertisement sell quite well. But a thousand pounds cash for my delivery from the King's custody? I turned my back on the moon and walked to Carmelite House where I had a talk with the legal adviser of the North-cliffe Press. I was told not to worry. The *Daily Mail* would be in court with £1,000.

That evening I wrote to Chrissie in Eilean Aigas:

Dearest child,

Just a line to say a bargain has practically been made and that if we don't fight the Government will not press the case, which means a fine of about £1,000, but not prison. Case will probably be January 12, but may be 15th or 16th.

Yours

M.C.M.

I had been told that I must call two witnesses for character. I should dearly have loved to call Sir Francis Elliot to whom *Greek Memories* was dedicated, but I did not feel justified in asking him to leave the Riviera and come to England in mid-January. Admiral W. F. Sells, as Bill Sells was now, was going to Portugal but he generously spoilt his holiday to help me. Then I wrote to Sir Ian Hamilton. I said I couldn't be sure yet of the date. It might be on the 16th, which would be his eightieth birthday. He telegraphed from Dunblane:

Will chuck any engagements and come down when you wire.

Sir Ian had been elected as Rector of Edinburgh University in the autumn of 1932. It is safe to prophesy that never again will a Rector of Edinburgh University be heard giving evidence at the Old Bailey about the character of a Rector of Glasgow University. When I reached the Old Bailey on that morning of January 12th I was moved to see that old veteran sitting beside Mrs Shield, his secretary, amid the encaustic tiles of the entrance lobby and dictating notes to her, perhaps for the Rectorial address he would soon be delivering.

Having ascertained that my case would be heard in Number One Court, I asked a constable to show me the way to the dock and then where I should hang my hat and coat.

"Ah, now that's a bit of a problem, sir." He called out to another constable. "Where could Mr Mackenzie put his hat and coat while his case is being heard?"

The other constable was equally puzzled. Then his face lightened.

"Couldn't he put 'em in the barristers' robing-room?"

I demurred to this.

"I know several of them. It might be embarrassing if I butted in when they were getting into their wigs and gowns."

"Yes, I see what you mean," said the first constable. "I'll tell you what. Roll up your coat and put it in a corner at the back of the dock, with your hat on top. They'll be quite safe."

Then, as we approached the door of the dock, he said,

"Your case'll be in camera, sir, as they say. Coo, what a set out we used to have with those camera cases during the war. Those comics from M.I.5 used to come along and have brown paper stuck over the skylight above the Court. They were like kids playing at Red Indians. Well, here you are, sir, and we all wish you the best of luck."

With this the constable opened the door of the dock and I stepped inside. Looking back to wave him my thanks I saw that there was no handle to the door on the inside. My first emotion was one of surprise at the size of the dock. I had always fancied the dock as a cramped enclosure with just enough room to hold the accused and a couple of warders; the dock at the Old Bailey was large enough for a dozen couples to dance in it without too much of a squash. An old gentleman with silver hair who was sitting in a corner of it in police uniform got up when I entered and set a chair for me.

I am not self-conscious or I might have been embarrassed by the eyes all over the Court that stared at me. Yet self-conscious or not, it undoubtedly is a bit of an ordeal five days away from one's fiftieth birthday to stand in the dock of the Old Bailey. I was wearing the black suit I wore at my Rectorial address last January.

I looked round at the Court. In spite of the daylight coming in through plenty of windows and from the very large skylight above, the electric lights were all turned on and the combination was fatiguing to the eyes. The Bench opposite was as yet empty. Nothing there to look at except the blind figure of Justice and the scales. The jury-box, too, was empty, but in a gallery on the right-hand side of the dock were a group of figures in long black overcoats who would be described in a report in one of the Sunday papers as "world-famous figures of the Secret Service". Among them was Holt-Wilson. I had run into him on my way to the first hearing at the Guildhall and had said, "Hullo, what on earth is all this nonsense about?" Whereupon he had popped away like a scared rook. Now there he was again in that rooks' parliament from M.I.5 and the Home Office. I could not help feeling once more that Holt-Wilson had been dragged into this business against his better judgment. I could not understand how so intelligent a man had allowed Intelligence to undermine his own intelligence.

C.M. and Faith after the hearing at the Old Bailey

Marie Dauthieu, C.M., Marjorie and Eric Linklater and Chrissie

C.M. and Moray McLaren in mountaineer's
national dress of Poland

The public were squeezed into a corner of the Court to the left of the dock with a poor view of the proceedings. Then came the seats of the Press. Below the Bench Sir Edward Tindal-Atkinson, the Director of Public Prosecutions, was apparently presiding over a tableful of legal officials. On either side of a long table running down the centre of the Court sat counsel and solicitors—the Prosecution on the right, the Defence on the left. Behind them on both sides were more officials and bewigged barristers. Then everybody rose and bowed as Mr Justice Hawke came in and took his seat on the Bench. I looked at him with interest and wondered if what seemed an intelligent man could be really taken in by the self-indulgent harlequinade being performed by the people entrusted with the country's security.

I read in a Press report that I pleaded guilty in a quiet voice, and obviously the Judge thought that all he had to do was to deliver a jobation and fine me £500 with £500 costs. Luckily for me as it turned out the Attorney-General proceeded to open his case as if I had pleaded not guilty. The Judge grew more and more exasperated as the morning wore away. One point Sir Thomas Inskip made was that I had revealed the mysterious consonant by which the Chief of the Secret Service was known. This was dangerous because in the Army List those officers who were connected with Secret Intelligence still had M.I.1(C) after their names to show what they were engaged upon.

"But, Mr Attorney, if C is such a dangerous consonant, why is it still being used nearly fifteen years after the war?"

"That I couldn't say, m'lud."

"No, I shouldn't think you could. That consonant should surely have been changed by now."

In fact after my case those in Secret Intelligence were shown in the Army List with M.I.6 after their names. In the First War M.I.6 stood for the interpreters' set up.

The Attorney-General went on to say that not only had I revealed the mysterious consonant C but I had also said that C stood for Sir Mansfield Cumming, the Chief of the Secret Service.

"But surely this officer's name was perfectly well known during the war?" the Judge asked.

"I think not, m'lud."

"Come, come, Mr Attorney, in clubs you and I both belong to?"

"No, m'lud, with great respect I think not."

"Oh, well, have it your own way, Mr Attorney, but please be quicker. I'm growing excessively tired of this case."

A moment or two later the Judge broke in again on the Attorney-General's laboured explanation of the danger of telling the world who C was.

"But when did this officer die, Mr Attorney?" he asked sharply.

G

The sudden question floored Sir Thomas Inskip who looked round at his Junior. Mr Fulton did not know. The Attorney-General looked hopefully across at the Defence. Sir Henry Curtis-Bennett shook his head. Mr St John Hutchinson shook his head. Sir Reginald Lane Poole shook his head.

"It may seem a little irregular, m'lud, but as we are *in camera* perhaps I might ask Sir Vernon Kell to tell us."

For a moment I thought that the rooks in the gallery were going to take flight, such a flapping of black overcoats did this suggestion of the Attorney-General set up.

Major-General Sir Vernon Kell was none other than the mysterious K, the Chief of M.I.5, or as he called himself in *Who's Who*, Commandant of the War Department Constabulary. Three or four years before the war Commander Cumming and Major Kell had been entrusted with two branches of the Secret Service. C was to be responsible for espionage and for all counter-espionage outside the British Empire, deriving his funds from the Foreign Office; K was to take charge of counter-espionage within the British Empire, deriving his funds from the War Office. K was a fanatical believer in secrecy for secrecy's sake and now to hear his name mentioned like this in a law court, even if it was *in camera* at the time, must have been a mental agony.

But K didn't know when C died. I prodded the silver-headed old gentleman who was guarding me in the dock and asked for paper, intending to write down the answer to the Judge's question.

"Do you wish to tell me something?" the Judge asked, looking across to the dock.

"Yes, my lord, with great respect, the officer in question died in June or July 1922."

"Thank you." And then with what Cockneys call a perishing look, the Judge eyed the rooks in the gallery. "I *accept* that."

I had an impression from the Judge's tone of voice that at this moment he was feeling that he and the accused were the only sane people in Court.

The Attorney-General bumbled on for the rest of the morning until the Court adjourned for lunch.

Faith, Christopher Stone and various friends including Cunninghame Graham, who had had a boring three hours while the Attorney-General was bumbling away *in camera*, were lunching at Pimm's Chophouse almost opposite the Old Bailey. I drank a Pimm's Number One with more gusto than I had given to a drink since I was an undergraduate.

I recall nothing of our conversation at lunch except dear old Don Roberto's reminiscence of himself in the dock at the Old Bailey over forty years before.

When the Court reassembled, it emerged from *camera* and Curtis-

Bennett made a speech on my behalf, designed to persuade the Judge to lessen the fine of £500 and £500 costs which he had been told would be the amount required to save the face of the Prosecution. He mentioned that I was Lord Rector of Glasgow University.

"I didn't know that," the Judge put in.

"And I propose, m'lud, to call upon General Sir Ian Hamilton, the Lord Rector of Edinburgh University, to testify to Mr Mackenzie's service under him."

Sir Ian went up into the witness-box on the Judge's right-hand, more like a twenty-year-old subaltern than a veteran general, four days away from his eightieth birthday.

Curtis-Bennett opened his examination.

"I believe, General, that Mr Mackenzie served under you at Gallipoli?"

"Yes, he certainly did. And a very promising young officer he was, but his health wasn't too good. I remember on one occasion I was coming out of my hut and saw how ill he looked. 'I don't want to lose any more of you young writers. You'd better . . .' "

"Excuse me, General," the Judge broke in. "If you would give a simple answer to a simple question, you wouldn't waste *your* time, and you wouldn't waste *mine*, which is more important."

Dear old Sir Ian was a bit flustered for a moment by this interruption, but he soon recovered and answered the next two or three questions which, oddly as it seemed to me, included a question whether I was loyal to King George.

Down below, Vice-Admiral William Fortescue Sells in spite of the slight deafness that most gunnery specialists used to get had heard the Judge's remark about wasting his time and decided he would not expose himself to such an interruption.

"I believe, Admiral, that Mr Mackenzie served with you during the war when you were Naval Attaché in Athens."

The tremendous 'Yes' with which Bill Sells replied was almost as loud as one of his own big guns. The effect on the Court was terrific. It was like the scene in *Alice in Wonderland* when Alice upset the jury-box and all the jurymen started making notes. Indeed, in several other respects that trial of mine resembled the trial of the Knave of Hearts for stealing the tarts.

Bill Sells continued to thunder out affirmatives to Curtis-Bennett's questions which included a repetition of that odd enquiry about my loyalty to King George.

"Thank you, Admiral. That is all."

"May I add something, my lord?"

Nobody, not even a judge, would have ventured to refuse that aggressive hooked nose and chin.

"Certainly, Admiral."

"I merely wish to say that I've seen Mackenzie working when his back was arched with pain, in conditions of pain in which I've never seen any other fellow work and that every member of his organization would have laid down his life for him. Anything more you want to know, my lord?" he thundered.

"Nothing, thank you, Admiral. Your evidence has been of the greatest help to me and to Mr Mackenzie."

Bill Sells stepped down from the witness-box with a nautical roll, as grand a man as I have ever had for a friend.

Then the Judge preached a little sermon to me.

"I shall remove at once any possible anxiety you may have felt by saying that I do not intend to send you to prison. At the same time, you must realize that by quoting those telegrams exchanged between the Foreign Office and the British Legation in Athens you committed an offence against the Official Secrets Act."

Then he went on for a minute or two to say how necessary it was for people like myself to respect the law. But he said not a single word about the threat to the secrecy of the Secret Service which my book was supposed to have been. He wound up by fining me only £100 and £100 costs.

Some years later his son the late Sir Anthony Hawke, Recorder of London, told me that when after he retired from the Bench his father had a touch of indigestion he used to talk about my case and say what a damnable position the Attorney-General had put him in by paying attention to those cloak and dagger lunatics.

After Mr Justice Hawke's sermon I retired from the dock to be held at His Majesty's pleasure until my fine was paid. One descends a sort of slipway; half-way down it is a gate through which one passes, and I felt a sudden pang to remember the murderers who before me had heard that gate click behind them like life itself. I was not shown into one of the dim cells immediately below the Bench where the accused wait their turn to go up into the dock and convicted felons wait to be driven off in a Black Maria to whatever prison they are assigned. I was shown into a whitewashed kitchen on the side where a young policeman offered me a cup of tea and a cigarette.

"Chuck the fag into the grate if anybody comes along," he warned me.

Only barristers in robes are allowed to descend that slipway at the request of their clients; solicitors are debarred. So Sir Reginald Poole, who was much more at home in the Law Courts than in the Old Bailey, had a difficult time finding out where he had to pay my fine.

After I had drunk the tea and smoked the cigarette the young policeman led me along past the cells to an office at the other end of the passage. One of the cell doors was open as I went by and I read scratched upon it this cry of despair:

Eighteen months Oh God my poor wife and kids

Those words have haunted me ever since. When I first read them I thought, "Yes, it's all very well for you, a popular figure with powerful friends, you can laugh at all that solemn mumbo-jumbo of the law. But suppose you were some poor devil of a clerk in Balham who had embezzled from his firm in the City, what would the months ahead of you seem like?"

At the end of the passage was a room with a counter, behind which a police-officer with a walrus moustache was writing and rubbing out names on half a dozen slates hanging to the wall. He was reproaching his subordinates for entering names for Wormwood Scrubbs which should have been entered on the Brixton slate or on the Wandsworth slate.

"I don't know where you'll all end if you haven't yet learnt to count."

I was given a kitchen-chair on which to sit and wait until the order came for my release.

Presently in the middle of this argument about Black Marias, Sir Reginald Poole, looking indescribably dapper, came in and said:

"I am Sir Reginald Lane Poole, and I wish to pay Mr Compton Mackenzie's fine so that he can leave the Court."

"Take the first turning on the right out of the yard outside," said walrus moustache over his shoulder, "and then the third door on the left along the corridor you'll see on your right. Oh dear, oh dear, which of you put down ten for the Scrubbs? Tut-tut, will you fellows never learn?"

"I am Sir Reginald Lane Poole," my solicitor repeated, rapping the counter sharply. "I wish to pay Mr Compton Mackenzie's fine. The Judge said . . ."

Walrush moustache looked round and shook his head sadly at such impatience.

"What the Judge says up there goes," he sighed, with an upward gesture of his thumb. "What the Judge says down here doesn't go for anything except coming down here. First turning on the right out of the yard and then the third door on the left along the corridor you'll see on your right." He turned again to his subordinates. "I see what you've been and done now. You've got the Scrubbs muddled up with Brixton. That's what you've done."

With a deep sigh he took a sponge and wiped out all the names on one slate. The Old Bailey was becoming more like *Alice in Wonderland* than ever. Sir Reginald walked out in as much of a fret as the White Rabbit. Some ten minutes later an official came in and murmured something to walrus moustache.

"Right," the latter said. Then he turned to me.

"You'll find it easier to go back through the dock."

I followed a policeman back to the slipway, took my coat and hat from the corner, and came down into the Court. A high-up police official with a couple of rows of ribbons on his chest put out his hand.

"I want to shake hands with you," he said. "You've been badly let down in this idiotic business."

And then I was with my friends again.

A few years ago a member's guest came up to me at the Irish Club and said, "I've been waiting to meet you for twenty years to tell you an amusing story about that case of yours at the Old Bailey. When you left the dock the next case called was a little runt not much more than five feet high who was charged with having a love affair with a cow somewhere near Windsor, and with repeating the offence on a subsequent date. 'Oh, my dear,' exclaimed one of your lady friends, turning to her neighbour, 'what an anti-climax!' Yes, I've been waiting to tell you that ribald story for more than twenty years."

I laughed.

"Yes, yes, I remember a tiny little man going past on his way to the dock. I asked the young policeman what he was charged with and I recall now his embarrassed look as he muttered, 'Buglary'. An odd synonym for that other trisyllable. I wonder how he managed that buglary. He was so small he must have used a milk-stool as a jemmy."

I dined on the evening of the trial with Ralph Pinker in Brook Street. The only other guest was Richard Aldington. He looked at me with an expression of earnest indignation.

"You'll never forgive this, will you?" he exclaimed in a tone of funereal sympathy.

"It's been a damned expensive business, but the experience of human nature was well worth it."

"I'd never forgive them," he declared.

That supercharged egoism is why Richard Aldington never saw life whole. Compare that relish for persecution with Harold Nicolson's[1] civilized and objective approach. He had written to me from Sissinghurst on December 5th:

My dear Mackenzie,

I am glad to hear that the verdict will be only technical. I hear nothing but sympathy expressed for you, and the feeling that you have been made a scape-goat of to cover the potential crimes of others in the future. The worst of those sort of incidents is that they are a strain on the nerves and that a sense of injustice and bitterness begins to creep in. But you are sturdy enough to throw away such unhealthy virus out of your system. A grievance, however justified, becomes like a poisoned

[1] Hon. Sir Harold Nicolson, K.C.V.O.

tooth. I only hope that when it is all over you will look back on the thing as a curious experience which, at the cost of several thousand pounds, enabled you to realize how many unknown supporters you possess in the country.

Yours ever

Harold Nicolson

Another letter which gave me much pleasure came from D. J. Macleod, the finest School Inspector I ever knew and a Gaelic scholar of the first order:

Will you allow me to say that so far as I know the Highlands and Islands—and no one knows them better—everybody wishes you well and their admiration and esteem for you continue at probably a greater level than hitherto. We are sorry you have been caused such heavy financial expense: that is the worst of law cases. My wife and I were delighted Sir Ian Hamilton whom she knows well spoke up like the soldier he is: that was enough for us in the North. What he says and you say go with the folk in the North. The Highland students are very proud to have you as Lord Rector.

Indeed, the telegrams and letters I received after the result of the trial at the Old Bailey would alone have made that 'curious experience' worth while. I will quote only from a letter of Calum MacSween in Harris:

My poor Dear Friend, I was glad you are back home once more. How I have felt for you and prayed earnestly for you these eight weeks. I am confident you are coming out of this indeed purified like fine gold and more to the Fore than ever you have been. . . .

Your Devoted Friend

Calum MacSween

Those who read my Octave Six will know what a delight that letter was to me.

The attitude of the Press about the case was sympathetic and in a leader *The Times* gravely warned those with more important secrets than mine to beware. I had clearly been used as a warning. The London correspondent of *The Times of India* observed that I had been lucky to escape with a fine. This same correspondent on the first day of the case had observed that I had always gone in for sensationalism and that when I was elected Rector of Glasgow University the academic authorities had been horrified to hear I was proposing to take the chair at the sittings of the University Court. That paragraph coupled with his comment on the verdict suggested malice.

After months of argument *The Times of India* forked out £400 and apologized in court. Of the £400 I had £220; the lawyers had the rest.

Anybody before the public, whether he be an actor, a novelist or a politician, knows that from time to time he will be made aware of somebody who dislikes him without ever having met him.

When the two Athenian papers started rival translations from the copies of *Greek Memories* which had been in circulation before the book was withdrawn Count Mercati, the King's Chamberlain in 1916 (and Michael Arlen's father-in-law later) wrote to Sir Francis Elliot to protest about something I had said about him. On January 7th Sir Francis had written from Cannes:

> *I have not found it easy to answer Mercati without saying too much, but I enclose a copy of what I have written. I hope you will win through all right next week, and that the book will be released. I am most anxious to see it since your last letter, in which you speak of its doing me justice, for I am not aware of any injustice having been done me!*

To Mercati he had written,

> *I have heard from Compton Mackenzie, who has enabled me to refresh my memory in regard to the events of the last days of November 1916 at Athens. It is a fact that at that moment, when passions were running high and a landing from the French and British ships was imminent, measures of precaution were suggested (by me), and among them the arrest as 'hostages' of prominent Royalist Greeks, including you. (It is perhaps unfortunate that it was not carried out, as it might have prevented the bloodshed which ensued.) It was not suggested that any of them was a dangerous intriguer, least of all yourself, and indeed, when I was shown your name on a French list of proposed expulsions, I had it struck out, Mackenzie disclaims having moved against you, and when, in the passage which you quote from his book, he said 'even Mercati, the King's Chamberlain' the 'even' was intended to suggest the extent to which it was proposed to go in order to secure the safety of our friends in Athens.*
>
> *I hope this will satisfy you that there was no implication of hostility to the Allies on your part. The period was one when a series of unfortunate msitakes were being committed by all parties.*

On January 19th Sir Francis wrote to me:

> *So you have capitulated. I am sorry, but it is evident from the Judge's remarks that you could not have done otherwise. The actual penalty is not heavy, but you are pretty severely punished by the other expenses. I fear it is dead loss, as I suppose you would not care to publish a bowdlerized edition. The writer of* The Times *leader seems to have had an inkling of what you suggested in one of your letters, that the prosecution was undertaken to put a stopper on certain other revelations believed to be contemplated.*
>
> *Will you now be able to send me the book without danger?*

The financial problem was so acute that when the case was over we wrote to the Director of Public Prosecutions to ask if the Constabulary of the War Department would indicate what exactly they objected to in *Greek Memories,* when we would delete the offending passages and reissue the book. A reply came to say that inasmuch as several copies had got into circulation before the book was called in a foreign agent would only have to compare the two editions to know what the British authorities considered dangerous and that therefore the book could never be allowed to appear. On February 9th Laura Lovat was writing from 1c Hyde Park Mansions:

Simon has just come in from interviewing Sir Robert Vansittart[1] at the F.O. The conversation does not seem to have been too happy as Vansittart, tho' personally v. friendly to you and Simon, feared he had not much power over the Public Prosecutor and that short of moving that Dept. he had no hope. He (Vansittart) was going to put 2 of his men on to the job and see what cd. be done but gave S. only v. faint encouragement.

Simon also went to see Sir Stewart Menzies[2] and told him some of the facts of the case, upon which S.M. took back all he had said, and seemed genuinely shocked at such 'dirty work'.

Both Van S. and S.M. agree that you have been made the scapegoat of their Depts. and are sympathetic but late. Van S. is to let Simon hear what his sleuths discover (precious little I expect) in a few days.

It was not so little. Those who moved in the matter of *Greek Memories* had secured the approval of King George before they took action.

Lord Buckmaster had offered to ask a question in the House of Lords but when Simon heard what had been going on behind the scenes he knew it was useless to do anything more.

"So that's why Sir Ian Hamilton and Bill Sells were asked if I was loyal to King George. Well, when Inspector S— said to Jack Hutchinson at the last hearing in the Guildhall that it was a dirty business he was right."

It was at this moment that the Inspector of the Inland Revenue in Inverness notified me they were assessing my income for the previous year at £6,500 and my wife's income at £900.

When my lawyer in Inverness had sent in my first income-tax statement after quitting the shelter of the Treasury in Jethou the Inspector had exclaimed: "But surely he must be earning at least £50,000 a year." This assessment was an example of bubble-blowing to which Inspectors of the Inland Revenue are prone: this particular Inspector's head was in fairyland. However, in justice to them much of the blame for that bubble-blowing rests on authors who brag about the imaginary sums of money their books have made.

In the previous autumn I had had long talks with the Duke of Montrose

[1] The late Lord Vansittart, G.C.B., G.C.M.G.
[2] Major-General Sir Stewart Menzies, K.C.B., K.C.M.G.

and Lord Dalziel, the newspaper proprietor who for thirty years had represented Kirkcaldy in Parliament and was now an advocate of the limited Home Rule called 'devolution'. I argued in vain for a measure of Home Rule as effective as that won by the Irish Free State. The Moderates' proposals were strongly supported by the Glasgow *Daily Record* and opposed as strongly by the *Glasgow Herald* which was afraid that Scottish Home Rule would encourage Republicanism and Communism. I had been urged to offer myself for the Chairmanship of the Scottish National Party but I declined because I was not prepared to spend my time in administering sedatives to calm internal quarrels.

I was thankful, indeed, that I had not committed myself to such a task when that confounded case started. In this January, so far as I could see, chairmanship for me for the next few years would consist of occupying my own chair and forcing my Swan fountain-pen to lay eggs.

My bill of costs with Lewis and Lewis was over £1,100. I still had an overdraft with the Westminster Bank of over £3,000 which I was pledged to reduce by £1,000 each year. I had to repay Cassells the £500 I had been paid for *Greek Memories* and ought to pay them a further £900 odd for the cost of publishing the book. However, Newman Flower had generously forgone £400 of this, so that when the novel I proposed to write for autumn publication was finished for which I was to be paid £1,500 I should have £500 in cash. I had to refund the £200 put up by the *Daily Mail*; so I should not be getting any more for my reviews until March. I asked the manager of the local branch of the Commercial Bank of Scotland in Beauly to persuade his head office to sanction an overdraft of £500 which could be repaid by May at latest. He did his utmost but his head office refused.

Eric Linklater came up to stay for a night or two at Eilean Aigas. He had decided to contest the by-election in East Fife as a Scottish Nationalist and I had promised to come and speak for him.

Eric talked about his desire to marry Marjorie MacIntyre and wondered whether he was justified in embarking upon matrimony. I told him that I recognized in him genuine creativeness and had no doubt whatever that he was justified in backing his future as a writer. I may have asked what he had to worry about compared with myself. Just when he was leaving for St Andrews for his election campaign he suddenly asked me if £200 would be any help at this moment.

"But, my dear man, you can't spare that amount of money at this moment. You've got that election! You're hoping to get married. No, no, no . . ."

"Will £200 be any help at this moment?" he repeated in his deepest voice.

If there was even the faintest trace of bitterness left in me after my time in London that gesture by Eric Linklater obliterated it.

"I'll take your £200 on one condition, Eric."

"What's that?"

"That you spend your honeymoon on Barra if you succeed in marrying Marjorie MacIntyre by next June, by which time I hope I shall owe nothing but a cherished friendship."

The bargain was made.

I was planning to start work at once on a skit of the Secret Service which I was proposing to call *I Spy*. When I found that title had been used I proposed to call it *Peep-Bo*. Finally the title was *Water on the Brain*.

Before I started on it I went down to help Eric Linklater in the East Fife by-election. There were five candidates, a National Liberal, a Labour, an Empire Free Trader, a Liberal and a Nationalist. The Empire Free Trade party with Beaverbrook footing the bill had a jolly time at one of the hotels near the links of the Royal and Ancient. I cannot remember where I stayed. My chief memory is of George Scott Moncrieff looking like the Bellman in *The Hunting of the Snark*, ringing a large bell to attract an audience from passers by but never gathering more than half a dozen. Sometimes he went wandering round between a couple of sandwich-boards. David Keir was the Liberal candidate, advocating a cautious measure of Home Rule. There was a large audience in one of the halls at St Andrews after the enthusiasm of which I began to feel that Eric Linklater would make a good showing. I was too optimistic. When the result was declared the National Liberal had a large majority, with the Labour man second. I fancy the Empire Free Trade candidate lost his deposit. Certainly the Liberal did and so, a hundred or so votes behind him, did the Nationalist.

I was more than ever convinced that the policy of the National Party in contesting seats at this date was wrong.

Ralph Pinker was naturally alarmed about my financial future but he made a bad mistake when he persuaded me to let Sotheby's auction many of my manuscripts and rarer books. I argued that this was a hopeless time for such an auction. The financial crisis injected by the banks to save the pound did not look as if the National Government was going to soothe the patient's anxiety. However, I had to give way and sell for £370 books which today would be worth more than ten times that amount. The manuscripts, too, were being sold when the market was lower than it had ever been and immensely lower than it is today. The second part of *Sinister Street* was in the Bodleian: the first part was bought by Hugh Walpole for £46 and presented by him to King's School, Canterbury. Years later I offered to give four manuscripts in exchange but the headmaster would not agree. It was a depressing business and one on which I prefer not to dwell. At the same time Ralph Pinker arranged with the *Referee* that I should do the weekly column called 'Mustard and Cress' which had been started by G. R. Sims in

1877 and had gone on for forty-five years. D. B. Wyndham Lewis had been writing it but had recently gone over to the *Daily Mail* with that amusing column of his which rivalled J. B. Morton's Beachcomber in the *Daily Express*. The *Daily Mail* were annoyed when I took on 'Mustard and Cress' and I was able to assure the Editor with complete sincerity that I was just as much annoyed. However, £750 a year was going to be helpful.

'Mustard and Cress' mercifully did not last long. At this time the popular Press were making a to do about musquashes escaping from furrieries. They were a threat to our own small rivers several of which had already been choked by them. Steps must be taken to deal with musquashes before the Severn, the Trent, or even the Thames were menaced by them. I wrote this verse:

> We *must* squash the musquash,
> The musquash, the musquash,
> For if we don't squash the musquash,
> The musquash must squash us,
> And we ought to squash Hitler, too.

Hitler had become Chancellor in January 1933.

Just after I had posted my contribution for the following Sunday, March 26th 1933, I had a letter from the Editor to say that he had received a quantity of letters from readers protesting against my sneer at that great man Hitler. In future I was not to mention Hitler in my column. I wrote back to say I could not accept such a prohibition, and my column in next Sunday's *Referee* was the last I wrote for them.

I needed the money badly enough, but I did not feel I could go on writing for a paper whose readers admired and trusted Hitler.

However, the House of Commons was equally trustful. In that very week Ramsay MacDonald came back from Geneva and Rome with a cloudy pact by which Germany was to have equal status with France in military strength. With the exception of Winston Churchill it was an amenable House of Commons. *He* maintained that disarmament conferences did more harm than good and that "French military preponderance was the great safeguard of peace in Europe—all the more so after the recent events in Germany.[1] He charged the Prime Minister with having through his intervention in foreign affairs . . . brought Great Britain nearer to war, and he scornfully bade him devote his attention to the urgent domestic tasks which awaited him and to leave the conduct of foreign affairs to be transacted by competent Ambassadors through the normal diplomatic channels.

"Mr Eden . . . declared the charge brought by Mr Churchill against the Prime Minister of being responsible for the deterioration of inter-

[1] *Annual Register*, 1933.

national relations to be a mischievous absurdity . . . Mr Eden's champion-
ship of his chief was warmly applauded by the House."[1]

The National Government elected by credulous voters to save the
pound was by now apparently unaware of its national obligations and
alas, this was equally true of the Labour Opposition.

Early in March I wrote a review in the *Daily Mail* of a book by Sir
George Turner[2] called *Mary Stuart: Forgotten Forgeries*. Sir George was a
distinguished surgeon, two years away from his eightieth birthday. He
was in the English Rugby team against Scotland in 1876 and could not
be accused of Scottish partizanship.

"This is a book so much after my own heart that I can hardly bring
myself to admit that Sir George's grammar is a long way behind his
judgment. It is no mere matter of splitting an occasional infinitive. Sir
George smashes his infinitives to smithereens wholesale. However, he
deals just as ruthlessly with the enemies of Mary Queen of Scots.

"There is precious little left of that sandy-haired *demivierge* Elizabeth
by the time he has finished with her, and who except an obstinate Whig
would not prefer the unvarnished truth from Sir George to the smoothly
varnished lies of Froude or the poison of that reptile Buchanan?

"John Knox emerges in his true colours as a concupiscent and un-
grateful Hun. The treacherous hypocrite Moray and the cold-blooded
Cecil are painted as black as their black souls were. In fact, Sir George
deals with all Queen Mary's accusers as remorselessly as he deals with
the accusatives of the English language, and I am sure he would have
hanged them as high as he hangs his own nominatives.

"Yet, in joking about Sir George's grammar, it will not do to suggest
that this book is merely one more piece of special pleading for a shame-
fully misused lady. The analysis of the forged letters is a damning piece
of destructive criticism, and the whole book is so valuable that the
publishers should have taken the trouble to have the proofs properly
read and thus avoid the many really bad misprints which extend even
to the index."

Warden, the editor, sent me a bundle of protests and one ingenious
reader cut up the review page to send me a clerical collar of the sixteenth
century. Warden pressed upon me the importance of avoiding the
expression of religious or political views. The *Daily Mail* was a bit
worried at the moment by the birth of the *Scottish Daily Express*.

I think (but my date may be wrong) that it was in this Spring of 1933
that Chrissie and I were being driven in to some function in Inverness
and just before the Ness flows into the Beauly Firth we saw on the shore
an Atlantic seal. It was the largest Atlantic seal I have ever seen and one
of its flippers was evidently out of action. It was already dusk and I told

[1] *Annual Register*, 1933.
[2] The late Sir George Turner, K.B.E.

Ashie Macrae to stop the car until darkness fell. I did not want some sportsman to shoot at the wounded seal.

Next day or the day after there was an announcement in the *Scotsman*, I think, of a strange monster's having been seen in Loch Ness. The *Daily Mail* sent up to investigate and finally announced that the monster was probably a seal. In a burst of outraged patriotism most of the readers of the *Daily Mail* in Inverness-shire and Easter Ross gave up their paper and went over to the *Daily Express*. The *Daily Mail* realized that their circulation was being damaged and sent up another investigator who finally came to the conclusion that the mysterious creature seen in Loch Ness might indeed be a prehistoric monster. I think I am right in saying that the *Daily Mail* never recovered its former popularity in Inverness-shire or Ross-shire. Was the original Loch Ness monster that wounded seal which made its way into Loch Ness and was seen so often for six weeks until its flipper was sufficiently healed to let it get back to the sea? That would account for the frequent reports at the time of its having been seen ashore. One report went so far as to say that it had a sheep in its mouth.

I have been turning over the pages of the reviews I was writing for the *Daily Mail* during this period. I find that on January 12th the day of the Old Bailey trial there was an enthusiastic notice of a war book by Guy Chapman called *A Passionate Pilgrimage*. Have any of the paper-backs reprinted this really first-class book? If not, why not? I find on the same page an equally enthusiastic notice of *Down and out in Paris and London* by George Orwell.

I was not impressed by David Garnett's *Life of Pocohontas*:

"The first part of this pseudo-novel or pseudo-history reminds me of a precocious Bloomsbury child who has dressed himself up as an Indian brave from the equipment of a toy-shop to go stalking his young companions through the shrubberies of Gordon Square while critics stand round and applaud like so many fond uncles.

"He reveals in a preface that his ambition was to draw an accurate historical picture, and to make it a work of art.

"Had he with a humbler sense of responsibility to the future confined his aim to the achievement of historical accuracy, possibly the work of art might have made itself, in which case this compilation of still life and letters might have been flushed with a more sentient hue than that which incarnadines the cheeks of waxworks."

I am glad to find that in February I was extolling Sinclair Lewis's novel *Ann Vickers*; immediately afterwards, in a notice of William Faulkner's *Light in August* I was writing:

"To the intellectuals on both sides of the Atlantic the work of Mr William Faulkner will appear more profound that that of his senior. . . .

"Unquestionably *Light in August* is a good book; possibly it is a great book. Yet with all its qualities . . . the book is rank with the odour of decay, and it is noteworthy how much this deliquescence of imagination is affecting even the very texture of Mr Faulkner's prose."

I went on to quote an example of that prose which wound up "the nearly adjacenting chimneys streaked like black tears".

"What on earth is the point of writing 'adjacenting'? What is gained by adding an English present participle to an already existing Latin present participle? While he was about it Mr Faulkner might as well have added a French present participle and written 'adjacentingant'.

"Nevertheless, I must not suggest that the whole book is written with such a barbarous disregard of verbal decency. Mr Faulkner is still too good a writer to believe that he can attract the world's attention only with the kind of noises that a third-rate trumpeter makes in a jazz-band.

"Arnold Bennett proclaimed that Mr Faulkner 'writes generally like an angel'. For this book he has plucked a quill from one of his own wings; it would not be a bad experiment if he wrote his next book with a thin steel nib."

About now the undergraduates of Oxford had decided in the Union that in no circumstances would they fight for King and Country.

"*Red Rags, Essays of Hate from Oxford* comes appropriately.

"Sixteen young men and two young women set out to dance round John Bull, no doubt with the confident expectation of putting him in a temper. Will they succeed? I doubt it.

"Mr Justice McCardie, who writes the Epilogue, is evidently not perturbed by the most extravagant feats of these young picadors. Nor, let me add, am I; but whether our placidity is a sign that Oxford remains essentially old-fashioned or whether it is a tribute to the comparative youthfulness of Sir Henry McCardie and myself might be hard to decide.

"Anyway, whatever the subject I nearly always found myself in complete agreement with the writer, so completely indeed, as to remind myself that I wrote from much the same point of view in various University publications when I was an undergraduate thirty years ago.

"The weakest pages in the book are those devoted to the personal introduction of the various essayists, because most of them suffer from that tiresome and self-conscious facetiousness which is apparently inseparable from the early attempts of the young to see themselves as others see them.

" 'How this book of *Red Rags* is stirring me,' says Sir Henry McCardie in his Epilogue. Well, I would not go quite so far as to echo that. The effect on myself was tenderly sedative, and in retrospect *Red Rags* seemed to possess the delicacy of old lace, to which clings a faint perfume of eau de Chypre or lavender water."

Among those young men were Quintin Hogg, John Connell, John Boyd-Carpenter, Lionel Hale, and Robert Speaight, none of whom could have been among the 'Ays' in that deplorable Union debate which, incredible as it now seems, did delude Hitler and his gang into supposing that Great Britain was soft, a belief that was confirmed by the appeasement that started in 1937.

It was a shock when two months after I wrote those words about Mr Justice McCardie he shot himself. I had met him once or twice and had been as much impressed by his personality as I always was by his judgments. He was only in his sixty-fourth year when he died, a very severe loss to British justice.

When I read those old reviews of mine I am more than ever grateful to the impulse which led me to withdraw from any attempt to be 'with it' in the twittering 'twenties. In every one I wrote I expressed my own opinion, completely unaffected by the fashionable opinion of the moment.

After that case had messed up my financial affairs I knew that it would be impossible for me to live at Eilean Aigas and I asked Simon Lovat if he would consider letting me break the lease. He told me he thought that could be managed and then on February 16th he was at Little Tew near Chipping Norton, watching the Magdalen and New College point to point in which the Master of Lovat, who had come of age last July, was riding; he had just been commissioned as an Ensign in the Scots Guards.

Shimi was winning the race and Simon Lovat was hurrying up a muddy slope to get a better view of the winning-post when just as Shimi won he stumbled and fell, unconscious. Laura was with him and he was driven to Chipping Norton hospital. There that evening he died. His body was taken to the Jesuit Church in Farm Street where it lay until it was brought to Beaufort Castle. On a snowy day the coffin was carried on a farm-cart from Beaufort to Eskadaile churchyard where he was buried. It was an almost unbearably moving occasion. The monks of Fort Augustus chanting the plainsong of the Requiem Mass said by Archbishop MacDonald, the guard of honour of the Lovat Scouts, the Provost and Town Council of Inverness who were given the Eilean Aigas pew, the words of the burial service spoken by Father Aeneas Geddes, the mourning lairds of the Highlands, the last pibroch of lament for a great chief, a great patriot, and a man loved by all.

The financial complications that the death of a landed proprietor involved made it impossible for me to consider breaking the lease.

I have told already how all my comic books had been written when worried and in physical pain. *Water on the Brain* was no exception. I kept on being laid out with that infernal sciatica and as well as the worry over money I had to answer endless letters, write that weekly column for the *Referee*, read a book a night after glancing through a couple of dozen, write my *Daily Mail* reviews, write my quarterly survey of records for

The Gramophone, and go down to Glasgow each month for the University Court. Looking back I do not know how I managed to finish *Water on the Brain* by the first week in May.

Newman Flower had been a bit worried when I told him of my intention to write a skit on the Secret Service. However, I was able to reassure him that it would be free from libel and official secrets. I dedicated it to Robert Rait who had just been knighted:

"My dear Principal,

" 'There is something wild in letting a pair of spurs be carried into the sea out of a boat,' Dr Johnson observed during that 'boisterous sail' from Skye to Raasay. And there is something wild in dedicating to a scholar of your renown a novel called *Water on the Brain*. Yet I am glad that you so amiably accepted the inscription to you of this farcical interlude, because it gives me an opportunity of expressing my profound gratitude to yourself and to the University of Glasgow for a hospitality inclusive of everything that hospitality can mean in the widest sense.

"I have always attempted to extract from the disagreeable experiences which have come my way in life a compensation from the experience itself, and a recent annoyance of mine was thus transformed into something akin to pleasure. In effecting such a transformation the good-will and sympathy of yourself and the University were prepotent.

"*Water on the Brain* represents the measure of my own amusement at the end of it all. It is the friendliest archery; not a shaft has been barbed with malice or poisoned by vexation of spirit. As a historian you will at once detect an air of improbability about this novel; but I am sure that on this occasion you would prefer improbability to probability, since the latter would have involved me in the odium of striking at men incapable of defending themselves except *in camera*. Nevertheless, the mercy one may show to individuals cannot always be extended to a system, and although *Water on the Brain* is a deliberate caricature of Intelligence there are features in the system which will be recognized even by those with a great deal less humour and knowledge than yourself.

"In brief: actual facts, real people, and existing organizations have been eliminated from the first page to the last. You may think after reading *Water on the Brain* that such a disclaimer was superfluous; but recently on one or two occasions the farcical has been mixed with the tragic in a way that might encourage even the sophisticated to accept farce as history. Hence my anxiety to insist that *Water on the Brain* is only a grotesque fairy tale.

Yours ever
Compton Mackenzie

Eilean Aigas 5th May 1933."

These words tried to express the gratitude I felt to the way the Vice-

H

Chancellor had carried off the appearance of his Rector at the Old Bailey. *Water on the Brain* was a reading success. I was gratified when the late Duke of Westminster told me that it was the only realistic book about secret service he had read.

A year or two ago *Water on the Brain* was reissued as a Penguin. I had a letter from a doctor in San Francisco to say how glad he was to have his favourite book again. Two former copies had been 'borrowed' by friends. He went on to say that I might be amused to know that during the war the O.S.S. (Office of Strategic Services is the full title, I believe) had found a copy of *Water on the Brain* in Cairo and had had a hundred photostat copies made to coach young American Intelligence officers in secret service work. I thought my leg was being pulled, but the very next day I received a letter from Cleveland, Ohio, to tell me the same. I mentioned this in an article I wrote for an American weekly and the *New Statesman* commented on it. There was no contradiction. So, however incredible, the story must be true.

Another Glasgow figure who had earned my gratitude was that staunch old Liberal Sir Daniel Stevenson.[1] He had wanted to raise a fund to pay my legal expenses but I had said I did not think he would get any newspaper to co-operate.

He wrote:

As you said, I find that the plan I had in mind of getting a fund raised through one of the newspapers won't work. I think the Editors would be quite willing to insert a letter from me, but there is an aversion to taking sides in what is more or less an official question.

My idea now is to try them with a letter asserting that the trial was worthy of the Star Chamber; that here we have a man well known to the whole country tried in camera on what is alleged to be a very serious charge, and the public kept in ignorance of the case for the prosecution and for the defence.

I knew that such a letter would merely annoy the other side and Sir Daniel agreed with me. I was deeply touched by the liveliness of that octogenarian; a year later I had an opportunity to pay him a tribute.

Sir Daniel was a persevering friend but he was an equally persevering enemy. David Cleghorn Thomson had gone to war with him about the Glasgow orchestra subsidized by Sir Daniel, who was President of the Scottish Academy of Music. Glasgow had for some time resented the headquarters of the B.B.C. being in Edinburgh. London had felt that David Cleghorn Thomson was taking too independent a line and the end of it was that Sir John Reith called for David Cleghorn Thomson's resignation.

I thought at the time that David had been hardly treated. He had built up Scottish Regional from its beginnings and had been responsible

---

[1] The late Sir Daniel Stevenson, Bt., LL.D.

for many fruitful experiments in broadcasting. However, he *would* make the mistake of telling his seniors what they ought to do and Sir John Reith was not of malleable material.

The new Controller of the Scottish Regional was the Rev. Dr Melville Dinwiddie, D.D.[1] who had had an outstanding record for gallantry in the war, and been awarded both an M.C. and a D.S.O. Dinwiddie divested himself of his clerical collar and would remain Controller of Scottish Regional for the next quarter of a century. He was just over forty when he succeeded and at that time in spite of his courage in the field he was obviously a little nervous of the greatness thrust upon him. One of the future programmes to which he found himself committed was an unscripted conversation in the Scottish Arts Club between Norman Sturrock, Willie Mackay Mackenzie and myself. If this was successful David had planned to have talks in other Edinburgh clubs.

The new Controller was worried at the beginning of his reign by having to accept the responsibility for what I might say in such a conversation, and he asked Norman Sturrock and myself to dine with him at the Edinburgh Café Royal. Norman made up one of his sagas about the evening in which I was supposed to have ordered caviare, oysters, lobster and champagne and made the new Controller so nervous about the size of the bill for the entertainment expenses he would have to present that he himself ate nothing during this banquet except the drumstick of a chicken.

Lord Reith and Melville Dinwiddie are such good friends of mine that I know they will forgive my telling the next story.

After dinner when Dinwiddie had been relieved about the proposed Club conversation by my telling him that I should not be able to manage it, he said to me,

"I know you're interested in psychical matters. I wonder if you have any explanation to account for an extraordinarily unpleasant dream which is recurrent. Almost every night just now I dream that I am followed down a dark corridor by a fearful monster. I cannot see the monster but as it draws nearer and nearer to me I suddenly find a door at the end of the corridor and just manage to escape as I wake up gasping with fright. And the really unpleasant thing about this dream is that every night the monster gets closer to me. Have you any explanation of this alarming experience?"

"Yes," I said. "Reith. You are worried about this new job. And your worry expresses itself symbolically in your anxiety not to let down Sir John Reith by disappointing him. You're going to make a success of your new job. So give up worrying and you won't have this dream again."

"Joseph is right," said Norman Sturrock.

An unnamed American poet about now threw out a challenge by

[1] Bailie Melville Dinwiddie, C.B.E., D.S.O., M.C., D.D.

naming what he considered the ten most beautiful words in the English language. Here it is:

Dawn, hush, lullaby, murmuring, tranquil, mist, luminous, chime, golden, melody.

The Editor of the *Daily Mail* suggested I should write an article giving my own choice of the ten most beautiful words. I include that article because the two lists I gave have a strange magic for me now in my eighty-fourth year, a sort of elixir of youth.

"A choice of the ten most beautiful words in the English language offers as lively and endless a topic for discussion as any that could be raised.

"I started arguing about beautiful words when I was twelve, and I devoted six months of strict rural seclusion at the age of twenty-one to the discovery and pursuit of beautiful words. I wish I had those lists by me now, though, no doubt, it was a wise act on my part which destroyed them. A writer chained to beautiful words is in peril of never expressing himself, and in that sentence I find a beautiful word which is at the same time completely simple and at anybody's disposal.

"*Peril* shall be my first choice. Its chief rival is 'danger'. They are of equal antiquity, both going back to the 13th century; but danger originally meant more particularly the risk of hurt from the power of a lord. *Peril* included every kind of risk, ghostly or otherwise. Take a line from a hymn that everyone knows. 'For those in peril on the sea.' Substitute danger, and the line is ruined. Compare the adjective 'perilous' with the adjective 'dangerous' and there is no need to quote Keats to demonstrate the superiority of 'perilous'. *Peril* sounds beautiful because, although it has no broad vowel sound, it has a perfect combination of consonants. You get a sense of the efficiency of the words in a phrase like 'at your peril'.

"After such a simple word it is tempting to choose some tremendous word like 'incarnadine' or 'incommunicable' or 'amaranthine', but I do not feel that one is entitled to choose such obviously decorative heavyweights except for competition in a special class of their own. Indeed, how far is it legitimate to choose a colour word when the choice is liable to be affected by one's own pleasure in that colour? It is impossible to claim that 'orange' is a beautiful word. Yet, I am so fond of this colour that I always enjoy an opportunity to use the word for it.

"Still, there is one word for colour which, I think, must have a place in my list, and that is *azure*. Long ago, when the word was first discovered in Arabia or Persia, there was an 'l' in front of it, the same 'l' you find in lapis lazuli, and 'lazure' competed for a time with *azure*, being used occasionally even until the end of the 17th century. But *azure* was the more beautiful form and if it meant the dreariest brown I should still include it in my list.

"What applies to colour words applies equally to flower words; but again I must allow myself one, and that is *carnation*. There is some doubt whether the flower was originally 'coronation' or 'carnation', and we should associate carnation more with flesh-colour than with the flower.

"Remember that it is both noun and adjective. Early in the 17th century 'carnation' was used to describe the horse that, presumably, we now call a strawberry roan. As a word combining fragrance, colour, and beauty of sound, 'carnation' seems to me in the first rank.

"I am tempted by some of the words ending with 'ilion', like vermilion, postilion, pavilion; but I shall pass them by, and choose *silence*. The list of the American poet, which started this discussion, included lullaby, hush and tranquil, none of which to my fancy can compete with 'silence' any more successfully than 'stillness' or 'peace' or 'quiet' or 'calm'. *Au cœur blessé l'ombre et le silence*, wrote Balzac, and in translating his exquisite phrase 'Shadow and silence for a wounded heart' we may find two more of the most beautiful words in the English language—*heart* and *shadow*. Some of the beauty of 'heart' lies in the spelling of it, and a curse be upon those who would simplify English spelling. The beauty of 'shadow' need not be insisted upon, and it carries with it a wonderful adjective, which is more than 'heart' does, for 'hearty' is a detestable word, whereas 'shadowy' is full of mysterious suggestion. I pause for a moment at 'sombre', but reject it as too modern and too easily debauched by American spelling. Somber! What a word!

"There are some glorious words ending in 'oon'—barracoon, rigadoon, lagoon, dragoon, typhoon, doubloon, galloon, macaroon, picaroon, maroon, gadroon, ducatoon, frigatoon, but such words are not so much beautiful as strange and romantic. Nevertheless, I am determined to have one word in 'oon', and who shall blame me for choosing *moon*?

"I am left with only three more words. This is getting serious. I have already chosen one ending in 'l', but I cannot omit *April*. 'The uncertain glory of an April day.' 'The April of my time, the sweet of youth,' 'The April's in her eyes, it is love's spring.' I doubt if any word has inspired so many beautiful phrases.

"And now I cannot exclude *apricot* from the chosen ten, whether it be spelt as we do now or whether it be spelt as once upon a time 'apricock'. Partly this love of the word 'apricot' is due to the association of the word with the beautiful Latin word, *apricus*, which is the most sun-coloured word I know. Yet, actually 'apricot' had nothing to do with *apricus*, but is connected with *praecox* in reference to its early ripeness not to its sunny qualities.

"I am left with one word, and I shall choose *forlorn*. The oldest meaning was 'morally lost' in the sense in which we still use 'abandoned', but early in the 16th century 'forlorn' had already acquired its woeful significance of to-day. 'Forlorn! The very word is like a bell . . .'

"Here is my final list in blank verse:

> "Carnation, azure, peril, moon, forlorn,
> Heart, silence, shadow, April, apricot.

"But I can put ten equally beautiful words into an Alexandrine couplet:

> "Damask and damson, doom and harlequin and fire,
> Autumnal, vanity, flame, nectarine, desire."

This article produced a surprising amount of attention and comment in the Press. Correspondents of the *Daily Mail* sailed in with rival lists, and in a book of cuttings I find that over two dozen papers (none of the London dailies, of course) had something to say about that list of words.

I was pleased to find that so much interest was being taken in words, but I was a little saddened by some of the rival lists which seemed to me a threat to the future of English prose. A correspondent of *John O'London's* wrote to offer a list of writers who used the most beautiful words in English—de Quincey, Lamb, Oscar Wilde, James Elroy Flecker, Aldous Huxley, John Masefield and Beverley Nichols; Shakespeare, Spenser, Milton and a few more were overlooked. This correspondent gave lists of the words used by the above writers and wound up with Beverley Nichols in apparent seriousness. Here they are:

Prelude, marionette, Riviera, Oxford, epigram, saxophone.

I wonder if 'escalation' would have been added to that list today.

Toward the end of May Chrissie and I went to Barra where the Crookle was going to put the pair of us up at 5 Ardveenish for £3 a week. Faith held the fort in Dryden Chambers and contrived to work on *The Gramophone* as well as get on with a book she was writing about the nieces of Mazarin. Nellie Boyte stayed behind at Eilean Aigas with the cats to do the typing of the fair copies and refuse the various requests for me to talk all over the place.

It was decided to celebrate my return to Barra by an expedition to Mingulay. That long June day remains in my memory as one of the supreme days of my life. Just before eight o'clock we went aboard the Coddie's boat in Northbay—the Coddie, the Crookle, Neil Sinclair, the headmaster of the Northbay school, John Johnston, the headmaster of Greian school, and Calum MacNeil, the headmaster of Eoligarry school.

I had provided two bottles of whisky, and nominated the Crookle as steward for the voyage. At eight o'clock the anchor was weighed and the Coddie said to me:

"All shipshape with a fair wind. What about tapping the steward?"

That phrase became current in the Isles for suggesting a drink, and I am told it may still be heard. We tapped the steward by emptying six drams of whisky, and the dream began. We did not call in at Castlebay or Vatersay but we landed on Sandray with its seven sandy beaches. None of us, even with the help of another dram, was able to see all seven beaches at once. So we failed to find the crock of gold, which is buried where the searcher can see all those seven beaches at once. Sandray was used at this time by the crofters of Vatersay for their common grazing.

Our next stop was Pabbay (Priest's Island) where there are the remains of the holy man's abode when Pabbay was populated. From Pabbay on to Mingulay, an island three miles long evacuated by its population hardly thirty years ago. The rich grazing of the island covers a large hollow the westerly sides of which rise to an awe-inspiring line of cliffs over 700 feet high which hold the Atlantic at bay. John Johnston told of a time when he had been collecting sea-birds' eggs from these cliffs and had slipped. He claimed that he had clung on for some hours and that at last the *sluagh* or fairy host had helped him to hoist himself back to safety.

Before we left Mingulay we knelt by the *làraichean* or stony remains of the houses which had once been lived in by a happy community to say prayers for those who were now dead.

We went on to cross the narrow swift-flowing stream of water between Mingulay and Berneray or, as it is always called, Barra Head. Here we were entertained by the lighthouse-keeper and his wife. The Barra Head lighthouse illuminates a large space of the Atlantic, and may be the first light of Europe sighted by voyagers from America. The grandfather of Neil Sinclair, known as the Barra giant, lived here once. He was indeed a giant, being over seven feet tall.

On the way back to Northbay we sailed along those stupendous cliffs on the west side of Mingulay, and as we steered to starboard for the east side of Pabbay (I think) we saw the famous blow hole known as *snaoisean* or snuff-taker and, sitting on a rock beside it without paying any attention to the sudden spurt of water, the largest sea-otter I had ever seen or ever saw again.

We were back in Northbay in the glimmering northern dusk after that day of days. Back to work again.

Ralph Pinker had arranged with Rich and Cowan, a new firm of publishers, that I was to write in a series they were publishing about various subjects "in my time" on *Literature in my Time*. I had planned to get on with a novel to be called *The Darkening Green* and was annoyed with Pinker for landing me with a pot-boiler I was in no mood to write and in which I feared I might scald myself. He reminded me of the financial situation and there was nothing for it but to get down to a job I had no heart for. My mood may be realized by a paragraph I wrote in the dedication to Francis Brett Young.

"*Literature in My Time* has been written with hardly any books of reference, and in a place remote from the ability to indulge in consultation with literary people. This method has destroyed any value the book might have possessed as a guide; but at least it has preserved it from any bias except my own, and, I hope, from some of the conventional jargon of criticism."

That paragraph was cut out. Lieut.-Commander C. R. St J. Rich had written at the end of August when I sent in the balance of the book:

"I am sure you will see the uncommercial aspect of this, and I don't think it is necessary, because neither you nor we suggest that the books in this series are in any way guides, and this book is what it sets out to be, merely Literature in *your* time. I am sure you will see this point."

I gave way, of course. To my surprise it was well received by the critics, and I was gratified when the *Annual Register* called it a "brilliant survey" of the century's literature.

Francis and Jessica Brett Young had left Westmorland and were now living in a perfect Adam house in Worcestershire, his native county. From there he wrote:

> *Craycome House*
> *near Pershore*
> *October 27.33*

My dear Monty,

The book arrived safely yesterday and I read it right through at a sitting, absorbed and delighted. This is not to say that I didn't frequently disagree with you. It seems that the effect of the whole thing was (as I had expected it to be) intensely stimulating, full of the vitality which you always have to spare, the wit that I look for, and the steadiness of judgement that puts you apart from the other critic-novelists. When I say that you're so reasonable, so sensible, I mean, of course, that you generally think what I do; but there's rather more to it than that. We have both of us, in fact, lived remote from the sweaty melée of 'literary' men who congregate in London, and we have neither of us been identified with any chapelle. I'm glad you had so much truth to say about Lawrence. The Messianic legend grows so strongly and can be discovered flourishing in such unlikely quarters that the world looks like being divided between him—poor hag-ridden (literally) creature!—and Dr Buchman, who must surely be one of the world's worst Babbits.

There are so many things in the book I enjoyed that I can't attempt to catalogue them; but I thought the dedicatory letter a perfect piece of tact; though, indeed, the last thing you should do is to apologize for being egoistic, since egotism of your kind has always been one of your major charms, and the reminiscent mood has always suited you to perfection, from the days of Sinister Street *onwards. In any case you know how proud I was of the dedication and how pleasant it is to think that, though we are members of one of the most spiteful and jealous professions on earth, we can still with complete honesty call each other friend. . . . God bless you.*

> *Yours always*
> *Francis*

One of the Professors at the University for whom I had the highest regard was W. Macneile Dixon who had been Regius Professor of English Literature since 1904. Macneile Dixon had taken every academic honour going at Trinity College, Dublin. I put him in the same class of Professors of English Literature as George Saintsbury, Walter Raleigh or Quiller-Couch. He was now sixty-seven but did not seem nearly as old.

With some misgivings I sent him a copy of *Literature in my Time* but those misgivings were allayed by the letter he wrote to me. Indeed, his letter compensated me for what I had fancied was the intolerable drudgery of writing that book.

> *The University; Glasgow*
> *Nov. 17.1933*

Dear Lord Rector,

Please accept my best thanks for the copy of Literature in My Time, *which reached me safely. I have spent a couple of delightful hours with it, and rather to my surprise, I must confess, found myself in much closer agreement with your verdict than I had anticipated. It has always seemed to me that a man's age could be estimated within ten or twelve years by his fancies in authors, more especially poets and novelists. Except here and there I don't seem to be 'a back-number.' But here and there I am dated beyond a doubt. I am interested to see, however, that D. H. Lawrence was not a test-case. A year ago I made a valiant attempt to discover what all the fuss was about.* Horribile dictu *he seemed to me quite a second, if not third rate writer. I could not in the least make out what the devil he wanted us either to think or to do. Is it time for me to resign my Chair? Times are hard and I trust you hold that the evidence of senility is not sufficient. There's a young fellow, Peter Fleming, whose* Brazilian Adventure *does seem to me well written. So perhaps I'm not yet wholly out of touch with the rising generation.*

> *With kind regards*
> *Very gratefully and sincerely yours*
> *W. Macneile Dixon*

I must go back to that month of June when I was still struggling with *Literature in my Time.*

I find in a letter to Faith:

Linklater and bride arrive on Friday next. We are to have a lobster supper which should keep the newly wed awake as successfully as the torch of Hymen.

How vividly that June 9th stays in my memory. Just as the Coddie and I were walking along to the pier in Castlebay, one of the Barra shop-keepers who was not on good terms with the Coddie beckoned to me. I went in and with an air of mystery he took me upstairs to his bedroom. There on a table was a bottle of whisky.

"It is my birthday," he told me, "and I want you to drink a dram with me and then I will read to you a poem I am after writing."

We drank our drams, and the poem in Gaelic was read to me. It was a kind of ode to himself on his birthday. Then we drank another dram and I hurried down to the pier for the *Lochearn* to come alongside.

"Well, Coddie," I said. "I've just been given something you were never given. R— M— has just given me a couple of drams. It's his birthday."

The Coddie jibbed.

"*A Dhia na Gràs* (O god of grace), fancy a man like that to be born in the beautiful month of June!"

Eric Linklater picked up his bride and carried her down the gangway to the pier. There was a cheer of greeting—and of relief perhaps that he had not dropped her into the water. To quote from a letter of Chrissie to Faith who was now in Jethou:

What grilling and glorious weather! But oh dear, what work there is to do. Mr Mackenzie has just finished The Gramophone *Editorial, and has gone out for a walk or rather to lie in the sun somewhere.*

First of all I'll tell you about the Linklaters. When they arrived nearly all Barra were at Castlebay to meet them, Mr Mackenzie included. There was a triumphal arch of ribbons made for them. Crookle's car was gaily decorated with ribbons of all colours, old shoes, horse-shoes, and all the other usual things. Dr Bartlett took them to his house and there they had champagne, which was unexpected and all the more enjoyable. Then they drove to Northbay, where Peggy Crookle and I had prepared a really very nice supper of lobster and mayonnaise and salad. I thought the bride would be so excited that she wouldn't be able to eat anything, but she ate lots and lots, which was a great satisfaction to the cooks!! I made the mayonnaise (the first time ever) and everyone said it was very good. They ate it all, so it must have been.

Then they were piped across the traigh mhòr to the house at Eoligarry where they are staying, and they seem very happy. She is a very very nice girl, and adapts herself wonderfully well to conditions here. I'm afraid, however, their landlady is just not a good cook, so they've had supper several times with Mr Mackenzie.

Mr Mackenzie is beginning to get very brown, and tries hard to get at least one walk a day. He has been out to several islands, too, in boats. It's a great pity he has such a great lot of work to do, for he should have a holiday. The book will not be done by the end of June. He is finding it hard to do, but he is dictating it all, and lying down to do it. He's had shoots several times, but except for two bad goes when we first arrived he has been well . . .

Much love
from
Chrissie

That mention of shoots reminds me of a letter I had from Ursula Maxwell that May. Misprints are not responsible for the spelling:

Champneys,
Tring,
Herts
19th May

Dear Monty

You simply must come down here and get your siatica cured—Lief, who runs this place, said he could amost guarantee to cure you. I believe he has never not cured a siatica case. That is if they did the cure properly.

Couldn't you come down now for two or three weeks—you could write all the time as there is nothing to do here at all! You could lodge Crissie in the village or she could come here as a guest on a reduced fee.

. . . If you do come and Crissie cant I'll write your letters for you!! also drive you about if you send your car down! . . .

The rooms are from £9. 9. to £18. 18 a week and there are also most attractive little challets at £10. 10. This includes treatment etc.

I must stop
        Do come

                    Love
                        from
                            Ursula

I resisted that expensive temptation; it was all I could do to find the £3 a week for the cottage life of Chrissie and myself. I resisted, too, the temptation to go down to Glasgow for the degrees that June, and it was a temptation because we were giving an honorary degree to a man whom I held in high esteem as one of the few European statesmen who seemed to have even a glimmering vision of Europe's future. That was Edmond Herriot. Apart from opening sales of work in Castlebay, Craigston and Northbay to raise funds for the cathedral being built in Oban I did no public speaking. Incidentally nearly £700 was raised by these sales of work in a small island with a population of less than 2,500. The only other public appearance I made that June was as one of the quartet of middle-aged gentlemen carrying the canopy for the Northbay Corpus Christi procession, and that was quite a job in a lively north-west wind. The Coddie led that procession, carrying the cross. I see him now coming out of the sacristy of St Barr's little church by the water's edge. He is in a laced cotta and is suddenly aware that his youngest son Ninian, aged about ten, is saying something to make the other altar-boys laugh. The Coddie for a moment feels self-conscious but recovering his inimitable *sang froid*, points to his chest and says to me in a voice that sounds in my ear today,

"Direct from the Vatican."

I see Morag Macdonald, the infant mistress of Northbay school, picking up one after another of her small charges as they fall over walking backwards to scatter flowers before the Blessed Sacrament, and seem in danger of holding up the procession, five hundred strong; there were 1,250 at Castlebay. Chrissie spoke in her letter to Faith about my expeditions to the small islands in the sound between Barra and South Uist. These were made either with the Coddie or the Sgoileir Bàn. Both of them were inexhaustible tellers of tales, and those little islands long empty were populated again by the folk who had once lived on them. I recall sitting on top of Fuday among the nests of the eider-duck and telling fairy stories to Flora, the Coddie's youngest daughter who was then on the edge of four. One day some twenty years hence I should have the privilege of giving away that enchanting little girl when she was married in Edinburgh.

I recall seeing the Sgoileir Bàn bringing ashore at Northbay two female English tourists whom he had taken for a sail in his boat. They asked him how much the trip was to cost.

"It will cost you nothing, ladies. I am an aristocrat of the democracy."

And indeed that was one of the secrets of the joy life was to me on Barra. They were all aristocrats of the democracy.

I had hoped that Veronica, who was now twelve and a half, was going to come and stay for a while during her holidays in August. Alas, Laura Lovat wrote to say that she and Hugh and Magdalen were going to Greece and that Veronica was to spend August with her sister Diana Westmorland.

Veronica wrote on July 11th:

Darling Monty,

Thank you so much for your lovely long letter, I did like it. . . . The problem for the holidays is at last solved. . . . The worst of it is that I won't be able to come to you by myself which is heart-breaking, and that I will have to wait till they come back from Greece till we all come on to dear old B. At any rate Magd. and me will be able to stay for quite a long time. . . . My dates are rather vague but I think we will get to Barra about Sept. 20 or thereabouts. How are you? Please forgive this rather selfish letter, for I think I have talked only about myself but I had to tell you our plans, didn't I? Love to Chrissy, Crookell, Coddy, etc. and a great deal to yourself. Lots of l. from

Veronica

In the letter Laura Lovat wrote to tell me that they were going to Greece and that Magdalen and Veronica would not be able to come in August she told me that Ethel Smythe was making a tour of the Outer Isles and would probably arrive in Barra.

Dame Ethel Smythe aged 75 did not seem the perfect compensation for losing Veronica Fraser aged 12½. I had not yet met that prodigious personality, but when I did I was grateful Laura had impressed upon her that she must begin her tour with Barra. The two days I spent in her company would be memorable indeed. She was very deaf, but as active as one of the Barra ponies that ran wild on the *machair*. As she and I tramped over that *machair* we talked about many things, my conversation being one long shout which left me often gasping for breath in the wind. I had recently read for the first time Goethe's conversations with Eckermann, and we shouted our enjoyment of those talks of long ago. We talked of Greece about which she had written that delicious book *A Three Legged Tour in Greece*, an arduous exploration of the Peloponnese she had made when just seventy. She told me about her time in Holloway when she was a militant suffragist, and I remembered Laura Lovat's telling me how Maurice Baring had visited her there and how when he was asked what relation the prisoner was to him he had replied 'ex-mistress' and left the prison officials blushing. Dame Ethel told me about her excitement when she was studying music in Leipzig and was asked to lunch to meet Brahms.

"Such a disillusionment for a girl," she declared. "I was so thrilled, but he said hardly a word and when a tin of sardines was passed round he ate all that were left and then picked up the tin and greedily sucked up the oil."

She went on to tell me how when she used to go out to dinner she used to bicycle with the skirt of her evening dress tucked into her bloomers and when she reached the house retire into a shrubbery and pull her skirt out of the bloomers before she rang the bell.

Father John Macmillan arranged for a waulking at the little parish hall of Northbay. This is the vigorous ceremony of shrinking the tweed. On either side of a trestle table sat six women who swayed backwards and forwards as they lifted a length of tweed and banged it down on the table and rolled it towards one another; the length of tweed would have been previously dipped in urine. Usually one of the women sings a waulking song of verse after verse while this is being done. However, that evening at Northbay the singer of the song was over eighty years old and sat away from the table as she sang verse after verse of the waulking songs.

When the exhausting process was over Dame Ethel asked Father John if it would be in order for her to offer the women a dram.

He replied,

"Yes, indeed, but I'm afraid there isn't a dram to offer them."

"Oh yes, there is," said Dame Ethel, as she lifted her skirt and pro-duced from a pocket on the inside of it a bottle of whisky with which she went round filling the dram-glasses fetched from the hall pantry.

"How do you say good health in Gaelic?" she asked me.

"Slainte mhàth," I shouted.

"Can't hear you."

Simultaneously Father John and I bellowed "Slainte mhàth."

"Can't hear you. Never mind. Good health to all you nice people and thank you for giving me such a splendid evening."

She left for Lochboisdale next evening and sent a bottle of whisky to Father John from Castlebay.

"A noble glorious woman," he declared in his richest tones, with which the pop of the cork seemed to express enthusiastic agreement.

Dame Ethel went on from South Uist to cross the South Ford to Benbecula and from Benbecula by the North Ford to North Uist, and thence on to Stornoway. From Lochmaddy she wrote me a very long letter in which she criticized severely two of the hotels at which she stayed and praised warmly a third.

Just after Dame Ethel left I received from Dr Agnes Habermann a printed thesis she had written for her Doctorate of Letters at the University of Bonn. It was entitled "The Romantic Quality of Compton Mackenzie" and ran to seventy pages. There was nobody on Barra who could read German. We used to pile the papers and letters in a corner of that tiny sitting-room for we had no files to put them in. That thesis vanished in the confusion of paper that was accumulated during the next two years and could not be found when somebody did come to Barra who knew German. I could never understand why people considered my books romantic. I was always under the impression when I wrote them that they represented a realistic approach to the novel.

It was at the beginning of this August that John Lorne Campbell, Younger of Inverneill, came to Barra for a week-end and stayed there until he acquired the island of Canna in 1938. We had met first at St Andrews, and I had been impressed by the potentiality of that young man in his mid-twenties. Like myself he had an American mother and like myself he was able to take a more objective view of both sides of the Atlantic than the average Briton or American. He had just published an invaluable book called *Highland Songs of the Forty-five* and was devoting himself to the study of Gaelic of which he would become one of the leading scholars. Over thirty years later Oxford would give him a D.Litt. for a thesis, and Glasgow would give him an Honorary D.Litt.

When he came to Barra he was wearing the kilt. I recall his saying a day or two later that he was going to stop wearing it because it made the people reserved with him as with a laird. I told him to give up thinking when he was in Barra that he was still in Argyll.

"The people here are shy. You have to pierce that shyness. But it's nothing to do with your being a laird. Lairds mean nothing to them in Barra. The last genuine MacNeil of Barra died a century ago."

Within a week John Campbell was as much in his element as I was.

Sir Godfrey Collins, the Secretary of State, did not come on the annual Scottish Office run around the Islands. Skelton,[1] the Under-Secretary,

---

[1] The late A. N. Skelton, M.P.

was on the fishery board cruiser *Minna*. The Prime Minister had told me at Spean Bridge that he would look into the question of the illegal trawling. I suppose Skelton like most politicians was afraid of committing himself and therefore he dodged an interview with me. His plus-fours bodyguard from the Scottish Office got him ashore unobserved by me. What I did observe, however, was the *Minna* lying sleepily at anchor off Castlebay while a Fleetwood trawler was at work hardly a mile away and a full mile inside the three-mile limit.

I at once sent a telegram to the Prime Minister:

At this moment the fishing cruiser Minna *is lying at anchor in Castlebay, Barra while a trawler in full view is at work inside the limit*

I followed this up with a letter giving details and adding my surprise that Mr Skelton had avoided seeing me.

I received this reply:

> "10 Downing Street,
> Whitehall
> 27th September 1933

"Dear Sir,

"The Prime Minister caused enquiries to be made into the matters raised in your letter to him of the 6th instant, particularly with reference to the visit paid by Mr Skelton to the West Coast.

"The purpose of Mr Skelton's visit was to supplement the enquiries made by the Secretary of State on the subject of illegal trawling and, especially, to enquire as to the extent to which white fishing was prosecuted and could increasingly be prosecuted in the Islands.

"The Prime Minister is informed that it is not the case, as you point out, that Mr Skelton did not bother to land at Castlebay. He spent the afternoon on shore, saw work in progress at a curing establishment, and discussed fishing questions there. It may be that the idea that he had not landed arose from the fact that, after proceeding to the pier to put ashore one of the crew of the *Minna*, he went to look at the Castle before landing himself, which he did, not at the pier but at a curing station.

"The Prime Minister understands that Mr Skelton was not holding formal conferences with fishermen during the tour, though he would, of course, have been very glad to receive a deputation had a request been made to him. He preferred, however, to make informal enquiries from a number of people, which he had found most instructive and helpful.

"The Prime Minister is also informed that no trawler was at work within the three-mile limit within sight of the fishing cruiser while that vessel was at anchor at Castlebay: the cruiser would not have remained at anchor in such circumstances. If it were the case that a trawler was then working within the limits, it is difficult to understand why information was not at once conveyed to the cruiser by those who observed the trawler.

"The Prime Minister is satisfied that Sir Godfrey Collins and Mr Skelton are fully alive to the situation in the different ports of the West Coast, and that the question of the best means of preventing trawlers from operating within the three-mile limit, as well as what steps can be taken for the further development by any possible means of the local white fishing are receiving their most earnest consideration.

Yours truly"

And it was signed by the Prime Minister's Principal Private Secretary.

John Campbell and I realized that the Prime Minister had obviously rapped the knuckles of the Under-Secretary who had, we knew, deliberately dodged seeing me. The poaching trawler was a fact for which we could have called fifty witnesses and the suggestion that we ought to have put out in a boat to teach a fishing cruiser her job was of course absurd.

John Campbell now decided that the best way to keep the agitation against illegal trawling hot was to form a Sea League like the old Land League of the 'eighties. Then Cameron-Head of Inverailort told us something that amazed us. In 1895 an Act of Parliament had provided for the formation of fishing districts all round Scotland, provided a sufficient proportion of those connected in any way with fishing applied to their various County Councils to move in the matter. Further, this Act of Parliament said that a 14-mile limit would be imposed as soon as the North Sea Convention met and approved such a limit. In 1895 the North Sea Convention consisted of delegates from Great Britain, Denmark (including Iceland and Faroes), Holland, Belgium, France and Germany. Scandinavia (Norway and Sweden) for some reason did not join it. That 14-mile limit would certainly have been approved by Scandinavia and Denmark which would no doubt have imposed it themselves. It is unlikely that France and Holland would have opposed such a limit being set in Scotland.

Those who did oppose it were the trawler owners of Hull, Grimsby and Fleetwood, and to such purpose that the Scottish Fisheries Act with Queen Victoria's signature was never acted upon because the North Sea Convention was not summoned. As for the fishing districts, not one was formed. County Councils involved were afraid of the extra halfpenny on the rates.

John Campbell and I distributed a leaflet in Gaelic and English:

WHAT THE SEA LEAGUE STANDS FOR

The Sea League has been formed to demand the same protection for the livelihood of the crofter fisherman as is given to the sporting fishing of the landowners themselves.

The objects of the Sea League are:

1. That the Minch between a line from Barra Head to Tiree and a line from the Butt of Lewis to Cape Wrath, shall be closed to trawlers, and that the fishing in this area shall be regulated to the benefit of the fishermen who live around it.

2. That the penalties for illegal trawling shall be increased, and the policing of the inshore waters made more efficient.

3. That the fines for illegal trawling shall be used for financing fishermen who have lost their gear through illegal trawling, or who want to commence inshore fishing for the first time.

The Sea League intends to fight unceasingly for these objects.

JOIN THE SEA LEAGUE

Subscription one shilling

Write (in Gaelic or English) to The Secretary, Northbay, Barra.

Late in that autumn John Campbell and I addressed meetings of fishermen in Barra, Eriskay and South Uist, when every single person who caught, bought or sold fish signed the petition for a fishing district. In the early part of 1934 we should speak in Benbecula, North Uist, Harris and Scalpay and receive equally unanimous support. Nobody connected with the fishing interests in any of the Islands under the Inverness County Council failed to sign that petition. We shall see later what was to happen or rather not to happen.

One thing the Sea League did achieve and that was to stimulate the Government into proposed legislation to increase the penalties for illegal trawling. Sir Andrew Lewis, a wealthy Aberdeen trawler owner, was protesting in letters to the Press about the injustice to trawlers involved in the proposed legislation. He also circularized all M.P.'s. The Sea League decided to do the same.

"Barra, Outer Hebrides
20th December 1933

"Sir,

ILLEGAL TRAWLING AND THE KING'S SPEECH

"In a Circular Letter sent to all Members of Parliament and published in the Press, Sir Andrew Lewis drew your attention to the opposition of the Trawler Owners to the legislation proposed in the King's Speech to increase the penalties for illegal trawling. We therefore feel certain that in the interests of fair play and justice you will be ready to give a hearing to a reply on behalf of the inshore fishermen of the West of Scotland.

"Sir Andrew Lewis suggests that the issues involved in this controversy

I

are not understood outside Scotland. We desire to point out that under all fishery conventions to which Great Britain is a party the Nationals of each country have the exclusive right of fishing within three miles of its coast, and to protect this inshore fishing, trawlers of any nationality whatever, including that of the country itself, are prohibited from trawling in such waters.

"Sir Andrew Lewis implies that trawlers will be victimized if Sir Godfrey Collins's Bill is passed. This can only be the case if illegal trawling is already regularly practised, for the proposed legislation only intends to increase the penalty for what is already a recognized offence. Unless the law is being broken now, there can be no grounds for a protest against increasing the penalties for breaking it.

"Sir Andrew Lewis implies that the West Coast of Scotland is closed to British and open to foreign trawlers. Nothing could be more misleading than this suggestion; the territorial waters off the West of Scotland have always been prohibited to all trawlers.

"The crofter fishermen of the West Coast of Scotland depend largely for their livelihood upon the inshore fishing, which cannot be perfectly conducted unless trawlers are effectively prevented from poaching in inshore waters.

"Ample experience proves that present penalties do not provide a sufficient deterrent, and that this Bill is only too urgently necessary.

"Surely the idea of laissez-faire has been so far abandoned that no British Government will consent that the sturdy sea-faring population of the West of Scotland and the Hebrides, a splendid source of manhood alike for the Merchant Service and the Royal Navy in time of national emergency, should have their principal livelihood illegally destroyed to the greater profit of a few big trawler combines.

We are
Yours faithfully
Compton Mackenzie (President of the Sea League)
Neil Sinclair
J. L. Campbell, Yr., of Inverneill } Secretaries"

Just after that telegram to the Prime Minister I was laid out and had to spend a fortnight of cloudless weather in bed. It was particularly annoying because Douglas West was staying at the Coddie's annexe to the post-office and general store he presided over.

Others had come to spend time in Barra during that summer. Colonel Haldane was one. I had not seen him since he showed me the infallible filing system of M.I.5 in Malta of which I wrote in Octave Five. He had been in Ireland during the troubles and had been so much upset by the way the British Government was handling them, of which the Black and Tans were the climax, that he had had a kind of nervous breakdown which had ended in his losing all his hair. He was a genial and lovable man; he still could not bring himself to speak of that time in Ireland.

Terence de Vere White came and the impression of his ability made upon me when I was in Dublin in the previous year was confirmed.

Two Capuchin friars came from Oxford—Father Paul and Father Alfred. The latter had been a naval chaplain during the war and we had many mutual friends to talk about. Father Paul, a tall man with a beard that made the few small trees on Barra look even smaller, might have been one of those who followed St Francis of Assisi when the Friars Minor started. One day he and Father Alfred were lunching with me in the Crookle's cottage and Father Paul said in the kind of tone somebody might use to say it looked like rain tomorrow,

"I think the end of the world is getting very near."

At that date the Devil had not given man the atom bomb. Father Paul's voice echoes in my memory and I feel inclined to believe he may have been right.

I had intended to start on a novel called *The Darkening Green* as soon as I was finished with *Literature in My Time* but Peter Davies wanted me to do a volume in his companion series to the short biographies under the general title of *Great Occasions*. I suggested writing about the Syracusan expedition but he felt doubtful whether such a disastrous affair could be called a great occasion, and so I substituted the two Persian invasions of Greece for a book which was to be called *Marathon and Salamis*. Although I was rather disappointed not to be able to present my picture of Alcibiades, I was glad to be reading Herodotus instead of Thucydides. My admiration for the latter could not be deeper, but for enjoyment Herodotus is captivating and a better companion for pain. Moreover, with my knowledge of the scene I felt I might be able to support Herodotus where contemporary scholars and commentators had been inclined to doubt his accuracy.

On the 30th of that September Lady Oxford wrote to me from Bedford Square:

How very kind and nice of you to write to me. I telegraphed to hope you would defend me from what Mrs Alfred Lyttelton wrote in Spectator of 23rd. It was meant to be nice and I don't mind her attacking my "slovenly, overloaded, re-repeated sentences" at all. What I do mind is her saying that I disappointed the women of England in the war. It is true I did and do scoff at female and other committees; but I worked day and night in the war and weighed under 7 stone when we left 10 Downing Street.

My sister's sons, my brother's sons, and many old friends and lovers were all killed in the war—why should anyone suppose that I was callous or idle! It is the old Daily Mail *'pro-German' cry which ruined my husband's reputation with fools—of which there are many. And it is for his sake, not for my own, that I wanted you to write to the* Spectator *but you are far away, and should not be troubled with such trivialities. So you will forgive your friend*

Margot Oxford

I love your letter and your promise and thank you for them.

I am proud to think that whatever I wrote gave pleasure to that superlative woman, and as I transcribe those pencilled words of hers to the page of my manuscript I see those bird-bright eyes of hers as we sit talking in Holyroodhouse and I hear from sixty-three years ago the tone of Guy Bonham-Carter's voice in Compiègne as he says to me of Arthur Asquith,

"You know, Monty, it's frightful for poor Oc. His stepmother smokes!"

John Campbell and I thought it would be a good idea to celebrate the growth of the Sea League with a firework display. In those days one could have a display of Roman candles, golden rain and Catherine wheels for £2 to which we added half a dozen rockets at five shillings a piece.

The fireworks were to be let off on a tiny islet in Northbay and there was a large crowd of spectators on the road beside the bay.

Hardly any of those spectators had ever seen a firework display. The Fifth of November had never been celebrated in Barra, and by having our fireworks in the middle of October John and I were careful to ensure that it was not being celebrated now.

With us on the islet were the Coddie and the Crookle, and also Dr Bartlett. The latter was inclined to know better than anybody else what to do and this led to a ludicrous incident. When the fuse of one of the rockets was slow in responding to John Campbell's lighter, the Doctor with a compassionate smile said,

"I'll show you a much simpler way to set off a rocket."

With this he leant down and applied the end of his cigarette to the fuse. It set off the rocket right enough but instead of shooting up to the sky it shot up Dr Bartlett's kilt and he leapt in the air while the rocket went zigzagging about on the islet until in one zigzag it dived over the edge into the water.

Next morning I noticed one of the old ladies of Ardveenish walking about and bent over as if she were looking for something.

"What can old Bean —— be looking for?" I asked.

I was to hear later that old Bean —— aged over eighty was looking for the gold that had fallen from the sky the evening before. Am I not to be envied for having spent so many years in close communion with such people?

A week or two after this Malcolm Douglas-Hamilton's flying-boat *Cloud of Iona* landed, or rather watered, in the harbour of Castlebay with Lord and Lady Londonderry. She was anxious to consult Father Mac-

millan about a concert of Gaelic songs she was proposing to give in
Londonderry House to bring a young Lewis pianist before the public.
While she and Father John were closeted in the dining-room of the
priest's house at Northbay Londonderry and I talked in the sitting-room.
I recall from that conversation his saying to me as he stood in front of
the empty fireplace:

"Why won't they make me Ambassador in Paris, Mackenzie?"

"I suppose the professional diplomats feel that *they* are entitled to
Washington and Paris, the two plums of the service, now that we are
at peace—for the present. They don't see why what they consider
amateurs should enjoy them."

"Yes, I know. But I want to be Ambassador in Paris. I feel I could be
useful. And don't you think Edie would make an absolutely first-class
Ambassador's hostess?"

"Of course. She'd be wonderful. All the same, I can't see the F.O.
agreeing to hand over Paris to a non-diplomat."

"I expect you're right, and I *am* Secretary of State for Air, which I
suppose in a way is just as important. All the same, I want to be our
Ambassador in Paris. Ramsay MacDonald did have a shot at persuading
the Foreign Office to agree but Vansittart opposed it. He thinks this new
régime in Germany is a menace. I don't agree."

As Londonderry said that, I thought of a walk I had taken a day or
two before with a young German *wandervögel*. He was an agreeable young
man; when I criticized Hitler, he had said with emotional earnestness
as we sat in the sun of St Luke's little summer at the edge of the cliff by
Faire na h'Abh,

"He is necessary to us. We must follow him to recover belief in
ourselves."

I remembered that poisonous black swastika on the outskirts of Danzig
and shook my head.

I shook my head again when Londonderry suggested that we should
encourage Hitler.

"I'm afraid I think we've already done too much to encourage Hitler."

Later that month there was to be a marriage between two of the young
people at Northbay. That island wedding in the real old style was an
unforgettable experience. About ten days or a fortnight before the actual
wedding the *rèitach* or betrothal was held. At this the future bridegroom
comes to ask the father of the bride for his daughter's hand, bringing
with him either his best man or an eloquent friend to make a speech and
point out what a fine fellow the suitor is and what a grand husband he
will make. The father, after some witty exchanges, at last allows himself
to be persuaded. His daughter is given away, and the guests make a
night of it.

In the late afternoon of a crisp October day we gathered at the bride's

house and set out for the church. A piper led the way. Then came the
bride and bridegroom, and behind them the bridesmaid in white with
a veil like the bride. They were followed by a few relations and particular
friends, two by two and arm in arm. On the way to the church beside
the sea-loch some of the young men fired off blank cartridges at intervals.
The marriage ceremony in the church was brief, for, being afternoon,
there was no nuptial Mass, and within a short while we were all back
again in the house of the bride's parents for high tea, at the end of which
healths were drunk and speeches made in Gaelic, with perhaps one or
two in English. The evening was taken up with a dance in the parish
hall to which came all the neighbours; a glorious evening of reels,
schottisches, quadrilles and 'strip the willow', which is the best of all
country dances. The dance opened with the bridal reel, danced by the
bride, the bridegroom, the bridesmaid and the best man while the guests
stood round, applauding and shouting and showering confetti upon
them.

The climax of the evening was a second bridal reel, the prelude to a
strange ceremony which must go back to the very beginnings of our race.
One of the senior married women present tapped the bride on the
shoulder and led her away and out of the hall by a back door, her place
being taken in the reel by another dancer. Then by one of the senior
married men the bridegroom was spirited away and his place taken,
then the bridesmaid by another married woman, and finally, in this
case by myself, the best man was eliminated, their places being taken by
other dancers, so that the reel was still apparently going on while the
principals were on their way back to the house of the bride's parents.
This may be a relic of marriage by capture, though some believe it was a
device to cheat the fairies and prevent their kidnapping either the bride
or the bridegroom.

By this time it was getting on for two o'clock in the morning, and
while the guests down in the hall were still carrying on with the dance
it was the business of a few intimate friends who had accompanied the
bride and bridegroom to bed them. There was much laughter when the
bride's garter had to be captured before she went off with her attendant
women to be bedded. It was now the duty of the men left to undress the
bridegroom and put him to bed beside the bride. This task accomplished,
with laughter that rang out to the great white billowy clouds racing
across the sapphire sky in the October moonlight, the guests had a final
deoch an doruis, which means literally a drink at the door, and reached
their own homes at four o'clock in the morning. You might think that
this was the end of an island wedding. Not at all.

The following afternoon just before dusk we mustered again at the
house of the bride's parents and set out in a second procession, arm in
arm and two by two, led by a piper, to walk to the house of the bride-

groom's mother. At every cottage we passed, little flags or coloured handkerchiefs were flying from a pole and we fired off the guns and got a cheer as we went on our way over the wet pasture land. Then another grand tea and afterwards another bridal reel in the kitchen, but we were all pretty tired by now, and I think we were home about midnight.

About three weeks later the bridegroom went off to sea; I saw him again in Buenos Aires nearly a year afterwards. I saw him next, home from the sea, with a little girl in his arms.

A few days after the wedding came a letter from T. E. Lawrence, now calling himself T. E. Shaw. It was written on paper stamped Union Jack Club, 91 Waterloo Road, S.E.1, but the address had been stroked out and Lawrence wrote,

> *In next fortnight probably at*
> *13 Birmingham St*
> *Southampton*
>
> *1.xi.33*

Dear Mr Mackenzie,

A few days ago I bought in Southampton a copy of your Guy and Pauline, *signed by you for 'C' and with his bookplate in it.*

Possibly this may have a sentimental value for you: and if so (as it cost me only 4/6: the bookseller was no good) I will be glad to send it to you in exchange for any other copy of the book you may have by you.

If however you don't need it, I shall be gladder, for it goes very well on my shelf with your three Levant books: and in that case please don't bother to answer this letter. I get lots of useless letters from unknowns, and refuse to beggar myself by writing back to them, wantonly.

At the same time, if you do answer, I'd be glad to hear that Vol IV has not been aborted. Holt Wilson and Kell made such asses of themselves over III that I fear they may have disgusted you. Also I am sorry you took Basil T. so seriously; all the documentation sometimes made III a little dull. I'm hoping for a really sporting IV to wind the history up with a bang. The picture of war-time Greece given by you is splendid. I spent a fortnight with R. in Athens and sympathize.

No answer, as I said, please—unless you need the relic.

> *Yours*
>
> *T. E. Shaw*

I agreed with 'T. E. Shaw' that *Greek Memories* was over-documented but I was led away by my anxiety to present the facts incontrovertibly. I had been irritated by the way the reviewers had sucked and swallowed the lies in Basil Thomson's book *The Allied Secret Service in Greece* as kids suck and swallow lollipops.

To my regret I never met Lawrence but I hope that the letter I wrote to thank him expressed some of my admiration.

A month after that letter I went down to Glasgow to attend the

University Court and speak at the annual dinner of the Caledonian Catholic Association. I quote from a letter to Faith of December 5th:

I had a tiresome journey. After a baddish crossing with the boat 8½ hours late I was met at Oban with the news that Alastair couldn't be there with the Austin, the coil of which had gone. I regretted I had had to let Christopher take on the Sunbeam last March. As it was I had to hire a car—a maddening expense—and the hired car broke a shaft at the back end of Loch Lomond. There I sat in that damned car all rigged up for the dinner. After waiting for nearly two hours without a soul passing a baby Austin came along, the owner of which kindly offered me a lift into Glasgow where I reached the dinner about 10 p.m. just in time to make my speech. Archbishop MacDonald insisted on staying to hear it, and so missed the last train back to Edinburgh. A Dominican in attendance on His Grace said, "He doesn't mind. Archbishop Mackintosh will lend him some pyjamas. It'll be I who'll have none."

An appalling week's correspondence waiting here at which Chrissie and I have been working all day. Eilean Aigas for Christmas is out of the question. Quite apart from money time forbids it. I'm very hard pressed, but if Jethou goes I shall begin to see daylight. Mrs G— evidently wants the island, but I imagine the husband is being dragooned into it. She sounds a tiresome woman. . . .

Young Campbell of Inverneill is being invaluable to me and relieves me of a lot of correspondence over the Sea League. He writes a good letter and is likely to be an outstanding Gaelic scholar. I've just had a letter from South Uist asking me to take up the cause of the kelp-burners. I think you'd be pleased by the confidence all these dear people have in me. . . .

I've just had a wee line from Magdalen to tell me she's engaged to Jack Eldon.[1] Laura will be glad. . . .

I've just read the most enchanting child's book Bibi *by a Danish woman. I sent it to Veronica for her birthday. She'll be thirteen, darling little girl. I've given* Bibi *a good notice in the D.M., but I've not seen a single decent notice of it yet. The reviewing of children's books is contemptible.*

If it can possibly be managed next summer I want to go to Denmark and Norway and urge the various fishing ministers to defy any attempt by the British Government to interfere with the limit they impose against trawlers. The Fishery Board, meanwhile, has just notified me that they hope to send Mr Fiddler to act as fishing officer in Barra for 3 months and asking me to supply him with all the information I can obtain. The fight is just beginning. The vested interests of trawling are now beginning to rig the Press.

I am issuing a challenge to Sir Andrew Lewis to meet me anywhere and publicly debate the question. . . .

I was very glad to get your wedding-day telegram on November 30. I made a good speech that night but the reporters couldn't get it down. They said I was speaking at the rate of nearly 300 words to the minute. . . .

----

[1] The Earl of Eldon.

The hope of finding somebody to take on Jethou was disappointed; Mr G— refused to be dragooned. Faith was now back in Dryden Chambers and decided against coming to Barra for Christmas. She was working at her book about the nieces of Cardinal Mazarin and doing reviews for *The Gramophone* which was being steered through this difficult period by Cecil Pollard with skill. Christopher had had a book published called *Christopher Stone Speaking* which did not have the success expected for it. The public wanted to hear Christopher Stone speaking, not to read him doing so.

Faith had tried to tempt me to retire to Jethou instead of the Outer Hebrides but throughout my life it has always been impossible for me to go back, and in spite of her tempting letters about the garden I had made Jethou for me was a vivid and cherished memory like Cornwall, like Capri, like Greece. Faith would write about Jethou in her three volumes of reminiscences with tenderness and grace.

On December 16th Laura Lovat wrote to me from Beaufort:

Monty dearest,

This is the first quiet minute I've had since (1) Magda had her appendicitis operation (2) engaged herself to be married.

You wrote her an enchanting letter, and I am glad abt. it. She is marrying a man who is "bon comme le pain" and has considerable character too. I do pray they may be happy. They have the Faith in common. He is the negation of the artist—she has lived in a world of them since birth—However one had to adapt one's self to many changes in life and I expect it's easier at her age than at ours. I think she is very happy, tho. she dreads 'home-sickness'. Poor sweet, she remains so much younger than Veronica. The latter will start on any venture, however dangerous and grim with a gay heart. Anyway, in this case the elements of danger is very remote.

I saw Faith 2 or 3 times in London but not since all this to do. I've had no heart to go to E.A. but believe all goes well. The memory of our lovely Xmas and b.day parties is too overwhelming.

Write to me soon and tell me your plans.

Dear love

L

I was delighted by the news that Magdalen was engaged to Jack Eldon. He had been in love with her for a long time. His father had been one of Simon Lovat's intimate friends at Magdalen and had married one of his sisters. Encombe had died young before succeeding to the earldom.

Just after Christmas Magdalen wrote in answer to my letter of congratulation:

Darling Monty . . .

I did so love your letter. It was much the nicest I got of all the other hundreds.

I do too so much wish you were not so very far away. We all miss you so much and Christmas wasn't half such fun without you.

Do change your mind and come back again—just for yours and Mummy's and Hugh's joint birthday. . . .

Uncle Alligator's[1] figure is to be seen to be believed. Hugh has grown a nose like a tapir but he's sweeter than ever. Shimi opened a shooting school in Beauly, and had to fire the first shot. We all went to watch—and he missed.

The shinty match of Lovat v. Beauly ended in bloodshed. . . .

With dearest love
Your loving
Magdalen

By the same post came a letter from Veronica:

Darling Monty,

Thank you so much for your lovely book. I am glad you gave me an Arthur Ransome. I simply love them.

Thanks for your lovely letter.

On Xmas Eve we went monster hunting on the banks of Loch Ness complete with telescope, binoculars and bible to swear on, cameras, etc, but alas we did not see a thing.

Do come back soon. I loved your story in No. 11 Joy Street[2] and next time I come to Barra we simply must see Sandray. I am glad you called the nice girl Veronica.

Love to all. Please write. I simply love your letters and I'm getting much better at reading them.

xxxxxxxx
From your
Veronica
Hugs

The comfort letters like those were to me in the middle of money worries and pain is beyond expression.

I had just sent off the final typescript of *Marathon and Salamis* to Peter Davies and was planning to start *The Darkening Green* as soon as Christmas was over, but when that letter from Laura Lovat arrived I wrote the dedication *A Wedding Bell for Magdalen* and started the new novel at once, determined to have the manuscript bound in time to be among Magdalen's wedding presents next year.

On December 18th I was writing to Faith:

Glasgow was too much for me, and I have been in and out of bed ever since. It's like the winter before last. The perpetual fatigue does not allow me time to recover. However, it's no use lamenting. The situation has to be faced and the

---

[1] Hon. Alastair Fraser.
[2] *The Enchanted Island.*

difficulties defeated. The transference of Jethou would keep the bank quiet until next autumn. They have been pestering me continually. Income tax is the grand problem. I paid off £450 this year—a fearful effort in the circumstances. . . .

The correction of Marathon and Salamis *was finickin' work. So many names and dates to check. I must tell you an exquisite bit of typing by Nellie. I had written "they sailed away to the Phoenician coast in two triremes" which N. hoping for the best typed as two 'tureens'; even the Owl and the Pussy Cat would not have got far in a pea-green tureen. . . .*

I am sorry you are so depressed over Jethou. But what can one do? I have always lacked the ability to establish a prudent security . . .

It's suddenly struck me this will be a Christmas letter. The next mail may not reach you in time. I'm sorry it's such a weary letter, but when this 'flu depression passes I shall be my usual optimistic self again. Anyway, I've succeeded in knocking Father John completely off whisky, and a halo is beginning to sprout on his head like a circle of crocuses in Spring.

I have to go to Glasgow again in February and I have promised to address the University of Wales on Feb. 9. Then you could come back with me and we could perhaps motor up together in your Hornet. But health, health. I dread making plans.

I can't think of any Christmas present for you. Is there anything you want for the car? Do get it and let me know what it is. I do hope you're keeping fit. Bless you, darling. I shall be glad to see you again.

Christmas Eve was mild and still; as I walked along to midnight Mass each candle burning in the windows of the little houses seemed a star of Bethlehem.

On December 29th I was writing to Faith:

I'm up and about and survived the Christmas round. The Darkening Green will probably lay me out again. But I must finish it in time for Cassells to publish in late Spring and give them another book for the autumn. Yesterday was an exquisite day. Calm and blue with a terrific swell in the west. Rollers half a mile long and 20 feet high. This isn't a proper letter, but just to let you know how I am and to wish you a happy happy New Year.

Dearest love

I was relieved when the *Daily Mail* renewed my contract for another year. The reviewing was a great strain but the money was a better sedative than any pain-killing drug. The object I set myself was to find about half a dozen books every week which I had read right through with enjoyment and could recommend to the public. However, I realized that to make my praise worthwhile it would be necessary to damn occasionally.

I was happily situated for a reviewer because my remoteness from the centre of things left my judgment completely independent and I was always careful to stress that my judgment of a book was an expression of my personal feelings about it and was not to be regarded as anything else. On the whole I found that if I enjoyed a book and was able to express that enjoyment the public would do the same. There were of course one or two authors whom I admired but failed to persuade the reading public to admire. There were also one or two authors whom I did not admire but whom the reading public did. I was not taken in by Axel Munthe's *San Michele* because I had been behind the scenes, as it were, and knew how much of it was the fruit of his rich powers as a romantic improviser. And those powers were rich indeed as the success *San Michele* had and still has with the reading public demonstrated. On the other hand I was completely taken in by Halliday Sutherland's *The Arches of the Years* and so was the reading public. It was only when Halliday Sutherland came to Barra a year or two later that I discovered he was as much a romantic improviser as Axel Munthe.

I turn over the pages of the reviews for this year 1933 and read among them a notice of Duckworth's series of 'Great Lives':

"Mr Bernard Darwin's *Dickens* is entirely satisfying. He has succeeded in painting a vivid and sympathetic portrait of a great man which the younger generation will not despise and which the older generation will not resent. . . .

"With Mr Pryce-Jones on the subject of *Beethoven* I would argue incessantly. His biography lacks imagination, common sense, musical judgment, and charity.

"Mr Pryce-Jones may feel that a great deal of nonsense has been written about Beethoven. That may be true; but there is something distasteful about the spectacle of a cock-sparrow picking at the plumage of a dead eagle."

In one of those recurrent guides to the Hebrides which were as superficial then as most of them are today, I was irritated to read,

"Any signs of lack of education are only to be found among the older members of the community. The present and younger generations have received, and are showing, the fruits of education."

Of that exasperating poppycock I wrote:

"The older people in the Hebrides are among the wisest and best educated in the whole of the British Isles; I should hesitate to claim that for the younger generation."

Of the journals of Arnold Bennett I wrote:

"The vanity, which only very seldom becomes tiresome, is never the vanity of the artist, but always the vanity of the successful business man. Occasionally the determination to show a dignified independence sounds smug, as when he pats himself on the back for not addressing Princess Marie Louise as 'Ma'am' and on not having been 'effusive when she wrote to me about the *Queen's Doll's House*'.

"As I remember, the Princess gave herself the trouble to write a personal letter to every author who contributed to the miniature library, so that Bennett's fear of 'being dragged into St James's Palace' may have been unwarranted."

I am glad to find a review of *Twenty Years a-growing*, by Maurice O'Sullivan.

This is a small classic and should be re-issued by my publishers Chatto and Windus. They were not yet my publishers when I thanked them for "issuing this entrancing book at a reasonable price (8s. 6d')". I fear a re-issue would be less reasonable today.[1]

I extract from my long review:

"The effect of this book on the reader is that by a profounder magic than any at the disposal of Mr H. G. Wells's time-machine he has been privileged to step back into the heart of the Middle Ages.

"Mr E. M. Forster, in the enthusiasm of his backward journey, has receded a little too far when he suggests in his introductory note that *Twenty Years a-growing* is 'an account of neolithic civilization from the inside'.

"To his sophisticated modern mind, the difference between neolithic and mediaeval life may not seem even as much as distinction, but if Mr Forster wants to experience neolithic life from the inside he will have to betake himself to what is left of the aborigines of Australia, none of whom has so far produced a work like *Twenty Years a-growing*. . . .

"Here at last is an authentic picture of a life (in the Blasket Islands off Kerry) which cannot maintain itself much longer against the ruthless externals of progress, and I commend this revelation of vanishing enchantments to those whose fancy demands a lovely dream which is at the same time a perfectly matter of fact and attainable reality."

Presently I was reviewing two of the biographies in Peter Davies's series and quote extracts:

Of *Richard Cœur de Lion* by Clennell Wilkinson I wrote:

"Mr Clennell Wilkinson has written an interesting book, but I do not feel he was really at home with his authorities. The touch that brings the 12th century to life is wanting, and though he alludes slightingly to Maurice Hewlett's romance *Richard Yea and Nay* Hewlett was years nearer to understanding Richard's time than Mr Clennell Wilkinson.

"I am not making this criticism lightly, for I happen to have read all the Chronicles of this period and can claim to know it as thoroughly as I know any period of history.

"Mr Eric Linklater's biography of *Mary Queen of Scots* is on another plane. . . . Those who may be inclined to think too much has been written about that tragic lady will be astonished by the imagination at work on

[1] Available in a school edition published by Chatto & Windus and in the Oxford World Classics series.

an aspect of her character to which no justice has yet been done.

"With brevity and humour, with lucidity, eloquence and beauty the heartrending story is told again, and on the last two pages the reader may learn why Mr Linklater was able to tell the old tale as if it had all happened but yesterday."

An excellent life of *Dryden* by Christopher Hollis came out this year. I wrote:

"No one has suffered more than Dryden at the hands of Macaulay, and Mr Hollis knocks another nail into the coffin of Macaulay's historical reputation.

> The dotage of some Englishmen is such
> To fawn on those who ruin them the Dutch,

wrote Dryden in 1662. Could a better epitaph be chosen for that coffin?"

When I wrote those words I was wondering if the dotage of some Englishmen was leading them to fawn upon Hitler.

A Glastonbury Romance by John Cowper Powys still has its doughty worshippers. I record what I thought about it thirty-three years ago and what I still think of it:

"Ordinarily I should have shirked attempting to digest such a mammoth; but reading on the jacket that J. D. Beresford believed *A Glastonbury Romance* to be one of the greatest novels in the world, to be classed with Tolstoi's *War and Peace*, that Hugh Walpole considered it equal to Thomas Hardy 'in power and poetry', that Gerald Barry discovered in it 'the mighty pantheism of Rubens', and that Eleanor Farjeon held it to be 'the greatest work of the greatest living writer of fiction' I decided that it was my inevitable duty to read it from cover to cover.

"It is certainly a grandiose book, and it is sometimes genuinely impressive: but the testimony of those distinguished sponsors is as near to being nonsense as does not matter, and dangerous nonsense at that, because when uttered by such names it carries with it the glamour of sense.

" 'I can call spirits from the vasty deep,' Owen Glendower boasted. 'Why, so can I or so can any man; but will they come when you do call for them?' Hotspur retorted.

"Mr Powys with his mystical Ancient British Celticism has called upon the spirits as portentously as Glendower, but not one of them in questionable shape has appeared from the vasty deep of time to obey his summons. That lack of effective authority was perhaps excusable, for unsuccessful necromancy should not be counted against a novelist; but when Mr Powys summons human creatures to move across pages and they fail to do so he becomes as much of a failure as a novelist as he was as a necromancer.

"It would be an unsporting refusal to play the game if a critic demanded probability from the principal characters in a romance like this; but a great creative imagination makes the improbable credible while we are under the spell. In compensation for the grotesque liberties taken with human nature we are given a rich and accurate and beautiful observation of the natural scene, but the prolixity and stiffness of the prose often destroys the effect of it. If the sponsors of this book had been content to claim less for it, the cool-headed critic might be able to grant more.

"Let it be admitted, at any rate, that Mr Powys deserves admiration for the courage and endurance with which he has carried through his huge task. Let it be admitted that when he does it in King Cambyses' vein he sometimes does it as well as that particular channel of expression allows.

"It is clear from the stirring fanfare played by the heralds of this grandiose book that the author is capable of convincing some people that it has unusual substance, breadth, and profundity. I think they are deceived. I distrust a wizard who mumbles such very elaborate incantations and hangs up so many stuffed crocodiles."

That autumn Methuen published a short book by Lord Raglan. I was amused to find myself mentioned as a 'war monger'.

I wrote:

"*The Science of Peace* provides a capital entertainment with its happy blend of sense and nonsense, logic and fallacy, knowledge and ignorance, all neatly and provocatively set forth in a lucid polemical prose.

"Lord Raglan's argument in a nutshell is that war is harmful, unprogressive, unproductive and absurd with one exception, and that is when England is painting any other part of the inhabited globe red. At the same time it is right to mention that he does suggest the advantage of handing over the Bengal Presidency to Germany, part of Australia to Japan, and half of South America to Japan and Russia.

"He wishes to abolish 'small and savage languages' and he finds 'the notorious inability of the Welsh to think clearly due to early bilingualism'. He even congratulates the B.B.C. on its 'valuable work in abolishing dialect.'

"There is a style of overcoat called the Raglan. If it is as impermeable to weather as Lord Raglan himself to the fundamental desires of mankind, it must be a useful garment.

"However, it is a pleasure to meet an opponent who can hit out like a man, and I hope that some of our more emotional pacifists will protect themselves against the moisture of their own tears with Raglan overcoats."

In that letter to Faith I quoted I mentioned a book for children called *Bibi*. I shall quote what I wrote about it because that enchanting book should be republished.

"Not merely the best, but *by far* the best children's story published this year or for many years is *Bibi* by Karin Michaelis translated from the Danish by Rose Fyleman (Allen and Unwin).

"It is the tale of a little Danish girl whose father is a station-master, so that she has a free pass to travel by train all over Denmark. . . . The result is a series of absolutely enchanting adventures related with the exquisite simplicity of Hans Andersen himself. It was all I could do when I had finished reading *Bibi* not to pack up and leave immediately for Denmark. I never read any book which made me long so much to visit the country which had inspired it.

"After *Bibi* I found the elaborate juvenile humour of *Dr Dolittle's Return* by Hugh Lofting (Cape) more than usually irritating; but the rapturous tributes Dr Dolittle receives each year from my colleagues compel me to suppose that I have a blind spot. That being so, I feel bound to announce that this tiresome gentleman has returned from the moon."

Inasmuch as Dr Dolittle is still at large I must presume that I am wrong in thinking that he is a bore. His admirers must try to forgive me as I must try to forgive 'Oliver Edwards' of *The Times* for his inability to enjoy *The Pickwick Papers* or *Alice in Wonderland*. Fortunately my heart is still sound or I might not have survived to write these words after reading that article of his on a recent Thursday morning. I hope I shall not miss much when in future I shall avoid the books he likes.

FIFTY-ONE YEARS OLD: 1934

O N that New Year's morning I was wondering if the year 1934 was
going to give me as difficult a time as the previous two years. A
letter from Lady Elspeth Campbell made me feel optimistic.

> Inveraray Castle,
> Argyll.
> *Dec. 30. 1933.*

My dear Mr Mackenzie,

*Just a few lines to wish you 'Bliadna Mhath Ur'. I hear you have sublet
Eilean Aigas to some people who are after the Loch Ness Monster. I hope they
won't catch it. . . . You may be amused to hear that I have had a great craving to
own the 'Dead March in Saul' and ordered it a year ago in order to play out the
old year. I was sent a vile jazz tune. I re-ordered it this year and an almost equally
vile vocal duet by Langston [sic] and Johnstone was sent. I gave the right Columbia
number and I have loved the tune ever since I saw a lifeguardsman's funeral
procession passing down the Brompton Road over 50 years ago and saw his black
horse and the boots (reversed I think).*

*It does seem hard that I can't fulfil this humble desire. I have not been buying
records as I have had to get a new piano for the people's concerts here, but I could
not resist that really enchanting McCormack record of 'The Fairy Tree'. I delight
in it. . . . I have been given an enchanting new Phillips D.C. mains wireless set
that is a great joy. My greetings to Father John and Miss MacSween.*

> *Is mise do charaid dhileas*

> *Elspeth Campbell*

Your new book is delightful.

Somehow I managed to finish *The Darkening Green* by the middle of
March interrupted by arguments with the Income Tax, reading and
reviewing for the *Daily Mail*, writing promised articles, answering about
fifty letters a week, long *Gramophone* editorials, correcting the revised
proofs of *Marathon and Salamis*, work on the Sea League, and most of all
by pain.

My diversion was the behaviour of two kittens and their mother.
When Chrissie and I came to stay with the Crookle we found a small
grey cat which was being treated kindly enough and well fed but always
as the cat to be put out every night. I gave this little cat a name—Grigi,
and Crookle was fascinated by the way she became a personal friend of
Chrissie and myself. He had been proud of the way she would catch eels
for herself from the burn but under our example she became a personal
friend of his. In due course she produced two kittens—a grey one like

herself and a tortoiseshell. We named them Rum and Eigg, and they were a continuous joy to me from the moment they arrived. Rum had a passion for melon and would growl over the thin rind of a slice of melon as fiercely as if it were the drumstick of a chicken. The longer I live the more clearly I see that the love of cats and dogs provides one of the great human dichotomies like Liberals and Conservatives or Platonists and Aristotelians. I have already written four books about cats and I hope to write two more before I leave this world—*Whiskers Galore* and *The Mews of the World*.

A letter came from Veronica in the middle of that February:

Darling Monty,

Thank you so much for the lovely long letter you sent me ages ago.

Don't blame me for this delayed letter, for you told me in yours that I need not write till the beginning of the term.

I hope your siatica is better, but if you will go and shut yourself up in Barra for years on end without seeing anyone, why then I think you richly deserve it, but all the same I think 'flu on top of it was a bit thick. There is too much (and yet so little). I demand an instant response to this. I suppose at any rate you will come for the wedding. If you don't I will leave you to choose your favourite death. . . .

Mummy is in London, so is Magdalen, Jack and Shimi. Shimi is starting or perhaps has started with an astrakhan waistcoat and a scarlet fez for Austria, Checko (etc) and Rumania for a month's leave. He is staying with different people Mummy knows . . . about the 24th of this month she is making us come down to London. Ugh! You've no idea how I hate it but M. is quite firm and I am resigned. I wonder if you will be coming down while we are there. I hope to goodness you will and then we can go and see a cinema or something together. Please give my love to Chrissie, Crookle, Coddy, Peggy etc.

Love and X's

From your very loving

Veronica

Before I went down to London in March I was visited by a deputation from those on the dole in Barra to say that they would be willing to work at making the road round Barra tolerable and accept the dole as part of their wage. I put this offer up to a couple of leading Labour M.P.'s in London. I thought it would give them something with which to jab the 'National' Government. I can see the dismay on their faces when I made this offer. "Work on the dole?" one of them exclaimed. "The Trade Unions would never stand for that."

Jack Eldon and Magdalen Fraser were married that April in Brompton Oratory. I bought a top-hat and exhumed a frock-overcoat I had not worn since before the Great War. It had to be sent to Forster's to be let out two inches. Mr Grammel, the head cutter, sighed when he looked at that frock-overcoat.

"We shall never see cloth like that again."

And as he fingered that example of pre-war tailoring he murmured,

"Well, sir, I don't mind confessing that when I look at my work of thirty years ago it brings a tear to my eye."

In Octave Five I wrote of that last occasion in Devonshire House before the great building was knocked down. I think it must have been in this April that I saw another great ducal house on the verge of its disappearance from London. This was Norfolk House in St James's Square where George III was born. I had taken Ursula Maxwell to the Gargoyle where we had dined and danced, and driven her back to Norfolk House; as she opened the front door with her key I asked if she wasn't nervous, sleeping in that great house with only a caretaker. She shook her head.

"They're going to begin pulling it down in a week or two. Gerald and Carrie hadn't a room left in Eaton Square and so Bernard Norfolk told me I could have a room here."

Gerald Maxwell who had been an air ace in the war, was married to a charming American, and there were few houses in London where I enjoyed dining so much.

A day or two after this Philip and Nellie Guedalla invited Faith and me to dinner, and I was asked by Philip if I felt like undertaking a lecturing visit with him to South America. It would mean leaving England on July 28th and being away about two months. I would give five lectures in Buenos Aires while he was lecturing in Rio de Janeiro and then I would go up to Rio and lecture there while he was lecturing in Buenos Aires. The lectures were to be given under the auspices of the Ibero-American Institute, which was supported by the Foreign Office. The Prince of Wales was keen on encouraging relations after his visit to South America.

I could not resist the chance of seeing South America and agreed. A day or two later Philip Guedalla told me that the Foreign Office had objected to my going on account of Official Secrets.

"So I got in touch with the Prince of Wales, and he squashed the objections of the Foreign Office."

My fare and Faith's were to be paid but if I was to keep the *Daily Mail* reviews going I knew it would be vital to take Chrissie and that would mean finding the money for her fare, besides having some extra money for my own personal expenses.

Newman Flower had been pleased with *The Darkening Green* and I asked him whether, if I could finish a book I proposed to call *Prince Charlie and His Ladies* before the end of July, he would publish it this autumn. I had suggested this as a subject for Faith when she finished her book about Christina of Sweden but she was more interested in the nieces of Cardinal Mazarin.

Newman Flower liked what I told him about my subject.

"And if you think you *can* do it before the end of July we'll publish it this autumn."

Faith was going to Jethou in the hope of somebody's being lured by the island into paying me £3,000 for the Crown Lease. She told me she believed that this time luck was going to be with us.

"For the last ten days there has been a ladybird in my room. I can't think how it found itself in Oxford Street."

And indeed that ladybird was a good omen. Suddenly in May three people within a few hours of one another telegraphed their willingness to pay £3,000 for the lease and pay down immediately £300 to confirm their offers. In the end a Mrs Fortington won it, being willing to take on both MacDonald and Kemp. Victor Carey thought the Treasury would accept Mrs Fortington, and after some six months of bureaucratic humming and hawing and legal delays I ceased to be the Crown Tenant of Jethou. There had been moments during my long wrangle with the Inland Revenue, while I was writing *The Darkening Green*, when I had considered going back to Jethou but it has been against my rule of life ever to go back to a place from which I felt I had exhausted all the creative urge it could give me. To have gone back to Jethou would have seemed a surrender; such a surrender would have shaken my self-confidence.

By the time the news came that at last Jethou had been taken I had been working hard for a month in Tarbert where Chrissie and I were staying with her parents.

From those six weeks of hard work upon the book I had to finish by the middle of July I recall two brief interludes cherished by memory. The first was the ascent with Calum MacSween of the Clisham, a 2,000 ft. ben in Harris, which did not involve anything like mountaineering. However, the long trudge up to the top was rewarded by the view. As we sat contemplating the sweep of country Calum said,

"Man, what it must have been to have seen the animals going two by two into the Ark!"

Always responsive to the mood of *sancta simplicitas* in those I love, I began to see a long train of animals marching two by two across that sweep of country led by two giraffes.

On another occasion when Calum and I were passing Loch Fincastle on our way to take a boat to the island of Taransay he told me of a battle he had once witnessed between a stag and a bull.

"And which do you think won?" he asked.

"The bull I should guess."

"Not at all, not at all. The stag kept jumping over him, back and forth, and every time he came down he ripped the bull with his antlers until at last the poor beast had to retire without as much as a bellow.

It was in October month and that stag roared with triumph. He was not standing for any nonsense from that bull among his hinds."

Taransay is the most uncanny island I have set foot on. When we approached it the three or four cottars, who lived in shallow caves in front of which were turf-covered huts, insisted on our drinking tea with them, apologizing for the absence of milk. They were not allowed by Iain Mòr to keep a cow. Iain Mòr who held the feu of the island lived in a gaunt grey house among his cattle and his sheep, and was so careful that when he had to leave the island he used to lock up the store cupboard so that his wife could not waste money on casual hospitality. The only living creature on the island that did not fear Iain Mòr was his white mare. To the frank delight of the cottars she had just bitten his arm and he had gone over to Tarbert for Dr Ross to attend to it.

There was a tiny school on the brae above the beach where we landed, in which four small boys and one small girl were being taught by a young schoolmistress. From her we heard more tales of Iain Mòr's ruthless economy. Then Calum and I walked across the island to see the natural arch. Legend said that there had once been a great battle on Taransay between the invading Norsemen and the Celts, and that relics of the battle could often be picked up; Calum and I did not find any rusted arms.

The cliffs on the western side of Taransay are fairly high and the natural arch is like a gateway to the Atlantic through which the ocean flows into a narrow cove with steep sides. Near the top of one of these we saw a small cave which we managed to reach with some difficulty. On the floor of it we found the ashes and bones of what I decided was a neolithic meal which I said must not be disturbed. After that we ate our own sandwiches on the grassy slope above the head of the cove, watching the tide come in. And then I was lucky enough to see a magical sight I had never seen before and shall never see again. Two otters were teaching their cubs to swim, and we looked on spellbound by a display of choreography beyond the grace and skill of the greatest ballet-dancers in the world. The parent otters tossed their cubs to one another in swift arcs or swam round them and among them in what seemed a kaleidoscope of curves and circles to compose a deliberate pattern of movement. I cannot hope to evoke in dull words the beauty of that scene, but by the kindliness of memory it is still vivid as I try vainly to record its magic.

In that June my aunt and godmother Isabel who had been Mother General of the Community of St Mary the Virgin, Wantage, died. In 1931 when she was 78 years old her mind had been afflicted by a kind of dark night of the soul. Then for several weeks before her death her mind became clearer and clearer as her body became weaker and weaker.

Mother Anne Louisa her successor, who was a sister of my dear friend

Willie Erskine, wrote a beautiful letter to the Community which I cannot
resist quoting:

St Mary's Convent,
Wantage, Berks
June 17th 1934

Dearest Sisters,

*We have been given re-possession of our great Mother Isabel Mary as she
appears for us in God's presence with all her faculties restored and enriched by her
entrance into the fulness of joy.*

*Those who have lived in homely intercourse with her in the past love to dwell
on her wit, her shrewdness of judgment, her undaunted courage in matters of
principle, her absolute integrity. She swept aside all artificialities and subterfuge,
and saw all things in the light of truth. This wit and aptitude were present with
her even when many of her faculties failed.*

*She wrestled and laboured for the perfection of her Sisters and spared herself no
pains for the physical, material and spiritual good of individuals and households.
She was dead to the praise of the world and shrank from publicity, which makes it
the more incongruous that the daily papers should have seized upon details of her
life so eagerly. Some of her last words were: "I am beyond all that" when certain
questions were put to her. The nearer she approached to God the smaller such things
appeared. The decision to resign was the result of a clear and undisputed call
during a day's Retreat. Her experience of the last years demanded of her the
uttermost farthing of surrender to which she yielded completely towards the end,
though not without a struggle. It was no easy matter to press through the darkness
of the last stage of her sacrifice in to the Presence of the King. When I was trying
to help her she said: "It is too hard for you," and so it was. But peace came at the
end and was unbroken for the last eighteen hours or so, when she looked like the
contemplative Saint of a Spanish old Master, emaciated and intent. This gaze
continued after death until the eyes were closed, the Habit once more enfolded her,
and a happy smile appeared on her lips. She calls us to a deeper intensity of Faith,
an abounding love of souls for Christ's sake, and above all to the naked reality of
Poverty, Chastity and Obedience.*

*"May God bless you all" was the message she gave you through me when I
asked her to keep us all in her heart in Paradise.*

Your loving Mother in Christ,
Anne Louisa

I owed much to that aunt and godmother in my earliest childhood.
It was she who gave me Kingsley's *Heroes*, Scott's *Tales of a Grandfather*,
Church's *Story of the Iliad and the Odyssey*. She herself had read Rollins'
History of Greece when she was four and undoubtedly it was she who made
me a philhellene. I have told in an earlier Octave about her life on the
stage when she played Ophelia to Irving's *Hamlet*.

My mother and she were the two most devoted sisters I have known and the death of Isabel in this her 81st year was naturally a deep grief. She herself with her Theatre Girls Club to look after, with the priceless aid of Nessie Bell, who is 80 years old herself now and just retired, felt she still had work to do in this world.

I had to go down to Glasgow toward the end of June to be present at the Graduation. Calum MacSween drove with me to catch the boat from Stornoway. Just as we were passing Loch Seaforth I saw the new moon through glass.

"I hope this doesn't mean that something has gone wrong with the transfer of the Jethou lease," I exclaimed.

Calum had not encountered the superstition of believing the sight of the new moon through glass is an ill omen, and was inclined to be sceptical about it.

When we reached the quayside at Stornoway the *Lochness* was already fifty yards on her way. From that moment Calum MacSween became as firm an opponent of seeing the new moon through glass as I was. Fortunately I had not cut it too fine for the Graduation, and when I arrived in Glasgow, Rait with that continuous kindness to me thought it would be a pleasant memory if I performed the capping ceremony in Bute Hall.

After the death of Sir Donald Macalister earlier this year Sir Daniel Stevenson had been elected Chancellor instead of Lord Macmillan whose candidature had been supported by all the present members of the Senate.

"You will have to propose his health at the lunch," Rait told me.

"But really that's the Vice-Chancellor's job."

"I know, I know, but I can't bring myself to do it. None of us can."

"I don't think you're being very far-sighted. He's a very very wealthy old gentleman, eighty-three years old with a deep love of his native city, and if he's made to feel welcome as Chancellor he'll probably leave the University lots of money. However, I'll propose his health. I shall do it with complete sincerity because he was very good to me at the time of my case."

I had indeed been much touched by the way old Sir Daniel had stood by me and I suppose I managed to convey that. At any rate, when the new Chancellor replied to my speech he broke down for a moment or two. The Rector of Edinburgh University had come over for this Glasgow Graduation.

"I wanted them to see us together outside the Old Bailey," said Sir Ian.

After the speeches were over my former commander-in-chief said,

"You're a terrible chap. The last time we were both at a speech-day function you proposed the health of Annie S. Swan and reduced her to tears. Now you've done the same to an old boy two years older than I am."

While I was in Glasgow some of the students told me that they were asking Sir Iain Colquhoun to stand as an Independent in the next Rectorial. I knew that my Assessor had been immensely popular and I was certain that if he consented to stand no other candidate would have a chance. I saw John MacCormick and told him that I thought he should advise Cunninghame Graham to withdraw his consent to stand. MacCormick, at whose prompting the G.U.S.N.A. had invited Don Roberto to stand, refused.

"Very well I shall write and urge him as strongly as I can to withdraw. He had his triumph in 1928. What on earth is the sense of asking him now six years later to be defeated as he certainly will be by Iain Colquhoun? Moreover, why expose the weakness of the National Party as you are all doing by contesting these hopeless seats?"

However, John MacCormick was obstinately set on repeating his own triumph of six years earlier and could not bring himself to admit that he was no longer 'King' John as he had been hailed when Stanley Baldwin had only scraped in by 66 votes. I had seen at the beginning of the Rectorial campaign for my candidature that the students did not want to be told what to do by a graduate and I felt sure that the students of next October would be equally averse.

I do not remember whether I wrote to Don Roberto or gave my advice verbally when I went to see him before going to the South America he knew so well, but I have a letter from him after Iain Colquhoun had won the Rectorship by a large majority and Don Roberto had been only third, in which he says *How right you were, Don Monti. I ought to have heeded your warning.*

Before I went back to Barra I attended the International P.E.N. gathering in Edinburgh over which H. G. Wells was presiding. Eric Linklater and I were amused to find ourselves at one of the 'also ran' tables at the opening dinner. I find a long letter from William Powell to explain he was not responsible for the mistake. Eric and I knew our Edinburgh and were amused.

On the evening of the grand final assembly and ball we were dining at the Pompadour, and seeing H. G. Wells with the Baroness Budberg at another table I took Eric across at the end of the dinner to introduce him to H. G. Then we sat talking till 10.30 when H. G. decided it was too late for him to appear at the assembly.

"I'm glad you gave me an excuse to dodge it," he said when Eric and I left him and Moura Budberg to join the assembly, a little late.

Back on Barra where somehow I managed to finish *Prince Charlie and His Ladies* in a fortnight, I had arranged with the Coddie to move into the Bungalow, as it was called, when Chrissie and I got back from South America in the autumn. Then Chrissie went up to Harris to say farewell, taking with her Rum who became a dearly loved cat in the MacSween household. She used always to accompany Calum MacSween who was the precentor almost to the church door and then go and meet him when she saw the people coming out from church on the other side of the loch. She would be killed one day like so many other beloved cats by a damned car. Her sister Eigg was given to an old crofter to be his sole companion for some years.

I should have no opportunity of reading the proofs of *Prince Charlie and His Ladies* and I asked Alastair and Henrietta Tayler, whose knowledge of Jacobite history was outstanding, to correct them. I was amused when the book appeared that autumn to find a footnote by Tayler protesting as an Aberdonian against a disparaging reference to Keith, the Earl Marshal. The book was dedicated to Laura Lovat.

I began to wonder whether I had taken on more than I could creditably perform when Philip Guedalla gave me the programme for Buenos Aires where we were due to arrive in the R.M.S. *Alcantara* at 7 o'clock on the evening of August 16th.

August 17th. Lecture at the 'Little Theatre' for members of the Argentine Association of English Culture.
August 20th. Lecture at the University.
August 22nd. Lecture at 'Amigos del Arte'.
August 24th. Lecture under the auspices of the Argentine Association of English Culture for the Argentine and British Schools (in Prince George's Hall).
August 27th. Lecture at the 'Little Theatre' under the auspices of the Argentine Association of English Culture, for the general public.
August 29th. Departure to Rio de Janeiro in Blue Star SS *Avila Star*.
N.B. A broadcast might also be arranged.

"Five lectures in eight days," I commented.

"Yes, but you can give the same one to the University and the Amigos del Arte. It's only three really."

"It won't be quite the same. I'll be talking without any script. How long ought each lecture to last?"

"A full hour," said Philip Guedalla firmly. "But another quarter of an hour would be all to the good and you should offer to answer questions from the audience afterwards."

"Do you seriously mean to say you're going to get up and talk about the English novel and what not five times in eight days without having it all arranged definitely?"

This question came from the clipped voice of Rose Macaulay whom Faith and I were meeting for the first time. That first meeting was the beginning of a friendship that would last until that unique woman left our world too soon.

"I'm so glad I came to dinner after all. I nearly didn't. I thought I wasn't going to like you," she said.

"I didn't think I was going to like you."

"What fun it is when two people expect to dislike one another and find they are wrong."

I shall have one or two stories to tell about that unique woman in years to come.

When I look back to that voyage of three weeks I seem always to be looking across a vast extent of pale blue ocean and watching the silver flying-fish leap and go skimming across the tranquil water to escape from some unseen enemy below. Why people wanted to waste their time playing deck quoits when they could watch those flying-fish was beyond me.

Our first port of call on the voyage out was Coruña and I recall being far from impressed by the externals of the new Republican régime. Philip Guedalla was determined to see the grotto of St James at Compostella but I did not feel I could face the nervous strain of getting back in time to go on board when the *Alcantara* sailed some hours later. And indeed Guedalla did get back only just in time.

When we were in Lisbon, the next port of call, possibly inspired by the *vino verdhe* we were drinking at lunch, I made some criticism of the way England had treated Ireland. Guedalla who normally found any topic an excuse for an epigram succumbed to an outburst of rage.

"I've no patience with all this talk about the wrongs of Ireland. What has Ireland suffered compared with what the Jews have suffered? What I remember about Cromwell is that he gave asylum to Jews."

We battled for a while and then Guedalla said,

"I can take a completely objective view about this because my origins are not Palestine but Carthage."

"No wonder you haven't got any sympathy for the persecution of Roman Catholics, my dear Philip."

At Pernambuco, our first port of call after Lisbon, the *Alcantara* stayed only long enough for the ex-President of Brazil, Dr Bernardes, to come on board and return to Rio de Janeiro under the terms of an amnesty granted by the government which had exiled him. From Pernambuco we went on to Bahia de Todos Santos which we should have all day to explore. Only once or twice have I sent a character in a novel of mine to a place I have never seen, and I was a little apprehensive about Bahia where I once sent Sylvia Scarlett. To my relief I did not have to kick myself for having made any mistakes. What I did regret was my ignorance of the lifts that went up from sea-level to the city itself. Those lifts smelt strongly of the castor oil with which they were greased and the only more unpleasant smell in my experience is a whaling station.

The Guedallas left us at Rio. Faith and Chrissie went ashore with them, but I was so staggered by the scene the harbour presents that I remained on board to sit staring at it for a couple of hours. I was not surprised I had never read a description of that bay which had given me the least idea of what to expect; the bay of Rio de Janeiro is indescribable.

On southward across the equatorial Atlantic, that pale-blue calm immensity twinkling with flying-fish, on southward with the fun of crossing the line and the excitement of the Southern Cross rising in a cloudless sky.

We dropped anchor in the estuary of the Plate, to waste an afternoon in an orgy of officialdom. When Franklin D. Roosevelt enunciated his Four Freedoms it is a pity he did not add freedom of travel as a fifth. I can still see those three boatloads of bureaucrats coming out from Buenos Aires to spend two hours over the passport formalities before we could go ashore to spend another hour in the customs. I must add quickly that those were the only three hours of boredom we spent during our fortnight in the Argentine.

We stayed at the Plaza Hotel, which at this date was one of the classic hotels of the world, to rank with the Savoy in London and the Ritz in Paris. I should like to think that the Plaza is today what it was a generation ago but since the shock I have received from the garish modernization of the *Illustrated London News* as I write these words I have given up hope of anything's being able to avoid being brought up to date, as the pretentious phrase goes. The Plaza was splendidly old-fashioned and serenely comfortable.

Without any diary or notes I can only give a disjointed account of that crowded fortnight. There are some friendly press-cuttings of the lectures from which I gather they were well received by the audiences, but not one of those audiences can I evoke in memory. I find that I was the guest of the Chamber of Commerce and of the Rotary Club. I find the menu of a dinner of Argentine Old Paulines. Among these I was glad to meet Talbot Carr whom I had not seen since I told in Octave Two of his arrival in school wearing a Union Jack waistcoat during the first excitement of the Boer War. I find a letter from 'Daddy' Roche whose rooms at Magdalen were on the same staircase as mine when we both went up in 1901.

Dear Monty,

It is over thirty years since the bonhomous days at Coll: Magd: and it is also many years since you wrote me that you hoped some day to visit Buenos Aires, and now I see that those hopes are in course of realization.

As guest of the Asociacion de Cultura Inglese you will receive every attention and be shown everything worth seeing, and your time will probably be very fully occupied, but if your official engagements leave you any time to spare, I trust that

I may have the pleasure of seeing you, and if possible that you may take a meal with me.

Yours very sincerely

E. M. Roche

We had that meal and a good talk about those 'bonhomous days at Coll: Magd:'.

Sir Henry Chilton, our Ambassador, gave a lunch for me at the most luxurious club I have ever known. The Círculo de las Armas (I hope I have the name right) was also the most exclusive club in Buenos Aires and when I was made an honorary member for my visit I was told that I was receiving the greatest compliment it was in the power of Buenos Aires to offer. I see now that grey outside with a bed of pink Chinese primulas on either side of the door.

Sir Henry Chilton[1] had a rich sense of humour.

"You'll be amused to hear," he told me, "I received a warning from the Foreign Office that I was not to give a dinner for you at the Embassy but that I might give a lunch for you, preferably not in the Embassy."

"Official Secrets, I suppose?"

"Exactly. Aren't they gloriously ridiculous?"

However, after I got home I received a letter from Sir John Simon, the Secretary of State, thanking me for the success of my visit to South America which had been much appreciated by the Foreign Office. There was a congenial Military Attaché, Major Andrews, who took the trouble to have sent to me a kilogramme of mast from the Patagonian beech (*fagus antartica*). I had told him of my anxiety to persuade the Forestry people in Scotland to try this tree in the Highlands. After a long paper battle with the customs they were at last allowed to enter Great Britain, but the Forestry people were much too busy spoiling the Highland landscape and depriving the Highland crofters of good grazing with their dreary rectangles of Norwegian spruces for making pit-props as soon as possible to bother about a hardwood tree that needed time.

It was at this lunch given by Sir Henry Chilton that I tasted for the first time an avocado pear—alligator pears they used to be called. They had hardly heard of them yet in London.

Mention of that first avocado pear reminds me of the *chili con carne* at Harrods' restaurant. This was beef roast in the hide. I have never much cared for meat but this was delicious; I could believe at last in the roast beef of old England once upon a time. One last tribute to Buenos Aires food, and this to the prawns which taste exactly like our prawns but are about four times as large.

One day a Norwegian arrived at the Plaza Hotel from Patagonia and asked to see me on a matter of importance. When he came up to our

---

[1] The late Sir Henry G. Chilton, G.C.M.G.

sitting-room he told me he had read in one of the papers that I had been at Oxford and he was anxious to know how he could get in touch with the Oxford Group. I was as much irritated as A.P.H.[1] by the way Dr Buchman was making Oxford responsible for his Moral Rearmament racket. As it happened, I had just written a review of Rose Macaulay's book *Going Abroad* and gave this earnest Norwegian the carbon copy to read:

"The fun is concentrated on a minor group of Buchmanites. The satire is a little too gentle for my taste; indeed, there were one or two uneasy moments when I felt that Miss Macaulay was in danger of being sympathetic.

"The disgust of Oxford at the way this Buchmanite business is being unjustifiably foisted upon the senior University has filled with malicious joy the light-blue soul of Miss Macaulay, and when we remember the contempt with which Oxford regarded such distinguished Tabs as the late Lord Macaulay, we have to admit her right to a sweet revenge. Yet in jeering at Oxford, Miss Macaulay should not emulate her distinguished namesake's inaccuracy by attributing 'bedmakers' to Oxford. Bedmakers, like the swallow-tail butterfly, are found only in Cambridgeshire.

"*Going Abroad* is a charming entertainment, and I trust the mobs of Buchmanites searching for 'guidance' in the courts of Cambridge will persuade Miss Macaulay to use a little more gall in her ink next time she writes about them."

"I fear you are without faith, Mr Mackenzie," said the earnest Norwegian.

"No, no, but I'm afraid it's rather an old-fashioned faith. It's called Catholicism."

Then I offered him a drink, but he refused it and went back to Patagonia, a sadder and not even a wiser man.

By a coincidence I was due to give a broadcast to Patagonia at six o'clock that evening. That was quite an experience. I was put into a kind of glass sentry-box with the microphone in the middle of a large studio filled with spectators goggling at me. Broadcasting was evidently still something of a novelty in Buenos Aires.

"Don't start yet," said the announcer as I looked at the big clock the hands of which were at six o'clock's straight line. "The shepherds and farmers, most of them Welsh but quite a few Scots, will just be getting back indoors at six. We'll give them ten minutes to settle down."

When my broadcast started, the flashes of the camera-men taking photographs accompanied me at intervals; children's faces were glued to the glass. I had some jolly letters after it from Patagonia, and from the broadcasting company the equivalent of £10 in pesos.

[1] Sir Alan Herbert.

I had had a letter from Mr Donald MacRae, the President of the St Andrew's Society of the River Plate, which gave me proud pleasure:

"This is a note of welcome from the members of the St Andrew's Society of the River Plate—1,650 no less—who, one and all, trust that your visit to the Argentine will be full of interest to you and of benefit to both the Argentine and the British Communities.

"One of the annual events connected with our Society is the Scottish Dancing competition, which will take place on Saturday, August 25th from 9 to 10 p.m., and the Committee would be very grateful if you could spare the time to present the prizes, and address a few words to the competitors (boys and girls all under 16 years of age), many of whom are Argentines."

I read at the head of the notepaper:

RULE 5. The object of the Society shall be to foster the Scottish National sentiment, and to promote Benevolence, Education, National Literature, Customs and Accomplishments amongst persons of Scottish origin or race.

It was for me a moving occasion. Hardly any of the younger dancers round about ten years old could speak anything but Spanish. Yet there they were with Highland names in kilts of their own tartans, dancing their Highland reels. I thought of Burns:

> And I will come again, my love,
> Though it were ten thousand mile.

It is sad to find so many young Scots of today unable even to dance a foursome reel. It is no doubt enterprising to be 'with it' by indulging in Spanish dancing but unfortunately hardly any of the competitors in these television contests can transform themselves into Spaniards; they should stick to dances which they can perform naturally and well.

We had the good fortune to be invited one evening to a fashionable night club the name of which I forget; it was built to resemble the inside of a ship. There the tango really was the poetry of motion, and if any of the judges at these dancing contests had ever seen a tango danced as it should be danced they would award hardly any marks to the competitors from whatever part of Great Britain they come. Formation dances, yes. The military two-step, yes. The tango, the rumba or the pasodoble, no, no, no.

Our wind up to that full fortnight in Buenos Aires was an invitation from the Jockey Club to the races at the Hippodrome. I was due to go on 24 hours in advance of Faith and Chrissie to Montevideo, where I was to give a lecture for the Instituto Cultural Anglo-Urugayo. The *Avila Star* in which we were sailing to Rio de Janeiro would stop at Montevideo.

I got hold of a racing paper to decide on which horse in the eight races I should put the £10 I had been paid for the broadcast. As I turned over the blue pages I found that a horse called Montevideo was running in the eighth race and thought this was an omen to which I should pay attention.

The Jockey Club's stand at the racecourse was the perfection of luxurious comfort. After a lunch that Lucullus himself would have respected we sat in comfortable armchairs from which we rose to go out on the great balcony to watch the races. Liveried footmen came round before each race to place our bets with the bookmakers. When I announced that I intended to back Montevideo in the last race our hosts all assured me that Montevideo was a hopeless investment. Then I was given expert advice on what I ought to back. I backed the recommended horse in the first race for £2 and lost. I did the same in the second race and lost. Then I put £1 on the various runners suggested to me, all of which lost, and by the time the eighth race was reached I had only £1 left of my £10.

"Well, I'm going to put this on Montevideo," I declared.

"It hasn't a chance," I was assured. "It's a hopeless outsider."

"I am going to back Montevideo."

Compassionate looks from the experts watched me hand those pesos to the footmen.

Montevideo won at 18 to 1. I was £9 up on the afternoon, but if I had refused to pay any attention to other people's advice I might have been £180 up.

I was much impressed during that fortnight in Buenos Aires by the freedom from insularity of the British community. I never heard any of them criticizing the Argentine way of life; wisely they had adopted it. This was equally true of the British community in Uruguay. It was not surprising. From that brief visit I carried away a feeling that Montevideo was the brightest example I had seen of a happy and prosperous democracy. When I was being shown over the Chamber of Deputies I felt as if I was being shown over their first house by a newly married couple. That indomitably active man Eugen Millington-Drake[1] had recently been appointed Minister but unluckily for me he was away at the moment. Equally enthusiastic in his encouragement of art and sport he must have been an ideal representative of his country. Football had by now become a passion in South America. Indeed, it was almost too exciting. I think it was in Montevideo that the grandstand of the football ground was covered with wire netting to prevent the spectators from attacking the rival players with missiles. The contemporary elevens of the Argentine and Uruguay may doubt if such a precaution was ever necessary. A freak of memory has left me forgetting completely the lecture

---

[1] Sir Eugen Millington-Drake, K.C.M.G.

I gave but remembering vividly the big nests of the weaver-birds in trees beside a road along which I was driven to get a glimpse of the country-side.

The *Avila Star* was one of Vestey's Blue Star line, decorated in the mock baronial style. I remember saying I supposed the Barons de Beef lived on board this line. There were few passengers, of whom I recall only two—a female fortune-teller and an elderly male hypochondriac travelling with a nurse. The weather was stormy for the first two days; we hit the gale which St Rose of Lima is supposed to have summoned to protect herself from some unwelcome advances by mariners. However, as the Southern Cross went dipping down we reached the tranquil pale blue equatorial waters and the silver flying-fish.

Our first port of call was Santos where the ship was to spend the day taking in cargo. Arthur Abbott, the British Consul at São Paolo, had written to suggest our driving up to lunch with him. We found a taxi at the dock in Santos and drove up that steep winding road through sublime scenery for an hour and a half. Unfortunately the scenery kept getting shut out by mist at intervals which was tantalizing. When we reached the Consulate Mr and Mrs Abbott were waiting for us with three Horses' Necks. I never enjoyed a drink more in my life.

After lunch we were taken to visit a snake farm where remedies and prophylactics for snake-bite were produced. At this date São Paolo was expanding in every direction and new buildings were going up every-where. I felt that this was going to be one of the great cities of the Western Hemisphere; today it is.

On our way back the taxi ran out of petrol just as we reached the outskirts of Santos; we were in a panic that the *Avila Star* would have sailed before we reached the dock. What a half-hour that was, as we waited for the taxi driver to come back with some petrol. We need not have worried. The *Avila Star* did not sail until nearly midnight. I stood watching the huge bunches of bananas being carried up by the dockers to join the frozen beef in the hold.

We were staying at the Copocabana Hotel which looks out over a long sandy beach where life-savers are always on the look out to rescue bathers in trouble with the Atlantic rollers. I had been told about the Copocabana Hotel by a tycoon who had taken over the MacBrayne shipping company and enabled them to replace the old *Plover* and *Cygnet* with the *Lochmor* and the *Lochearn*. When he heard I was going to Brazil he told me to be sure to stay at the Copocabana.

"Finest hotel in the world."

In fact the Copocabana compared with the Plaza in Buenos Aires was like the Dorchester or Grosvenor compared with the Savoy or Claridge's.

Chrissie distinguished herself on the first evening by her dancing performance in a melodious number of worldwide popularity. After the dancing we went to the roulette tables where when Faith and Chrissie had won the equivalent of a pound each in reis I insisted, despite their indignant protests, in coming away while they were still in pocket. The lesson of that Kursaal in Geneva when I was seventeen was still potent. I attended a gramophone evening at the local gramophone society, where I was presented with a set of records of Brazilian music on which the confounded customs at Southampton insisted on charging a steep duty.

I had been warned it was a breach of good manners to wear tropical clothing in Rio, which prided itself on never being too hot. Nevertheless, I felt pretty warm when I was walking round that superb Botanical Garden from which I recall most vividly an avenue of palm-trees over 100 ft. high along which danced blue butterflies twice as big as swallow-tails. I recall, too, the green humming-birds shimmering over tropical flowers, the first live humming-birds I had ever seen.

I was due to give one lecture in Rio but at dinner with the Counsellor of the Embassy—the Ambassador was away—on the previous evening I was suddenly seized with one of my infernal goes of sciatic neuritis, and was completely laid out for two days. My lecture had to be cancelled. Headlines in the Rio papers announced:

O ESCRITOR COMPTON MACKENZIE ADOECE GRAVAMENTE
O CONHECIDO LITERATO INGLEZ ATACADO DE PARALYSIA

The Times announced my paralysis; cables from Reuter, from the *Daily Mail* and about two dozen friends came in.

We sailed from Rio in the R.M.S. *Arlanza* and to my agreeable surprise the first name I saw on the passenger list was that of Oc Asquith.[1] I have written in Octave Three of the Easter vacation spent with him and Guy Bonham-Carter at Compiègne in 1903. Guy had been killed in 1915 and Oc Asquith had lost a leg in the war. He and I played chess daily throughout the voyage and I did not manage a single checkmate. He used to shake his head over my reckless moves just as thirty years ago he had been wont to shake his head over the night life of Guy and myself in France.

I was rather excited to hear that our next port of call after the palm-trees of Pernambuco sank below the horizon would be St Vincent in the Cape Verde islands. Alas, it was dark when we reached St Vincent and there was nothing to be seen but great heaps of coal along the quay. The flowers in Madeira were more rewarding.

I was disappointed that we could not reach home in time for the Mòd at Oban, particularly as the Castlebay children had won the Shiant Shield. This was a triumph for Annie Johnston, their teacher, than

[1] The late Brig.-Gen. the Hon. Arthur Asquith, D.S.O.

L

whom no better teacher of small children ever lived. She was renowned throughout the Gaelic world on both sides of the Atlantic, for her ability to teach children was just as much for teaching the grown-ups who attended each year the Gaelic Summer School. She was a perennial spring of Gaelic folk lore; her tales were inexhaustible. A truly lovable woman, she was utterly unspoilt by the esteem in which she was held. I only once saw her put out of countenance. I was having tea in her cottage on the east side of Barra when she went out to get something from the store-cupboard and came hurriedly back to say there was a monster in it.

"A monster?" I exclaimed.

"Och, well, it is not so very large but it is terribly fierce-looking."

I went along to investigate and found it was the caterpillar of a puss moth making its strange grimaces and arching itself to frighten any bird that seemed likely to attack it.

"You must be the largest bird, Annie, that a puss moth ever tried to frighten."

One story I shall allow myself of the many she told me during our long friendship.

There were two small boys in her class, one a Protestant, the other a Catholic. The latter was holding up his hand.

"What is it, Donald?"

"Please, miss, Hughie is after making a big swear."

"Hughie has been swearing?"

"Yes, miss. Hughie is after saying that God is a Protestant."

Annie Johnston told John Campbell and myself that the Barra children had been teased by the children from schools on the mainland competing in the action songs because they talked Gaelic among themselves.

John Campbell and I had gone to Harris that December to ask every-body with any interest in the problem of illegal trawling to join the Sea League and enable us to send in our request to the Inverness County Council to form a fishery district in the Outer Isles and thus carry out the Act of 1895 which had never been put into operation. We had an enthusiastic response from the island of Scalpay which had a larger number of active fishermen than the whole of Harris. We drove all over Lewis with Calum MacSween and, although Lewis came under the County Council of Ross-shire and was therefore not concerned with Inverness-shire islands, we were much encouraged by Lewis support. As owner of the Shiant Islands I was a Lewis ratepayer, and did not feel an 'outsider'. The shameless infringement of the three-mile limit by Fleetwood trawlers and the havoc they were doing to the whitefish were exacerbated by their continuous sheep-stealing.

John Campbell and I were feeling in a belligerent mood, and after

Annie Johnston's report we felt it was time to stir up An Comunn Gaidhealach.

I shall reprint those two letters we wrote in that December of 1934 because, alas and alack, the criticism we made then could be made even more trenchantly a generation later:

> Tarbert, Harris.
> Outer Isles.
> 10/12/34

Neil Shaw Esq.,
Secretary, An Comunn Gaidhealach
212 West George Street,
Glasgow
Galltachd na h-Alba

Dear Sir,

With reference to the Mòd to be held in Edinburgh next year, we are glad to observe from notices given in the Press that the Mòd held at Oban this year has had such a success and yielded such a handsome profit.

We are very anxious to persuade the schools of the Outer Isles, where the national language of Scotland, although not officially recognized, is in everyday use, to send their children to compete at the Edinburgh Mòd. It would be an opportunity both to acquaint these children with the capital city of Scotland and its monuments and associations, and to impress upon the inhabitants of the Capital itself the enthusiasm and zeal of the children themselves for the ancient culture of their country.

Money, however, is scarce in the Outer Isles, the people being of moderate means and there being no landowners to call upon for assistance as in Argyll; therefore it is necessary that we should have some assurance of outside financial assistance.

We should like to feel that we could depend upon your organization for three hundred pounds. If we can have this assurance, we intend to approach Messrs MacBraynes and the County Education Authorities of Inverness and Ross-shire in order that the most suitable arrangements can be effected.

It is, of course, to be understood that such an assurance will not cause the relaxation of local efforts to raise money for the same purpose. When it is remembered that it cost £50 to send the Castlebay choir to Oban this September, it will be realized to what an extent outside assistance is essential if the Islands children are to be properly represented at the forthcoming Mòd.

We have to add that we have been deeply shocked to hear, on impeccable authority, that the children of the Castlebay choir were teased during the Mòd at Oban by the children of the Mainland choirs, because they spoke Gaelic. We think that, in view of the deplorable inferences which may be drawn from this incident, it is desirable that the Gaelic-speaking children from the Islands should be sufficiently *represented at the Edinburgh Mòd to render the repetition of such an incident impossible.*

> *We are, Sir,*
> *Yours faithfully,*
> *Compton Mackenzie*
> *J. L. Campbell yr of*
> *Inverneill*

We received the usual evasive assurance that all Secretaries give on such occasions.

On Christmas Eve John and I wrote:

We are obliged to you for your answer to our letter and are glad to hear that our suggestions are to be referred to the Mòd and Music Committee; but, as the time for making the necessary preparations is short, we are anxious that our proposals should be referred to a quarter from which we can obtain a definite reply as soon as possible, as if we are refused by An Comunn it will, of course, be necessary to make a public appeal on a national scale. We regard the moment as critical for the future of the Gaelic language, and wish to emphasize as strongly as we know how the vital necessity of impressing on the genuine *Gaelic population the importance of An Comunn and thus remove the unfortunate impression which is gaining ground among them that the Mòd is an academic festival remote from the problems of everyday life.*

We wish to make it perfectly clear that there was no suggestion in our letter of any lack of warmth in the reception of the Barra children at Oban; what we want to point out is that the presence of children speaking Gaelic as their natural *language apparently struck with surprise the more sophisticated products of the Movement.*

It has occurred to us that the final decision of An Comunn may be influenced by being asked to hand over £300 for application outside their control. We make haste to disclaim any desire to administer this fund. All we wish to know is that the money will be there if any Outer Islands schools apply for a grant towards their expenses. It will be readily understood that we both stand in an exceptionally favourable position for the exercising of personal persuasion in this area; and we should not take up the time of your Committee unless we felt unusually optimistic of a local response.

Alas and alack, I repeat, An Comunn Gaidhealach has never attempted to penetrate with the Mòd even as far as to the wilds of Dingwall since 1931 let alone to cross the Minch and hold a Mòd in Stornoway. The financial help we asked for was never forthcoming. As things look now, Gaelic will disappear as a spoken language as line-fishing has disappeared from the island economy.

After reading those letters when revising my manuscript in October

1966 I read in the *Scotsman* that An Comunn had failed to raise more than £100 toward the £1,000 hoped for from which money was to be found for making gramophone records for Gaelic lessons. Lady Elspeth Campbell and I managed to get such records made over thirty years ago without any help or encouragement from An Comunn.

When the weight of Jethou was lifted from my shoulders in May I had decided to build a house on Barra but I could not commit myself to this until the consent of the Treasury to the transfer of the Jethou lease had been received. By the time we returned from South America this had been granted. Meanwhile, the Department of Agriculture in Edinburgh had granted me a feu of one acre provided I undertook to do and not to do three pages of feuing regulations. Among these I promised not to use any building erected on the acre of ground as a "Common Inn, Tavern, Alehouse or Spirit Cellar". I promised not to cause to be erected a "Brewery, Distillery, Tannery, Foundry, Manufactury for keeping gunpowder or gas, candles or soap". I promised not to "keep any horse, cattle beast, sheep, goat or pig on the feu except with the written permission of the Department". I could not resist writing to ask if there was any objection to my keeping four Siamese cats on the feu and received a courteous reply to say that the Department had no objection.

The site chosen by me with the Coddie's approval was an acre of the sandy machair close to Tràigh Mhòr, the great cockle beach, and about 300 yards from the long beach called Tràigh Iais which faced the Atlantic. According to Father John Macmillan this was where Macneil of Barra used to eat his lunch when out snipe-shooting and was called Suidheachan—the sitting down place. So we decided to call the three sided bungalow I proposed to build Suidheachan.

In October I was able to give Malcolm Maclean of Tobermory the all clear to go ahead and he was writing to say that he hoped to start work in February or March.

The 27 crofters of Ardvore, the township on whose common grazing I proposed to build had all given their assent to my feu. Malcolm Maclean at his own risk had laid a water pipe from a spring on the brae south of the machair.

I had taken the Coddie's bungalow for a year. There was a sizable sitting-room and kitchen on the ground floor with two bedrooms above. Although it was always called the Bungalow it really was not a bungalow. Chrissie had one bedroom above and the other was kept for guests. I myself slept in a tiny room off the sitting-room.

I was determined to start *The Four Winds of Love* as early as possible in the new year but before I started I had to write *Catholicism in Scotland*, one of a series called the Voice of Scotland which Routledge were publishing under the editorship of J. Leslie Mitchell (Lewis Grassic Gibbon). I also wrote a fairly long account of Barra for *The Book of Barra* which John Campbell was compiling. I began to yearn for my books which were all packed waiting for the new library that was going to be built for them. All that I left behind in Jethou was a complete set of the bound volumes of the Journal of the Society for Psychical Research and about thirty volumes of books about psycho-analysis—Freud, Jung, Adler and the rest. I had realized by now how much psychology was being administered to literature and did not want to swallow any more of it.

I turn over the pages of my reviews that autumn and find I wrote of a book by Beverley Nichols called *A Village in a Valley*:

"A keen observation of nature, so keen that Mr Nichols had observed what nobody has observed before him: for instance, the young moon rising in the western sky, orange-tip butterflies sucking honey from nasturtiums in late summer, and a species hitherto unknown to entomologists, which, I think, must have been the male of the painted lady. This was observed in the garden of his friend the Professor, whom Mr Nichols roguishly salutes as 'the King of the Butterflies'.

"When we read that autumn crocuses give Mr Nichols a lump in the throat, it looks at first as if he had been chewing colchicums, which are poisonous; but it soon transpires that the lump is due to emotion over the fact that they are not spring crocuses.

"Thousands will revel in this tender, this almost juicily tender book."

John Galsworthy died in January 1933 and Cape published this autumn *Letters From John Galsworthy* (1900-1932) edited with an introduction by Edward Garnett. I found it "an astonishing revelation of the way some authors work. Mr Edward Garnett has never been conspicuous for a sense of humour, but even he should have avoided writing 'I wrongly challenged Galsworthy's knowledge of the aristocracy. He knocked me off my length by sending me a list of one hundred and thirty upper class men and women he had met or known.' In that letter about *The Patrician*, the author himself added, 'I have left out of the enclosed list nouveau or parvenu aristocracy (except perhaps half a dozen); they are nearly all old stock.'

"It is like an argument with a wine-merchant over that last lot of port.

"I wish I could add that there was one nutritious sentence in this volume for aspiring young writers; but there is nothing, and, that being the case, it might have been kinder of Mr Garnett to leave the correspondence between him and Galsworthy unprinted. Nevertheless, it does possess an unholy fascination and may fairly be called one of the curiosities of literature."

I am glad to find myself writing of *Storm in Shanghai* as *La Condition Humaine* by André Malreaux was called in the translation published by Methuen:

"It is a magnificent book, perhaps the best that has come out of France since the war, and it makes the boasted novelties of Bolshevik literature from Russia look like old-fashioned feuilletons.

"*Storm in Shanghai* is a tale of the Communist rising in 1927 which, beginning with a murder by a Chinese terrorist, carries the reader through one terrific scene after another to a ghastly conclusion.

"Yet, the profound psychology of the author and his ability to make the most insignificant of his characters live unforgettably in the imagination prevent the book from ever deteriorating into a monotonous catalogue of horror.

"*Storm in Shanghai* is not for the squeamish, but it is one of the few modern books in which the matter not merely justifies the manner of narration but makes such a manner imperative. If ever some of the younger American and British writers get hold of themes like this they may wish they had not wasted so much blasphemy and obscenity and shell-shocked prose on inadequate material."

Let me say again thirty years later what a magnificent book *La Condition Humaine* is.

I had just written that review when Wilfred Macartney arrived in Barra. His wife Jane had written to tell me he was due to be released from Parkhurst that November after serving eight and a half years of that disgraceful penalty of ten years to which he had been sentenced by Lord Hewart whose career as Lord Chief Justice made Judge Jeffreys look like Dr Barnardo. I have told the story of Macartney, my former subaltern, in Octave Six.

I had written to Macartney when he was released and urged him to come at once to Barra and immediately get his experiences of prison down on paper. Macartney arrived in the last week of October.

As if it was yesterday I see Macartney sitting at tea in the Bungalow and hear Chrissie saying to him,

"If you want anything, ring. I'll be in the kitchen."

I was on my way out to go along to the post office and tell the Coddie, in whose house near by Macartney was to stay, that he had arrived. On being told to ring he looked much embarrassed.

"I haven't been used to ringing bells for some time," he said.

And I still see him on that first evening fidgeting with his hands and hear him say apologetically,

"I'm afraid I'm not used to having pockets."

Father Donald Campbell had just been transferred from Castlebay to Oban as Administrator of the new Cathedral which was about half finished. Father John MacQueen was now the parish priest of Castlebay with whose arrival began a friendship which is as intimate as ever today. Father Dominic MacKellaig who had the parish of Craigston was an equally intimate friend but he to my sorrow is no longer alive. I told Father MacQueen and Father MacKellaig about Macartney's past. I also told the Coddie and Neil Sinclair. Nobody else in the island was ever aware of it.

By happy timing Macartney arrived in Barra just before Hallowe'en when we had all been invited to a party by Neil Sinclair and his dear sister, Annie. It was a memorable evening with all the traditional diversions of that happy date, and before we joined hands for 'Auld Lang Syne' at midnight Parkhurst was something in the past for Macartney.

I thought of a title for the book he was to get down at once to writing, *Walls Have Mouths*. I promised to write an introduction and comments between every chapter.

The handicap I imposed on myself by electing to write of *My Life and Times* year by year is becoming increasingly heavier as my memory wrestles with dates and incidents nearer to the present. On consideration, I believe that something which I had been supposing occurred in this year 1934 in fact occurred in 1933.

When Sir Oswald Mosley left the Labour Party and formed the New Party with John Strachey and Harold Nicolson it was dissolved less than a year after he had been defeated in the Glasgow Rectorial election. Mosley started the British Union of Fascists; John Strachey became for a while a fellow traveller with the Communists; Harold Nicolson became National Labour. There was widely spread sympathy with Hitler and Mussolini, which people have conveniently forgotten. Lord Rothermere came out in favour of Mosley and helped the B.U.F. with considerable funds besides instructing the *Daily Mail* to indulge in propaganda for the movement. A member of the Savile asked me to attend a dinner in Claridge's at which Mosley would expound the Fascist gospel. After that various people present were invited to speak, among them Salvemini, the distinguished historian, who presented Italian Fascism in roseate hues. To my surprise I was asked to speak, and I warned the British Union of Fascists to keep out of Scotland. In his reply to the various criticisms of the speakers Mosley made as able a speech as I have ever listened to. I wondered what he would say to me. Unexpectedly instead of tearing my speech to pieces he assured me that he had the greatest sympathy with the aims of the National Party and that the British Union of Fascists would abstain entirely from campaigning in Scotland.

At the end of the evening I was taken to meet him and my eye caught sight of a note beside Mosley's place at the table. *Urgent. Be sure to answer Mackenzie.* Sir Oswald Mosley invited me to visit the headquarters of the B.U.F. in King's Road, Chelsea. I was no more impressed by the young men in black shirts and jackboots than I had been by the young blackshirts in Capri before the march on Rome. Nor did their female associates inspire admiration. I recall walking across Hyde Park with Mosley and saying to him that I thought his attempt to provoke anti-Semitism in the East End was likely to lead to dangerous developments and that his crusade against the payment of tithes by farmers was comparatively harmless. He said,

"Yes, but you don't realize what strides we've made forward since we were recognized as anti-Semitic. Our membership has doubled."

In the summer of this year 1934 there was a great Fascist rally at Olympia at which interrupters were treated with such brutality by the young Blackshirts that public indignation was loud and the Home Secretary was asked questions in Parliament. Like most Home Secretaries when asked awkward questions he gave a reply that committed him or the Government to nothing. Soon after this the British public was shocked by Hitler's massacre of his opponents in Berlin and Munich, the night of the long knives as the Nazis called it. People in Great Britain who had been expressing their admiration of Hitler kept quiet; the British Union of Fascists became rapidly smaller.

In a Christmas letter to Faith from Tarbert:

Young Inverneill and I had a great time in Lewis. Wonderful weather. Driving with the hood down all the way. I feel very fit. You'll have to visit Lewis next summer. The Standing Stones at Callernish on the west side of the island are as good in their way as Stonehenge. The MacSweens were disappointed you didn't manage to come for Christmas. I'm going back to Barra on January 4th. I shall be glad to get a church again. I do find Presbyterianism a bit heavy, though the Church of Scotland minister here, the Rev. Duncan Macleod, is a splendid chap. He's over eighty and his hair is still as black as a crow. He is a great smoker, but I hold my own with black twist. He was in Canada once and told me he always found the company of the French Canadians a great relief.

I was telling Calum MacSween about Mosley and his B.U.F. He decided they must be like the Freemasons who he assured me had secret dinners at which there was a goat sitting at the head of the table. Such a tale is obviously a survival of witchcraft stories in the 17th century.

One last memory of 1934. Father John had just discovered Wordsworth's poem about the Highland reaper. Neil Sinclair and I were with him.

"Read it, Neil," he commanded in his richest tones.

"I don't seem to have my glasses, Father," said Neil.

"Read it, read it, Neil."

The Sgoilear Ruadh saw there was nothing for it but to read the poem which he proceeded to do very nervously. I hear now,

>   "Of old unhappy far off things
>   And bottles long ago."

"Och, holy smoke, Neil," Father John roared. "Battles not bottles!"

FIFTY-TWO YEARS OLD: 1935

M Y original idea had been to spend £3,000 on building the bungalow, the amount I had received as premium for the Jethou lease. I suppose it was making an excuse to my conscience for any extravagance I had in mind. There was not much left of that £3,000 by now. As usually happens when one is planning to build a house the original estimate mounted up and the final estimate was £4,155 to which had to be added surveyor's and architect's fees and legal fees. The Standard Life Insurance gave me a £3,000 mortgage which involved another insurance policy and Malcolm Maclean the builder gave a secondary mortgage of £750 which would leave me to find £405. This worried me.

On January 9th I was writing to my friend Harry Paterson, an Edinburgh S.S.C. who had managed what had seemed last year the too formidable problems of financing the building of that bungalow.

The finding of the extra money required during the next six months is an acute problem, for I have given post-dated cheques covering every half-penny of spare cash to the Income Tax people. Here are my possible solutions,

(I) To postpone building the house till next year.
The arguments against this are obvious, the most serious being the storage of my books and furniture meanwhile.

(II) To cancel the billiards-room;
But as this is to hold practically all my books it would be infernally inconvenient.

(III) To re-enter into negotiations with a possible purchaser of the Shiant Islands and ask him a considerably lower price. But I do not want to sell the Shiant Islands if it can possibly be avoided.

(IV) I am starting to write a very long novel which cannot be finished till the end of June, but the £1,500 which I shall get for that will be swallowed up by paying off what remains of my overdraft, the rent of Eilean Aigas, the Insurance premium, and what is left of my bills. The Daily Mail *£120 a month leaves me with just enough for living expenses after the Income Tax post-dated cheques are met.*

Harry Paterson wrote back, strongly advising me to go ahead. He had arranged with Maclean, the builder in Tobermory, that the £405 would not be called for until the house was finished.

Now that everything seems to be arranged to your satisfaction, I shall press for the Feu Charter. On January 9th the Department of Agriculture wrote regretting

*any inconvenience caused by the delay and stating that the Draft Feu Charter would
be sent on the* following week *but the 'following week' expired ten days ago.*

A month later Paterson was writing:

*I note that you have pegged out the site of the house with Maclean. . . . I note it
is vital that Mr Maclean gets starting to unload the bricks in the puffer with the
first Spring tide in March, but notwithstanding all promises, the Draft Feu Charter
has not reached me. The Feu Charter is the basis of the whole transaction, and the
Department's failure to produce it mucks up everything. Urgent letters have failed,
and I shall now try personal application.*

On February 20th Paterson was writing,

*I to-day had an interview with two of the Officials at the Secretary's Office,
Department of Agriculture, and have definitely ascertained that the Draft Feu
Charter has been passed by the Department Solicitor and a Plan of the Feu prepared.*
*A point has arisen regarding the water supply to the Pendiclers[1] and your Feu.
The Draft Feu Charter has been returned to the Solicitor for insertion of a clause
limiting your right to a joint supply along with others presently entitled to a supply
from the same well or source in the Pendicle.*

I wrote back at once:

*The water supply we are proposing to use is from a new source entirely, but in
order to show my appreciation of the action of the Ardvore crofters in letting me
have a piece of their common pasture I am proposing to give them a tap to water
their cattle from the pipe which we are laying on the understanding between me
and them that in case of any shortage of water the house will be supplied first, and
this tap temporarily cut off. The existing water supply which would be used jointly
by myself and the pendiclers is in an inconveniently placed tank. If the Department
wished to exercise any rights over the new water supply they ought to pay the whole
cost of the installation. I hope I have made it clear that nobody else is using the
water supply I propose to use which is up the hillside a quarter of a mile away
from the pendicle.*

On March 3rd I wrote to Paterson,

*I telegraphed to you suggesting that one of the Department's representatives
should come here and look at the situation on the spot. It will be perfectly possible
to make a road up to the house from the east, but it seems a fearful waste of money
to make the kind of road necessary for the transport of heavy building material,
especially as the tenants of Ardvore themselves use and expect me to use the other
road. They are anxious to sign a protest against what they consider the arbitrary
and deliberately obstructive attitude of the Department. If you think that a statement
signed by the tenants to say that they are perfectly willing for me to go through what*

[1] Pendicle is not to be found in the *Concise Oxford Dictionary*, but the big one
defines it as "A small piece of property, especially when separately sub-let".

may be called a potato patch, but is in fact common pasture, would be useful, let me have word, and I will get it done. It is clear to me that the officials in Edinburgh are being deliberately misled, and I have a shrewd suspicion which of their Commissioners is responsible, for I have good reason to suppose that this man has done all he could to prevent my having the feu.

I have forgotten the name of that suspect, but he was an enemy of the Coddie and because the Coddie had suggested the site of Suidheachan he was anxious to thwart him.

I could fill many more pages of this Octave with the correspondence over that Feu Charter. I have given this sample of it because it will explain why one day in Suidheachan I should write my novel *The Red Tapeworm.*

After Maclean had pegged out the ground which the house was to occupy I had one of those bad goes of pain which with me used nearly always to succeed the construction of a book in my mind. I had told Eric Linklater of my conception of *The Four Winds of Love* in 1932. The action of the East Wind was to take place mostly in Spring and I should make use of the Polish visit in the Autumn of 1932. The action of the South Wind should take place mostly in Summer with Italy and Greece to mark its direction. The West Wind's direction should be for America, Ireland and Cornwall, with the action mostly in Autumn. The North Wind should be based on Scotland with Winter as its main season.

I came back with Coddie from that pegging out and felt that the decisive action taken over the site and direction of the house demanded that I should begin *The Four Winds of Love.* I sat till the small hours with half a sheet of typing paper in front of me, jotting down slowly one by one the names of the chief characters. It is improbable that a bottle of wine stiffly corked suffers any conscious reaction from being uncorked and slowly poured out into glasses until it is empty. Yet if a bottle could feel, that is what I felt like on that February night when at last I had constructed the fundamental design of *The Four Winds of Love* and told Chrissie that she need not put any more records on the gramophone. I slept all night but next morning I woke with that infernal stab in the heel which was always the signal of a fierce attack.

While I was out of action Maclean altered slightly the direction of the house as it was shown on the plan. Hence the interminable correspondence with the Department of Agriculture. He had already laid that pipe from the spring on the brae at his own risk, and now he took the risk of bringing the puffer with masses of bricks to the Tràigh Mhòr where during the low spring tide of March they were unloaded and carted up to the site of the house.

The Silver Jubilee of King George V was celebrated that May. We had a great picnic for the children of Northbay and Eoligarry Schools with sports. I think the most exciting event was a 50-yards race for four-year-olds and under. I can see now two of these 'infants' falling on their faces within a yard or two of the winning post.

The Silver Jubilee celebrations were followed by the ceremonious laying of the foundation stone of Suidheachan.

To quote from an Edinburgh paper:

"Mr Malcolm M'Lean, building contractor, presented Mr Compton Mackenzie with a handsome silver trowel as a souvenir of the occasion at which 200 of the island residents were present. Father M'Millan of Northbay performed the ceremony of blessing the foundation stone and sprinkling it with holy water.

"The good wishes of the community were expressed by Father M'Kellaig of Craigston, the Rev. Ian M'Dougall of Cuir, parish minister, and Mr John M'Pherson of Northbay.

"Mr Mackenzie thanked all those who had helped him in his project, and mentioned particularly the people of Ardvore, the adjoining township, for their goodwill in helping him to acquire the site."

The *Daily Record*, a copy of whose Jubilee colour number had been buried in the foundations, had a leader on Saturday May 11th:

A SETTLER FOR BARRA

"Preparations for Mr Compton Mackenzie's settlement in Barra are surrounded by a glamour which seems rather more than is ordinarily inspired by a change of residence.

"It is essentially a personal matter and our curiosity must be curbed. But Mr Mackenzie is a public figure, one of our foremost men of letters, and his way of life is a matter of public interest. We wonder, therefore, whether this exile signifies a spiritual adventure, an evasion of life's problems or merely a glorified holiday.

"Father Macmillan blessing the foundation stone of the author's new house at Vaslain, said 'You came to assimilate our life . . . we need his help . . . by blending together, by mutual transfusion of our ideals and grafting of sentiment and character. A golden circle of nobleness and character used to surround Eilean na h'Oige (the island of Youth). That circle, although not broken and shattered altogether, suffered the coming of a world whose ways are artificial and insincere. It is up to us, with your co-operation and help, to repair the damage done to that golden circle.'

"That is more than an eloquent welcome; it is a dedication to an ideal. Mr Mackenzie, it seems, is to be no mere recluse, though the transformation is reminiscent of the escape of other authors.

"Stevenson and Samoa are evoked. Tusitala, as the natives called him, also built himself an island home and in time fashioned a 'golden circle' with servants and retainers around him and became a benignant island chieftain. If Mr Mackenzie has not forsaken politics, we may see the analogy further realized, though Scotland's future will probably remain his sphere of service, Barra may be the core of things inspirational.

"Whatever the reason for the change, Mr Mackenzie's own account of his experience, whether translated in fiction or given direct, should be unusually interesting."

I wonder if the writer of that leader would have felt that *Whisky Galore* justified it.

Our next excitement that summer was a visit from Lord Moyne[1] in his yacht. The yacht was anchored off Northbay so that Lady Londonderry could consult Father John Macmillan about another Gaelic concert she was giving at Londonderry House next autumn.

I fancy Sydney MacEwan and Duncan Morrison, a brilliant young pianist from Lewis, came to Barra that summer. The latter owed much to Lady Londonderry's patronage. 'Major' as he was called was an unique product. I recall visiting him in his Stornoway rooms and fancying myself back in the artistic mood of the fin de siècle 'decadence' of the 'nineties.

Sydney MacEwan had been on the Nationalist Committee which ran my Rectorial. He was in much demand as a singer and I seem to remember saying to him I thought he was mistaken in supposing himself to be a baritone. Anyway, he discovered that he was really a tenor and went to study singing at the Royal College of Music. I asked Plunket Greene to let me know what he thought of his voice and was so much encouraged to find him enthusiastic that I decided to write to John McCormack and ask him to be kind enough to hear a young singer. John McCormack did so and became a friend and infallible adviser of young Sydney. I also recommended him to the attention of Oscar Preuss of Parlophone. He had a great success on a tour in Australia and made many records. Then he felt a vocation for the priesthood. The Scotland hierarchy were sensible enough to let him continue to give concerts in America and Australia when he was a seminarist in Rome and after he was ordained. The money he earned was enough to finish the beautiful Roman Catholic Cathedral in Oban. After many years at Lochgilphead where he restored the little church with perfect taste, as I write these words, Canon Sydney MacEwan has just been given the charge of St Andrew's, Rothesay, in succession to Canon John MacQueen.

In July I turned aside from *The East Wind of Love* which I was finding hard going to write *Catholicism in Scotland*, which was published later on that year. The preliminary announcement brought me several anony-

[1] The late Lord Moyne, D.S.O.

mous letters, in one of which was enclosed a consecrated Host. As Gibbon wrote about the Gordon Riots:

A dark and diabolical fanaticism which I supposed to be extinct, but which actually subsists in Great Britain perhaps beyond any country in Europe.

What puzzles me about anonymous letter writers is their cowardice. One might suppose that if somebody felt strongly enough to express his disapproval of another person he would not be afraid to sign his name. I used to receive anonymous letters regularly when I was in Barra, denouncing my Popery; when I went to live in Edinburgh I expected my anonymous mail would grow. Yet in the last thirteen years I have not received one anonymous letter about Popery, although from time to time I used to get anonymous letters from frustrated teetotallers denouncing me for corrupting the youth of the country by giving a testimonial to the good whisky called Standfast.

When John Campbell and I started the Sea League in 1933 the following anonymous letter was sent to various leading members:

Sir,
    This is to warn you and put you on your guard against Edward Montague Compton Mackenzie, active agent at present in Scotland of the British Secret Service. *Be wary of the* Sea League *and any future schemes sponsored, framed or concluded by him for the apparent restoration of Scottish National life and prosperity as so much camouflage to cloak his real activities of paid informer and secret destroyer of all efforts in general towards any form of national unity or concerted national action.*
    Division, betrayal, and chaos are all that Scotland and every genuine Scotsman who prizes his nationality and his country's wellfare may expect from Compton Mackenzie and his associates.
    Take warning therefore
                    CLANN SCOTLAND

While we were in South America John Lorne Campbell had been sensible enough to fall in love with Margaret Fay Shaw, and this June he and she were married in Glasgow, the service being conducted in Gaelic. Margaret was a Pennsylvanian who as a girl in her 'teens had bicycled all over the Outer Isles with two other young American girls. She had been captivated by this tiny world by which I had been equally captivated, and had been spending more and more of her time there. She was completely at home in South Uist, her favourite island, and the people took her to their hearts. She was an artist with her camera, and would one day compile a remarkable book. *Folk Songs and Folk Lore in South Uist* is indispensable to all students of either.

I am writing these Octaves in the wooded recesses of the Quercy, where the people of this magical countryside of south-west France look and think so much like the people of the Outer Isles and West Highlands that I begin to play with the notion that, when the Romans were bringing Gaul into the Empire, many Gauls took ship and voyaged to Ireland whence the Gaels or Scots as Tacitus called them landed in Argyll and along the northwest of Scotland. Experts of ethnology may dismiss this as idle fancy but I shall continue to cherish it. One of the benefits conferred by old age is the experience that has taught me how often experts are wrong.

As my thoughts turn to those Gaels or Gauls of Barra with whom I spent years of such rich fellowship, two stories of this year 1935 recur to me.

One evening when I was toiling away in the Bungalow either at a *Daily Mail* review or a *Gramophone* editorial or the book I was writing there came a knock at the door and Chrissie took off the record that was being played to answer. It was Sgiuridh (Skewry) back from the Oban cattle sales. It was in the house of Sgiuridh and Bean Sgiuridh that Eric and Marjorie Linklater had spent their honeymoon. Chrissie murmured to him in Gaelic that I was working and that he must not stay too long. He explained that he had had a successful day at the sales and that he wanted me to take a dram with him. With this he dug down among his clothes and produced a bottle of whisky. Chrissie fetched two small dram glasses. Sgiuridh eyed them with a touch of disapproval before he filled them both.

"Slainte mhàth (good health)," he said draining his glass.

"Slainte mhòr (great health)," I answered, raising mine.

When we had drunk to each other in a single gulp, Sgiuridh was on the point of refilling the glasses when Chrissie shook her head.

"He has to get on with his work," she told him.

It was now Sgiuridh's turn to shake his head sadly as he put the bottle back in his pocket, and set out on the long walk to his croft in Eoligarry.

On his way across the great Cockle Strand, the Tràigh Mhòr, he brooded over that call he had made at the Bungalow and when he reached home he woke up Bean Sgiuridh who was in bed asleep.

"A terrible thing, wife, happened to me this night," he told her in Gaelic. "I went to the Coddie's bungalow to give Compton a dram, and Chrissie Chompton gave us two glasses I would be ashamed to give anybody in the poor house."

In Barra I was either Compton or Mr Mackenzie. I recall on one occasion the Crookle's being shocked when he heard the Doctor address me as 'Mackenzie'. 'Compton' was a term of respect from those who knew me well, 'Mr Mackenzie' was a term of respect from those who knew me less well. 'Mackenzie' seemed to dear Crookle a piece of vulgar familiarity.

One afternoon I was driving with three old ladies from Ardveenish, the township beyond Northbay, to the east side of the island. I was sitting by my driver in front; the three old ladies were sitting in a very tight squeeze behind. On our way we passed a rather gloomy-looking man in blue dungarees and I heard a great babble of laughter behind. I turned round to ask what the joke was but the three old ladies were still speechless with mirth. At last one of them managed to ejaculate,

"That was X— Y— we were after seeing."

The laughter bubbled and babbled again.

"What was so funny about that?" I asked.

"He does not believe there is a future life when we are all dead."

And all three of them, tightly squeezed though they were in the back seat, rocked with unquenchable mirth.

The disbeliever in the immortality of the human soul had never before been presented to me as a comic figure; now I, too, laughed with them.

Some time in this summer Eric Pinker in the U.S.A. sold the film rights of *Sylvia Scarlett* for £1,000 on which I had to pay Eric's percentage and an American agent's percentage. On top of that there was American income tax. So I had only £700 of the £1,000. Katherine Hepburn was to play Sylvia. A young English writer whose name I have forgotten wrote the script. I never saw the film but from what I was told by people who did see it Hollywood made as much of a mess of Sylvia Scarlett as Crippen made of his wife.

Some of the reviews I was writing during that year express what I was feeling about the contemporary trends of the moment:

"Authoritative novels about theatrical life seldom achieve popular success, and even less frequently gain critical esteem. Indeed, a survey of fiction would probably end in laying down as a general rule that all novels written round the arts are severely handicapped.

"I can recall two good English novels about music during this century —*Maurice Guest* by H. H. Richardson and a novel by Romer Wilson, the title of which refuses to come back to me; and there have been not more than two or three good novels about the stage.

"The popularity of *The Good Companions* was due to the fairy-tale treatment of theatrical life; nobody with first-hand knowledge of strolling players could accept it as anything else than a fairy-tale. I was therefore a little amused to read on the jacket of *Double Turn* by Audrey Lucas (Collins) that its setting lends the story much of that spirit of glamour and vagabondage which made *The Good Companions* so popular.

"Now, one of the merits of *Double Turn* is that it completely destroys the glamour of stage life and turns vagabondage into bondage. Miss Audrey Lucas, who is a daughter of the greatly loved 'E.V.', has not only written a first novel of extraordinary competence as a piece of technique and presentation of characters but she has also produced a

M

devastating commentary on the contemporary English stage and English acting.

" 'Most of all he admired Sacha Guitry, that master of effect, who can hold the house with a whisper and a minute later shatter it with a tirade. The English have been taught to call this over-acting, but the prefix is superfluous; it is just acting as the world has understood it before our leading men knew quite so much about public schools.'

"I should like to have that passage printed in large type and stuck inside every young English actor's box of make-up. Moreover, until our dramatic critics occupy the first two rows of the gallery on first nights instead of the front two rows of the stalls they will never learn how to rebuke the present fashion, and it will continue."

I am glad to find myself writing of Christopher Isherwood's *Mr Norris Changes Trains* (Hogarth Press):

"The ruthlessness of observation might be almost repellent were it not warmed by the affection which the Comic Muse bestows on her favourite votaries. All the greatest humorists have loved their victims.

"His is indeed a rare talent."

Of *We Have Been Warned* by Naomi Mitchison (Constable) I wrote:

"These ineffective Socialist dons playing with free love, these credulous enthusiasts of the Labour Party who think that peace on earth is sitting down to high tea with enthusiasts of other nations and talking platitudes in Esperanto, the mumbo-jumbo of pseudo-science, pseudo-hygiene and pseudo-psychology, they are all in Mrs Mitchison's novel and if it were not for the publisher's assurance that *We Have Been Warned* is 'full of the deep passions and implications of political partisanship'. I should have been tempted to believe that the work was a satire on modernity written by a devout student of Aristophanes.

"However, grateful though I may be to Mrs Mitchison for her give away of the other side, it is not for that reason I urge people to read her book, but because it is a completely engrossing novel."

Of *D. H. Lawrence* by E. T. (Cape) I wrote:

"This comes as a great relief after so much of the rubbish that has been written about the dead novelist. I opened it in trepidation, expecting to find the usual hysterics inside; but this exquisitely written account of Lawrence as a boy and youth and young man . . . is a profoundly moving record without a trace of false sentiment or morbid egotism."

Of *Early One Morning* (Faber and Faber) by Walter de la Mare I wrote:

"One might suppose from his modest introduction that Mr de la Mare had done no more than prepare an anthology of childhood. *Early One*

Morning certainly is the loveliest anthology of childhood ever gathered, but Mr de la Mare, with his own exquisite art, has designed an unparagoned floral arrangement amid the varied greenery of his own prose.

" 'How to describe this book?' ask the publishers justifiably lost in admiration. The reviewer who, in a couple of evenings, has had to race through nearly a quarter of a million words in which he would fain have lingered for a month, can only echo 'How?' . . .

"A few pages later on we are reading:

" 'A chimney of 1818 might be made only seven inches square; and, that being so, not only a tiny but a naked child was necessary.

" 'A master sweep, Thomas Allen, testified that he had been articled in 1795 at the age of three and a half. I have been obliged myself to go up a chimney naked, but I do not like to see my children do so.'

" 'Yet, do not let us be in too much of a hurry to impute righteousness to ourselves. In 1933 one thousand and thirty-eight children were killed on our roads and sixty to eighty children were injured or crippled every day in road accidents, while the N.S.P.C.C. has to deal with about 40,000 cases annually of various forms of cruelty to children.'

"There is no phase of childhood overlooked in this wonderful volume, and no reader will lay it down without a great enrichment of his knowledge of human nature, without a quickened sense of beauty, and without a glow of gratitude to Mr Walter de la Mare."

Is that 'wonderful volume' in print today? I hope so; it might be an antidote to some of the dregs in the Freudian cup which are being administered to University students by contemporary academic psychologists.

I am glad to find myself writing of *Peace by Ordeal* by Frank Pakenham[1] (Cape):

"From time to time, but the times are few and far between, one closes a book with an impression left upon the mind less of having read a book than of having personally assisted at some long-drawn-out, tense drama . . .

"Yet in pressing this magnificent book upon the attention of readers, I am doing so less with the idea that they should make themselves acquainted at first hand with facts which have been twisted out of all true shape by national, sectarian, and party beliefs than out of an anxiety that no reader should miss the opportunity Mr Pakenham affords him of being a well-placed spectator at one of the great dramas of history.. . .

"Without exaggeration *Ordeal by Peace* can be called a truly noble book, for it is infused with wisdom and charity and justice."

The self-conscious modernity with which too many young writers try

[1] The Earl of Longford.

to shock their elders or betters in the sexy 'sixties was already apparent in the thin-faced 'thirties.

Here is one of them:

"In a note at the end the author claims that 'the history of literary English is the history first of the adaptation of English words to Latinizing minds, and then of the making of that artificial Latinistic lingo more and more flexible, as if to disguise it as natural English. . . . For this reason one of the basic tasks of a proletarian writer . . . is to try to write a normal English based solidly on spoken English. . . . This new novel of mine is in a language which I am confident is a step forward towards what is needed.'

"Is it? Here is our pioneer novelist's final sentence:

" 'Out of the volition of the body in the gloom of the room passing through the twilight passage of sleep into another day.'

"The author's confidence in his normal English seems misplaced."

It is sad to reflect that the two four-letter words with which the young literary Adams and Eves have stripped off their fig-leaves are both of them of Latin *not* Anglo-Saxon origin. The good old Anglo-Saxon five-letter word for it went out with Chaucer.

In July of this year I wrote:

"It can hardly be much more than a year ago that there appeared a remarkable volume of personal experiences called *Down and Out in London and Paris*. It is not six months ago that there appeared an even more remarkable novel called *A Clergyman's Daughter*. Last week there was published by the same author a more remarkable book than either of its predecessors and after reading *Burmese Days* by George Orwell (Gollancz) I have no hesitation in asserting that no 'realistic' writer during the last five years has produced three volumes which can compare in directness, vigour, courage and vitality with these volumes from the pen of Mr George Orwell. . . .

"Let me make it quite clear that *Burmese Days* is not a comfortable book. . . . Every character, male or female, is presented without mercy, and with such startling actuality that the reader is left without any chance of blaming the author for looking only at the worst side of human nature. Yet in spite of its brutality there is something in Mr Orwell's writing which excludes the slightest suggestion of deliberate malice.

"Whatever may have been the motive underlying the writing of this book, the sole apparent motive is a desire, an almost passionate desire, to tell the truth. This is apparent even in his handling of the natural scene which makes us feel and taste and smell and see the tropics to a degree that has rarely been managed by the pen.

"I cannot but hope that a writer like this who can see with such horrible clearness in the dark, will find it worth while to gaze with equal determination at the light, for if Mr Orwell were equally successful in doing that it would tax imagination to set a limit to his potential achievement."

Soon after that review appeared in the *Daily Mail* I received a letter signed *Eric Blair* and underneath in inverted commas *"George Orwell"*. In this letter he told me that I was the only reviewer who seemed to understand what the three books were about. I was pleased about this because it encouraged me to suppose that I was able to distinguish between authentic contributions to English literature and anxious toadying to the mood of the moment.

In a letter to Faith from Florence that September Norman Douglas wrote:

Delighted to hear that Monty is writing the book of his life. Do give him my love.... Tell him I found Down and Out *an excellent book, and a most interesting document. Davies' Tramp book is just piffle in comparison.... I also enjoyed vastly the* Burmese Days. *I should like to make the fellow's acquaintance. . . . The* Clergyman's Daughter *would be welcome.*

For some reason I wrote to my mother this summer to ask for her memories of Karl Marx whom she had known while still in her 'teens. Among my papers I have discovered the account she sent me when she was in her eighties:

"We used to go to see Mr and Mrs Marx on Sunday afternoons, taking that awful vehicle, a four-wheel cab. They lived in a horrid little house (I thought) with a high flight of steps to the front door—a dull small street in the St John's Wood neighbourhood. I don't remember any garden at the back. Nor do I remember having tea with them, but tea wasn't by any means universal in those days. I remember as an innovation five o'clock tea as we always called it.

"Distinctly I can see Mr and Mrs Marx. I thought of him as a big man in every way, with a very large head and hair rather like 'shock-headed Peter's' way of wearing his. Mr Marx was always very kind and apparently liked us to come; he used to make fun with us. There was certainly one cat to whom he was devoted, and I think there were more than one.

"Mrs Marx was most gentle, motherly and kind, but I don't think anything much in the way of looks. Eleanor who was always called Tussie, pronounced like Pussy, was very like her father and had exactly the same frizzy hair—a sort of dust-coloured hair. She was very fond of me, and I used to be at their house more often and more intimately. Her father and mother liked me too—I expect probably because I had no notion Mr Marx was a great person and was not in the least in awe of him. I am sure he was very fond of young people.

"Eleanor was most anxious to make me take Shakespeare seriously, indeed she used to drag me to Furnivall's Shakespeare Society meetings. I was shockingly volatile and insisted on making fun of everything and everybody. Karl Marx sent his books to my mother, all of them inscribed. No doubt they were all sold at her death with everything else.

"Eleanor Marx never married, but when your father produced *Twelfth Night* at the Strand Theatre in 1886 she came to see me as Viola and was delighted to find me in Shakespeare at last. She was living then with Edward Aveling (he was called Doctor, *not* of medicine.) He had deserted his wife. After a time he deserted Eleanor Marx, and she committed suicide. I don't think any of them had any religion at all. At the time we first knew Karl Marx we had very little religion ourselves. At any rate we did very little churchgoing. Aunt Isabel and I never left off going to church, but nobody else in the family did.

"I wish I could remember more, but I'm going back to the 'sixties. I do remember what a pathetic figure Mrs Marx was, of course *devoted* to her husband and daughter, the only one left of a large family; and I do remember a sort of weight one felt in being with them which I expect caused me to be utterly flippant. Indeed, at that time of my life it was the only way I managed to get through and help Aunt Isabel through also. One looks back and thinks how different one might have been, but one did not see how, and I still doubt what else one could have been."

My mother, now in her eighty-third year, who had started the Theatre Girls Club at 59 Greek Street, in 1915, had the pleasure in September 1935 of getting it incorporated by the Board of Trade. Here is an extract from the advertisement in various newspapers:

"Notice is hereby given that in pursuance of the 18th Section of the Companies Act, 1929, application has been made to the Board of Trade for a licence directing an Association about to be formed under the name of The Theatre Girls' Club to be registered with limited liability without the addition of the word 'Limited' to its name."

Thus the preliminary to a quarter of a column of small print telling what the Club was doing and winding up by warning all and sundry that if any people objected to this application they must notify the Comptroller of the Companies Department at the Board of Trade by October 10th.

What amused me was the permission to leave out 'limited' from the Club's name: its inclusion would suggest to the public that it was a money-making concern and not a charitable institution.

In a letter to congratulate my mother that October I wrote:

You mustn't believe too much of what you read in the English press about the Italians. I'm afraid the possibility of having to fight for our cotton interests in the Sudan is dictating the tune. We have behaved on many occasions just as badly as the Italians and would do it again if there were any land we wanted to grab. If it was justifiable for the French to overrun Morocco and for us to overrun Egypt the Italians can hardly be blamed for supposing it is equally justifiable for them to overrun Abyssinia. I hate all these imperialistic wars, and I find this orgy of self-righteousness in which we are indulging extremely unpleasant. . . .

I'm rather hoping that the Bishop of Argyll will be sufficiently recovered of his cataract operation to say Mass in Suidheachan—pronounced Sooyechan—on St Andrew's day. Faith is doing a terrific job over the furniture.

And indeed she was. She had come up to Barra in August with Colin Summerford for a fortnight when the house had been far enough advanced for her to see what the various rooms would want. Her book *The Cardinal's Niece* had gone into a second edition and she was full of plans for future work. *The Gramophone* was growing stronger all the time and she was devoting herself to the editorial side of it, her brother Christopher being now much preoccupied not only with his work for the B.B.C. but also with Radio Luxemburg. The flat in Dryden Chambers was being given up and Faith had taken on what she called the Loosebox. This was three rooms over the stables of Bridgefoot which Martin Secker had made and in which as I write these words he now lives in his eighty-fifth year. Nicolas Nadegine's marriage had broken up and his ex-wife was going to marry Kerensky. So he was given temporary asylum in the Loosebox.

I had finished with *Catholicism in Scotland* and had gone back to *The East Wind of Love*, when my financial plans were badly upset at the end of November by receiving a letter from the new editor of the *Daily Mail* to say that they were not going on with a star reviewer after the New Year because the expense of the Abyssinian war was making it necessary to rely on the newspaper's staff for reviewing. In one way I was relieved by the news because five years of reviewing had been a strain. Apart from a month off during the South American trip and a month off this year I had not missed a week. At the same time, the furnishing of Suidheachan, the extra £500 on the building due to be paid by the end of the year, and the need to maintain my monthly payments for Income Tax was going to make it difficult for me to find the money for current expenses.

The East Wind of Love had grown in bulk and I could see no prospect of having it and *The South Wind* finished before June in the following year. So I wrote to Newman Flower and asked him whether if I let him have another novel by the end of January it could count as an extra to our agreement. The novel I proposed to write would be called *Figure of Eight*. With his usual quick sympathy he told me to go ahead.

He did have one disappointment for me. Macartney who had finished *Walls Have Mouths* was now in London, and I sent him along to Cassells,

feeling pretty sure Newman Flower would accept the book for publication. However, he turned it down at once because he thought it might
involve Cassells in libel actions.

On November 25th I was writing to Faith:

*Just a line to let you know we hope to get into Suidheachan on Thursday, but
in any case Mass will be said there at 10 a.m. on November 30th, our thirtieth
wedding anniversary. I hope all goes well in the Loosebox. I'm in an inconceivable
state of business with books, curtains, records, furniture arriving and everything to
be transported after landing for 8 miles. The house is exquisite, thanks to your
marvellous furniture-shopping. The cats and Nellie Boyte have arrived and decided
that Suidheachan suits them.*

The Bishop of Argyll was unable to say Mass on St Andrew's Day,
and Father John Macmillan was in Glasgow. So Mass was said by Father
Dominic MacKellaig with Father John MacQueen and P. J. Martin,
the headmaster of the Castlebay school, managing the music. There
were about 200 crofters with their wives and children present. That they
all squeezed themselves in was almost a miracle.

A week later just as I was going to start *Figure of Eight* I went down
with an acute chill.

On December 20th I was writing to my mother:

*I have had a nasty go of bronchitis, a chill on the bowels and sciatica coinciding,
and I've been in bed for a fortnight. However, I was lucky to avoid pneumonia and
must not grumble. Still, it is a great bore with so much to arrange. I'm beginning
to wonder if I'll be up for Christmas. Yet we are having exquisite weather here—
cold but windless and clear—with the Aurora Borealis very brilliant every night.
I'm sorry to hear of so much fog in London. This island is mercifully free of fog—
only three days of sea mist in the year. . . .*

I know the loss of the Daily Mail *is a blessing in disguise but the disguise is a
heavy one at the moment because I am pushed for money. The Four Winds are
now as windless as the weather and somehow I must finish a different novel by the
end of January. I had meant to start this novel a fortnight ago but perhaps the
extra time to meditate on its construction is another blessing in disguise.*

I was meditating on the international situation more than *Figure of
Eight* during those days in bed. What seemed to me the ill-inspired
emotion of the British public about Abyssinia and their apparent
indifference to the persecution of the Jews launched by that 'bloodthirsty
guttersnipe' as Winston Churchill would one day call him in a broadcast,
was perturbing. I had had no belief in the effectiveness of the League of
Nations since they had climbed down to Mussolini after his outrageous
onslaught on Greece. I had no vestige of admiration for Mussolini but
it was impossible to pretend that he was not securely in power and I was
afraid that the sympathy he was getting from the Nazis over Abyssinia

would lead him to abandon his attitude over Austria. Whatever might have been Sir Samuel Hoare's prejudice in favour of Italy I felt he was more likely to be a successful Foreign Minister than Anthony Eden with his prejudice against Italy as Minister without Portfolio for League of Nations Affairs.

The only thing that cheered me up that December was the statesman-like behaviour of King George when he returned to Greece as monarch.

Mrs Roebuck came up to spend Christmas with us and from that visit I can date the passion Chrissie conceived for cooking, a passion which would inspire her to ever more remarkable culinary achievements for the next quarter of a century. Christina Roebuck, Christina MacPherson of Skye before she married, was a cook of genius who had had many years in America before she separated from her husband and came to live in Edinburgh with her only daughter Betty, who was now about sixteen and a student of the piano of which she became a teacher. That flat at One South Charlotte Street was the centre of all that was most truly gay in the Edinburgh of those years. Moray McLaren lodged with her until he came down to London in this autumn of 1935 and took over 16 Dryden Chambers. I shall not attempt to evoke Christina Roebuck herself because those who knew and loved her will reproach me for failing to bring her to life on the printed page and those who did not know her will suppose I am indulging in fantasy.

I could recall so many festive ceilidhs lasting until the small hours but *où sont les neiges d'antan?* Where are the snows of yester year? One story only I shall allow myself, to which I cannot give an exact date.

When David Cleghorn Thomson left the B.B.C. he took a cottage in Sussex but the call of Edinburgh was not to be denied and he made up his mind to start a literary monthly to be called *Scottish Bookman*. One day in the Savile he told me of this project and the more enthusiastic David became over it the more I felt inclined to cool that enthusiasm. Finally I left for Edinburgh by the first train around 9 p.m. and next morning when I emerged from the Caledonian Hotel I ran into Eric Linklater.

"The very man I wanted to see," I exclaimed. "David Cleghorn is proposing to start a literary monthly in Edinburgh and he must be dissuaded from doing so. Let's go along to the Roebucks' and we can talk over a way to dissuade him. You realize what it will mean? You and I will be called upon to contribute to it every month. It will cost David a lot of money because no literary monthly in Edinburgh can possibly make money. Yes, I know *Blackwood's* is still full of life but the *Edinburgh Quarterly* could not survive."

When we reached South Charlotte Street I told Eric of my plan for David's future.

"He should become a minister," I said. "He will be a fashionable young minister and in due course he will be called to a fashionable church. In time he will undoubtedly become Moderator of the Church of Scotland, and you know how much David will enjoy the ruffles and the three-cornered hat and the knee-breeches."

Eric in his deepest voice agreed.

"Then it's our duty, Eric, to persuade David to become a minister."

As I said this the door of that room in South Charlotte Street, with its view of the Castle, opened and David Cleghorn Thomson whom I had left in the Savile the evening before came in.

I have seldom been completely taken aback in my life; I have certainly never been so completely taken aback as I was at that moment. In my confusion I lost my presence of mind.

"Hullo, David," I said, trying not to look surprised by his presence in Edinburgh. "Eric and I were just talking about you. We were saying what a splendid idea it would be if you became a minister."

"Thanks very much," said David. "But I happen to be an Episcopalian. After our talk yesterday evening I decided to come up to Edinburgh. I just had time to catch the train after yours. I'm glad I've found you both. I want to talk about this literary monthly I am going to start."

Eric Linklater and I were defeated.

Mrs Roebuck and Chrissie had a great time with our Christmas goose, and knowing what a disappointment it would be if I did not get up for dinner I made the effort to do so, but was back in bed next day.

I had written to Veronica for her fifteenth birthday on December 2nd and she wrote back on December 11th:

Darling Monty,

I loved your book and letter, thank you so much for remembering. How horrible to be laid up with sciatica just when you are moving in to the new house. . . .

Do you think 15 is a great age? It seems to have come very slowly to me, and the only thing which has really marked its arrival is a beautiful, long pale pink summer dress, which I shall wear with much assured self-assurance and, I hope, great effect during the holidays. . . .

I wish you would come to the mainland just for a week, Christmas week, and then we could have the usual family party and play 'Chase' after tea.

I have got a beautiful new pair of scarlet tap dancing shoes, they will make an 'effet bœuf' at the dancing class as all the others have dull black or brown ones.

When will The Four Winds of Love *be published? You must surely have finished it by now.*

.   .   .   .   .

Please give my love to everyone I know in Barra.

            Lots of my love and a fifteen years old kiss

                                      Veronica

Zelle sends her love.

I wrote to that beloved child for Christmas and she wrote back on December 26th:

Dearest Monty

I loved your letter although it makes me a trifle gloomworthy.

I should love to have lunch with you at Eilean Aigas again—and pine for the sight of someone conducting 'Carmen' with the hearth-brush!

. . . . . .

I am being coddled back to perfect health again with maddening ease. I had my appendix removed in August and of course did much too much after it was out—with the result that I have been treated as a (pseudo) invalid ever since. I languish on sofas and call for sal volatile at frequent intervals.

A blessing is that I can't go back to the Convent—of which I had my last bitter experience last summer. . . .

I'm so glad you are awed by my immense age. I do hope I look it but I'm afraid I shall always seem hopelessly young till my hair is permanently up. I put it up already now and then but I have to live up to it to such an extent that it really is a nuisance!

I think I have got on quite well with my piano (smug?) I am going to learn the moonlight sonata in the holidays, I think—but at the moment I am playing Rachmaninoff's prelude in C minor—and am struggling with reels for Shimi's amusement.

I think it is mostly through your influence that I love music and poetry and books so much and I shall never stop being grateful to you for awakening it in me.

Your always loving
Veronica

Very few things in my life have given me as much pleasure as that letter. The letters of that beloved child from nine years old until now are very precious manuscripts.

I had written to thank her for that last letter and on January 15th she wrote for my birthday:

Darling Monty

Guy and Pauline is quite lovely and thank you a million times for sending it to me. . . .

I am so glad that you were pleased to know that I was grateful to you for beginning my artistic education. It is absolutely true and I shall never stop being grateful, although I was terrified of your thinking me affected when I said so.

I have like the rest of the British public school class (curse their silly conventional blockheads!) a horror of being thought in any way different from my fellow humans. The thought of expressing any deep emotional or artistic feeling in words, and then not being understood and laughed at, sends me into quite idiotic panic.

Luckily I have the grace to laugh at myself and condemn my folly—still I never have the courage to speak of my real feelings about books and music to anyone, even Mummy. Yet I haven't grown shy, I promise you that! I am continually having my forward behaviour repressed, but I don't care much. I hate the bashful—wriggle and finger-in-the-mouth attitude. It's much more fun to have a million usual friends in the world and a few real ones than knowing just a few family ones already broken in by one's relations' approval.

I really do love G. and P. It and Carnival are both upon my favourite books list (that sounds rather like a reviewer's cliché). I showed Hugh the bit about undergraduates and their silly synicism (?). It might really be an epigram on Hugh— so exactly like is it. I have been teasing him a lot about it and it proved my point beautifully.

I makes me feel frightfully old, seeing through Hugh's synic and bitter pose at Balliol. It only makes him look frightfully young and inexperienced (because everyone knows that he has got the kindest heart in the world). Yet here he goes on, trying to be grand and sophisticated by pretending to have a ruthless and warped nature! His every word tastes of lemon and Oscar Wilde, yet he makes me laugh till I cry— which naturally enrages him!

I now hate my Rachmaninoff. It seems just an empty thump. I always thought it must have some morbidly passionate meaning behind all that noise but if it has I haven't found it yet, and I have grave doubts of its just being one big 'blague'.

By the way I refuse to read Scott! It isn't his stiffness I hate (give me 30 Dickens 20 Jane Austen and 10 Trollopes to 1 Sir W.), but I always feel he isn't a bit genuine and anyway the border country is very disappointing. The whole of the lovely Tweed valley is marred by Abbotsford's monstrosity. . . .

We had a dance 3 days ago. It was simply lovely. There were 100 kilts and about the same skirts so altogether about 200 people came. I danced every dance and my dress which was tulle was so torn at the end that it had to be pinned up in a bustle by the kilt pins of Colin Mackenzie and Allan Cameron which they nearly skewered through me.

I do hate my writing, it won't grow up and looks just as bad in ink or pencil. I think I'll learn speed writing which disguises bad handwriting in illegibility, like someone I know!

Your very loving

Veronica

Isn't this a monster letter

I had just written to wish my mother a happy New Year and many happy returns of her 83rd birthday. '83!' I had written, how little realizing that when I became 83 a note of exclamation would seem absurd.

On that 83rd birthday of my mother I started *Figure of Eight,* packed with thermogen and praying to keep bronchitis and the spasms of sciatica at bay.

FIFTY-THREE YEARS OLD: 1936

IN the autumn of this year I was to give a broadcast from London called *Living Off the Map*; the next two years of this Octave will be easier to follow against that background and therefore I give it here, in a way in order to postpone recalling that infernal January.

"In most maps of Scotland the Southern islands of the Outer Hebrides break through that thickened line of longitude by which maps are commonly framed, and find themselves in the margin, and so it really is not too fanciful to call life on the island of Barra living off the map. To be frank, I am not so very anxious to talk about that life, because one of the charms of such a life is its genuine remoteness from much of what many people consider important, and I should hate to give an impression that living on a small island on the edge of the Atlantic Ocean is intended to convey any kind of a challenge to those who live elsewhere. So before going any further do let me protest that the last reason for spending all my time on a small island some eight or nine miles long and at its greatest breadth scarcely four miles across is a desire to escape from the world. Why, one does not escape even from motor cars and lorries on Barra; we have about twenty of them on our twenty miles of degraded roads. In calling our roads degraded I refer to their surface. In every other respect those twenty miles could hold their own with any twenty miles over which I have driven.

"Here is the round. Southward, to Castlebay, the port of Barra, with its fleet of drifters all through the summer, its herring-gutting stations and its ruined mediaeval castle on a rock in the middle of the harbour, and beyond in the sun's eye, the shapes of green island after green island merging into a sea of molten silver. Eastward, the slate-blue waters of the Minch, and on a clear day, in winter for choice, the mountains of the mainland sixty or seventy miles away, riding along the horizon like snowy galleons; and nearer, the jagged peaks of Rum and Skye, and Canna like a great whale, and Ben More of Mull floating free from the rest of that lovely island from here invisible. Westward, the Atlantic, pale blue or golden or crimson-flecked in the sunset, rolling in upon desolate beaches of white sand. Nothing now between you in your car and the coast of Labrador except that ocean, by the edge of which runs the machair as we call it, which means the grassy sward dressed with lime by the blown sand and powdered shells, where white and red clover grow thick, and, in their season, primroses and a hundred other flowers. Northward, an absolutely level square mile of beach composed of thousands of years of cockle-shells over which the tide flows sometimes sky-blue, sometimes dove-grey, sometimes a pale green, the colour of a cowslip spathe. Beyond this cockle strand stretches the sound between Barra and South Uist, which can be a richer ultramarine than any stretch of water on this side of the Mediterranean; beyond, Ben More of Uist, not unlike Vesuvius from here, and the white beach of Eriskay, the first Scottish ground trodden by Prince Charles Edward. I suppose we ought not to grumble at the metal of the road, for as Hamlet says 'Here's metal more attractive'.

"The heart of the island consists of a rolling moorland rising to a highest hill of 1,300 feet, with glens and lochs and burns and heather; in fact, a miniature of the Highlands without the pines and birches, and though I would not sniff at a few grand old *pinus sylvestris* of the aboriginal stock, I would far sooner have no trees at all than endure the outrage to the landscape which is usually inflicted by departmental afforestation. Some people think the Scottish countryside is improved by plastering it with slabs of monotonous green in the shape of Douglas firs planted in straight rows at regular intervals. I do not. Spinach is all right with a poached egg; a landscape apparently smeared with spinach is all wrong. And that is the usual effect of the afforestation going on at present.

"The heart of the island provides all the solitude a normal human being should want, but do not suppose that Barra is a melancholy spot in which the few remaining inhabitants left behind by the tide of progress are eking out a parlous existence by the uncertain glimmer of the Celtic twilight.

"On the contrary, Barra has as many people as it can comfortably hold—two thousand two hundred and fifty at the last census with an extra four or five hundred in the summer months when the herring boats are at work. What do the people do? Well, they cultivate their crofts—many of them would fish if the inshore fishing had not been ruined by the intensive trawling since the war. The young men go to sea. The young women go away to service or work at the gutting of the herring as far north as Lerwick or as far south as Yarmouth. But there are always plenty of young men and young women on the island, and the dances which are held all the year round except during Lent and Advent in one or other of the three parish-halls are, often enough, too full. Barra is an extraordinarily happy place. Laughter is the keynote. There is always a good story going the rounds. Gaelic is a great language for wit, and with three-quarters of the population of Barra speaking both Gaelic and English, the native Gaelic wit salts the English. And it is not empty laughter. Barra passed through some fierce ordeals during the last three centuries in the way of persecution, evictions and famine, but I do not want to harrow your feelings by dragging up the old unhappy past. The point I would make is that the laughter of Barra has experience behind it. It is a mellow fruit which has ripened after a frosty spring.

"Nine visitors out of ten, when asked how they are enjoying their stay on the island, reply not with praise of the scenery but with praise of the people. One of the reasons for that is the remarkable cosmopolitan outlook of the people due to so many of them having travelled the world over. It is a curious, but an extremely pleasant, combination of shyness with good manners and savoir faire. I have a habit of working all night when I am interested in some book. When I am doing that I do not get up before the afternoon. Now, you can do that sort of thing in Italy, and you can do it in Ireland, and you can do it in Barra, and have it accepted for what it is—perfectly natural behaviour for a man who orders his life to achieve some end. In lots of places it would be deemed eccentricity, and no sane man wants to be surrounded by people who consider him eccentric. The tyranny of time, so excessive in some parts of the world, does not exist in the Outer Isles, nor, indeed, anywhere in the West Highlands.

"There is a story told of the late Lord Leverhulme explaining to an old Lewis man what he wanted him to get through in a day's work and of the old man's replying: 'But, my lord, you are not giving us any time for contemplation.' Early to bed and early to rise makes a man healthy, wealthy and wise. Wealthy it might make him. His health it would certainly not interfere with. But wise, no! The people in the Outer Hebrides go to bed late and rise late. They are certainly not wealthy but they are profoundly wise. And there is a great deal to be said for living off the map in that unchartered sea of margin if wisdom is esteemed above wealth. In high summer nobody goes to bed till late because the pearly shimmer of the Hebridean midnight simply cannot be wasted in sleep. And in winter nobody goes to bed till late, because there is no point in getting up before the long protracted morning twilight has become full day. A dance in Barra seldom starts properly until well after midnight, even in winter. And apropos of winter, let me disabuse you of the notion that the Outer Islands have a savage wintry climate. On the contrary, they have one of the best winter climates I have experienced. That there will be gales goes without saying, but gales beside the Atlantic give you your money's worth, and between the gales there are halcyon interludes, days of such surpassing loveliness and clarity that the islands seem to float suspended between earth and heaven in a crystal globe, nights when the shafts of the Aurora Borealis dance across the sky above the curlews fluting in greedy triumph by the ebb, above the wild swans on the loch, and the otter at his supple sport. I remember driving the Christmas before last about sixty miles in an open car from Tarbert in Harris to the Butt of Lewis, the sun warm upon our backs all the way. Our mean temperature is the same as Devonshire, and in Barra the rainfall is well under 40 inches, for we are away from the great hills of Harris and Skye. As for snow, we seldom see it, and when it does fall it

lies only for a few hours. With a proper sense of commiseration I have to
inform people in the warm south that this summer from the end of April
until the end of July we hardly had a wet day. There were a couple of
wet, gusty weeks in August, but they were followed by a most exquisite
September. I shall not pretend that gusty summers are unknown in the
Outer Hebrides, but during the last five years I have not known one
intolerable winter. As for the mist in which we are popularly supposed
to be wrapped, I can assure you that few parts of the British Isles are so
free from it.

"Still, it is not the magic of the seascape, unequalled away from the
Aegean Islands; it is not the climate, which if you can stand plenty of
wind really is most agreeable; it is not the pleasure of having at least
twenty small desert islands easily within reach of a boat; it is not the
variety of the flora and fauna; it is not the relief of getting only three
posts a week; it is not the convenience of having an aeroplane from
Renfrew land on the beach not fifty yards from your door in case you
must go away; it is not even the absence of Sunday newspapers which
for me gives its greatest charm to living off the map in that particular
gap in the line of longitude made by Barra; no, it is not any of these things.
For me it is the pleasure of living intimately in a small community which
is a microcosm of the great world, with one important difference, however, and that is that everybody in it is a real person; the way that life
on the map is moving just now does make it more and more difficult for
people to be themselves. Just as the life of the island as a whole is marked
by a certain completeness and distinction, so are the lives of the individuals who make up this small community. The mere fact that so many
of the men have nicknames is an expression of this individuality. You
will remember that the award of a nickname at school always used to
be a pledge of individuality, even if sometimes it was not a complimentary nickname. That completeness of the place and people undoubtedly creates a sense of detachment, which I daresay many would
call self-sufficiency, but we are a large enough and vital enough community to be able to be self-sufficient, and, as I have said before, the
wide experience of the world from seafaring which you will find all over
the island destroys the self-sufficiency that springs from ignorance.
Throughout the whole length of the Outer Hebrides there is no decline
in population, such as is going on all the time in most of the Inner
Hebrides and on the mainland of the West of Scotland. . . . Liberty is
still esteemed out there, and the continuous sapping of liberty is the first
thing of which I am painfully aware when I find myself on the map
again.

"I shall not brag that we can escape altogether from the minor horrors
of civilization. Rates and taxes are still demanded. Forms have to be
filled. Licences have to be taken out. The abominable state of the roads

C.M. describes the size of a baby seal to Lord
Moyne's party who came to Barra

Christina MacSweer.
in Buenos Aires

The Coddie and his wife

Father John Macmillan

is not considered an excuse for carrying more passengers for hire than the regulations permit. Still, departure from the islands always oppresses my spirit with the fancy that I am exchanging freedom for restriction, and I will claim that so far as it is possible to preserve a semblance of liberty in the Europe of to-day we do preserve it in the Outer Isles. So much of the land has been fought for by the people and won within the last fifteen years. In 1886 they had to send the Royal Scots and the Royal Marines to deal with the crofters of Lewis, and the crofters won. In Harris not ten years ago men were in prison for raiding land, but the land has been won and kept. In Barra the last big raid took place about fifteen years back, and where for centuries the larks sang in spring above a desert they sing now above forty cultivated crofts and well built homesteads. The cry of depopulation goes up not only from all over the Highlands of Scotland, but also from the rural districts all over Great Britain. On this little island off the map we have six schools with over four hundred pupils.

"In a neighbouring island owned by one man, the most fertile in the west, there has been a solitary marriage during the last quarter of a century. In Barra marriages are a rising market, though unfortunately it has become a habit of the young people to go to the mainland for a dull, commonplace ceremony vastly inferior in every way to the wedding they could have at home."

I have dug out that old broadcast at this point because the memory of Barra it brings back to me explains to myself how I was able to write and revise and send off the typescript to Cassell's of a novel of over 100,000 words in exactly thirty-one days. Nellie Boyte typed away all day at my manuscript; Chrissie MacSween sat up playing the gramophone with the huge E.M.G. horn till 3 a.m. I sat on in my chair till 6 a.m., went to bed and slept till 2.30 p.m. Sensibly I made Sunday a night of rest and recreation. Every Sunday evening we had a gathering in the billiards-room and library at which we played one-life pool and later a variant of slosh I invented. At this gathering, sometimes as many as twenty, there were usually present the priests, the doctor, the schoolmasters, the Coddie, the Crookle and other Barra personalities with Inverneill and an occasional visitor from the mainland. Young Inverneill as I think of John Campbell in those days performed within my experience an unique feat of concentration in a billiards-room. He used to sit back on the narrow ledge in front of the bookshelves deep in one of the books without paying the least attention to the performance of his rivals. Then when the time came for him to play his ball the book would be put down on the ledge and his shot played, after which he would return to the book until his turn came again. In spite of his apparent complete remoteness from the game he would sometimes preserve his one life and scoop that penny pool.

N

Good news came from Faith the day after I had started *Figure of Eight*. William Collins had agreed to take the volume of autobiography she was proposing to write under the title *As Much as I Dare*:

They are going to give £100 advance. When I shall be able to start on it I don't know but they are not hurrying me. 'Billy' Collins is a dear young man rather like Eric Maschwitz to look at. He said the loss of your reviews in the Daily Mail *was a very serious one for publishers. I said "then why didn't you all advertise and keep them going?" He said your reviews were the only ones that definitely made a difference to sales.*

I had been cheered up by getting about half a dozen letters from publishers to say how sorry they were I was no longer reviewing.

Chrissie was very tired by the middle of the month and I was relieved and grateful when her mother came down from Harris and really took on all the household work. I had written to Faith on January 13th:

The real strain of the house falls on Chrissie who is working like a drudge—scrubbing, washing up, cooking, etc. . . . .

I am sending with this the two essays in the Bach Competition, which I want printed. I really had rather a job deciding, because so many of them were excellent. However, I don't think any of the other competitors will grudge my awarding the prize to the colliery fitter.

I am up till six every morning with Figure of Eight *and two-fifths through. I have had to forbid Chrissie to sit up and play the gramophone. It is too tiring for her. Luckily the Marconi wireless set is behaving marvellously. I now amuse myself at about 4 a.m. by the American stations of yesterday cutting in on the Russian stations of to-day.*

We used to get America easily and clearly with a small Marconi set all through the war. I heard clearly every one of F. D. Roosevelt's fireside chats.

I was writing to Faith on my birthday:

This is all I can arrange for the February Gramophone *editorial. I'm too tired after working till 6 a.m. to dictate when I wake up next afternoon because it makes me tired when I start off again on the book. . . .*

Chrissie's mother arrived yesterday evening for a fortnight and has been a great help already. She did the whole corridor herself this morning and I didn't hear a sound! I have given myself the book half finished for a birthday present.

On January 21st I was writing to Faith:

Chrissie is much better. I shall complete 2/3 of the book to-night. I wish so much time did not have to be wasted on letters—forty by the last post. There's a new Inland Revenue chap at Inverness and of course he has to suspect everything that was settled with his predecessor. That is the first job an Inspector has to do when he moves to a new area. So I've had to dictate endless replies to endless questions all of which were answered when we came to Eilean Aigas. But why do I moan? I have a house I like, furniture I like, a study I like and people round me I love. As long as I don't expire I shall be pretty well all right in 3 years, and after all I do really enjoy work better than anything else. . . .

The cold down south is reaching us now. It seems to be all over Europe. . . . Owing to not going to bed till 6 and not waking until 2 or 3 I find it difficult to deal with problems like the matting for the corridors. I start work again as soon as I've done my post. I'm coddling myself a good deal. In fact I haven't been out of the house for six weeks. Plenty of exercise every Sunday at billiards. . . .

I think the B.B.C. are overdoing the King's death. Baldwin was quite intolerable last night. He impresses me with complete insincerity, but in justice to him I daresay he doesn't think he's a humbug, so perhaps he cannot be called a humbug.

On January 24th Faith wrote:

I'm going to see the funeral from the roof of St James's Palace with the Godefrois. . . . Did you read that the cross fell off the crown at the feet of Edward in the procession from King's X to Westminster Hall? It was picked up by a Guardsman and refixed by Crown jeweller for the lying-in state. An ominous occurrence.

On January 29th Faith wrote:

I had a grand view of the funeral—a really most beautiful sight. From this roof of St James's one could see it coming behind the trees of the Mall and then turning the corner and right beneath us. What was most moving was that the gun carriage was preceded by a mass of pipers, more than 100, playing 'Speed bonny boat' which no doubt you'll disapprove of as Charles Edward's own song, but the thrill as it came nearer and burst upon us was indescribable. The King marched with studied nonchalance, but his hands were clenching and unclenching.

The death of Rudyard Kipling while the bulletins about the health of the King were being issued made much less impression on the public than it should have. With the foolish belief of young men that older men will last for ever I had never taken the opportunities I had had from time to time to meet him, partly because I was out of sympathy with his point of view and partly because we supposed he was always rude to young men. By now I had realized his genius and in my depression about the will o' the wisps of Safety First and Collective Security which were leading the 'National' Government deeper into a morass I began to appreciate what Rudyard Kipling had stood for.

This year was to see the deaths of many people by whom the tenor of my life had been affected. I had been much concerned when Venizelos had associated himself with that abortive republican coup in the previous year but I had been much relieved when King George II had shown so much generosity on his return to Greece. I have already written much about Venizelos. Let me say no more now than reaffirm my conviction of his true greatness as a statesman and a man.

Cunninghame Graham had gone out to Buenos Aires in that spring to be present at the 'christening' of a new town which the Argentine Government were calling 'Don Roberto'. He died just before the ceremony took place. I have many letters from him which I should have liked to publish but they are almost all of them literally undecipherable owing to his increasing blindness. In the last of them written from Buenos Aires he had told me that he was determined to visit me in Barra when he returned to Scotland. Alas, only the mortal remains of that modern Bayard *sans peur et sans rapproche* came home.

G. K. Chesterton died. Mrs Chesterton wrote from Top Meadow, Beaconsfield that June:

Dear Compton Mackenzie,

It was good of you to write: I know he always spoke so warmly about you and valued your friendship. Much of what he stood for will go under, but not everything, because as he wrote
"My name is Lazarus and I live."
Thank you for your Mass for him on St Peter and Paul's Day—my birthday and our wedding day.

Yours gratefully

Frances Chesterton

G. K. C. left St Paul's only five terms before I went to the School. Yet he was nine years older than I. I can add nothing to the epitaph on his memorial card written by a great English poet:

> Knight of the Holy Ghost, he goes his way,
> Wisdom his motley, Truth his loving jest;
> The mills of Satan keep his lance in play,
> Pity and Innocence his heart at rest.
>
> Walter de la Mare

In the following month Robert Rait died. I have tried elsewhere in this Octave to express some of the warmth of my gratitude to him, and to his wife and two daughters for their kindness during my Rectorship. I was deeply touched by Lady Rait's letter in reply to mine.

I need not tell you how fond Bob was of you, or how much he enjoyed working with you as Lord Rector. Those years were so happy, happy for us and for the University.

Gerald Gould died. He was at Magdalen just after me and I did not know him intimately. I could be grateful to him for many generous reviews in the *Observer*. His son Michael Ayrton who at fourteen seemed rather older than his father is a much valued friend for whose genuinely creative criticism I have a high regard and with whom talk at the Savile is one of the pleasures to which I look forward on my rare visits to London.

Maxim Gorky died, bringing back memories of Capri. Charles Aitken died, bringing back memories of Church Row, Hampstead. My cousin Emily Symonds died. She followed in the tradition of women writers by calling herself 'George' Paston under which pseudonym she wrote some successful plays. My old friend Henry Lygon died after a long and painful illness. And what memories he brought back of Oxford. A great loss to the Savile and to English singing was the death of Plunket Greene.

Faith's elder brother E. W. Stone died early in that year. 'Foxy' Stone as he was called at Eton was as unlike a fox as can be imagined. I was all that he disapproved of theoretically and *Sinister Street* all that he disapproved of in literature. Nevertheless, he always showed me the greatest kindness, and although he was worried by my dedication of the first volume of *Sinister Street* to his father I like to think that he would have been pleased by the dedication of my Fifth Octave to his son Reynolds.

And now back to that financially backward spring of 1936.

On February 7th I wrote to Ralph Pinker:

The complete manuscript of Figure of Eight *has gone off to you to-day. I couldn't get it off on Wednesday because the boat did not come with the gale. . . .*

Besides the £500 for Paterson I am now overdrawn in the Beauly bank for £68 and they are pressing for this to be covered immediately, in fact they have been pressing for the last month. Something must be done to keep me going while I am finishing off the first half of The Four Winds.

I have fended off the Income Tax people with post-dated cheques, but I must have enough ready money to keep my household going or I shall crash. A fortnight's work would finish the first quarter of The Four Winds *ready for press; if it appeared as* The East Wind of Love *it would have as much chance as the first part of* Sinister Street.

I am not in favour of publishing it in two big lumps, but if that is considered imperative, the means must be found to support me while I am doing it. I could sit down to-morrow and finish another novel in six weeks but that would only mean postponing progress with The Four Winds. *No very large sum of money is required, once this £500 is sent to Paterson and the overdraft on the Beauly bank has been covered, but I must have some assurance of being able to carry on during the next six months.*

A fortnight later the £500 was sent to Paterson for the extras to be paid over the building of Suidheachan. I had been in a good deal of pain all through February after finishing *Figure of Eight*. A letter from Ralph Pinker on March 2nd was not an analgesic.

I had rather a shock at the end of last week when Newman rang me up in a state of great agitation to say that Figure of Eight *was not really a novel in the technical sense of the word but a volume of stories and, as such, could not be expected to sell anything like a sufficient number of copies to justify the advance they have paid on it. I took the galleys home this week-end and I find it hard to combat Flower's assertion. . . . It is essential for us somehow to obtain payments on account of the next book spaced out for the next months but the trouble over* Figure of Eight *has made things difficult. Flower also raised the point of the book that has just been announced by Routledge—I was in a bit of a hole there, because you had not told me anything about it.*

To that I replied on March 6th:

"I do not accept either your or Newman's opinion that *Figure of Eight* is a collection of short stories. The construction of the novel was made perfectly clear in the synopsis I sent and if that criticism was going to be made it should have been made then by you or Newman.

"It would be impossible to get eight complete short stories out of the book which would stand publication *without* the weaving of the various incidents into the pattern I have made. However, it is idle to argue about my own work like this; the only possible test is criticism and circulation. If the book is regarded by reviewers as a collection of short stories, and if the advance is not earned Newman knows perfectly well that I would never dream of letting him down and that I should be willing to have the deficit subtracted from another novel.

"At the present moment I have been in bed nearly three weeks with severe influenza and this damned sciatica. The possibility of coming down to London as you suggest is out of the question before the weather improves. In any case I haven't the money to travel. This is not a figure of speech. I have in actual cash less than £30 and my account at the Beauly bank is now overdrawn for £148. I have to meet these Income Tax cheques every month. £30 at present and next month £50.

"I have just refused, because Newman objected, £100 from Hodder and Stoughton with another £400 as soon as the Pericles biography was delivered any time during the next year. *Catholicism in Scotland* was asked for nearly two years ago and I wrote it to help a man who is now dead (Grassic Gibbon). It was written at odd moments and sent off last summer. There was no secret over the book; it was announced by Routledge long ago in a series called *The Voice of Scotland*. The £100 I received was devoted to religious and political objects. I suppose the next thing that will be resented is that I am writing an introduction for Macartney's penal servitude book which Gollancz is publishing only after Flower turned it down.

"My position is that by the end of this month I shall have the manuscript ready of what would be considered a complete novel if I had not revealed that it was the first quarter of a novel. This is regarded by people who have read it as the best thing I have written, but after your reception of *Figure of Eight* I am thoroughly shaken about other people's opinions. It was my intention to complete the second part by the end of June and offer Newman what will amount to two long novels as one.

"Both you and Newman seemed to desire to keep me in spite of the temporary inconvenience of such a client. I gave you both a chance sometime ago to be quit of me, because I was feeling then that I was a burden. Either you and Newman are able to see me through this year because you have confidence in my work, or you have lost confidence in my work and are not willing to see me through this year. Give me a candid answer whether you do want me to continue with you both. To be frank, this reception of *Figure of Eight* suggests that you are both looking for an excuse to force a rupture."

The day after that letter to Pinker I wrote to Faith:

I am involved in a painfully worrying financial crisis. I may have to come to London but I am very weak after this influenza and I dread the journey in this weather. However, I may have to come.

One thing is vital. I must have £100 from the Gramophone *to pay the second 10% of the furniture account and the first instalment. I can pay that back in 3 months and will give a bill. Talk to Christopher and Pollard and wire "What you want possible".*

The Coddie is lending me £200, half of what he has in the bank. He offered it. Thank God for the generosity of humble friends.

I can see the expression on the Coddie's face as I refuse at first to accept that warm-hearted offer and hear echoing from the past those inimitable accents as he looks down that aquiline nose and says,

"You'll be after taking this £200 from me. It was I who persuaded you to build Suidheachan. Och, a' Chompton, you'll be taking this £200. I'll still be having £200 with Roderick Macleod."

This was Roderick Macleod who was Manager of the local branch of the Commercial Bank of Scotland.

"But you'll have to be changing your account from Beauly to Castlebay," he added.

Mr Campbell at Beauly had fought so hard for me with his Edinburgh-rocky Head Office that I hated transferring my account. However, he understood my motives, and poor Roderick was saddled with that Edinburgh-rocky head office of the Commercial Bank.

With Coddie's £200 and the *Gramophone's* £100 the financial storm was calmed for a short while.

On March 16th Ralph Pinker wrote:

"Cassell's are not wishing in any way to be 'quit' of you. Their difficulty is a straight-forward one in that, while, perhaps, the words 'volume of stories' are too strong to use, the book-sellers would inevitably regard it as a volume of sketches and, if they put it out as a novel, they would get the book returned in large numbers. If they put it out as a volume of sketches, then it would only sell approximately a third of the number. . . . I have been racking my brain to try and find a constructive suggestion, first of all to get over the difficulty of *Figure of Eight*, and the only way we can think of is that when you deliver the first two *Winds* there should be a deduction for the advance on this to make up the difference on *Figure of Eight* as you yourself suggest but, would this course enable you to carry on? Can you make a suggestion? In any case, please believe that the last thing any of us want to do is to give you the impression that we want to 'be quit'."

On March 18th Pinker sent the first batch of slip-proofs of *Figure of Eight* with a note from the Cassell's editor:

There is a point on slip 2 which I should be glad if you would raise with Mr Mackenzie, and that is the remark, put in the mouth of Mrs Pilkington, about the police and their ways. Without in the least doubting the truth of this remark of hers, I feel it is not desirable or politic to make suggestions about the police making overtures to girls.

Also, several times the word 'bitch' is used as an epithet. We do not like the use of the word in this sense in our books. I hope the author will not mind changing it.

I had, with what seemed audacity in 1912, used 'bitch' once or twice in *Carnival*. Martin Secker with equal audacity had ventured to print it, but in the U.S.A. Appletons had asked me to take it out. Their readers were not prepared to see 'bitch' in print. I removed the 'bitches' but left in 'mare' which of course is a much stronger pejorative to apply to a woman in Cockaigne but was apparently not used in America.

On March 23rd I wrote to Pinker:

"I am sending off by this mail the first 535 typescript pages of *The Four Winds*. I should like Newman to read these at once and by what he feels about it the future must be decided. If he is sufficiently interested I will send some more along, but the whole of this typescript will have to be sent back to me as there is still a final revision to make in order to avoid printer's corrections which might be heavy in a book like this."

On March 25th Pinker wrote:

"I have had another long discussion with Newman. . . . I pointed out how essential it was for you to receive a regular sum to enable you to keep going for the present and suggested Cassells should pay £150 a month, beginning next month, until the first two *Winds* are published. Any remaining part of the £1,500 advance could then be paid in a lump."

On March 27th I wrote to Pinker:

"By this post go back the galleys of *Figure of Eight*. I have taken out the 'bitches' with the exception of one which I am afraid must stay in. I have also taken away from the mouth of a Cockney cleaner of twenty years ago her aspersions upon the police. I hope I haven't left in any derogatory remarks about the Albert Memorial.

"After reading through the book again I am more than ever convinced that the criticism of it is without justification, and it is a pity you did not read through the whole book before you aligned yourself with Cassells in the matter. Perhaps it will be better to take out the names of the eight girls and substitute numbered chapters. . . .

"I want to know as soon as possible about *The Four Winds*. Never again will I expose a book of mine to the treatment *Figure of Eight* has been given."

On March 30th Pinker wrote:

"I hope I may hear something from Newman to-day regarding *The Four Winds*. I owe it to myself to explain that there was no question of my 'aligning' myself with Cassells against you. It would not have been honest if I had not given you my opinion. This, however, does not alter the fact that if you consider *Figure of Eight* to be a novel, then I shall do my best arrangement for you, irrespective of my opinion. That was formed on a comparatively small portion of the galleys, but it was all that was available at the time and the matter seemed urgent."

On April 6th Pinker telegraphed:

Flower enthusiastic winds but cannot make him advance further money till manuscript delivered in spite utmost effort

On April 11th I wrote to Pinker:

"If no money can be forthcoming until I have finished both *The East Wind* and *The South Wind of Love* it is clear that I shall just have to finish off *The East Wind*, which I should have done this week if I had not been plunged back into bed again with another attack.

"I'm out of pain now and I will send you the balance of *The East Wind*, and Newman will have to decide immediately whether he is going to publish it or not. If he refuses I shall have no alternative but to send it to another publisher. I wish to act perfectly fairly and shall make no attempt to negotiate with another publisher until the final decision is taken.

"At the present moment I owe no money to Cassells. I have agreed to allow anything lost on *Figure of Eight* to be deducted from the advance on a future novel, and surely this argues the greatest good will on my part. I'm sorry you should be hurt by my thinking you had aligned yourself with Cassells over *Figure of Eight*, but I hold to my opinion that you should have read the whole book before you agreed that it was not strictly speaking a novel. . . .

"I am faced by the depressing fact that the whole of Cassells have made up their minds that the book won't be a success, which means that advertisements will be cut to a minimum and that their travellers will lack confidence. If in spite of this the book should achieve success no credit will rest on anybody except myself.

"In deference to Newman's wishes I declined a £500 advance from Hodder and Stoughton for a 75,000 word life of Pericles, £100 payable immediately, which would have been worth £300 to me at the moment! You wrote to me about a proposed book on *My Island Home*, but you feared Newman would not agree to that.

"What I am asked to do now is to sit down without a halfpenny in the bank and with a manuscript of already about 150,000 words ready for press and continue to write without a halfpenny in the bank another 150,000 words. It is hardly necessary for me to say that this cannot be done. I contend that any advance up to £1,500 is covered by the manuscript in hand, and that if I am to write any more of this book I must be given the means to do it. You assure me that Cassells have no desire to see me out of their list, but I cannot believe their attitude can be dictated by anything else.

"When I negotiate, if I have to negotiate, *The Four Winds of Love* with another publisher I shall negotiate for one volume a year and that will allow me, after finishing off *The East Wind* for press, to get to work at once on another novel under my contract with Cassells, for which I will give them a choice between three, and which I will deliver by the end of July. If on the other hand they do not want this, I will carry on with *The Four Winds* for another publisher.

"The Commercial Bank are worrying me for £148 of an overdraft, and I shall have to give them a definite answer when I shall be getting money in. I am really risking a good deal by not entering into negotiations immediately with another publisher; by not doing so I am showing my earnest desire not to make a break if it can possibly be avoided, but money I must have somehow if only to achieve some peace of mind to get on with my work."

On April 16th Pinker wrote:

"I have given a great deal of thought to the situation and had another talk with Flower. The position at the moment is, of course, a deadlock in that you cannot sell a book elsewhere unless Cassells turn it down, and, technically speaking, they are strictly within their rights in refusing to make an advance before a manuscript is delivered. What I was most anxious to avoid was any suggestion from our side that we might cancel the contract entirely and go elsewhere because if you have a contract, as you have now for three novels at £1,500 advance, that is an asset and a good one and not lightly to be given up. But Flower this morning said in the course of conversation that he might, seeing the position you were in, think of cancelling the contract. So I took him up on his words and asked him whether he would consult the other directors and let me know if they would be prepared to cancel it, making it clear, however, that we, as your representatives, are not committing you in any form to be willing to cancel, but we were just interested to know if they were willing.

"The situation is also complicated by the fact that Cassells are guarantors of the payments to the insurance company on the house, so that any fresh publisher would have to take these over. I hope you feel I manœuvred the situation correctly? What I should like you do do, if you will, is to let me know your opinion of what publisher you would like to go to should Cassells be willing to cancel and what sort of contract you want."

On April 22nd I wrote to Ralph Pinker:

"I am not at all anxious to leave Cassells. On the contrary, I would sacrifice a great deal to stay with them. Still, if you think that Newman and his other directors really would in their hearts be glad to be quit of me I've no desire to hold them to an engagement of which they are tired.

"What I had hoped was that Newman would be sufficiently keen on what he has seen of *The East Wind* to publish it this autumn and pay me the advance on my completing it, which should be next week. That you say is out of the question. If he is firm on this point I must try to find another publisher for *The East Wind* who will accept it as the *first* of four books. I am assuming of course that if Cassells do not see their way to publishing *The East Wind* separately they will allow me to consider that book my own to dispose of. Naturally I should prefer to complete the present contract with them by writing other books to be chosen from a list I would send them. If they want a book for early next spring I will postpone writing *The South Wind* until I have written another book for them, for which, as I have told you, I would agree to have deducted any part of the advance unearned by *Figure of Eight*. In offering to do this I think I have made a gesture, but as you do not allude to it I presume that it has not been appreciated. All I asked you to say was that I still do not accept the contention that *Figure of Eight* is anything but a novel completely up to my standard, but that my offer was made to show my anxiety to do everything possible on my side to be amenable.

"The immediate situation for me is so serious that I must have a quick answer about *The East Wind*. I have had to borrow £200 from a friend to pay wages, household bills, rates and income tax instalments. This loan *must* be repaid very soon. I have also to pay off my overdraft of £148 unless I wish to lose all credit. Then next month I have to pay more income tax. In June I have to meet the insurance premium and interest on the house.

"The loss of the *Daily Mail* was fatal for me in this heavy year, and to that my present straits are due. Had I known a year ahead this was going to happen I could have planned my books better. . . .

"It is a bitter disappointment to me that Newman is not keen enough on *The East Wind* to make an effort to let me finish *The South Wind* and publish it. However, he isn't and so I am on the rocks. I must get myself off them.

"And now for the possible future of *The Four Winds*. It seems to me much better that I should handle this book myself. I may have to make a special arrangement and I have in mind to take a big chance and offer it to a firm which you would think it madness to offer it to."

The firm I had in mind was Secker and Warburg. Martin Secker had been taken over by Fred Warburg, and Roger Senhouse who had put money into Martin's business had agreed to join Warburg. Believing as I did that *The Four Winds of Love* would be the *Sinister Street* of my middle age, I wanted to see Secker's name on the title page.

"Anyway, I wish to negotiate *Winds* myself. I have put all I know into the first of them, and as you are unable to pull me through the four months necessary to write *The South Wind*, I feel that you should with good will let me have the satisfaction of doing what I can with it. You have already had one novel this year on which I have paid your commission; if Cassells wish me to go on you will have a second in the autumn. If Cassells insist that the whole contract is void by my failure to hold out long enough to write both *The East Wind* and *The South Wind* you still have a chance to make a contract with any publisher you like. But *The Winds* will not be in it. In any case I profoundly hope that there will be no question of any other publisher, except for *The Winds*. I should like you to tell Newman that I am without any money except what I have borrowed from a friend in humble circumstances; if you do this I am sure that Newman will agree to let me negotiate *The East Wind* right away. If I am sued by the Inland Revenue it can only mean bankruptcy, and he must realize what it will mean if I can't meet those monthly cheques. . . .

"With regard to America: the *Winds* can go to Dodd, Mead if they really want them, but I was not encouraged by their wanting to change the title. However, as far as America is concerned, you will do what you think wisest and handle the book there.

"Please telegraph me if Newman releases the *Winds*, and you agree to my handling them myself: *Winds Are Free*.

"I'm afraid you'll feel hurt over this determination of mine to handle the *Winds* myself if Cassells turn them down; but I don't expect you've ever had to face what I'm facing at the moment. In such circumstances one loses confidence in everybody except oneself. My worries are not diminished by Faith's having gone into an isolation Hospital with scarlet fever last week, and when you realize that in order to get down to London I should have to borrow the money for my fare, you may appreciate my anxiety."

Fortunately Faith's scarlet fever was of the mildest kind. It was an extraordinary complaint for a woman of fifty-eight to catch; she always believed she caught it from a Chinese author whom she sat next at a Pen Club Jamboree.

On April 27th Newman Flower wrote:

"Thank you for your letter and for the copy of your letter to Ralph Pinker which, of course, I shall treat as confidential.

"Let me say at once that I never wished that you would leave Cassell's, and I liked very much indeed the 125,000 words I read of *East Wind*.

"The position with me was this. About a year ago you wrote to me and said that you were starting on *East Wind* and you might require me to help you before you delivered the book by the beginning of this year. To this end I advanced you in October last £500. It had been suggested that *Four Winds* should be divided into two books, and it was your intention at that time that we should have the first book for publication this spring.

"I was therefore very surprised and perturbed when in December you told me the book could not be done in time, and that you would do a quick novel in the meantime. On a lot of these novels which you have done hurriedly, we have lost money. To be quite frank we have paid too much for them, especially as you have hardly any sale in cheap editions. Apart from one book you did we have made very little money out of you at all. In fact I think I can say with truth that, if we counted in the interest on money advanced before it was due, and 'overheads' which any publisher must charge against a book, then we should have done no more than break even, or we may not have broken even.

"When *Figure of Eight* came in I liked the excellence of the character work, but I cannot agree with you that this is a novel. It is not a question of splitting hairs as to whether this is a novel or whether it is not, or whether in paying £1,500 we paid too much, but it is question of the acid test which is about to follow. If we go to the trade and say this book is a novel, we know quite well now that we are going to get 60% of the copies back when they find out it is a set of sketches, in addition to getting the trade up against us for subscribing this book as a novel. We have had this trouble before. Whether you think this is a novel or whether you do not, I can tell you for certain what the trade is going to say about it.

"But let us for the moment drop that side of it and consider *The Four*

Winds. I asked Pinker to find out (when I had read the first 125,000 words you sent) how long the book was going to be. In due course he replied that the book would be a quarter of a million words, and the second book likewise. Therefore it seemed to me that I had read over half of the first book, but that half did not appear to be anything like finished. It also appeared to me, that if *East Wind* was going to be hurriedly rounded off it would be ill balanced, because you had obviously spread yourself on the early portion of it and had written rather at length.

"Another point. As you had taken practically a year writing this portion, it seemed absolutely impossible to me that you could finish this *East Wind* and the completed *South Wind* by the summer. Therefore, if I agreed to paying £150 a month, I felt that the whole situation would become more involved than ever, and in about a year's time it would be a proper tangle; unless you wrote a quick book or two which might be a financial advantage to you, but a financial disadvantage to us. I, therefore, had to tell Ralph Pinker frankly that I could not agree to this monthly payment, but that the moment a complete book was sent in I would pay £1,500 for it in accordance with the agreement. What more to suggest I do not know. I have been hoping that some suggestion would come from you which might have straightened things out.

"I am sure you are not right in thinking that Ralph has not helped you and I can only say that Ralph has spent a lot of time with me over schemes to get you out of your difficulties, and has put up a strong fight for you on each occasion.

"I still hope there may be a way of straightening out the tangle."

On April 29th I wrote to Newman Flower:

"I cannot do more for *Figure of Eight* than offer that you should deduct the amount of unearned advance from any advance paid on one of those 'hurried novels' in the future, and if you really mean that you do not want me to leave Cassell's that can be done when you want it.

"The problem of the *Four Winds* is not quite so simple. At the present moment I have done of *The East Wind* as near as I can calculate 150,000 words and I think another 15,000 will finish it. With every inducement of financial stress and worry, to do what you feared and 'hurriedly round it off', I have not done so. I will agree with you that I cannot finish the *South Wind* with certainty by the end of the summer, because in a work of this magnitude calculations are easily upset to the tune of some thousands of words. It is, I venture to think, a compliment to *East Wind* that after reading 125,000 words of it in typescript you should feel it wasn't nearly finished; I must assume that this implies the book's readableness whatever its other merits may be. I am working as hard as I can to finish *East Wind* and I really believe that next week will see it finished.

"What I should like to do is to send you the balance of the typescript and let you make then your final decision. *The East Wind* closes in October 1901 and *The South Wind* resumes the story in March 1913 in different scenes with different characters, although of course the chief characters go right through. If you approve of *East Wind* what I would then suggest is that you paid me £1,500 advance on it, but that for *The South Wind* you should only pay me in advance what I earned from *East Wind*, and similarly for *The West Wind* and *The North Wind*, i.e. the advance earned by each preceding book.

"But I am so near the rocks that unless you can give me a line by return to say that you think there is a probability of this arrangement's being come to I shall have to ask you to let me offer the *Winds* to another publisher; otherwise there will only be *The East Wind* and the other *Winds* will be dust as far as I am concerned. It is perfectly clear that I cannot write another long book, such as *South Wind* will be, *on nothing*. Even if I could fend off all claims until it was finished, the worry would inevitably kill my conception because I should never feel able to develop any incident to its full extent.

"The whole point of my settling here was to give myself the surround-ings necessary for me to produce the large novel I wished to write. I admit that my first conception of *The Four Winds of Love* was less ambitious than it is now, but that only means that the book is a bigger and better work than I thought it was going to be.

"I hope you understand that I am not trying to force your hand by the proposals I have made in this letter; but it is vital for me to know within as few days as possible what I may hope your attitude will be toward publication in four volumes. Unfortunately the time has gone by when by making me an allowance of so much a month I could have fended off the immediate calls long enough to finish *The South Wind* and enable you to publish the two together; I have been fending off people for the last two months."

The day after I wrote that letter to Newman Flower I received a letter from Ralph Pinker:

"I must start by saying that I am sorry I omitted to make mention in my last letter of your 'gesture' relating to *Figure of Eight*. I did tell Flower about this and he is very appreciative.

"I am a bit confused by what you say regarding *The East Wind* because Cassells have always been definite that the *Winds* were to be published in two volumes, and this is borne out by all the correspondence. Also, you are wrong in thinking that Newman does not want to read any more of the *Winds*. He does—and he is not willing at present to consider abandoning the idea of publishing these books, because he has always had it in his mind that this is one of your major works. Cassells are going to have a Meeting of all the Directors on the whole question of whether they should offer to release you, but my impression is that they will say 'no'. Even if they say 'yes' it might not be to your advantage to agree to a release. The main reason why Cassells are difficult about paying money before a manuscript is delivered is that they have huge sums of money out which, of course, entails great loss of interest and the Board decided to cut down on this kind of thing. They are willing, and ready, to pay the money the same day a manuscript is delivered but not before.

"There is, of course, the additional point that if the Cassells agreement were cancelled and we went to another publisher, the other publisher would have to take over the guarantee given by Cassells with regard to the house. However, possibly this might be arranged. But, as I say, at present, and until they have their Meeting, they are expecting to receive the manuscript of the first two *Winds* in due course for publication in one volume.

"As far as we are concerned, I suppose there would not be much point in going into a long discussion now as to who should handle the *Winds* if it should go to another publisher, but, I must be honest and say that I think we ought to—apart altogether from the question of the agreement between you and this firm."

On April 30th Pinker wrote:

"Cassells are planning to publish *Figure of Eight* on June 25th. They have raised a point with regard to the proofs. This may seem very trivial and niggly, but, owing to the horrible complications of libel law they feel we cannot be too careful, and, although the point is trivial it *might* cause trouble.

"On page 150 there is the reference to the Café Royal and a faintly derogatory mention of it as being now a German beer-hall. There is the danger that the proprietors of the Café Royal will turn round and say that you are libelling their place."

On May 9th Newman Flower wrote:

"I am afraid I do not see that the suggestion which you made simplifies the position, at all, but rather complicates it.

"We should not be prepared to publish four separate volumes of *The Four Winds of Love*. If we did, we should quite expect to be in 'rough water' with the last two.

"As you will remember, the book started as a one volume scheme; then it got to two. You, yourself, told me you did not want it to exceed two. All our plans have been on the basis that *The Four Winds* was going to be in two volumes of two *Winds* each.

"You cannot sell *East Wind* to another publisher with a three book contract unfulfilled with Cassell's, especially as Cassell's are co-guarantors

Hugh Fraser, Father Geddes, Laura Lady Lovat with Rose, Veronica Fraser, Lord Lovat;
at Beaufort cn Jubilee Day

Front Row: Mary, Hon. Bernard Constable Maxwell, Michael, Mrs Maxwell, Oona
Back Row: Ian, Gerald, Joan, Betty, Ronnie, David, Ursula, Marjorie, Andrew

for you in another direction. If you do, and that book were issued, we would very reluctantly injunct it.

"It seems to me that the friendliest suggestion I can put up to you, to help you out of your difficulty, is to offer to cancel all the unfulfilled contracts with Cassell's at once, provided that the guarantee is transferred by you from Cassell's to another publisher at the same time. This would enable you to raise money at once on *East Wind*. But it must be clearly understood that we shall have to be released from this guarantee before we will sign away the contracts which are outstanding.

"Will this help you? Heaven knows I do not like to see you going from Cassell's, but I do not see any other way of your raising immediate funds.

"You admit in your letter that you cannot complete *South Wind* by July. This only goes to show that I was right in my surmise that, if we start paying £150 a month, we might be doing so for very much longer than the time suggested, namely, until the end of June.

"If you are going to take the same care with *South Wind* as you have with *East Wind* it is obvious to me that you will not have the book finished until next spring; by which time on the £150 basis, all the advance would have been swallowed up in advance payments. Then how are you going to get the money to carry on while you do *North Wind*? It is this situation I have foreseen all along.

"Well, I make the above suggestion in the friendliest spirit, and if you decide to accept it, no one would be more sorry than myself to see you disappear from our list."

The monetary maze I was in forced me to accept Newman Flower's offer as sorrowfully as he made it. *Figure of Light* was to be the last book of mine published by Cassell's.

Newman Flower's forecast of its reception by the Press and the Trade was fortunately for me completely wrong. Not a single reviewer found it a set of sketches and almost everyone said it was one of the best novels I had written. Their bouquets smelt very sweet in that radiant June on Barra almost exactly thirty years ago as I write these words.

Figure of Eight was published in a Spanish translation but to my regret has never been translated into French. The theme anticipated that exquisite film called *Carnet du Bal*.

In 1941 I used the central character for a broadcast play of an hour called *Lucy Arnold*. This was produced at Manchester by Val Gielgud and Moray McLaren, but it was so badly cast that I had to cut it off when I listened to it in Barra. Dear Val Gielgud recognized this and in 1946 it was done again with success. But the best repeat was a year or two later when Dora Bryan played Lucy Arnold, and when for the first time I heard an actor or actress speak my words as I heard them when I wrote them.

o

By an agreeable coincidence while I have been telling the story of *Figure of Eight* a letter came from the B.B.C. to say that they were proposing to do *Lucy Arnold* for a fourth time.

I have related the story of the beginning of *The Four Winds of Love* at such length because I cherish a fancy that it will be recognized in time as a justification for the kind things said over half a century ago about *Sinister Street*. I was encouraged to go on cherishing this fancy when Edmund Wilson whom I regard as the most vital critic of contemporary letters praised the book.

In September John Campbell and I decided it was a time to expose the "insolence of office and the law's delays" by calling a meeting of protest about it. He and I had founded the Sea League in the Autumn of 1933. We had secured the signatures of every fisherman and everybody connected with the fishing industry from Scalpay to Vatersay to a petition for a Fishing District Committee to be constituted in accord with the Sea Fisheries Regulation (Scotland) Act of 1895. Such a Committee in the Outer Isles under the Inverness-shire County Council would be of great advantage by maintaining an efficient local patrol and in regulating the use of the ring-net and trawl by local small boats.

On January 7th 1935 the County Clerk had acknowledged the receipt of the petition in Inverness. On March 9th he had written to say that the petition had been considered by the Parliamentary Bills and Law Committee of the County Council, which had remitted it to the Convener and the County Clerk to prepare a report for the subject for submission to the next meeting. The County Clerk had then written to ask in what way the Petitioners believed that the creation of a Fishery District would help their industry.

On May 3rd 1935 the County Clerk had acknowledged receipt of statement giving reasons which the Petitioners had for believing that the creation of a Fishery District would help their industry. He regretted that the statement had arrived just too late for consideration at the May meeting of the County Council.

On June 17th 1935 the County Clerk notified the Secretary of the Sea League that the Parliamentary Bills and Law Committee had considered the Petition and had instructed him to inquire whether the fishing interests in the Inverness-shire Outer Isles were prepared to be responsible for the expenses incurred by the creation of such a district and its administration.

On July 10th 1935 the Deputy County Clerk acknowledged the receipt of a letter from the Secretary of the Sea League to say that the fishing interests in the Inverness-shire Outer Isles were not prepared to be responsible for the expenses.

On August 21st 1935 Sir Alexander MacEwen, ex-Provost of Inverness, submitted a memorandum on the Fishing District question with an estimate of expenses at £20 to £25 per annum.

On the very next day with nervous promptitude the County Clerk wrote to Sir Alexander MacEwen and protested that the expenses would probably be much severer than his estimate.

On September 7th 1935 a big protest meeting had been held in Castlebay to object to the suggestion made by the County Council, against the intention of the Act, that the local fishing interests should bear the expenses of a Fishery District. Meetings were held simultaneously in North and South Uist.

A motion was passed unanimously, congratulating the Norwegian Government on its imposition of a four-mile limit outside all the fiords. This was sent to the Norwegian Embassy in London, expressing a hope that public opinion in Norway would support our attempt to close the Minch and the Moray Firth to trawlers, British or foreign.

On October 25th 1935 the County Clerk had written to say that the County Council had agreed to make formal application to the Secretary of State for Scotland for the creation of a Fishery District as petitioned for.

In May of this year 1936 the Sea League wrote to ask the County Clerk what the Scottish Office had replied, whereupon the County Clerk wrote back to say that no answer had yet been received from the Scottish Office.

On August 14th we enquired again. The County Clerk enclosed a letter received from the Scottish Office dated June 29th 1936 in reply to his of October 31st 1935, May 4th 1936, and June 15th 1936 saying that the Secretary of State would like "to receive a statement of the grounds on which the County Council consider that the creation of such a District would be expedient and would serve a useful purpose", and to be furnished with the County Council's views on the composition of such a Committee, which in any case could not come into existence before the next County Council election in *December 1938*.

Exasperated by the behaviour of MacDilly at the Inverness-shire County Council and MacDally at St Andrew's House, Edinburgh, we had another crowded meeting in Castlebay that September which was well reported in the Scottish press. We passed a motion protesting "against the delay set in the way of putting into action, in the Inverness-shire Outer Islands an Act passed in 1895 for the better regulation of Scottish Fisheries, by adding one unnecessary delay after another, and authorizing the President of the Sea League to put the case personally before the Secretary of State for Scotland at the earliest possible moment." I then proposed that the Secretary of State for Scotland, on his official visits to the Outer Hebrides, should travel to the Islands by the government-subsidized Macbrayne mail boats in winter, in order to obtain a better insight into existing conditions in the Hebrides than would be got in the course of a summer cruise in the fishery cruiser *Minna*.

The *Scotsman* gave a column to reporting this meeting. I find I said after commenting on the evasive delaying tactics of the Scottish Office and the County Council:

"If this kind of behaviour continues, the question of the creation of a Fishery District will be carried over from one County Council election to another, and we shall be lucky if we get it by 1950. We want a Fishery District before the next war when the absence of trawlers may lead to an improvement in the fishing as it did after the last war. This procrastination and red tape is typical of the Scottish Office and all other Government Offices, and also in the Government's handling of international politics, which is leading us steadily toward chaos."

I was too sanguine when I hoped we might get a Fishery District by 1950. In April 1955 John Campbell was writing to the *Scotsman* that, although a staff correspondent of the *Scotsman* had drawn a doleful picture of the dire consequences likely to be suffered by the British trawling industry if the Icelanders were to be allowed a four-mile limit on the Norwegian principle, the increased catch of fish landed by British trawlers from Icelandic waters had been £3,838,876 in 1954.

"Meanwhile, the trawling industry has been allowed to get away with the imposition of a ban on the landing of Icelandic fish in Britain since 1951, to the detriment of British consumers and British exporters."

Reference was then made to the failure of F. Fraser Darling's *West Highland Survey* and Adam Collier's *The Crofter Problem* to support the case for extended fishery limits in Scottish waters.

A month ago as I write these words in July 1966 John Campbell sent me from his island of Canna a copy of the Fishery Limits Act of 1964.

"31 years almost to the day after the first Sea League meeting at Castlebay our policy had been put into effect—at least one if not two generations too late.

"When you write this up will you make some allusion to the weak-kneed attitude of various 'experts' on the Highlands and Islands . . . who were too timid to support the policy in their books? The *Stornoway Gazette* did not print a letter from myself in 1964, pointing out that the Sea League deserved some of the credit." See Appendix D.

It is melancholy to reflect that if the vested interests of English trawler combines had not succeeded in preventing the Act of 1895 from being put into operation the Hebrides today would be an example instead of a problem. Seventy years is too long a delay even for Mr MacDilly and Mr MacDally or the Rt. Hon. Mr Shilly and the Rt. Hon. Mr Shally.

A few days after that meeting of protest MacNeil of Barra arrived on the island with his newly married wife, the widow of an American Army officer. His claim to be the 45th hereditary chief was presently to be allowed by Lord Lyon, but there were many on the island who believed that a MacNeil in Nova Scotia had the better claim.

The people of Barra, always glad to turn a heyday into a holiday gave MacNeil a warm welcome. He was piped up the hill to the Castlebay Hotel and the occasion was celebrated by a concert and a dance that evening. MacNeil of Barra makes the now usual mistake of calling himself *The* MacNeil in *Who's Who*. There are three 'The's' in Scotland— The Chisholm, The Pope and The Devil; in Ireland, of course, there are many 'The's'. MacNeil is far from being the only offender; 'The's' are becoming as thick as midges. Cameron of Lochiel is so unquestionably the chief of a great clan that he requires no 'The' to reassure himself.

When Newman Flower had turned down the idea of publishing *Walls Have Mouths* by Wilfred Macartney, I wrote to thank Victor Gollancz for a warm-hearted letter in which like several other publishers he said how much my giving up the *Daily Mail* was regretted. In the same letter I told him about *Walls Have Mouths* and in January this year he asked Macartney who was now living in London to bring him his typescript. He wrote at once to me.

Like you I found the book quite enthralling—in fact, having started it last night and read half of it then, I started on it again at six o'clock this morning.

He then went on to make various criticisms and suggestions. I was in the middle of that desperate effort to finish *Figure of Eight* in a month. But I find a letter from me to Victor Gollancz of over a thousand words from which I extract a sentence or two.

I thought it wiser not to criticize the style while Macartney was actually writing it because I feared he would grow stilted at once. He started one chapter on sexual life in prison, which was hopeless because he became self-conscious in telling it. So I told him to give me the facts and I would put them down.

I went on to say I would write a prologue, comments between each chapter, and an epilogue, and that I should make every effort to let him have the result by the end of February.

One of my troubles at the present moment is lack of money, owing to building a house and the initial expense connected with it. Therefore I cannot afford to spend a great deal of time on Macartney's book, but must press on as soon as possible to finish the first half of my 'magnum opus'. So you may rely on my getting the material to you as soon as possible for my own sake.

On February 26th I was writing to Gollancz:

I have been laid up with a good deal of pain since I finished my Cassell novel, but I am gradually wading through Macartney's book and hope to send it off to you next week. . . . I have read through the proof you sent me of Keep the Aspidistra Flying *which confirms my opinion that this chap, George Orwell, is a real crasher, and I flatter myself on having as quick a nose for the genuine slice of life as anybody. Not a line in this novel suggests anything but the truth. And it is a little masterpeice of construction.*

The following remark is not for your quote:

I was amused to find that the same novelists he chooses to express his contempt for are the very ones Macartney mentions as being laughed at by convicts. I was naturally pleased to hear that such books of mine as they were allowed to read were read and re-read. Am I foolish in wondering whether the judgment of a book's vitality by men cut off from life is the judgment of 'time' in every sense of the word?

Victor Gollancz called on D. N. Pritt to vet the book not only for libel but for anything that would give Them an excuse for gagging *Walls Have Mouths* with an injunction.

I was receiving agonized letters from Macartney to say that Pritt had practically disembowelled the book.

On May 4th Gollancz wrote:

We had a rather dreadful evening at Pritt's (from half past nine to about four o'clock in the morning) at which we went over the galleys point by point. . . . I do not think its 'punch' is in the least diminished—in fact I did not dare to hope that we should get out of the thing with the stuff so little mutilated.

I wrote on May 12th:

I have considered very carefully my prologue after the excisions made by Pritt, and I think much the best thing to do is to leave blanks after the excisions. That will impress on the public better than anything else the tyranny of the Official Secrets Act. As it stands now the prologue is unfair to Macartney, for it leaves in all his misdeeds and omits all that illustrates from my point of view the cause of them.

Gollancz thought the blanks were a good idea but Pritt disagreed:

I don't want to thwart Mackenzie's efforts to repair the damage I have (or have not) done; but I don't like this scheme of blanks. I do not veto it, but I express the fear that this slightly ostentatious treatment of the problem will invite the authorities to use an even finer toothcomb than they would anyhow.

However, I insisted on the blanks being retained, and wrote:

I do not want to be unreasonable, but I cannot see that a few blanks are going to challenge the authorities. Moreover, the prospect of being asked on oath what the words originally were so far from perturbing me delights me. I do not fancy the authorities will enjoy cross-examining me if I may judge by the efforts that were made in my own case to keep me out of the witness-box.

Walls Have Mouths was published in September and was a resounding success. On the same day as Victor Gollancz wrote about that long night battle with Macartney over Pritt's cuts, Ralph Pinker telegraphed:

*Flower informed me contents his letter. Rich and Cowan subject to Board
Meeting very interested possibility publishing* Winds *willing publish four volumes
paying £1,500 each. First advance signature second six months Bill which you can
discount now. House guarantee not obstacle.*

Pinker had been against my going to Secker and Warburg but in the
end Fred Warburg had felt they were taking on too much in *The Four
Winds*. So I had not to bother about them when I told Pinker to go ahead
with Rich and Cowan. The first proposal was that I should finish *The
South Wind* by the end of the year; when Newman Flower offered to
release me from my contract with them I had wired to Hodder and
Stoughton to say I was free to give them a life of Pericles by mid-
September if they still wanted to do it. The answer was 'Yes' and Rich
and Cowan agreed to wait for *The South Wind* till next year.

Rich flew up to Barra in June, and we all much enjoyed the company
of this genial retired Lieutenant-Commander. The Coddie was particularly impressed by him and that aquiline nose of the Coddie had a keen
scent for the right material. I was able to give Rich a notion of what he
was taking on with *The Four Winds of Love* which by now had grown to a
novel of nearly a million words. He was not daunted and agreed that I
should not attempt to promise more than *The South Wind* by the middle
of 1937.

On July 1st I wrote to Pinker:

I have to-day received the first eight notices of Figure of Eight *of which I send
you eight extracts. I think you will agree that I have a right to feel a little triumphant,
though I recognize of course that the acid test is sales not reviews.*

I will quote from one:

"Nobody can trace with a firmer pencil the historic wrinkles on
London's countenance . . . A love scene of a divinely touching awkward-
ness that ought to have a place in future anthologies of the innocent god."
The Times Literary Supplement.

Quite recovered from scarlet fever Faith was with us at Suidheachan
for about six weeks that summer. She had found a pleasant upper half
over a shop at 31A Connaught Street to which she now moved. One
agreeable feature of the Connaught Street abode was that it looked out
at the back over gardens in which archery was going on.

I find a scrawl to Faith at the end of August:

*Everybody, but far the most of all myself, misses you. I sat down last night to
start* The South Wind *and after 6 hours in my chair produced four names of
characters, but in my mind I more or less solved the problem of construction which
is very difficult. I hope to get the first few pages done to-night.*

The will to get started on *The South Wind* may have been stimulated by a letter I had received from Rich dated August 27th:

I think I should write to you, at this stage, to inform you that I have now finished reading The East Wind; *this has also been read by Mr Colin Still, Mr Wynne Thomas, and Mrs Eileen Bigland, our literary advisers, and we are of the unanimous opinion that it is magnificent! I do not think I need say any more.*

Proof correcting went on through September but I managed to get some thirty thousand words done of *The South Wind* before I went down to London at the end of the month.

An eddy of gossip was flowing about the King but I paid little attention to it and did not realize when I was told that the Archbishop of Canterbury was to dine with us at the Savile that the dinners to which he was being invited by various Clubs were propaganda to prepare 'Clubmen' for what can only be called the conspiracy into which he was entering with Mr Stanley Baldwin. He was to be presented as a wise and tolerant man of the world whose willingness to accept abdication as inevitable meant that it was inevitable.

It was Sydney Dark, the editor of the *Church Times*, who arranged the Savile dinner and we were given to understand that His Grace felt he was playing truant by dining without his domestic Chaplain.

"I'm being rather naughty, I'm afraid," I heard him say roguishly.

Archbishop Lang had been Dean of Divinity at Magdalen in the mid-'nineties, and when I was presented to him he sighed almost voluptuously.

"Ah, Magdalen! Happy man, happy man! I always feel that Balliol is my Alma Mater and All Souls' my loving wife and that the time I spent at Magdalen were enchanted years spent in the arms of a beautiful mistress."

I can see now the expression in his eyes and the gleam of the skin in his almost hairless eyebrows above them.

The night after that dinner at the Savile with the Archbishop I was given a dinner by my new publishers in Soho Square to wish good luck to *The East Wind* which was to be published in January exactly twenty-six years after my first novel. I liked Ashley Cowan, who was as I remember an Argenti on one side with a charming house in Cheyne Walk. I presumed that he had put up the capital for Rich and Cowan and I hoped all would go well.

I made my first appearance on television while I was down in London. The Alexandra Park studios had just been opened. In those days the victim's face was painted as yellow as a brimstone butterfly and he was put in a chair on a small platform. A tubular lamp about a yard long was fixed at the back of his neck and was so hot that he had an impression his hair was being singed.

"Now," said the producer, "try not to be nervous. And don't move your hands or your legs. Just sit there and talk quite naturally for five minutes."

"If I'm going to talk naturally," I told the producer, "I'll be sure to move my hands. I'll keep my legs still but I move my hands without being aware of it."

The producer paused for a moment.

"Oh, well, it doesn't matter. There are only two hundred sets in the country," he told me.

Macartney's book *Walls Have Mouths* had been a sensational success when it appeared that September, and being anxious to show he was as good as his words he asked me to draw up a petition for an amnesty for the Dartmoor mutineers. The idea was that the King should grant this amnesty at his Coronation.

I wrote as follows:

"At a special Assize Court held at Princetown in the month of May 1932, twenty-three men were sentenced to various terms of imprisonment for the part they had played in the mutiny at Dartmoor Prison in January 1932. One of these sentences was for twelve years penal servitude; two were for ten years; three were for eight years, and the rest varied from six months to six years. Imposed on top of sentences already being served by the mutineers, they involved men in serving as much as eighteen years penal servitude.

"One mutineer, T. Davies, was tried apart from the other mutineers at Exeter Assize Court; he was given twelve years penal servitude for wounding with a razor one of the prison officers two days before the mutiny.

"One man by the name of Ibbetson, who had only a few months to serve to finish a four years sentence, was given an additional ten years. It sent him mad and he is now in Broadmoor Asylum.

"It may be argued that the cases of these men have been tried before juries of their fellow countrymen and that therefore it is idle to draw attention at this date to the conditions in Dartmoor which directly caused the mutiny; but we have to remember that the very existence of a place like Dartmoor Prison is a reproach to national decency, and that being so Society is not entitled to exact too harsh a penalty from men who have violated laws which are based not as much upon the code of morality as of expediency.

"An opportunity approaches for an amnesty for these unfortunate men. At the last two Coronations considerable remissions of sentences were granted to prisoners. Is it too much to ask that at the forthcoming Coronation the suffering of these men shall not be forgotten? It may be hoped that those happy members of Society who will celebrate the

Coronation with flags will not grudge the celebration of it with freedom for a score of men less happy than themselves."

Owing to the Abdication the petition was never presented.

I still have the signatures of H. G. Wells, Augustus John, and others. A card from Bernard Shaw is of particular interest:

With Bernard Shaw's compliments
　　　I can't make sense of the 4th paragraph. Can you?
　　　　　　　I sign as revised. G. B. S.
4 Whitehall Court, London, S.W.1.
21st Nov. 1936

Here is the 4th paragraph as amended by Shaw.

"It may be argued that the cases of these men have been tried before juries of their fellow countrymen; *but the juries could not find the prisoners innocent and did not dictate the shockingly terroristic sentences.* We have to remember that the very existence of a place like Dartmoor Prison is a reproach to national decency, and that being so society is not entitled to exact too harsh a penalty from men *whose revolt was a revolt of outraged humanity against unbearable conditions.*

　　　　　　　　　　　　　　　　G. Bernard Shaw

I at once accepted Shaw's emendation and had just ordered a revised printing when the news of the Abdication made it impossible to send the petition.

Here are two letters both written on the same day—November 19th, 1936, but from what different hearts.

One is from Lady Oxford:

Dear friend, I will certainly sign this appeal, and you may add the names of my son—Anthony Asquith, and my daughter Elizabeth—Princess Antoine Bibesco. It makes my blood boil *to read of such* barbarous *sentences. Men are far worse than beasts who can do such things. . . . If you would like me to approach the King later on I will do so.*

　　　　　　　　Yours in haste
　　　　　　　　　　Margot Oxford

The other is from Lord Nuffield's secretary:

"I have been asked by Lord Nuffield to say that he very much regrets that he is not in a position to support the appeal for an amnesty for the Dartmoor Mutineers.

"He hopes it may be appreciated that as he is receiving such an over-whelming number of similar approaches just now, it is proving impracticable for him to cope with them."

Apparently Lord Nuffield thought that an amnesty was a financial transaction.

One other letter from the Archbishop of Canterbury's Chaplain and Secretary:[1]

Lambeth Palace, S.E.1.
23rd November, 1936

Dear Mackenzie,

We used to be at Magdalen together and I therefore drop titles.

The Archbishop of Canterbury has received your letter of November 17th with regard to an amnesty for the Dartmoor Mutineers. His Grace understands that it is not proposed to provide for any amnesties of prisoners in connection with the forthcoming Coronation. He does not think that this is a matter in which he can intervene.

Yours sincerely
Alan Don

Alan Don himself was a lovable man. One may suppose that His Grace was almost certain by now that there would be no Coronation of King Edward VIII, even although his head was on the stamp of this letter.

That great crusader William Gallacher had promised to ask questions in the House about the Dartmoor Mutineers, and Macartney was anxious for me to meet him and Harry Pollitt. So Macartney, bubbling over with the hospitality in which thanks to the success of *Walls Have Mouths* he could at last indulge again, asked us all to dine with him at Simpson's-in-the-Strand. Harry Pollitt and I gratified Macartney's zest for hospitality by ordering expensive dishes, to all of which Willie Gallacher shook his head as he looked down the bill of fare with a frown. At last his brow lightened.

"I'll have some of this," he decided.

This was shepherd's pie costing eighteen-pence.

"And I'll have a cup of tea with it," he added, looking severely at the bottle of champagne on ice which was waiting to be uncorked for the rest of us.

When dinner was over our ebullient host called for cigars. I noticed that Willie Gallacher was frowning again. Much as I should have enjoyed one of Macartney's Corona Coronas, I refused it and said I should prefer a pipe.

Willie's face lightened again as it had lightened when he found the shepherd's pie on the bill of fare. He plunged into the side-pocket of his coat and brought it back with a handful of well-rolled black twist.

"Will you take a pipeful of my tobacco?" he asked me.

"There's nothing I like better," I declared.

[1] The late Very Rev. A. C. Don, K.C.V.O., Dean of Westminster.

We lit up and puffed opposing clouds of smoke at the smoke from the large cigars of Macartney and Pollitt.

From that moment Willie Gallacher and I became great friends, and I salute the memory of one of the most genuinely sincere men I have been privileged to know.

A day or two after that dinner at Simpson's there was a letter in the *Daily Telegraph* (I think) from Ronald Squires complaining of having been gassed out of a famous restaurant in the Strand by the fumes of two pipes.

On my way to Barra in the middle of that October Chrissie met me in Glasgow and I decided to fly back. Earlier that summer I had flown for the first time when a Scottish Airways plane had taken Father Mac-Kellaig, the Coddie, Neil Sinclair and myself to the South Uist games. *8 minutes from the gate of Suidheachan to the ground* as I had written to Faith.

The flight from Renfrew Airport to Barra seemed more of an adventure. As we rose into the air I thought that an airport which was not surrounded by a large cemetery would have been more reassuring to the flying novice. I wrote to Faith:

I must say that flying in a gale is a most exhilarating experience. The only time I was at all nervous for a moment was when we suddenly swooped down 4,000 feet in order to find out the name of a steamer wrecked off Gigha. This we did at an angle of 45°. After that not a bump till we were off Barra and coming round into the wind to land. I certainly think you ought to fly next time. I'm sure you'd enjoy it.

That gale which I found exhilarating was the beginning of one of the fiercest I remember in the West. I was writing to Faith:

We had a 'socking' gale last night and by the wireless it isn't finished yet. 90 miles an hour at times. The damage here isn't too bad. 5 slates, the garden fence down, the top of the aerial (which hasn't hurt reception at all), and the whirling cowl on the billiards-room chimney whirled away on to the tràigh mhòr. Birds all round the house—geese, oyster-catchers, lapwings, gulls. It was a cannonade. The Barra lifeboat had an S.O.S. from a Norwegian ship off Barra Head but she must have foundered with all hands. The Lochearn was lying in Castlebay all night and couldn't reach the pier till eight this morning and for the first time the aeroplane didn't come to-day.

Earlier that summer Colonel Kenneth MacDonald of Tote had asked me if I was prepared to sell the Shiant Islands. It was the last thing I wanted to do but my financial position was in such a poor way that I said I would, and we agreed on £1,500 as the price. Then there was a hold up until he should be able to get hold of money he had in India. I said nothing to Calum MacSween at the time because I did not want to worry him until it was certain that Colonel MacDonald would be able to conclude the purchase. I heard from him this October and wrote from London to tell Calum the sad news, though I was able to say I had made his continuation as tenant a condition of the sale.

To my amazement Calum MacSween wrote to tell me he had expected my letter because on the night I wrote it he had dreamt I had come to him and told him I had been compelled to sell the Islands. Calum MacSween was always psychic and his brother Angus certainly had second sight.

I was very sad to sell the Shiants but I was immensely relieved when I heard they had been bought by Nigel Nicolson who would one day dedicate that admirable book he wrote about the Leverhulme experiment in Lewis and Harris to the memory of Calum MacSween, the tenant first of Leverhulme, then of me and finally of Nigel himself.

When I got back to Barra I had written to Calum of our flight. He wrote back:

I am afraid you may get a surprise some day: I have not much faith in motors. Even in a boat they are a risky business; to hang one's life in the air is extremely so.

My job now was somehow or other to finish my life of Pericles by the end of the year. I had just made the effort to get down to work again when I received a note from Louis MacNeice[1] to ask if he could come and see me. I sent back word to say I would send the car for him the following afternoon; he was staying with the Crookle. The editor of the chief Opposition paper in Belfast had been on Barra this summer and from him I had heard about the great courage the Bishop of Down had shown in criticizing the behaviour of the Orangemen. So the first thing I said to Louis MacNeice when he arrived with a young woman whose name I have forgotten was to express my admiration for the courageous attitude of his episcopal father.

"Oh, I'm not interested in what my father is doing." And as he said this he looked quickly at his young female companion as if for an approving nod. I suppose he was piqued because I did not express my interest in his poetry. As I had never read any of it this was unfortunately beyond me. He had just become a lecturer in Greek to the Bedford College for Women, so I told him I was working on a life of Pericles. That interested him no more than his poetry interested me. On the following evening he called about ten o'clock in an agitated state to ask if I would endorse his ability to honour a cheque for £10 he had just written. This I did.

In a book he wrote called *I Crossed the Minch*, which he seemed to think was a feat of condescension, he wrote with evident disapproval of my wearing a green jumper to match a green tweed suit and went on to talk about the rich white rug in the billiards-room as if it was an ostentatious

[1] The late Louis MacNeice, C.B.E.

display of luxury to find across the Minch; it was in fact a cheap Indian rug that cost eight guineas. He seemed to think that my courtesy in sending a car for him was an assumption of grandeur and self-importance. I never met him again.

I could not help contrasting MacNeice's cocksure air of knowing all about the Hebrides in a fortnight with that of H. V. Morton who had visited Barra that summer; after planning to follow up his fascinating book about the Lowlands called *In Search of Scotland* with another about the Highlands and Islands, he told me that he did not feel justified in doing so.

"Thank goodness I know when I don't know," he had said to me.

I was grateful to be far away from London in Barra during that December week when the country was waiting for news of the Kingdom's future. I think I should have been tempted to stick a knife into Geoffrey Dawson, the Editor of *The Times*, that Magdalen man for whom the white lilies of the College had become tiger-lilies.

I wrote in *The Gramophone*:

"What a strange thing music is! This platitudinous ejaculation was inspired by the Beethoven Quintet in C Major which has just been published by Columbia.

"It is a work with which I was not familiar and, whether or not my mind was preoccupied with other matters, it made no impression on me either the first time that it was played or the second time. It was played a third time when I was trying to exclude from my mind, in order to concentrate on my own work, all thoughts about late events, and most of all a black rage which had come over me at hearing immediately after the news of the Abdication the prices of the Stock Exchange read by the six o'clock announcer out of their usual order. Was that the true anodyne for a nation's sorrow, a rise in the shares of some wretched motor-car company? Had Elgar's *Land of Hope and Glory* been played as an overture to this eructation of bad taste? Financial anxiety is intelligible, but decency should have kept the Stock Exchange prices at such a tragic moment to their proper place in the lees of the news.

"I had cut off the wireless in a fury for some chamber music to be played, and was trying to get away from the present and back to the Greece of the 5th century B.C. about which I was writing when gradually I became aware of an exquisite melody that was washing away the sense of uncleanliness that was left by that conjunction of tragedy with commerce. On asking what the music was I found that it was the second movement of this Beethoven Quintet in C Major."

Faith had been spending a night or two with her brother Frank who was Chaplain to the Verderers of Windsor Park. She wrote:

It wasn't much better at Chaplain's Lodge as the flood of slander had spread

*over the Park and no one had a good word to say for Edward . . . some people came
in after lunch and the whole room began abusing him. So I up and said, "I think
it's disgraceful of you all to speak of him like this. Whatever he has done he has
gone now. Can't you remember the good about him?" There was a short silence,
but before long they were picking again at his poor carcase.* The Times *leader
is scandalous. I nearly wrote to them (only I knew it wouldn't be published) about
his going to Frank's church for communion, ringing up himself to find out if there
was a service.*

Then came that unforgivable broadcast by the Archbishop of Canterbury on the Sunday evening after the King had gone.

As H. G. Wells said, Stuart Hibberd should have announced,

"Now, ladies and gentlemen, you will hear the final talk which brings
Rat Week to its conclusion."

The December wind was sighing round Suidheachan as I listened to
that compound of oil and venom oozing from the wireless set.

Three days after what I felt was His Disgrace's broadcast I had a
welcome letter from Faith with news that W. H. P. Collins had rung her
up to say that he had read *As Much as I Dare* with intense pleasure and
was confident it would have a great success. By the same post Rich wrote
to tell me that *The East Wind of Love* was to be the January Book of the
Month of the *Daily Mail*, of the *Evening Standard*, of the Book Circle and
to be the Book Society's first recommendation.

I was grateful that the original intention to publish *The East Wind* in
November had been delayed. The Abdication crisis would certainly
have completely overshadowed it.

In spite of the financial future looking better I was still having a
terrible time over money. Rich and Cowan arranged to pay me for the
Winds with bills instead of cash.

On November 23rd I was writing to Pinker:

*The Castlebay manager of the Commercial Bank of Scotland has just called to
say with a good deal of indignation that his head office in Edinburgh had forbidden
him to extend the overdraft of £119 because they considered that the £500 bill of
Rich and Cowan discounted by them was the equivalent of an overdraft to that
amount.*

Luckily I had sent off the revised typescript of *Pericles* to Hodder and
Stoughton, and a day or two later was able to pay in their cheque. At
the same time, I was disappointed over the money for the Shiant Islands
which had not yet reached Colonel MacDonald from India.

It was about this time that Mrs Roebuck was again spending a few
days with us. Suddenly she said to me,

"Would £800 be any use to you?"

"It certainly would, but if there's any fairy gold on Barra I don't
know where to find it."

"I do," said Mrs Roebuck. "I've got it saved up."

I told her I was not prepared to dip into her savings.

"But it would be a help," she insisted. "It's not even on deposit, because I grudge paying income tax on it. If I hand it to you you can pay me five per cent. every six months and I won't have to pay income tax on it."

I knew only too well that Christina Roebuck was lending me that money with her heart not with her head and that my acceptance of her generosity was truly desired. So I accepted the loan with another thanks to God for the friends He has given to me. I had been able to pay back the dear Coddie his £200 which had saved the situation earlier.

I had also been able to pay back to *The Gramophone* money which had been advanced to Faith. She had been doing a splendid job for me as London editor. Christopher Stone had been entirely preoccupied with his broadcasts of popular music from Luxemburg but owing to the loss of a lawsuit about those broadcasts he was turning back to *The Gramophone* and obviously much less anxious for his sister's help. I foresaw that it would not be long before he would gently and affectionately squeeze her out of the editorial chair.

Let this year end with the dedication of *The East Wind of Love* to Eric Linklater dated in that November:

"Just over three years ago I told you that my next novel would be called *The Four Winds of Love*, and I asked you to accept the dedication of it. At that time my notion was that it would be a long novel, but not too long to be published in a single volume. When I sat down to weave the various themes into a whole it was soon apparent that the book would be twice as long as I had supposed; but after working at it for six months I was at last compelled to recognize that if the task I had set myself was to be completed without shirking, the book would be four times the length anticipated while it was just floating about agreeably in my fancy. So you see, instead of offering you a complete edifice I offer you no more than the foundations of one.

"When I was three-quarters of the way through *Sinister Street* the European war began and the large-scale book I had planned to build on the foundations of *Sinister Street* had to be abandoned on account of the inadequacy of such foundations for an edifice which would have to house the war and its effect upon the life of our time. For two or three books I tried to persevere with my original design, but the inadequacy of the foundations became increasingly apparent, and I was driven to accept the hard fact that many years must pass before I could hope to achieve the emotional detachment and experienced craftsmanship required to build my ambitious edifice to a new design. There was a moment when I believed I had discovered a formula for a novel about the war, but I threw that over in order to write the series which began with *Gallipoli Memories*, and came to an untoward conclusion with *Greek*

Memories. After the tiresome case brought about by the third volume, my publisher wrote to find out what the offended Authorities disliked so that the necessary excisions might be made and the withdrawn volume reissued—like a blank cartridge. The reply was that the offended Authorities could not assent to this because, inasmuch as a certain number of the copies were in circulation, a foreign agent would only have to compare one of these copies with the expurgated version to discover what it was the Authorities wished to hide from him! In other words *Greek Memories* could never be published and therefore the Authorities could feel sure that the fourth volume, *Aegean Memories* would probably never be written, and certainly never published in my lifetime. So I was left with another unfinished edifice, and I cannot help feeling that I am inviting fortune's mischief by setting out to build yet again a work in successive volumes. In view of what fortune may hold in store for this work, I hesitate to announce any more than that the next volume will be *The South Wind of Love,* and will take up the tale eleven years later and carry it on to the end of the war, that *The West Wind of Love* will deal with the years immediately after the war, and that *The North Wind of Love* will bring the action into the third decade of this century.

"Five years of reviewing have left me with prejudice against very long books, and I shall find it easy to sympathize with critics who groan at the prospect before them. I am hopeful that when the four volumes are published it will be clear that the size of the work was demanded by the design, but whether a design which involves such an accumulation of incident, such an amount of discussion, such a variety of scene, and such a crowd of characters will be approved is another matter, and I confess that I wait the final verdict with some anxiety.

"In dedicating to you the first volume of *The Four Winds of Love,* I have chosen a junior contemporary for whose existing work I have a secure admiration and in whose future work I have an equally secure confidence, but let that pass; a truer and better reason is that I hope to please thereby a friend to whose friendship I owe more than can be paid with words."

As I wrote that dedication I was back in 1912 and asking myself why I was going on with *Sinister Street* when a great European war would make such a novel seem out of date. Now I was wondering how far I should have reached in *The Four Winds of Love* when a second European war would begin.

P

FIFTY-FOUR YEARS OLD: 1937

I HAD tried hard to avoid coming down to London for the Foyle's lunch given at the Dorchester to celebrate the publication of *The East Wind of Love* on January 7th, but so much stress was laid on the advantage of my appearance from the point of view of the book's material success that I foolishly gave way and went to London. The result was that I succumbed to a particularly vicious influenza which was rampant that winter and arrived back in Barra to take at once to my bed, where I had to remain until almost the end of the month.

Laura Lovat had telegraphed her congratulations on *The East Wind* and on January 20th was writing:

After the exuberant telegram you must have been puzzled by my silence—but I have been caught and mangled and racked and stunned by this appalling 'flu (more like the Black Death) so that only to-day I can lift my head from the pillow. Despite this—and it's an enormous compliment to your book—I have been enthralled by it.

Yes, it certainly was a vicious influenza that winter.

Another letter from one of the Frasers and Maxwells galore to whom this Octave is dedicated came from Elsie Maxwell.[1] In the course of it she wrote:

It has always been a bit of a worry to me that all Catholic boys are so very young for their age. The boys I have known most intimately—my brothers, and my own sons particularly so. Simon was absurdly young and immature when he went to Oxford, but as no one could say he was immature in after life one came to the conclusion that it did not matter. But your book has brought up again the extraordinary difference between Catholic and non-Catholic education—not only in the obvious things such as that Religion is the pivot in one case, but in the way public opinion (which is the pivot in the ordinary public school) hardly counts in the Catholic ones. It seems to me this lack of the fetish of public opinion, tho' in some ways a good thing, in others is not so, and that it is the lack of this stimulus which leaves them undeveloped.

Elsie Constable Maxwell was one of the wisest women of whom I have had the good fortune to be a friend. She would live to a great age and as it seemed to me grow wiser and wiser all the time.

By the end of the month I was able to get going with *The South Wind of Love*. I was writing to Faith:

[1] The late Hon. Mrs Constable Maxwell.

I am sitting up in my chair again for the first time. There's no doubt I was very ill. Chrissie is definitely better, but her mother has been trying to get here from Harris for five days and is even now only at Lochboisdale. We hope to get her over to-morrow morning.

I was particularly gratified by Humbert Wolfe's review in the Referee. *I wrote to thank him. It really gave me great encouragement.*

I managed somehow to produce a 1,200 word review for the Sunday Chronicle, *Jan. 31 issue, but how I don't know. I'm sorry about the* Gram. *editorial but it's hopeless to attempt it. We had no boat on Wednesday. So I've no news of you since Monday.*

I admired Humbert Wolfe's[1] poetry and respected his criticism. His death soon after the Second War started was not only a loss to English literature; it was also a loss to the Ministry of Labour of which he was Deputy Secretary.

The other review of *The East Wind* which helped to make me feel that the task of writing the quarter of a million words I felt was the lowest estimate for *The South Wind of Love* was written by Douglas West in the *Daily Mail*. The last sentence was particularly gratifying:

"This is a book triumphantly alive, packed with thought, and mercifully free from the influence of coteries and the faint provincialism ineradicable from most English fiction."

James Drawbell, the astute and imaginative editor of the *Sunday Chronicle*, had persuaded me to take on a weekly book. I was glad to get a letter from him in February to say that my reviews had been well received by the readers of the *Sunday Chronicle*.

Throughout the previous year we had been badgering the Inverness-shire County Council to do something for our Barra roads which were full of pot-holes, deep in sand after a gale, and in every way a disgrace to the County Council. We received nothing but evasive replies from the County Clerk and there was no sign of any action's being taken. Finally we decided this January that the only way to stir the County Council up was to refuse to pay our car licences. Every car and lorry owner on the island except one agreed upon this course. There were about a dozen of us including two of the priests and the doctor. We invited the motorists of South Uist to join in our refusal to pay car licences but they did not feel bold enough to do so.

With our protest we sent the sum total of the money expended on repairs to cars and in replacing tyres. That sum total was larger than the money required for our licences.

The Press reported our strike fairly on the whole, though of course some of the asses who bray in correspondence columns were given hearing.

[1] The late Humbert Wolfe, C.B., C.B.E.

In April we again refused to pay the Road Fund licences and in July
we were summoned to appear before the Sheriff-Substitute at Lochmaddy in North Uist. Sheriff Inglis indulged in some pompous animad-
version which Justice Shallow would not have disdained, and imposed
ludicrously heavy fines.

Press comment was fairly intelligent on the whole but the *Observer* on
July 18th was fatuous:

"The Barra rising, in which Mr Compton Mackenzie figured as one
of eleven motorists in that island of the West who refused to take out
Road Fund licences as a protest against the poor conditions of the island
roads, has been summarily suppressed. Fines were imposed last week on
the rebels at Lochmaddy, where the case was a described by the sheriff
as 'a grievously ill-chosen example of endeavour to show parochial
independence of national obligations.'

"The fact that most of those concerned in the case are known to be
ardent Scottish Nationalists has lent the affair a piquancy not present
in its immediate circumstances, but it cannot be said that the Nationalist
Cause has benefited. There have been previous instances of irresponsi-
bility on the part of the movement's leaders that have alienated general
sympathy, and this latest escapade savours too much of 'playboys of the
western world' to inspire any feeling that the participants were more
sinned against than Synge-ing."

That last execrable pun was inspired by my having said in April that
unless more attention was paid to the Outer Isles the people would have
to consider secession to Eire. This had been reported in the *Observer* as
coming from that playboy of the Western world, Compton Mackenzie.

In fact the only Nationalist was myself; one could not imagine a more
patriotic Englishman than Dr Bartlett, even if he did sport the kilt.

In due course we appealed against the fines imposed by that pompous
Sheriff-Substitute and that autumn before the Lord Justice Clerk, Lord
Pitman and Lord Mackay our appeal was successful in reducing all the
fines. If Craigie Aitcheson, the Lord Justice Clerk, had been on his own
a perusal of his judgment suggests he would have abolished the fines
altogether. Sir Alexander MacEwen handled the legal side of the business for us. All the motoring papers commended our practical protest
and from all over Britain motorists sent contributions to our expenses
with warm approval.

Early in 1938 the Inverness-shire County Council set out to put the
Barra roads in order. The playboys of the western world had won.

During all this road business I was working twelve hours a day at
The South Wind of Love, and that I continued to do until I sent the last
10,000 out of 270,000 words to Rich and Cowan at the end of June. I was
compelled to work at this pace because they were set on publishing the
book by the end of August.

There were two names in the Coronation honours which I was glad to see. Iain Colquhoun was given the Thistle and Hugh Walpole was knighted.

Rupert Hart-Davis quoted from my letter of congratulation in his remarkable biography of Walpole because it had given Hugh such pleasure. Here is Hugh Walpole's letter to me:

> *90 Piccadilly*
> *W.1*

May 16. '37
My dear Monty,

Few letters I've had have pleased me as much as yours—Brett Young, Swinnerton, yourself—However much I have seemed tiresome or a joker or interfering in the past—somehow we've always stayed friends and I think I'm prouder of that than anything. In fact I'm not really between us, proud at all. I think the War stopped us from doing what we were really meant to do. But there in my library is the MS of Sinister S. *Vol. I and that I'm proud of*

> *Yours always*
> *Hugh Walpole*

I have already tried to explain to reviewers of *My Life and Times* that I am hoping to recapture the past in a contemporary mood. Therefore I had to tell stories of Hugh Walpole as he was at the time and as I was. Once upon a time he had been consumed by jealousy over the success of *Sinister Street*. Then as he himself became successful that jealousy faded. I have been lucky in never having known the emotion of jealousy. I knew what intense pleasure that knighthood must have given Hugh Walpole and therefore my own pleasure in it was completely sincere. Frank Swinnerton and I had laughed at Hugh but both of us grow fonder of the people at whom we laugh; we are in fact grateful to them for making us laugh.

Somerset Maugham in spite of his success remained jealous. In January 1935 when I was in Harris with John Campbell, crusading for the Sea League, a letter for him was inadvertently addressed to me. Here is his acknowledgement:

> Villa Mauresque
> Cap Ferrat
> A.M.
> *January 16th 1935*

My dear Monty

Thank you very much for sending me on the letter. I can only imagine it was sent to you because the postal authorities thought that you were the only author that mattered. Nice for you but somewhat chilling for the rest of us. I did not know you

*lived in the Isle of Harris; surely that is where they make the tweed. Couldn't we
have some sent.*

Yours always

W. S. Maugham

We had a visit in Barra at the beginning of June from Walter Elliot[1]
who was now Secretary of State for Scotland. He and Mrs Elliot[2] arrived
by plane with a stout bodyguard of plus-fours from St Andrew's House.

I think Mrs Roebuck was staying with us at Suidheachan and that
she and Chrissie had prepared a superlative lunch. But the bodyguard
was firm. Lunch would be waiting for Mr Elliot at the Castlebay Hotel.
The plus-fours felt that if he were left unguarded to lunch with me he
might be lured into promising us that lobster pool for which the Sea
League was pressing. He would not be able to plead ignorance of fishing
matters, having been Minister of Agriculture and Fisheries until last
autumn. Moreover, there was the question of the Barra roads; he might
be committed to some insufficiently considered promise to take some
action that the Scottish Office found so deplorable an intrusion on
Civilian caution. The plus-fours even tried to suggest that there really
was no time for an apéritif.

At this Mrs Elliot rebelled and sent off Walter Elliot to look for
something she had left in the plane.

"They're only fussing about the time for lunch in Castlebay," I told
her, "because our roads are in such a ghastly state that the cars will have
to crawl along from here to Castlebay."

The plus-fours frowned. They thought they had made it clear that the
Secretary of State was paying an informal visit to Barra.

In the *Daily Record* this had been expressly stated. " 'Mr Elliot is not
flying to Barra specially for the purpose of seeing the roads there,' said
an official of the Scottish Office in London yesterday. 'The roads do not
come within the jurisdiction of the Secretary of State, but he will take
the opportunity of acquainting himself with local conditions and circumstances during his tour of the isles. Although he will see the roads, no
formal arrangements have been made for this purpose.' "

"He'll not only see the roads," I said to one of the plus-fours, "he'll
feel them, however late you manage to be for lunch in Castlebay."

That June was to be an influential month for me. I had been increasingly indignant over the backwash of the wretched gossip which reached
me in Barra about the Duke of Windsor and Mrs Simpson while they
were waiting for the decree nisi of her divorce to be made absolute.
When they were married in France on June 3rd I sent a telegram wishing
them both long life and happiness, winding up with 'Floreat Magdalena',

[1] The late Rt. Hon. Walter Elliot, C.H.
[2] Baroness Elliot of Harwood, D.B.E.

the motto of the College at which the Duke had been an undergraduate some ten years later than myself. After I wrote those words I turned to the *Annual Register* of 1937 to check the accuracy of the date I had given for the wedding. The chronicle of the year's events records the Earldom and Garter conferred upon Mr Stanley Baldwin in May, and on June 2nd the victory of Mid-day Sun in the Derby followed by this:

"Earl Baldwin announced that a gift of £250,000 which had been placed at his disposal by an anonymous donor in appreciation of his services to the country was to be made into a new Imperial Trust to be administered by independent trustees for the purpose of strengthening the ties of Empire." Somehow it soon leaked out that Lord Baldwin himself had presented this £250,000.

Yet throughout that volume the man who as Prince of Wales had done more to strengthen the Empire than anybody else is nowhere mentioned.

To my surprise and pleasure I received a telegram of thanks sent off after the wedding breakfast. Macartney was in Barra at the time and urged me to write to the Duke and offer my pen to write a book which would put his case fairly to the world. Finally I decided to do this. The Duke wrote back to accept my offer and presently wrote again to say he would see me that autumn in Paris and discuss a synopsis of the proposed book.

I had made some strong remarks in the June number of *The Gramophone* about the failure of the recording companies to give the public a record of the Duke of Windsor's broadcast at the time of the Abdication.

Christopher Stone had been worried by my outspokenness but Faith had been firm. I received many letters from readers applauding my remarks: there was not a single protest. Faith wrote to say that the feeling the Duke had been given a raw deal by the ecclesiastics and politicians was growing stronger all the time.

It was in the middle of that June that the disastrous fire at Beaufort Castle happened. I had telegraphed and written my grief at the news to Laura Lovat. On June 18th she wrote to me:

My dearest Monty,

I knew you were grieving with us—and was so grateful for your wire and letter.

I never dreamt the death of anything inanimate could cause such a wound—(I mean quite apart from the unending losses and material worries in which one is enmeshed—).

I suppose the only thing is to get accustomed—as best one can—to this mental (spiritual?) amputation.

Strange to say the Chapel is unscathed and where all else is either a chaos of ruins, or smoke and water ruined 'saved' rooms—it retains the most fantastic

*serenity and peace, smelling faintly of incense and ready for Mass which was to be
said the day after the fire.*

*I am miserable about my books—most of yours gone—all my scrapbooks—
indeed everything I loved! A whole life's associations!*

*I must just try to rebuild it a little for Shimi's sake—just to make it habitable—
but I don't know if we ever can even do this. I am just done in.*

Dear love

L

As I read that poignant letter I was seeing that beloved little girl
Veronica playing a Mozart sonata in the twilight. I was hearing again
the sound of those Christmas parties with Frasers and Maxwells galore.
I was reading *Pride and Prejudice* to Laura when she was laid up with a
broken leg and converting Magdalen to a realization that Jane Austen
was much more interesting than she had supposed.

Somehow by the beginning of that July I finished *The South Wind of
Love*. Rich and Cowan had started setting it up when I let them have
the first 150,000 words. Now they suddenly took it into their heads that
50,000 words must be cut. I refused to do the cutting myself and after
their literary advisers had tried to make the cuts they had decided that
the most they could cut out of 270,000 words were 10,000. So Rich and
Cowan decided to go ahead without any cuts.

When I finished the book I dedicated it to Newman Flower and wrote:

My dear Newman,

*It was to you in your room at La Belle Sauvage that I first put into words my
conception of* The Four Winds of Love, *which alone would make your name at
the head of this dedicatory letter appropriate. That the long process of elaboration
ultimately resulted in my being unable to fit it into your list makes me more anxious
than ever to inscribe to you this volume so that I can have a chance to thank you
for an association of seventeen years without a single disagreement. You thought
(and you may yet be right) that four volumes would be a mistake. I could not squeeze
my tale into two. You could have compelled me to do so, but you generously allowed
our contract to be broken in order that I might write this tale in my own way.*

*That first volume was treated with such sympathy by almost all its reviewers in
this country, the United States and Australia that it is a temptation to make a bid
for the sympathetic treatment of the second by enlarging on some of the difficulties
by which I was faced. I hope, however, it will not be counted as an appeal for
sympathy if I insist that this volume must not be read as even veiled autobiography.
That I have drawn upon my own experience for certain historical incidents is
obvious, but it will be a waste of time for people to try to identify characters or
search for facts in what is a work of fiction. One or two of the subsidiary characters
have been drawn from life, but the originals of such are no longer alive. The
principal characters are pure creations of my fancy and are not even founded upon*

models. The two islands of Lipsia and Icaros are adumbrations of real islands but all their inhabitants are fictitious and also much of the topography. Mileto is a cloud-cuckoo place of my own. So is Citrano. These remarks on places apply to ships, and even where I have occasionally used actual incidents the people who played their part in such incidents have not appeared. I was never in Salonica, and that portion of the tale might have been placed equally well at any Base. Salonica happened to be the Base geographically necessary.

Goethe, well over a century ago, deplored the fact that the increasing publicity of an artist's life precluded the somnambulistic state in which a work of art should be achieved. And what was publicity then compared with to-day? Unfortunately when we begin to write we are not so sure of success as to preserve from the start a strict anonymity, and indeed anonymity nowadays is no longer recognized as the privilege of a writer.

The West Wind of Love *will take up the story where it stops with this volume.*

Well, with all its faults, my dear Newman, I offer you The South Wind of Love *and with it my gratitude for more than can be expressed with a book however long.*

Yours ever

Compton Mackenzie.

I was deeply touched by Newman Flower's generous acknowledgment and I sent him an advance copy of *The South Wind of Love* at the end of August:

Islehurst, Sevenoaks

Aug. 24. 37.

My dear Monty,

You have done some very human things in your time, and no one has better reason to know it than I. But I am quite certain that you have never been more generous than in your dedicatory letter to South Wind.

The book arrived this morning. I assure you, my dear Monty, that this is the greatest compliment that has ever been paid to me. I send you a thousand thanks for such a fine gesture of friendship, and a thousand thanks again.

There is a sense of affection in the way you put the reason for this book not appearing under the Cassell imprint—an affection responsive from this end. Of course I was all damn-wrong about the 4 volumes. I have been reading the book all this evening and, if I didn't know it before, I know it now. But all publishers make a bad 'break' sometimes—else they would retire early to gorgeous estates with more retainers than the books they ever published.

I am going on holiday the day after to-morrow and taking the book in my bag, to finish in quietude and leisure. . . .

Meantime I want you to know how much I appreciate a friendship for me which made you write that letter,

Yours ever

Newman

Newman Flower came up from Dorset to be present at the Foyle's lunch given for me on my eightieth birthday to usher in the First Octave of *My Life and Times*. Alas, he is no longer with us to read those heart-warming words he wrote to me twenty-nine years ago to a day as I write these words.

I look back forty years and in his room at La Belle Sauvage I hear a great publisher exclaim:

"You're the only reasonable bloody author I know."

The South Wind of Love was treated kindly by almost all the reviewers in Great Britain and the United States; perhaps if I had never offered my pen to the Duke of Windsor and started *The West Wind* instead of *The Windsor Tapestry* before the Second War started it would have been easier for critics to judge the complete novel. Circumstances would rule that the second volume of *The North Wind* would not be published until eight years after *The South Wind*.

I had notified the Duke that I was letting my publishers know about his letters to me in the strictest confidence, and I had insisted that the *Sunday Pictorial* in which I had done a weekly column about the gramo-phone and records for five years should have the first refusal of any book about the Duke. The terms of my contract with Rich and Cowan for *The Four Winds of Love* made it necessary for me to agree to allow them half the money from all serial rights. Otherwise they could have made it impossible for me to write the proposed book about the Duke. I was worried to hear about the sum offered by the *Sunday Pictorial* if the Duke gave it his formal approval. I argued that all I wanted from him was a private acknowledgment that the facts of the Abdication as I proposed to present them were accurate. I began to regret having suggested the offer of the serial rights to the *Sunday Pictorial*, because the prospect of big money was obviously too exciting. The *Sunday Pictorial* wanted an authorized biography: I had wanted only to write about the Abdication. Finally much against my better judgment I agreed that the synopsis I should send for the Duke's approval should be on a much larger scale than the history of the Abdication. I pressed upon Rich and Cowan and upon Pinker the need for absolute secrecy until the Duke had been able to read the synopsis of my proposed book and give the all clear.

On my way back to Barra I had to do a couple of broadcasts from Scotland and invited Norman Sturrock to fly back with me and spend a few days in Barra. The members of the Scottish Arts Club declared that such a journey would be fatal for Norman, but Norman himself was determined to fly for the first time and his heart was mercifully not affected by the experience. I look back to those few days we had together as an exquisite sunlit calm before the storm.

On August 4th I was writing to Pinker:

I had a nice shock yesterday when a fellow landed here in a plane sent from London by the Daily Express *to ask if it was true that I had been invited by the Duke of Windsor to go to Austria with a view to presenting his side of the business as a counterblast to* Coronation Commentary (presumably this was some broadcast)[1]. *This means there has been a leakage at your end.*

I had to do some extremely rapid thinking, for it was quite clear to me that the object of that infernal visit was to know which paper was to have the story if such a story became available, and I had practically to bribe the Daily Express *to silence by promising them the first exclusive information.*

At the same time, I was in a furious rage at having my hand forced in this manner. Grant, the Editor of the Sunday Pictorial, *has evidently not breathed a word about his offer, and indeed, I have absolute confidence in his discretion. The* Express *would not have bothered to send this specially chartered plane to Barra if they knew the* Sunday Pictorial *had agreed to serialize. For God's sake, do impress on Rich the vital necessity for secrecy. Faith left for Salzburg last week and before I know where I am a plane will be arriving with somebody wanting to know if she is going to Austria at the Duke's invitation.*

And do give up sending me telegrams in which the Duke is alluded to as Mr Jones. If any more of this sort of thing goes on I shall call the whole thing off.

I was badly shaken to read some days later in the *Glasgow Bulletin*:

ABDICATION SECRETS

"If a rumour I heard yesterday becomes fact, we may one of these days be reading the most sensational book of the century. It will deal with the Abdication, and the rumour has it that if the Duke of Windsor gives his consent to the publication of certain documents the country will be presented with a new and rather startling version of the inner history of the crisis. The British author whose name is linked with the story is read throughout the world."

I was thankful that there was no mention of my name yet in connection with the rumour, and I now got down to the synopsis of the book I was proposing to write. I find a letter of August 27th to Sydney Dark, the Editor of the *Church Times*:

Dear Sydney,

I have just been arguing with one of the priests here about the Anglican Church's divorce attitude and you can help me.

On what do you base the right for an Anglican priest to refuse to marry divorced persons? I remember Father Black protesting in various churches at the end of the last century against the re-marriage of divorced people, but I also seem to remember that he was hauled over the coals for it by Bishop Creighton. Have you the back files of the Church Times *which would put the case against re-marriage?*

---

[1] I had not yet heard of Geoffrey Dennis's book.

The argument arose over the visit from a friend who had been divorced and re-married at St Ethelburga's, Bishopsgate. I always understood G . . . C . . . was Anglo-Catholic.

Be a good fellow and let me have an indication of the authority for refusing re-marriage, outside of course the claims of the Anglican Church's Catholicity, which we mustn't argue about.

Forgive my being a nuisance.

Sydney Dark wrote back:

The Church Times
7 Portugal Street
London W.C.2.
September 2nd 1937

My dear Monty,

The law of the English Church is in the Canons of 1603 and in the Prayer Book Marriage Service.

Anglo-Catholics do not, of course, admit that the decisions of secular Courts, the Judicial Committee of the Privy Council, can override Canon Law.

G . . . C . . . is an eccentric and certainly not an Anglo-Catholic.

Looking forward to gossiping again at the Savile.

Yours ever
Sydney Dark

I sent off my synopsis to the Duke on September 9th, but was perturbed by the post next day.

A letter arrived from France dated June 10th. It was from the Secretary of the Duke of Windsor with formal thanks for my wedding telegram. I looked at the postmark, and it coincided with the date on which it had been written two months ago. I now examined the envelope and detected at once signs of its having been opened.

I presumed that all the letters acknowledging telegrams of congratulation had been handed by the post office to M.I.5 so that these protectors of the realm could learn who were likely to take part in another rising for the King over the water.

And now with the stupidity of so many sleuths in the Great War it was to send the letter on to an ex-sleuth two months after it was written and expect him not to spot at once that it had been opened.

Whether the letters of the Duke of Windsor to me had been opened I could not say; a microscopic examination would have been necessary and I was not prepared to let them out of my sight.

I cannot remember the details of the agreement that was being drawn up with Rich and Cowan, but I find the draft of an exasperated letter to Ralph written some time in the middle of that September:

So far as you personally are concerned you can rely on my intention to maintain our business relationship, but I will not continue it except as a personal arrangement between myself and yourself. If I have to deal with an organization of which you are only the mouthpiece and in which you are not completely your own master the personal relationship which makes a business arrangement possible for me is destroyed. I have given you and Rich and Cowan a tremendous chance. You and Roddie Rich may be personally interested; but I am not satisfied that either the firm of J. B. Pinker and Sons or the firm of Rich and Cowan are interested in anything at the moment except driving a hard bargain with me. None of you seems to grasp that I have twenty times as much experience of this kind of matter as the whole lot of you put together.

Of course there is going to be a fight and a very big fight and if all of you are not prepared to fight you had all better give up now before the fight begins. If you think this book is going through with the blessing of the authorities you were never more deceived in your life.

This book can only be authorized by the person whom it is about, and he may not feel able to do that. My own feeling is that pressure of every kind will be brought to bear upon him, when his advisers see the synopsis, to withhold his authorization and cancel the 'assignation' he made with me to meet him in Paris at the end of this month.

But whether he authorizes the book or not I shall write it. My motive in writing is to speak out on behalf of a man I believe to have been wronged by public opinion, for I believe that if the public learn the facts that opinion will be completely changed. Therefore provided I can get what I have to say into print the money side is immaterial to me. At the same time I am not going to stand for anybody's making a farthing out of this book who is not prepared to risk something more than £250 a month for an option to publish it.

The delay in acknowledging my synopsis made me more and more doubtful of the Duke of Windsor's second thoughts. People in London had obviously been chattering and I felt sure that everything would be done to stop that meeting in Paris, which he had suggested. My doubts were justified. Toward the end of October Sir Walter Monckton[1] asked me to come and see him and Mr George Allen[2] at his chambers in 2 Harcourt Buildings, Temple. Allen was the senior partner of the Duke's solicitors Allen and Overy. I made a note of that interview at the time for Rich and Cowan and give it here in its crudity to avoid 'writing it up'.

"Sir Walter Monckton said that if the book were written on the synopsis sent by me to the Duke he and Mr Allen who were the only people apart from the King who knew the true facts might easily find

[1] The late Viscount Monckton of Brenchley.
[2] The late Sir George Allen.

themselves charged under the Official Secrets Act. When he made this
remark Monckton moved to a desk in the window and picked up what
I saw was my synopsis. I replied I did not see how this was possible unless
they had communicated facts and there was no evidence of that. I
declared that my only object in writing any book was to present the
truth as it appeared to me and that it would seem in the course of trying
to do this I had already hit the truth. I added I wished to present the
position, character, and motives of the Duke fairly to the world. I felt
that both ecclesiastical and political influence had been unfairly used
against him. In fact I considered his treatment positively unconstitutional, but that no doubt would be a matter for legal argument when
I had put the case for unconstitutional behaviour. It was about this point
that Allen suddenly asked me if the Duke's behaviour *could* be defended.
I replied with some passion, but I cannot remember the details exactly.
One point I made very strongly was that nothing would induce me in
any book I wrote to throw the Duchess to the wolves, and Monckton said
quickly, 'that is very important from the Duke's point because that is
one thing he will not stand'. The argument then resolved itself into the
question of whether such a book would hurt the present King, and I
expressed strong confidence in my ability to be able to avoid that and
quoted to them a conversation I had with the present Queen when she
was Duchess of York about the future of the dynasty. I added that the
treatment of the Duke of Windsor since the Abdication was a steady
threat to the stability of the dynasty in this country and that if war came
my words would come true. I said that I was not so much keen on an
absolute authorization as a private assurance from the Duke or his
advisers that there was no misstatements of fact in my book. At this point
Monckton said, 'In other words what you want is a nihil obstat?' 'Yes,'
I said, 'as distinct from an imprimatur.' I pointed out it would be fatal
if the book erred in any trifle of fact. But I recognized that the Duke might
not want to be held responsible for my opinions, particularly about
individuals, and for that reason I did not seek an imprimatur. I pointed
out that if the book were to be of any service the widest circulation was
desirable and with that end in view my publishers had gone into the
matter of serial publication, but it was always understood that any such
serial publication was dependent on the Duke's decision. I added that it
was obviously impossible for us to let an editor down through any subsequent repudiation by the Duke. At the end of the interview, which lasted
about an hour, both Sir Walter Monckton and Mr Allen said that it had
been of the greatest help in clearing up the situation and that I might
consider the matter still open. Monckton asked me how long I would
be staying in London, and I said another ten days at least. On that he
said, 'Oh, that will give us plenty of time to reach a final arrangement.'
The interview came to an end because they were due for a conference

with Sir William Jowitt over the libel action against Heinemann.[1] One point I made very strongly when the matter of time was being discussed, which was that every moment was making it more and more difficult to guard against some premature and inaccurate statement in the press. The whole of Fleet Street knew that a book was being written, and so far it had only been my personal appeal which had prevented several disclosures already."

At the end of October I received a letter from the Duke to say that on consideration he felt that he would not authorize the book and suggested my talking it over with Walter Monckton.

On November 5th I wrote:

I am much honoured by your Royal Highness's gracious letter and hasten to assure you of my obedience to your will in this matter. I shall take advantage of the kind permission to consult Sir Walter Monckton and Mr Allen and when I have finished the book not a line shall be printed without your Royal Highness's approval.

On November 5th Walter Monckton wrote to ask me to dine with him at the Windham Club in St James's Square. That civilized Club almost next door to the London Library was destroyed by a German bomb. I recall the table at which we sat lighted by red wax candles and the charm of my host who eight years younger than myself shared a birthday with Lloyd George and me.

I asked him point blank whether the Duke wanted me to abandon the proposed book.

"He cannot give the book his approval."

"I shall make it perfectly clear that the book was written without his help, his encouragement or his approval. What I want to know is whether he does not want me to write the book."

"Nobody sympathizes more than I with your reasons for writing such a book, but I think you'd be wise to drop the whole business."

"I will only drop it if the Duke tells me that he wants me to drop it."

"I don't think he'll do that."

"Why not?"

Monckton did not answer. There was no letter from Paris and I resolved to go ahead.

Bob Boothby suggested I should ask Winston Churchill's advice about writing the book, and on November 16th he invited me to dine with him at the Savoy Grill to meet Churchill. It was the day Lord Halifax had gone to Berlin at Goering's invitation for the opening of the hunting exhibition, and it may be called the day on which appeasement was openly declared to be the policy of the Chamberlain Government.

To the question about the proposed book about the Duke of Windsor, Churchill answered,

---

[1] Over the Geoffrey Dennis book.

"Write it, but don't publish it for another ten years."

I protested that I was anxious to change current opinion. A book published ten years hence would be merely an historical curiosity.

I remember winding up by saying,

"After all, he *is* a Stuart."

"A Stuart?" Churchill exclaimed. "He's a Plantagenet!"

After that we went on to talk about the Dardanelles and I remember asking Churchill why he had not come out there when the Coalition Government had made him Chancellor of the Duchy of Lancaster instead of First Lord of the Admiralty.

"Ian Hamilton was greatly hoping you would come out and see for yourself."

"George Curzon," said Churchill. "I was stepping up the gangway of a destroyer at Brindisi when a message came that George Curzon wanted to see me urgently in London."

We talked on about Gallipoli, but alas, I made no notes of what Churchill said on what was for me such a memorable evening.

It was nearly one o'clock when Albrecht von Bernsdorf came into the Grill with Lady Jowitt.

"Who's that pretty woman with Albrecht?" Churchill asked.

"It's Lesley Jowitt," Bob and I said simultaneously. "You must have met her."

Churchill shook his head.

"I've never seen her. They'd better come along to our table."

We waved to them, and they came along to our table. I see Winston Churchill as he took the cigar out of his mouth and clipped off the chewed end of it with a pair of scissors from his pocket before he had another puff.

"Well, Albrecht," he said. "I suppose your countrymen are making a fool of Lord Holyfox tonight?"

"But, of course," Bernsdorf replied, with a gesture of agreement from two hands sweeping apart.

Albrecht von Bernsdorf had been Councillor of the German Embassy before Hitler came into power. He owned great estates in Holstein and with much courage had shown himself an opponent of the Nazis, travelling repeatedly back and forth between Great Britain and Germany. Hitler finally had him arrested when war came, and in that last April he was one of those who with Admiral Canaris and others were slowly hanged to death naked for Hitler to gloat over in a film made of those executions to gratify that 'blood-stained guttersnipe'.

I had gone back to Barra toward the end of November and was not in London when the *Sunday Dispatch* published a front-page sensational article headed THE TRUTH ABOUT THE DUKE OF WINDSOR BOOK. There were some disastrous paragraphs.

"So far it is understood, the question of royalties for the Duke and Mr Mackenzie has not been decided, and with regard to this and other questions there have been negotiations between Messrs Rich and Cowan Ltd and the Duke of Windsor's solicitors, Messrs Allen and Overy of Finch-lane, London, E.C.

"When the book first came to be discussed it caused some misgiving in high circles in London, and to make it easier for the Duke to give his approval, the *Sunday Dispatch* understands that it may be necessary for certain matters to be handled with circumspection.

"It is hoped, however, that any difficulties will be overcome.

"At first it was feared that the Official Secrets Act would interfere with the writing of the story, but an eminent Counsel has been consulted and an opinion has been given that there is little probability of any difficulty in this respect.

"Compton Mackenzie, stormy petrel of literature, has had a number of thrilling experiences."

Next morning, the *Sunday Dispatch* was quoted with inelegant variation by every newspaper in the country, and on that Monday afternoon Messrs Allen and Overy issued a statement:

"In view of statements which have appeared in the Press, it seems desirable to make it clear without delay that the Duke of Windsor has no intention of approving the contents of any biography nor is his Royal Highness prepared to supply information for such a biography."

This simple statement gave the Press another opportunity for headlines of which DUKE OF WINDSOR REPUDIATES COMPTON MACKENZIE was typical.

Rich and Cowan now issued a statement to the Press Association:

"We entered into an arrangement with Mr Compton Mackenzie in July 1937 to publish a biography of His Royal Highness, the Duke of Windsor, which Mr Compton Mackenzie was about to write with the Duke's approval.

"Correspondence was passing at that time between His Royal Highness and Mr Compton Mackenzie which showed clearly that the latter had asked for and obtained authority to write an authentic account of the Duke's life, more particularly of the events leading up to the Abdication, and to publish this after it had been submitted for approval to His Royal Highness.

"On the strength of this correspondence Messrs Rich and Cowan entered into certain commitments. Later, it was arranged by correspondence that a synopsis of the proposed biography should be sent by Mr Compton Mackenzie to the Duke. One of the objects of the book was to counteract the misstatements that were being circulated.

"So far from disapproval being expressed it was not until the beginning of November that any indication was given that a change of mind was

Q

possible, and not until last Monday November 29th that the publishers were informed that the Duke did not intend to proceed with the matter."

Messrs Allen and Overy now issued a supplementary statement to the Press:

"His Royal Highness's position has already been made clear. It is fair to Mr Compton Mackenzie and Messrs Rich and Cowan, Limited, to say that Mr Mackenzie approached the Duke and was given to understand that His Royal Highness would welcome a book to be written by Mr Mackenzie, but after full consideration of the synopsis supplied to him and of what such a book would necessarily involve, His Royal Highness at the end of October last wrote to inform Mr Mackenzie that he could not supply information for it.

"The recent announcements in the Press made it necessary for His Royal Highness to come to a final decision immediately in the terms of the statement already issued."

In fact it was Walter Monckton who had let me know that the Duke had changed his mind, and incidentally that his advisers had not found it too easy to persuade him to do so. If I had thought for a moment that the Duke was really opposed to my writing a book about the Abdication I should have abandoned the idea.

On December 1st Faith was writing from Connaught Street where I had been staying with her for the last two months:

The whole of London is plastered with you tonight. Not only News Review *in rows everywhere but posters DUKE'S BIOGRAPHY sensation—DUKE and AUTHOR all over the place. . . . I had an agonized letter from Mother but visited her before lunch and told her you were perfectly peaceful and not worried (I don't know if that's true but it was all she was worried about) and left her feeling happier.*

By the same post came a letter from Ursula Maxwell written from the Duchess Nursing Home in Beaumont Street, W.:

Dearest Monty,

What does the Duke of Windsor think he's doing? Has he backed out completely or were the reports in the papers just a newspaper ramp?

I do hope it isn't going to affect your plans for writing the book?

Has someone been 'getting at' the Duke of Windsor, or is it that he wants you to go ahead with the book without being publicly involved in the idea of it? I do hope it will be all right. . . . I've got to stay here for another age. . . . Much love

Ursula

Roddy Rich wrote on December 2nd:

Events have certainly moved with great rapidity during this last week and, by the time this reaches you, you will have seen our statement with the gratifying statement made by Messrs Allen and Overy. This is most gratifying because I feel sure it is now clear in the minds of this country at any rate—I must almost say the world—that it has been made impossible for Mr Jones to act as he would have wished over this book.

I think it would have done your heart good to have been in my Club last night. Members whose names I do not know and in some cases have never seen before, kept coming up with a general demand to know when this book would be ready.

The headlines had been bad enough, but they were accompanied in several papers by paragraphs of completely inaccurate and libellous comments. Even the respectable *Spectator* indulged in a silly little anonymous sneer. "Here is Mr Compton Mackenzie wanting for some reason or other to write a life of the Duke of Windsor."

As I remember we sent out writs for libel to five newspapers.

With an unusual contradiction of the law's delay the first action was heard hardly more than a month after the writ was issued.

"A settlement was announced in the King's Bench Division today of a libel action arising out of a paragraph in the *Leader*, in connection with a book which Mr Compton Mackenzie, the author, had proposed to write about the Duke of Windsor.

"Mr Compton Mackenzie was the plaintiff. The defendants were Associated Periodicals Limited and Newnes and Pearson's Printing Company Limited, publishers and printers respectively of the *Leader*.

"Mr Gerald Gardiner, for Mr Mackenzie, said that the paragraph complained of was published on December 11th under the heading,

" 'The Duke of Windsor angry: unauthorized life not wanted.'

"Mr Gardiner continued. 'Last July Mr Mackenzie formed a project to write a book about the Duke of Windsor. He was highly indignant about certain rumours that were current. He held the view—and still holds the view—that the Duke and Duchess of Windsor have not received from this country—and particularly from certain elements—the consideration which they deserved. He accordingly placed himself in communication with the Duke to ascertain whether such work would meet with His Royal Highness's consent and approval. The Duke's reply was that he would gladly welcome anything which Mr Mackenzie might feel inclined to write. Two or three months passed, and Mr Mackenzie had begun work on the book, when there unhappily appeared in a Sunday organ of the Press, a highly coloured and sensational article purporting to deal with the matter. The Duke thereupon did that which he was entitled to do. He changed his mind. His solicitors caused to be published a statement to the effect that, in view of what had appeared in the Press, it seemed desirable to state that the Duke did not intend to give approval or authority for the writing of any biography or to give any information for the writing of such work.'

"The *Leader* thereupon published the paragraph in question, which was to the effect that the Duke was very annoyed with Mr Mackenzie. It implies that Mr Mackenzie was falsely pretending that he was writing the work with the consent and approval of the Duke, and had made that false statement for the purpose of 'puffing' the sales of the book.

"As soon as the defendants found there was no warranty for any such implication they published an apology in the *Leader* and agreed to pay Mr Mackenzie's costs and a substantial sum by way of damages. Mr Mackenzie had agreed to accept those terms of settlement.

"Mr Cyril Hardy for the defendants said they welcomed the opportunity of retracting the implication made against Mr Compton Mackenzie. He asked Mr Justice Charles to agree to the record in the action being withdrawn on the terms endorsed on counsel's brief, and his Lordship assented."

I cannot help feeling rather proud that the counsel who pleaded my case is now the Lord High Chancellor of Great Britain. Indeed, I am inclined to fancy that I have been a bit of a mascot for Lord Chancellors. Lord Sankey, of whom I write in Octave Two, was my form-master at Colet Court. Lord Simmonds and Lord Jowitt were friends at Oxford. Lord Maugham was a friend of mine at the Savile. Lord Kilmuir succeeded me as Chief of the Inverness Gaelic Society. Equally, of course, those six Lord Chancellors might claim that they were mascots for me.

Mr Justice Charles was another friend of the Savile and also a great supporter of *The Gramophone*. He was the son of a judge and he had many stories of bygone judges which he told superbly.

There had been a difference of opinion about the status of the Duchess of Windsor. Debrett had given her third place in precedence: Burke had given her thirty-third. The precedence was settled in favour of Burke; in this December the Duchess was not given the rank of her husband by King George VI. In a preliminary announcement of *The Windsor Tapestry* the publishers had alluded to the Duchess of Windsor as H.R.H. and on December 22nd I was writing:

We can't possibly call her H.R.H. but the way I had changed it is without offence. To allude to her as H.R.H. in print is a direct discourtesy to the King, who has not granted her the title.

I am well away with the writing of the book now, and please never allude to it as a life or biography of the Duke, but always in my words as a study of the life.

It was my contention that, after King Edward VIII had been told by Mr Baldwin that morganatic marriage was unknown in this country, he was in fact given a morganatic marriage. I made this statement once on television and did not receive a word of criticism for doing so.

I was astonished to find Mr A. J. P. Taylor of all people supporting

Stanley Baldwin over this. In a note to Lord Beaverbrook's account of the Abdication published in this year 1966 he writes:

"Though the practice is common on the Continent there has been no case of a morganatic marriage in this country. The members of the Royal Family, such as the Duke of Cambridge and the Duke of Sussex, who are sometimes described as having been morganatically married, had not fulfilled the requirements of the Royal Marriage Act and were legally not married at all. Baldwin was therefore correct."

There may not be a Morganatic Marriage Act in the Statute book, but is Mr Taylor prepared to argue that Mrs FitzGeorge was not accepted as the wife of H.R.H. the Duke of Cambridge?

Here is Mrs FitzGeorge's obituary on January 14th 1890 when *The Times* had a very much better Editor than *The Times* of 1936:

"We regret to announce the death on Sunday, at the age of 74, of Mrs FitzGeorge, wife of H.R.H. the Duke of Cambridge . . . in the course of Mrs FitzGeorge's long and painful illness the Queen has sent to make frequent enquiries at her residence in Queen Street, Mayfair."

Is Mr Taylor prepared to argue that morganatic marriage was not recognized when Lady Cecilia Buggin (daughter of the Earl of Arran and widow of Sir George Buggin) was created Duchess of Inverness by Queen Victoria, as the morganatic wife of H.R.H. the Duke of Sussex?

The Times of 1843 recognized morganatic marriage in their obituary of the Duke of Sussex:

"He braved the resentment of the Crown, he risked the hereditary dignities of the Succession, in order to enjoy the blessing of domestic peace with the daughter of a British peer."

I went into this question of morganatic marriage exhaustively in *The Windsor Tapestry* and I should not have returned to it now if Mr Taylor had not maintained that Mr Baldwin was right. The cold fact remains that H.R.H. the Duke of Windsor was told there was no such thing as morganatic marriage in Great Britain, and then had his own marriage made morganatic by refusing to give his wife his own rank. Is Mr Taylor prepared to argue that the Duke and Duchess of Windsor are legally not married?

I started *The Windsor Tapestry* on December 10th, the anniversary of the Duke's broadcast speech to tell the country why he had abdicated. Joyce Weiner, not long down from Lady Margaret Hall with an Oxford degree, had been recommended to me as a young woman well qualified to do the necessary research for my proposed book. Since September she had been searching Parliamentary records, old and recent memoirs, and old and recent newspapers in the British Museum to provide the mass of material from which I should be able to detect what seemed significant for my contentions. She would come up to Barra at the beginning of the New Year and be of invaluable service while I was doing the hardest piece of concentrated work I had ever attempted. Indeed, without Joyce Weiner's devotion to her task, I should never have been able to complete my own.

That autumn I had begun to think I should be wise to have a small house of my own in London. Faith's first volume of reminiscences called *As Much As I Dare* was so good that I urged her to think about following it up with a second volume. Christopher by now was beginning to pay more and more attention to *The Gramophone*. It might not be quite fair to say he was deliberately making it more difficult for his sister to do her editorial work, but she certainly felt it would be a relief to him if she went to live somewhere in the country and concentrate upon her memoirs instead of musical criticism. The lease of 31A Connaught Place could be broken next summer, and I thought we should be wise to find somewhere else in London.

I felt that it might be necessary to be in London after *The Windsor Tapestry* was published and I wanted to be back in Hampstead where I had begun to write *Carnival* and had my first real success.

I saw an advertisement by Potters of Heath Street, Hampstead:

"Woodbine Cottage, Vale of Health, Hampstead.

"By the summit of the Heath, Whitestone Pond and Spaniards Road. A most unique and genuine Period Cottage, in quiet and very secluded Countrified Surroundings. Small Old-World garden. Freehold Price £2,500."

My publishers would receive half the money for the serialization of *The Windsor Tapestry* for which the *Sunday Pictorial* had agreed to pay £5,000, and my agents would have their commission from both of us. I agreed at once to Rich and Cowan's getting half the serialization money because they had already paid me the £1,500 for the copyright of *The West Wind of Love*. So the money was found to buy Woodbine Cottage when my offer of £2,250 was accepted. Faith would write of it one day in *Always Afternoon*:

"The Hampstead cottage is in the Vale of Health, still a village. It is the other half of Leigh Hunt's abode which is now a separate cottage. I have seen a print of it complete as Rose Cottage, notable among other things for having been the home of Alfred Harmsworth and his brothers when they were children. Leigh Hunt described it as a 'packing-case'. . . . Keats described in *Sleep and Poetry* the parlour which Hunt said was no larger than an old mansion's closet.

> 'For I am brimful of the friendliness
> That in a little cottage I have found,'

wrote Keats, who was a near neighbour, constantly dropping in. It was here that he and Hunt competed in a sonnet to the Grasshopper and the Cricket.

"Another frequent visitor was Shelley. . . . When he was in Italy he wrote that Jane Williams's singing transported him back to the little parlour in Hampstead. 'I can see the piano, the prints, the casts, and hear May's (Mrs Hunt's) "Ah! Ah! Ah!" ' . . . There was the charm, then, of age and association about the weather-boarded cottage which I spent the winter preparing for M."

On December 20th George Malcolm Thomson wrote to me from 3 Holly Terrace:

My dear Mackenzie,

You have been treated damnably. But I am glad to hear the book will be written. I know it will be good.

The South Wind—for which I owe you more thanks than I can ever utter—has held me absolutely enthralled. It is magnificent. The story grows all the time in pace and strength. I send you my warmest admiration.

That you are coming to join us in Hampstead is good news. We shall have some nights yet! And I think that this may have to be, after the Four Airts, a little wind blowing off the Heath!

If there is anything I could do, command me.

Yours ever

G. M. T.

We did have 'some nights yet' after wonderful dinners prepared by G. M. T.'s beautiful Norwegian wife.

After endless letters about the book I was proposing to write about the Abdication it was pleasant to hear from Oliver Gogarty about *Pericles*:

Is there anything that would lure you over from your island home to Connemara for Christmas? We shall have a party which you might find congenial. . . .

Your Pericles *is a liberal education. I bought a copy which I hope to review for the* Irish Times. *It is an urbane and very able book. Tout à toi.*

I wrote back:

Christmas in Connemara would be splendid, but I am tied up by too many responsibilities to enumerate, and the pleasure of visiting the further West must still be postponed.

I hope you came out of that tiresome libel business over that delightful Sackville Street book without being too much disappointed by the result. I have now been flinging writs at various papers over this lunatic fuss about the Edward book, but I hope they will all decide to compromise without going to Court. Meanwhile, I am working hard at the book. What people don't seem able to grasp is that the only reason for writing a book like this is because one feels passionately that it ought to be written.

The Irish Times *have already reviewed* Pericles, *and unfavourably at that. I am glad and encouraged that it found favour with you. I wish we all lived in Periclean Athens as Norman Douglas wrote to me the other day. We were not meant for this Austin-Seven age.*

WHEN I retired to Barra that winter I was already feeling doubtful whether Rich and Cowan would be the right publishers for the book I was proposing to write about the Abdication. However, I had no alternative. I had already committed myself to them by the contract for *The Four Winds of Love* and drawn money in advance for *The West Wind* which I was now postponing. I had to ensure that Joyce Weiner would be properly paid for the invaluable work she had done and was still doing. I had to fight for the 2½ per cent. which Macartney deserved for persuading me to write to the Duke and offer him my pen. I had stipulated that the *Sunday Pictorial* should have first refusal of the serial rights. So in the end I had agreed that whatever profit there was on this book about the Abdication should be divided equally between myself and my publishers and that J. B. Pinker and Sons should have 10 per cent. of my share of any profit.

On January 28th I was writing to Faith:

I think you can go ahead with the furnishing and decoration of Woodbine Cottage. There is good reason for financial optimism but as you know I will not blow unduly iridescent bubbles. However, Rich seems convinced that the book will sell. All I care about is that the Duke's case should be fairly presented. Monckton in his own charming way made it clear to me that his sole object had been in the Duke's own interest to dissociate himself from any semblance of authorization for what he realized in the synopsis would be an attack on Baldwin, the Archbishop, etc.

I believe the book will be weighted with honest indignation. Joyce Weiner, admirable creature, will give you news when she goes to London in 3 weeks. She and Chrissie are extremely harmonious, and it needs harmony with these masses of papers, Annual Registers and Hansards with slips, and dozens of other volumes.

I've done nearly 50,000 words. It will be about 150,000, I think, but perhaps longer. What do you think of Abdication Arras for a title with a jacket like the Bayeux tapestry?

I'm glad Collins are treating you so well. The Abdication book should help the sale of As Much As I Dare.

On February 3rd Chrissie was typing a letter from herself to Faith:

"No letters have gone for a week—such gales! This perpetual wind gets on one's nerves frightfully. I am getting really tired of it. The plane did come today after five days, the longest we've been without it since they started flying out here. The cable was broken, too; we had to send the *Sunday Chronicle* review by wire. Luckily the cable was mended just in time, but it is now broken again. I wish we could be in London for the winter. Perhaps we will after this.

"My mother is here just now. God knows when she will get off. I don't mind, as she has done nearly all the mending and baked us lots of cakes. I haven't a moment to spare just now for these things. . . .

"The book goes on well. I am typing it now and wish I could send it to you. I expect Joyce Weiner has told you about it, but I think what he has written since she left is the best of all. . . . He is shattering Baldwin now. . . . I saw a good blurb of *As Much As I Dare* in Collins' Spring List. It will make people want to read it. I do hope you will both have smashing successes at the same time. . . ."

Chrissie herself had a bad chest for three weeks followed by laryngitis. "But I am not ill with it," she wrote. I do not know what she would have been if her mother had not been with us.

On February 13th I was writing to Faith:

I've written and revised about 75,000 of the book and I reckon I've a good 100,000 still to do. I never wrote in such a fever, but I can't write more than about 1,500 words a day. I hope I'll get on faster with the 18th century part.

. . . I'm sorry Collins are too pressed for time to let you have signatures. Send me the galleys by all means, but it will be too late now to make any corrections, won't it? If not send them along, though my eyes are getting a little strained by continually referring to bad print in the books of reference. I'm going to call the book The Windsor Tapestry. *That's final.*

Rich and Cowan started to set up in galleys what I was writing; looking back at that winter I wonder Joyce, Chrissie and myself did not end up in lunatic asylums, because every galley went back pinned with typed corrections and additions.

On February 28th I was writing to Faith:

I'm now working 14 hours a day. This correction of galleys without having made a fair copy is damnable. I've sent off 45,000 for press and have written nearly as much more, and there's still another 110,000 at least to do. It's a tremendous grind but worth it. A bit of pain today but I hope I'll keep clear of it. A bad attack would be rather a business.

The exquisite weather we have had for a fortnight looks like breaking up this afternoon, but I prefer March to come in leonine, provided the lion doesn't bite my leg.

I'm glad you're getting over to Paris, and will see Norman Douglas. Give him my love.

Flame-coloured velvet sounds perfect for Woodbine. By the way, I have been wondering why Woodbine Cottage was vaguely familiar and I've just remembered that it was the cottage in Santa Claus in Summer. *So that disposes of my plan to change the name to Cherrytree Cottage. I hope the cherry-tree by the door won't mind.*

March came in like a lion and did bite my leg. I was laid out for several days and fuming because I could not get on with weaving the tapestry. The wind was infernal; apart from that serene fortnight in February it was the fiercest winter for gales that Barra could remember. Moreover, instead of going out like a lamb as it should have done March went out as an even more savage lion.

Faith's book *As Much As I Dare* was published at the end of the month. The reviews were all enthusiastic and a second edition in which she was able to correct some of the many misprints was soon on the way. She was doing a marvellous job with the furnishing and decoration of Woodbine Cottage. She would write in *Always Afternoon*:

"For the alterations and painting I had the assistance of Nadegine, who in the absence of any singing engagements worthy of his attention had become a decorator under the name of Nordiss, and could be seen striding along in huge paint-spattered overalls beside the handcart containing the implements of his trade, with his diminutive mate between the shafts. Russians have a refreshing freedom from class prejudice where work is concerned. They plunge into any career they think will give them a livelihood, and out of it something else with fatalistic fervour."

On April 7th I was writing to Faith:

I am utterly against any kind of attempt to 'appease' that evil mudlark with a Charlie Chaplin moustache but I feel that Chamberlain is doing the right thing by trying to detach Mussolini from Hitler, and I thought Eden's petulant resignation a display of vanity rather than statesmanship. I know that Mussolini is a puff-ball, or perhaps I should say a bullfrog, but I cannot believe the Italians will let him make a pact with the barbarians.

On April 13th I was writing to Faith:

Inverneill has put in an offer for the island of Canna. If he gets it it means he will be able to feed quite 40 people when we have the war this hopeless government of ours will land us in. It is a charming island four miles long by one—same configuration as the Shiants. It is in the middle of the upheaval a million years ago which begins at the Faroes and ends at the Giant's Causeway. South slope and marvellous soil. Small population is Catholic. Attractive church built by the Butes, with an £80 a year endowment. The price is £9,000 with stock at valuation, about another £4,000. . . . My old friend Francis Underhill has been made Bishop of Bath and Wells. So he'll have the best mediaeval city and the best 18th century city in which to wield his pastoral staff. Father MacQueen is just back after being kept for 6 weeks in Oban by the Bishop who couldn't bear to part with him. I'm not surprised; he's a gem of a man. I won't write more. I'm making a desperate effort to reach p. 400 before Easter.

That desperate effort laid me out after what had been a difficult four months of writing and research. Faith wrote in *Always Afternoon*:

"So the first scene was played through to the accompaniment of boisterous gales, rattling tiles, shrieking windows, deafening volleys of hail, catastrophic rain, short, washed days of brilliant blue sea, ivory cumuli and purple shadows, flashing through the grey heavy-laden clouds that swept the heavens in the wildest winter Barra had known for years. Never a soft smother of snow at the windows, but everything tac!—tac!—stimulating, quickening, goading into work, with Beethoven, Wagner, Sibelius training their great guns against the clamour outside. Fire racing up the chimneys and sometimes down again in gusts of blinding smoke, exhausted lamps fed in the small hours before they began to flicker. And pain-pain-pain joining the uproar, throbbing and hammering on hard-driven nerves.

*   *   *   *   *

"When he wrote at white heat it was inevitable that fierce attacks of pain would interrupt his labours. But I was not prepared for a blood-red Priority telegram announcing he had collapsed during an attack and that I must come at once. This was on April 18th when the book was nearing completion. It was Easter Monday, but I was able to engage a sleeper to Glasgow and rang up Scottish Airways to charter a private plane to Barra which would cost about £30. This was the only way to get there in reasonable time; the sea-journey took twelve hours from Oban and there was no boat for two days. Late in the afternoon I had another blood-red wire that the danger was past and I need not come unless I wished. Another wire an hour later said 'Definitely better condition steadily improving.' A few minutes after that another: 'Sorry to have alarmed you but condition made it necessary now out of danger and sleeping peacefully.' I cancelled the sleeper and the thirty guinea plane. A telegraph letter set my mind at rest: 'Mr Mackenzie just woke quite normal after good sleep . . . don't worry now think he will be all right.'

"After lying five hours like one dead he came back to consciousness and asked what all the fuss was about. On being told he had been insensible for five hours he said, 'A good thing, too. How do you think I could have stood any more of that pain?'

"His own comment in a scrawl written two days later was, 'If I was near death it's a much less trying business than I had supposed.' "

Joyce Weiner wrote to Faith:

I gave one look at him on Monday and was absolutely horrified: his face was the colour of grey clay and he was completely rigid. He did not yield to Chrissie's attempts to restore him and she was absolutely distraught. . . . The Doctor acted in the most sensible way. He applied artificial respiration and injected a restorative drug.

When he came to after five hours he fell into an easy sleep and woke up to find

*us in his room. He asked what all the fuss was about. "Thank God you are alive,"
said Chrissie and he looked at us as if we were mad.*

*I do hope he will not delay coming to London because you may imagine how
helpless one feels with him here. . . . The greatest burden has fallen on Chrissie this
time but the only thought in her mind is that of complete thankfulness; I know she
will no more spare herself in the future than she has up till now. But it is a great
responsibility and a frightening one too as you, of course, know. . . . You must have
had an awful two days and we were thinking about you all the time.*

In Chrissie's letter to Faith was this:

*I must tell you a sweet story about Coddie's youngest boy aged 4. When the
Coddie's family heard about Mr M's illness their mother sent the 3 youngest
children, Mary, Flora and Neillie to the Church to pray for him. This they did
and wee Neillie must have gone on praying for him when they got back to the house.
The first thing he said when he opened his eyes next morning was—"Well, I prayed
for Compton anyway all night!"*
The Coddie himself lit 12 candles in the church for his recovery.

On April 27th she was writing:

*He isn't right yet by any means and I had to send for the doctor at 3 o'clock on
Monday morning to give him something which would give him some relief and sleep.
He did this successfully and he slept from 4 a.m. till 4 p.m. But I was afraid to
go to bed and leave him alone until Nellie got up. He was fine all day yesterday
and dictated to Joyce in the evening.*

*The doctor has sent for Nurse MacNeil to be with him for the rest of the time
he is here . . . it is better to have a professional nurse in case of emergency and he
really is an invalid while he is working on this book. I only hope it will be appreciated
that it was not only his pen he had put at the disposal of this Windsor cause but
very nearly his life.*

Whoever it was that wrote that petty review in the Listener *must have been
jealous of you both. We all think here it must have been written by a woman.*

On May 6th I was writing to Faith:

After sending the first galleys to the Sunday Pictorial *through Ralph I've at
last heard that they are pleased with them, but I could not extract from him or Rich
what price they were paying for the serial rights. Then yesterday I had a wire to
say they must have completion by May 14th and have wired back to promise it by
May 16th, but I am getting pretty tired. I've dictated 36,000 words since that
tiresome black out at Easter besides correcting these damned galleys. Angus
Dunstaffnage is here for a week and I let him read the galleys up to date; he says
it is like floating down the Zambezi.*

*Chrissie is at last definitely better. The arrival of Nurse Annie MacNeil
enabled her to get some proper rest. Joyce will just hold out, but even she is beginning
to wilt now. Nellie is holding out well.*

I am so looking forward to seeing all you've done at Woodbine, and I'm sorry if I left the choice of the Morris pattern curtains to you, but the need to concentrate on finishing this book by May 16th is making it impossible to concentrate on anything else.

I'm so glad As Much As I Dare *is still going along so well. Don't bother about that silly review. It was probably written by one of your female acquaintances. You cannot expect to avoid an occasional jealous shaft.*

On May 4th Faith sent me a document that has just been handed in.

AIR RAID PRECAUTIONS   Area No 62

CENSUS

The Air Raid Wardens who have been appointed by the Borough Council of the Sector in which you reside will be visiting you shortly to register the sizes of respirators required by you and members of your household, in the event of emergency, and it will be appreciated if you will afford them the necessary assistance.

Wardens can be recognized by the silver A.R.P. Badge and Brooch which they wear. . . . Would you therefore complete the undermentioned form and keep same in safe custody until called for within the next two or three days?

I know perfectly well [Faith wrote] *that the whole business is to keep us quiet and that masks are useless after a few hours. All the shops are now offering to gas-proof rooms. It seems that in Germany an unfortunate person is detailed to stay on the top floor in every house and be ready to catch any incendiary bomb and pop it into a pail of sand while everybody else is waiting for death in a gas-proofed room below. What bloody nonsense it all is. They admit that there's nothing to be done about high explosive bombs.*

I wrote back:

When they issued gas-masks at Gallipoli the men used them as tobacco-pouches. I hope the latest gas-masks will be even as useful as that. It's a pity somebody can't invent a mask to protect oneself against the hot air being talked about the European situation by Tories and Socialists alike. The Germans are set on war and we think we'll stave it off with gas-masks! My bet is August 1940, though it might come in '39 to celebrate the silver jubilee of peace.

I had hoped to finish *The Windsor Tapestry* on May 16th but it was May 18th when I sent off the final chapter.

I wrote to Faith:

I'm still having a good deal of pain but the relief of writing Explicit *will probably quieten it better than any sedatives. It has been a really tremendous strain upon one's accuracy and one's style. I only hope all this effort will be of some avail. I never spent myself on any book so utterly.*

Chrissie took this letter with her and left for London where Joyce was meeting her. I set out for Edinburgh on Monday May 23rd. Dominic MacKellaig volunteered to travel with me, and Nellie stayed for some days in case any important letters or papers had been left behind.

When I got out of the plane at Turnhouse Norman Sturrock was at the airport.

"What have you been doing?" he said as he handed me the *Sunday Pictorial* of the day before.

"I saw it at Renfrew," said Dominic MacKellaig, "but he wasn't feeling too good, so I didn't show it to him."

I looked at the paper and began to fancy I was suffering from one of the delusions that sometimes came with pain.

Here is that front page of the dirtiest evacuation of journalism within my experience. I might have been excused for supposing that the Fleet river carrying the sewage of London was again flowing down Fleet Street. It began with a headline of letters $2\frac{1}{2}$ inches high.

THE DUKE:

Below this was a double headline of letters $1\frac{1}{2}$ inches high.

APPALLING
BOOK

Framed on one side was this:

"*As Much As I Dare* . . . that was the title of Mrs Mackenzie's autobiography.

"More Than Any Wise Man Would Dare . . . that should be the title of her husband's biography of the Duke."

On the other side was my face and under it in a frame:

"Compton Mackenzie: He set out to defend the ex-King. Instead, the book is an atrocious embarrassment to the present King and Queen— and a disservice to the Duke himself."

Under this was the reproduction of a cheque on Messrs Coutts & Co.

Pay to Compton Mackenzie
　　　　　Five thousand pounds

There was one illegible director's name; the second director was *Cecil H. King*.

Under this cheque was:

DESPATCHED LAST NIGHT . . . THE CHEQUE THAT ENDS A DEAL WHICH A SECTION OF MACKENZIE'S BOOK MADE INGLORIOUS.

Then began an article by the twenty-five-year-old Editor of the *Sunday Pictorial*:

"Today this newspaper takes a course unprecedented in the history of the British Press.

"Today this newspaper denounces a book which six months ago it acquired the right to publish."

Young Mr Hugh Cudlipp then proceeded to drivel on for two more pages with lengthy quotes from the chapter the *Sunday Pictorial* felt impossible to print.

When I had stipulated that the serial rights of *The Windsor Tapestry* should be offered to the *Sunday Pictorial* I had supposed that it was still under the direction of Macwhirter and Grant from whom I had received unceasing consideration during the five years I wrote my weekly gramophone article. I did not know that it had changed hands and that after 'modernising' the *Daily Mirror* Mr Cudlipp had been set the task of 'modernising' the *Sunday Pictorial*. The short leaders signed W.M. in the *Daily Mirror* which had been the sanest leaders in the Press had gone. They were written by R. J. Jennings of whom at school I wrote in my Second Octave. Now here was Mr Cudlipp in what seemed an epileptic fit of outraged morality trying to make up with headlines what his head lacked.

Woodbine Cottage was a joy when I saw for the first time how perfectly Faith had chosen its furniture and its decoration. As I sat in the big double room with its two eighteenth-century fireplaces and looked out through the french-windows opening to an elegant wrought-iron veranda and a small garden leading directly to the Heath I was back with Leigh Hunt and Keats.

I obviously had a case against the *Sunday Pictorial*. Presumably the cheque they photographed, having served its purpose, no longer existed. It was never sent to me. However, it was equally obvious that I could not bring an action against the *Sunday Pictorial* without involving the Duke of Windsor, and with the evidence I had of the lengths to which a newspaper was prepared to go I could not risk any attempt at further sensationalism at the Duke's expense. At the moment I was more angry with my publishers who, in their anxiety for the money of which they with my agents would have the lion's share, had made this deal and persuaded me to let them send galleys to the newspaper as they were printed.

On the following Sunday there were more scare headlines in the *Pictorial*:

ROYAL BOOK SENSATION:
A FRANK LETTER

Under this in a frame with a picture of me was the following:
"What is going to happen now about *The Windsor Tapestry*? Nine per

cent. of our readers supported Mr Compton Mackenzie. Ninety-one per cent. agreed with the *Sunday Pictorial* it should never be published.

"For £5,000 we had acquired the right to publish the volume in this newspaper—a right which, when certain chapters arrived, we refused to exercise.

"The cheque, as stated last week, was despatched.

"The next step lies with Mr Mackenzie's publishers.

"The *Sunday Pictorial* addresses this letter to them today."

This was followed by a letter addressed to Ashley Cowan which took up nearly a page, and in phrases of nauseating humbug entreated Rich and Cowan to join "with this newspaper in preventing certain parts of the book achieving the permanency of print".

I cannot find among my press-cuttings any compliment paid to the *Sunday Pictorial* for its self-denying ordinance; I find several gibes. The *Tribune* commented:

"Succeeding to a somewhat tardy attack of piety, the *Sunday Pictorial* devoted three precious pages to explaining why it will not publish an 'appalling book' about the Duke of Windsor. . . . Brushing away a manly tear or so, we turned to the customary leg show on the other pages and decided to bear up somehow."

The Bookseller commented:

"A week or two ago we ourselves saw galley proofs of the book; it is very long, very detailed and contains many words of more than one syllable. Hardly the book, we might think, for serializing in the *Sunday Pictorial*, which, judging from the issue we bought last Sunday, believes in the simplest message. SLEW BABES, BED IS PYRE are headlines in that issue which seem to be typical. . . .

"The *Pictorial* ran a long article, written in apocalyptic tones by Mr Hugh Cudlipp, the Editor, explaining how parts of the book were too shocking to be published in his newspaper. In bold type and across two columns, Mr Cudlipp reproduced certain uncomplimentary phrases which Compton Mackenzie had written about the early Hanoverians. 'There is one passage,' wrote the horrified Mr Cudlipp, 'Mackenzie shows his hand.'

"It is certainly to be hoped that nobody ever tells Mr Cudlipp about a terrible writing guy of the name of Thackeray. If the editor of the *Sunday Pictorial* were to find out what that fellow wrote about George IV there's no knowing what might happen."

The following week the *Bookseller* commented:

"With our hang-the-cost-get-the-story recklessness we splashed another twopence last Sunday on a copy of the *Sunday Pictorial* and were rewarded to find Mr Hugh Cudlipp, the Editor with Historical Responsibility, still doggedly maintaining that he had done the right thing by the early Georges in deciding not to serialize *The Windsor Tapestry*, although he had paid £5,000 for the rights.

"There was sandwiched in between pages devoted to pictures of pretty ladies with pretty thighs and to sadistic headlines (Thrashed! Starved! Chained!) a 'Frank Letter' addressed to Messrs Rich and Cowan urging them to consider carefully the *Sunday Pictorial's* warning about the book. Not all his liberal use of black type nor his direful style could quite hide the fact that Mr Cudlipp didn't seem to know what he was making all the fuss about.

"The skeletons which Mackenzie is supposed to dangle before his readers date from the reign of amorous George I and he observes of the period between that date and the death of Queen Charlotte, wife of George III: 'Throughout that history of outraged nature, smothered passion, perjured vows, of wives repudiated, mistresses discarded and children wronged, not one example is there of a Bishop intervening to denounce the sins against the sacrament of marriage which were being encouraged by the Royal Marriage Act.''

A few days after that fatuous letter to Rich and Cowan I received a note from Charles Eade who had just given up as editor of the *Sunday Graphic* in a last desperate attempt to increase the circulation of the *Sunday Dispatch* which was dropping all the time. He wanted me to lunch with him at the Savoy Grill to discuss a matter of some importance. When I reached the Savoy I was introduced to Lester Wilson, who would later start the *TV Times* on its career, a lovable man who lived at Richmond with his mother and a bulldog as kindly as himself. Both Charles Eade and Lester Wilson evidently felt that in offering me £1,000 to write a potted version of a 270,000 word book for serialization in the *Dispatch* they were committing themselves to a do-or-die adventure. I accepted the offer subject to my being able to arrange matters with my publishers who were planning to bring the book out at the end of June.

There was a big discussion at Woodbine Cottage because the publishers maintained that they were entitled to half the money paid by the *Dispatch* on top of which would be my agents' commission. So for what would be a tough job in my present state of fatigue I should only receive £450. I forget how the discussion ended. What I remember most vividly was a little dark man among the others.

This was H. R. Watson, who had been Chief Clerk to one of the leading firms of solicitors and was now representing Metcalfe, Copeman and Pettefar at 2 Clement's Inn. They were also the solicitors for J. B. Pinker and Sons and had handled the writ against the *Leader* and the apologies of the other three papers who had received writs. It was he who had realized the ability of Gerald Gardiner. When some months

R

later J. B. Pinker and Sons ceased to exist Watson took on the financial management of my affairs for the next fifteen years or so.

Whatever was decided about my share of the money the *Sunday Dispatch* was authorized to go ahead. For some preliminary publicity about myself I was asked if I would have talks with Peter Cheyney.

"He's rather down on his luck just now," said Charles Eade. "He was my News Editor on the *Sunday Graphic*, but he was too unreliable."

I have already mentioned a book at the back of my mind to be called *Great Liars I Have Known*. I am never likely to write it because I should have to call the liars improvisers and nobody would want to read a book about improvisers. I gave Axel Munthe, Halliday Sutherland and Ford Madox Ford first place but I should certainly have added Peter Cheyney to the company. He was superlative. Every time he came to Woodbine Cottage he told me a different tale about the way he got that hole in the side of his head. It was after he had told me a story of his experience as a Black and Tan when he had been captured by the 'Shinners' and buried up to his neck on a sandy beach for the tide to come in and drown him.

"What happened, Peter? Did some Canute come along and try to keep the tide back while he was digging you out?"

"Better than that, my dear man. A dog with whom I had shared some bully beef the previous day came and dug me out. But it was a close shave. Did I ever tell you how I got this hole in my head?"

"Yes, you told me last time you came to Woodbine."

But it was no good. I had to listen to the tale again. However, it was not as boring as it might have been because it was an entirely new version of the way he got that hole in his head.

"I can't think why you waste your stories on me, Peter. You ought to write thrillers."

"I wrote one last year, but it was a flop."

"If at first you don't succeed. . . ."

"Yes, you may be right, but I've led such a fantastic life that I haven't had time to get really down to thrillers. I went in for poetry at first."

I hesitate to claim any credit for launching Peter Cheyney upon that torrent of thrillers he was to write and out of which he was to make a huge amount of money, and what is more prevent the Inland Revenue from collecting a halfpenny of it in death duties. It is true he had already written one unsuccessful thriller when I first met him, but I like to think it was my encouragement as a listener to his tales that persuaded him to try again. It is amusing to reflect that Peter Cheyney had as big a vogue twenty years ago as Ian Fleming has today.

Each of the eight instalments of my potted version of *The Windsor Tapestry* was seen by Gerald Gardiner and each one duly passed as free from libel.

The first instalment was to appear on July 3rd and on that date the

Sunday Pictorial was covered with headlines from one to another of which Mr Hugh Cudlipp swung in a display of moral acrobatics. He even had the impudence to claim that in the potted version in the *Sunday Dispatch* I had been guided by his better judgment and refrained from criticizing the four Georges. Finally he was convinced that he had been invited to a gathering of the Octavian Society on the occasion of the Duke of Windsor's birthday at which I had been invited to speak but had declined the invitation because he felt *I* might have been embarrassed by having to sit next to *him*.

Truth commented:

"In a frenzy of righteous indignation the *Sunday Pictorial*—that pattern of clean journalism—announced that it would not publish Compton Mackenzie's *Survey of the House of Windsor*. If it is too disgraceful to be offered to the readers of the *Sunday Pictorial* it must be strong meat indeed, for the *Pictorial* is as bad as the American 'tabloids' or 'pulp magazines' at their worst. In any event, as Mr Mackenzie is a distinguished writer with a reputation to lose, it is unlikely that he would write anything unfit for the readers of *Truth* or *The Times*, let alone the *Sunday Pictorial*. I wondered what the milk in the coconut was.

"It is all very simple really. The *Sunday Dispatch* is going to publish the book, which has had an enormous advertisement from the *Sunday Pictorial's* attack on it. The *Dispatch* and the *Pictorial* are part of the same financial group. The *Dispatch* sells about a third as well as the *Pictorial*. This stunt should even things up a bit."

It certainly did. On July 31st the *Sunday Dispatch* was able to announce that since their publication of five instalments of *The Windsor Tapestry* its circulation had risen by several hundred thousands.

There were several other gibes at Mr Cudlipp. Let one suffice.

The *Bookseller* commented:

"Poor Mr Cudlipp was game to the last. In his own paper on Sunday he was still defending the early Hanoverians with a frenzied devotion which poor mad George III would have given America to command."

Before *The Windsor Tapestry* came out as a book toward the end of that July Gerald Gardiner advised me to send the proofs to Treasury Counsel for an opinion on the possibility of a prosecution for criminal libel. He did not think for a moment that there would be such a prosecution but it would be as well to make sure.

"You don't want any more experience of the Old Bailey," he said.

So the proofs were sent along and a few days later I went to . . . the actual place I have forgotten, perhaps because I was so much impressed by the Treasury Counsel. The Senior Prosecuting Counsel at this date

---

[1] The late Judge G. B. McClure.

was G. B. McClure,[1] the Recorder of Rochester. The junior Counsel present, a man for whom I have a great admiration, is still alive, and it might be a breach of legal etiquette to publish his name.

I was much surprised when the first thing McClure said was, "What's your brother doing now?"

"My brother Frank? Oh, he's in America, acting. But how did you know him?"

"He and I were in the same battalion of Territorials in the war."

"The London Irish."

"Yes, the 9th London."

"But you're a Scotsman."

"So was Fiery, wasn't he? That was what the men called him. They adored him. He won as good an M.C. as was ever won when he brought what was left of them back. He was badly wounded after that and when he recovered he was a musketery instructor at Hythe. Why didn't he stay in the army?"

"He had an impossible wife who was for ever moaning for him to go back on the stage. They're separated now and he has married again."

"The best adjutant we ever had and the men adored him."

My mind went back to Malta to nearly thirty years earlier when Frank was in the Royal Inniskilling Fusiliers and chucked the Army as I have told in Octave Three. I had not seen him for twenty years and I should never see him again before he died in 1965.

"Well, now, about this book of yours," said McClure. "Of course, it certainly is criminal libel because you have practically accused Lord Baldwin of high treason and to accuse a Prime Minister of high treason is certainly criminal libel. But I suppose if there were a prosecution you'd defend yourself?"

"I certainly should."

"And put Lord Baldwin in the witness box?"

"Yes, for at least a week. And the Archbishop of Canterbury. And several Cabinet Ministers. And several Court Officials. And Geoffrey Dawson, the Editor of *The Times*."

"Yes, and then I suppose you'd read to the jury those two letters you have from the Duke and stand on your defence?"

"That is exactly what I should do."

"Well, the jury would find you not guilty without leaving the box and the Government would have to resign next day. So I don't think there is any likelihood of a prosecution for criminal libel."

"Will you put that in black and white?"

"Well, not quite like that but we shall give you our opinion that there is no risk of an action."

I give the opinion of Treasury Counsel in Appendix E. It was well worth a hundred guineas.

The Windsor Tapestry was published by Rich and Cowan on July 30th and two or three months later by Stokes in the U.S.A. In the hostile reviews not a single one was able to demonstrate that any of my statements of fact were wrong, although *The Times* did have the satisfaction of catching me out writing Naseby in a moment of aberration when I meant Worcester. Howard Spring wrote in the *Evening Standard*:

"It is passion controlled, passion implemented by a master of his own art."

That appeared in the morning edition but it was suppressed in the next editions.

The *Manchester Evening News* warmed my heart by saying:

"When all the heat and argument over this book have died away, people will discover that its opening pages contain perhaps the most vivid and colourful picture of the 'nineties' that any author has created. . . . A masterpiece of description and sympathetic understanding."

I had received an anonymous letter from a Catholic prelate whose handwriting was recognized by Father John MacQueen. In this I had been rebuked for defending divorce. I shook my head over the stupidity even of a Catholic prelate and was relieved to read in the *Universe*: "Mr Mackenzie's pen is brilliant at any time. On a theme such as this, upon which his soul is stirred he is dazzling."

Quite a few public librarians were under the impression that *The Windsor Tapestry* had been banned and told anxious readers so. Incredibly, only the other day I received a letter to ask me where *The Windsor Tapestry* could be obtained because the local librarian had told him the book had been withdrawn from all public libraries.

Here is a revealing leaflet sent round by the head office of W. H. Smith and Son:

"TO ALL SHOPS AND STALLS

Windsor Tapestry by Compton Mackenzie
(16s Rich and Cowan)

"All 'A' shop, 'B' shop and stall managers will note carefully the following important instructions in connection with the above book which are to be adhered to rigidly.

"No objection will be placed in the way of any manager carrying such stock as is necessary to meet reasonable public demand, but special displays of the book, inside a shop, in a shop window or on a book-stall front are definitely forbidden.

"No advertising matter of any sort will be issued by head office for the book and no advertising matter is to be accepted from the publishers; neither will managers write 'homemade' tickets for the book. "We repeat that these instructions are to be rigidly observed."

I suppose some branch manager who disapproved of the attitude of what would presently be known as the Establishment gave me that leaflet.

The skunks who exude anonymous letters were busy. I received over a hundred, nearly all of them obscene, evidence of the foul rumours about the private life of the Duke which had been rife during the months after the Abdication. Fleas from the rats of December 1936 were still hopping about and infecting people.

What surprised me was the feebleness of the criticism produced by the clergymen who had been brought in by some papers to dispose of my arguments about the Anglican Church and divorce.

Among the people to whom I had been exceptionally rude was Beverley Baxter.[1] He was at this date M.P. for Wood Green and Editorial adviser to Allied Newspapers. Nevertheless, in a Canadian paper called *Maclean's Magazine* he had written immediately after the Abdication a scurrilous account of it.

One day going to lunch at the Savoy Grill I saw James Drawbell at the first table on the left of the door in.

"Do you see who this is?" Jimmie Drawbell asked with a grin.

I did not recognize the fellow-luncher.

"It's Beverley Baxter," said Drawbell, the grin widening.

"I'm afraid I had to be very rude about you, Mr Baxter. But I do not withdraw one word of what I wrote."

Beverley Baxter replied in an injured tone,

"I thought you took advantage of your greater experience than mine with words. I felt I was owed more consideration."

"Consideration," I exclaimed. "What the hell consideration did you show to the ex-King?"

As I said this I made an involuntary gesture to stress my words and in doing so swept one of those big Savoy decanters of water into Beverley Baxter's lap.

"I'll apologize for doing that," I told him. "But I don't take back a word of what I wrote about that miserable article of yours in that Canadian rag."

I did not meet Beverley Baxter again until not long before his death. He called on me in Edinburgh. When he was leaving he turned round in the doorway and said to me,

"You were right. I was wrong."

---

[1] The late Sir Beverley Baxter, M.P.

That was a piece of generosity which it is such a pleasure to place on record.

Readers may be thinking that I am going on too long about *The Windsor Tapestry*, but for a year it had occupied me so much in different ways that I could not make my story of it shorter.

Little did I think when Macartney persuaded me to write and put my pen at the Duke of Windsor's service that I was going to involve myself in such a complicated situation.

I have had to give a full account of the behaviour of Mr Hugh Cudlipp because in a book he wrote called *Publish and Be Damned* he suggested that I ought to be grateful to him for the extra money he put in my pocket.

I expect that at the time the Duke of Windsor wished he had never said he would welcome a book by me. However, I think he recognized I had not written *The Windsor Tapestry* for any reason than indignation at the way he had been treated. At any rate, a Christmas card used to be sent from the Bahamas when he became Governor. On the Sunday that war came the *Sunday Dispatch* published an article by me in which I was urging that if war came the Duke of Windsor should be given an opportunity to serve his country as he wished to do. He wrote to thank me for that article. And when his own book was published he graciously sent me an inscribed copy.

After I left Rich and Cowan, Chatto and Windus reprinted *The Windsor Tapestry*; I put all I knew into the writing of it and today I stand by every word I wrote.

Throughout the sometimes almost intolerable publicity of the Spring and Summer of this year the Vale of Health was true to its name. Of course, as the year went on I was having interludes of pain but I was lucky enough to be a patient of young Dr Michael Kremer who eight years later would become the Neurologist of the Middlesex Hospital.

Perhaps the proximity of the Whitestone Pond encouraged more dampness than there was in the rest of Hampstead but to live in what was really a small country village within half an hour of Piccadilly Circus was a continuous refreshment and stimulant of the mind.

Keats wrote "Souls of poets dead and gone". I could have echoed that apostrophe when I could fancy that the very room in which I was writing articles or correcting proofs might once have heard the sound of Keats's voice reading one of his sonnets to Leigh Hunt, might have heard the high voice of Shelley as he came in with a woman in his arms whom he had found lying unconscious on the Heath. When she recovered her senses she explained that she was on her way to Hendon, after hearing her son acquitted on a criminal charge. The emotion and fatigue had been too much for her. I heard the voices of Lamb, Hazlitt, Coleridge and even the voice of Byron who came to this cottage of which Keats wrote:

For I am brimful of the friendliness
That in a little cottage I have found.

Next to Woodbine was an even smaller cottage called Sydney where Stanley Jackson, a young barrister, lived with a charming young wife and baby. He had written some notes before to thank me for a review I had given of his life of Mr Justice Avory, and he was now hard at work on a life of Guy de Maupassant. A friendship began between us which I still enjoy.

Another friendship began that year. This was with Desirée and Edmond Segrave, who was and still is the editor of the *Bookseller*. I was to have the pleasure one day of being asked to be godfather to their daughter Lydia. She was my first girl godchild, and I thought it was absurd to give a girl a mug. So I gave her a hand glass, and made the gift a habit.

Some time that summer I dined with the Segraves at 5 North End House, Fitz James Avenue, W.14. I was amused to find that this sonorous address belonged to a block of flats which had been built in the big garden of the now vanished lunatic asylum called Otto House of which I wrote in Octave One. In my early childhood I used to fancy that one of the inmates might escape and hide himself under my bed. I was less amused to find that under a pompous name the Fulham Borough Council had also built hideous flats over the lovely garden of The Grange where Burne-Jones had lived and before him Samuel Richardson. I have so much still to write and unfortunately so short a time in which to write those books that I shall probably never succeed in producing, like the Newgate Calendar or Malefactors Bloody Register, a register of the crimes committed by Borough Councils and most flagrantly of all by the London County Council against the past. Between the vandals of the London County Council and the Huns who dropped their bombs is a distinction without a difference, and the Huns did much less damage.

Since writing those words the Edinburgh Town Council has been setting out to compete with the crimes of the London County Council. I hope that in my next Octave I shall be able to write that the Vandals have been defeated.

On June 8th there was a great meeting in Queen's Hall convened by the Association of Writers for Intellectual liberty under the title "In Defence of Freedom".

The invitation was as follows:

"With the spread of Fascism in Europe the lives and interests of men and women in the liberal professions are increasingly threatened.

"This Association of Writers is inviting members of its profession to take part in a large, non-political public meeting to express their abhorrence of this systematic attack on the intelligences. So far, Sir Hugh Walpole, Mr Desmond MacCarthy, Miss Rebecca West, Miss Rose Macaulay and Mr Philip Guedalla have agreed to speak, and many other writers are willing to support the meeting, either by their presence on the platform or by sending a message for the Chairman to deliver.

"The Association is anxious to make the meeting thoroughly representative of British letters and hopes that you will take part in what can be a most impressive declaration of the writers' essential future in the development of culture.

23 Haymarket,

London, S.W.1."

The Queen's Hall was packed that night, and on the platform was a gathering of writers to denounce Fascism, under the chairmanship of John Brophy. The most moving speech was made by Rosamond Lehmann. The other speeches were conventional and I was slightly irritated by the attention paid to Mussolini and the failure to denounce Hitler as violently as I felt he should be denounced. So when I got up to speak I let myself go, particularly on the foul persecution of the Jews.

Patrick Balfour[1] in his column said it was like a performance of *Hamlet* by Sir Johnstone Forbes-Robertson. "But he wasn't acting."

I had about fifty letters after the meeting, from which I print three. The first was from the late Basil Tozer, the husband of Beatrice Langley, the violinist, whom I had never met.

My dear Sir,

I am taking the liberty of congratulating you on your fine impassioned speech last night which came as a welcome relief amidst so much weak stuff bristling with platitudes to say nothing of Rose Macaulay's footling attempts to be humorous. You will probably live to see history once more repeat itself: and these bloody tyrants crushed out of existence. . . . I wish you would broadcast a talk with punch in it, which is what we need badly. My name is probably unknown to you but you can find it in Who's Who *if you want to.*

Yours truly

Basil Tozer

Victor Gollancz[2] wrote:

A line to thank you for your speech on Wednesday night. It was the first passionate speech that I have heard in the innumerable meetings I have both addressed and attended during the last two years. That is our whole trouble—passionate indignation is almost a thing of the past. I was more moved by your speech than anything I have heard for a long time: and I thank you for it, only 40% as a Jew and 60% as a man.

[1] Lord Kinross.

[2] The late Sir Victor Gollancz.

Professor Charles Singer[1] wrote from the Athenæum:

I was much moved by your noble and eloquent words last night at Queen's Hall.

I venture to enclose a pamphlet by myself with a foreword by my friend the Bishop of Chichester. It contains, I believe, some data on the subject which are not generally familiar.

Had I been writing the pamphlet at this moment I should have phrased differently the first paragraph on p. 21 excusing the Papacy.

Nevertheless, I think it would be fair to make these additional points:

A. The Pope, although he has now expressed himself decisively, on the race idiocy was, in fact, very dilatory in doing so.

B. Even Cardinal Faulhaber, while repeatedly attacking Nazi doctrine and practice, had almost pointedly refrained from doing so on the ground of there being an outrage on humanity as such.

C. The defection of the entire Austrian hierarchy has not only weakened the Catholic position in the world at large, but has also undermined the resisting powers of both the German hierarchy and of the Protestant 'Confessions'. (My latest information is that the latter have taken a step which is, in effect, complete submission to Hitler, but I am not quite clear on this point.)

Therefore whatsoever may transpire during the coming years, I believe that the last five years must always remain an extremely ugly interlude in the history of Christianity. For my own part, except for the recent action of the Pope—who, in the nature of the case cannot now live for very long—and a few isolated Christian leaders, I can see no sign of the ugly interlude being ended.

Again thanking you for your elevating and stirring speech.

Yours sincerely,

Charles Singer

One may wonder, if Pope Pius XI had not died in the following February, whether he would have been driven into excommunicating Hitler. What is certain is that his successor showed sad weakness in his attitude to Hitler.

I had had no doubt for a long time about the need to crush Hitler but I clung to the hope of detaching Mussolini and was irritated by the Left's quacking Collective Security, apparently under the impression that if they quacked loud enough they would lay it like an egg. Neither Mussolini nor Franco was a threat to civilization: Hitler was. I saw a news film showing Mussolini at his bullfrog best when he received Hitler at their meeting at which Hitler kept falling over himself and looked like a lavatory attendant beside the Duce. I was worried because the audience in that News Theatre in Piccadilly roared with laughter every time Hitler moved and evidently thought he was just a harmless clown who reminded them of Charlie Chaplin.

[1] The late Professor Charles Singer, D.Litt., M.D.

I find my mood expressed in a copy of what I wrote to thank Basil Tozer for his letter:

There is no chance of a broadcast with a punch because it is the one thing they do not want in a broadcast; it is a pity because it might be effective.

The proceedings at the Queen's Hall were solemn and gentlemanly, but Rosamond Lehmann made a really beautiful speech, though alas, I fear it did not carry beyond the first rows of stalls.

I think Chamberlain is doing his best with Italy after Eden's failure there but I shan't believe in this country's determination to stand up to Germany until Winston is brought into the Government.

To Professor Singer I wrote:

Words fail me to express what I think about the failure of official Christianity, whether Catholic or Protestant, to condemn by means of practical measures of ecclesiastical discipline this 'racial' hysteria.

I read your pamphlet with full agreement, and I was glad to find the Bishop of Chichester writing the foreword. I remember him as George Bell when he was at Christ Church.

I think the real trouble of the last five years has been the association of Judaism with Bolshevism by interested propagandists on both sides. . . .

Two days after that meeting in Queen's Hall I was much pleased when the B.B.C. let me celebrate White Rose Day by doing a broadcast about the Old Pretender who was born on the Tenth of June. The qualities of the *de jure* King James III and VIII have seldom been appreciated by historians; Thackeray's picture of him in *Esmond* was a pestilent caricature.

Eight days after that broadcast I was to enjoy in every sense of the epithet a delicious week in Paris.

In October of the previous year the Saintsbury Club had entertained at the Vintners' Hall a representative party from the Club des Cent—the famous club of the *gourmets* of France.

Now came an invitation for members of the Saintsbury Club to be entertained in Paris. The five who were able to accept were A. J. Symons, famous for his musical boxes and quest for Corvo, Curtis Moffat, the husband of Iris Tree, Dick Wyndham,[1] soldier and painter, David Tennant and myself. Of course André Simon, the doyen of the Saintsbury and the centre of its life was with us.

Dick Wyndham, David Tennant and I met at White's to fly over together. I recall from that flight that just after a bottle of champagne had been uncorked the plane flew low over Dick Wyndham's house in Sussex on that sunny Saturday afternoon.

[1] The late Major Richard Wyndham.

"Look at them!" Dick Wyndham exclaimed.

On the lawn in front of the house were chairs and small tables and about a dozen people. "The maids and my man are evidently having a party."

We stayed at the Hotel Lotti in the Rue de Castiglione and were to dine that night at Le Pré Catalan in the Bois de Boulogne. Paris seemed a little sad when we arrived because the decorations that were being put up for the visit of the King and Queen were only half finished, owing to the visit's being postponed until July on account of the death of the Queen's mother, Lady Strathmore.

I run the risk of being accused of hindsight when I say that the half decorated city gave me a feeling of dread for its future but even as I write these words twenty-eight years later I can still feel that ominous sadness as we drove along to the hotel.

The emotion quickly passed away in the warmth of our reception.

Sir Eric Phipps,[1] the British Ambassador, was to preside over that feast in the Bois de Boulogne. I took in to dinner Madame Cointreau and I was so captivated by her that I am ashamed to say I have forgotten the lady on my other side. Madame Cointreau was half Swedish and half Scottish but completely Parisienne. Few women are endowed so richly with both beauty and intelligence. Two or three years ago I was the *Weekly Scotsman's* Scot of the Year and at the dinner in the Westbury Hotel off Bond Street a young man in his twenties came up to me and gave me his mother's remembrances of that dinner and with those remembrances a double bottle of Cointreau.

Madame Cointreau was sitting on the Ambassador's left and he asked me if I recalled the last time he and I had met at dinner.

"Just twenty-one years ago," I said. "At the Ritz."

I have written of that dinner in Octave Five. He was then First Secretary at the British Embassy. I shall be telling in my next Octave of a third memorable dinner at which Eric Phipps and I met.

What a dinner that was at the Pré Catalan. Heidsieck Monopole 1928 (en jéroboam), Perrier Jouet 1928 (en double-magnum) . . . I feel it is my duty to print the three menus of those three meals in Appendix F.

Our lunch next day was at Le Pavillon Royale before driving to Auteil to see the Grand Prix from the Members' stand. For this occasion the close season for ortolans had been extended for five days to enable the visitors to taste ortolans. It is the only time I have eaten ortolans. They were served *en cassolettes*—little oblong coffins of cardboard.

Curtis Moffat asked me if I knew the proper way to eat an ortolan. I shook my head.

"I'll show you," said Curtis as he picked a bird out of its cassolette and put it into his mouth.

[1] The late Rt. Hon. Sir Eric Phipps, G.C.B., G.C.M.G.

Curtis Moffat was one of the most indomitable talkers in Europe, this was the only occasion on which I have known him silent. He had picked the little bird out of its cardboard coffin and put it into his mouth, The ortolan was very very hot and I see now its beak waving outside Curtis Moffat's mouth as he chewed with agony. I decided to eat my ortolans in what may have been the wrong way but less painfully.

After the races we were given a dinner by M. Laurens-Frings, the President of the Club des Cent, at the Yacht Moteur Club, and next day we flew home.

On a card with the three menus under the Tricolor and the Union Jack flying from the same flagpole there was a charming little address which began:

"It affords us great pleasure to greet in you the distinguished representatives of the illustrious Saintsbury Club on your short visit, much too short to really comply with our heart's desire."

It was indeed too short, for we revelled in every moment of it, and the memory of that visit would glow in my heart during the hideous German occupation and in some way assure me that one day Paris would be herself again.

Back in London I found waiting for me an advance copy of *Guy and Pauline* which the Oxford University Press had just added to their World's Classics. It was to be published on the same day as *The Windsor Tapestry* on July 23rd. Strange bedfellows, I reflected.

I had arranged before I left Barra that the weekly gatherings at Suidheachan to play our special brand of pool should continue while I was away, and I was glad to get a letter from the Coddie to 'report progress' in his favourite phrase.

> *Tigh-A-Choddie*
> *Northbay*
> *Isle of Barra.*
> *June 17th 1938.*

Charaid,

I hope you are well and the sun of prosperity shining on the present and the future and the hope of seeing you in the near future I would very much appreciate. I need not go over the ground and tell you how I felt the last night we were together, and will just leave aside until we meet in reality.

A big crowd at Suidheachan last Sunday, daylight up to 11 o'clock. The night was glorious, all the players in excellent fettle. . . . Father Dominic got the new car. He is quite proud of it and one of his opponents was the first to get in it.

At the moment staying with us is a young American artist who is over from Boston with a bursary. He will be one day a famous man. Murdoch was the first man to catch his eye, he exactly shaped him like the Apostle Peter. He says if I promised him to grow a beard he will cross the pond and do me next year. So you see that you have an artistic vote re the Coddie's beard.

Now the tide of spinsters has not yet started to flow, though a couple is coming to-night.

I shall be glad to hear from you when you find so convenient and I close with sincerest wishes, and in the near future I am going to write to Chrissie, please tell her that I am going to pose to the artist, even though the beard is not there.

Do charaid dileas

Choddie

That letter set me wishing that I was away from London and a packed engagement book; but I was beginning to get worried about my future with Rich and Cowan, and it was vital for me to remain in London. Nevertheless, I kept my eye on Island affairs, and find myself writing to Malcolm MacMillan, the Labour member for the Outer Isles, on July 5th.

"I have just read Wedderburn's[1] answer to your question in the House about the sand at Eoligarry and I have written a letter to the Secretary of State, of which I enclose a copy. It is damnable that these nincompoops of officialdom should be allowed to play the fool like this."

This was my letter to the Secretary of State for Scotland:

"Sir,

"I have just read with amazement in Parliamentary Debate of the House of Commons (June 30th 1938) the frivolous reply by the Under-Secretary of State for Scotland to Mr Malcolm MacMillan on the subject of sand encroaching on the land of the Department of Agriculture's holders on the island of Barra, Outer Hebrides, in which he claims that the Department has undertaken to repair damage by the planting of trees and bent grasses.

"A depth of ignorance is revealed by the Under-Secretary of State's reply. It would be as serviceable to plant hydrangeas on the terrace of the House of Commons to stop the flooding of the Thames as plant trees on the island of Barra to stop sand.

"At present the Department of Agriculture is neglecting its duties and making no effort to deal with the problem of encroaching sand, which has become a problem only since the Department took over the responsibility for the Eoligarry estate.

"It is insufferable that a Minister of His Majesty's Government should cynically display to the House of Commons so profound an ignorance of existing conditions in the Western Isles, and as soon as I return to Scotland I shall make it my business to expose such ignorance at public meetings and in the Press."

Mr C. C. Cunningham,[2] the Private Secretary of Mr Colville, wrote

[1] The Earl of Dundee.
[2] Sir Charles Cunningham, K.C.B., K.B.E., C.V.O.

to say that it was the normal duty of the tenants of machair land to prevent sand blow. In spite of this the Department of Agriculture had in the past undertaken the repair of damage of an abnormal character, and that they would continue to do so in future. The reply to Mr MacMillan, referring to the planting of bent grass and trees, was applicable to all estates owned by the Department. That reply did not justify the assumption that trees were to be planted at Eoligarry in the future.

The Department of Agriculture would keep the position continually under review and they would continue to take such remedial steps as were practicable.

To this I replied,

"Sir,

"I am obliged by your letter of July 14th and regret that I have still to insist on the delinquency of the Department of Agriculture in the matter of sand blow at Eoligarry. The blame rests entirely with the Department on account of its failure to continue protective measures practised from time immemorial in the outer islands and only abandoned at Eoligarry when the Department became the owners of the estate. Every year that passes now adds to the gravity of the situation and makes the remedy more difficult to apply. The tenants are not involved, because the tenants are under the control of their landlords and being reasonable men will at once cooperate in any reasonable and farmer-like proposal to grapple with the problem of sand blow. I recognize that you are at the mercy of explanations offered to you by interested but often incompetent officials, but the Department administration has become a laughing stock in the West, and so long as Secretaries of State and Under-Secretaries of State perform their annual pilgrimages escorted by Department officials so long will such pilgrimages be a waste of the Secretary's time and of the country's money. The particular problem at Eoligarry which has led me into this correspondence can still be solved with comparative ease, but I repeat that every year of further neglect will add to its difficulties."

Alas, those last words were to prove only too sadly true. The Department of Agriculture steadily evaded its responsibilities and today the sand blow is destroying good machair pasture faster than ever.

However, there was a stir in the lethargy of the Scottish Office when work began on a first-class road round Barra. John Campbell and I had the gratification of feeling that the refusal of the owners of motor-cars and lorries on Barra to pay their licences was worth the legal expenses in which we were both involved.

That new car Father Dominic MacKellaig had acquired suddenly arrived in London with its owner and his younger brother Neil Mac-

Kellaig[1] whom I had last seen in Barra when he was still a seminarist. It was nearly the end of July. I was tired out with two months of broadcasts, potting *The Windsor Tapestry* for its serialization in the *Sunday Dispatch,* dinner after dinner with speeches to be made at some of them. I looked at my engagement book. I had no engagements until August 5th. I asked Dominic if he and his brother were game to take Chrissie, Nellie, and myself on a pilgrimage to some of the places in my past. They thought it was a good idea and on Saturday, July 30th we set out for me to revisit the glimpses of the moon. Oxford came first. We stayed that night at the Eastgate Hotel which for me was haunted by the ghosts of the twenty-firsters of friends killed in the First World War. In the dining-room those ghosts and I were sitting round the big table once again with life before us, as we drank to our host's coming of age.

I was disappointed that George Gordon, the President of Magdalen and the next Vice-Chancellor, was not in residence. I never had the pleasure of meeting him, which has always been a regret. In Cloisters, in Chaplain's Quad, by New Buildings, in St Swithun's, and along Addison's Walk, ghosts everywhere. I took my companions to 43 High Street where to my immense pleasure Miss Allen was still the landlady. She was close on seventy, but full of reminiscences about that year thirty-five years ago when Harry Pirie-Gordon and I lodged at 43 High with the formidable Miss Prince and herself. According to her it had been the outstanding year in the chronicles of 43 High.

On the following afternoon we drove to Burford. At Lady Ham where the present owner received us kindly I asked if we might go up into what was apparently now a bedroom to see the bay window, looking down over the Windrush below and across the orchard, on which visitors to Lady Ham had once scratched their names and an appropriate quotation with a diamond pencil. I looked for Roger Fry and *The fresh green lap of fair King Richard's land.* The window was blank.

"I'm afraid that window was broken by the workmen when they were in," said the owner of Lady Ham, "but I'm glad this window wasn't broken. That's what interests me."

It was my record that on an August Bank Holiday in 1905 a Camberwell Beauty had flown out of that window. I was back again swinging down the pear-tree against the house and chasing that Camberwell Beauty till it flew out of reach.

I saw again in that bedroom the room as it once was. My books were again on either side of the fireplace. Twinkle, the Manx cat, was in the grandfather-chair. I was wrestling with a sonnet by the light of a reading candle. I was suddenly glad that window had been broken. On it on a June day in 1904 the Provost of Worcester had written *hoc erat in votis,* and it would be six months later in a letter from Mrs Daniel opened and

[1] Rt. Rev. Mgr. Neil MacKellaig.

read in this room that I should hear of the breaking off of my engagement to Ruth Daniel.

I think we stayed at the Lamb Inn that night. Anyway next day we had reached Wells where I went to call on my old friend, Francis Underhill, the new Bishop of Bath and Wells, which if I were an Anglican parson would be the most desirable see in Great Britain with the richest remains of the middle ages in one city and, except for the New Town of Edinburgh and Dublin, the finest eighteenth-century remains in his other city. And besides the glorious west front and octagonal chapter house of his cathedral the most beautiful palace of them all. Yes, as I went along to that palace and saw the swans in the moat raising their beaks to ring the bell for food to be served them, I felt that Francis deserved this after his arduous years once upon a time as Vicar of St Alban's, Birmingham and his valuable service as Warden of Liddon House and Grosvenor Chapel where my great-grandfather's adventure as a midshipman was recorded in my First Octave.

I recall saying to the Bishop when we had greeted each other,

"I can't understand, Francis, why none of your canonists have tackled my exposition of the Anglican Church and Divorce in *The Windsor Tapestry*. It's no use just saying I'm all wrong. Why doesn't one of them show where I go wrong and demolish my argument?"

"Because, my dear Monty, your argument was unanswerable."

I told him about the Archbishop's remarks to me at the Savile Club dinner.

"How like him," said Francis. "The other day he and I were both at some conference at which the Cardinal Archbishop was present. After it was over the Cardinal's car was missing. 'And so,' said Lang to me, 'I felt bound to offer him a lift. But I didn't like to drive him directly to Westminster. So we went to Lambeth first. But I did not invite him to come in.' 'No?' said I. 'Not even to partake of your evening glass of milk?' "

After that we talked of the old days at High Cross when I was a pupil at the Vicarage waiting for my first term at Oxford, and of the time when he was a curate at St Thomas's, Oxford.

While we were in Wells I saw advertised in the local paper a cottage in the small village of West Horrington, a mile or two away. What pleased me as we turned off to look at this little property was a large sign NO THROUGH ROAD. I found that Tor Vale as it was called was at the end of this welcome cul-de-sac consisting of a four-roomed cottage over a hundred years old to which had been added much later a wooden bungalow with two large rooms. The dwelling itself was not particularly attractive but the small garden above the wooded slopes of a deep coomb down which ran a stream was enchanting and the view away over the Vale of Avalon to Glastonbury Tor as lovely a view as I had ever seen.

s

The lease of Faith's upper-part in Connaught Street would come to an end on March 25th next year and she had already been looking at various possible country retreats in Dorset and Wiltshire. The years of hard work she had been doing for *The Gramophone* had made her weary of London. Moreover, Christopher's complicated advertisement of light records from Luxemburg and later from Lyons had come to an end and he was now devoting himself again to the London editorship. Faith herself after the great success of her first volume of memoirs *As Much As I Dare* was now full of a second volume to be called *More Than I Should*. She had been over to see Jethou and had been much distressed by the way the new tenants had allowed both the little garden she had made and the garden I had made go to ruin in order to plant geraniums, lobelias and marguerites in neat rows. She was longing to make another little garden and here in West Horrington was the ideal spot with that magical view away over Avalon and the sound of that bubbling stream in the coomb below. The price was only £800. I felt sure Faith would love this place and when she returned from Salzburg we drove down to look at it. She was completely captivated and at the beginning of September it was hers; she renamed it Peace Close.

Colin Summerford had been in Barra all the summer but he was soon coming back; Nicolas Nadegine had given up the idea of a singing career and was planning to write his autobiography.

Faith was delighted to get a letter from Calum MacSween on the day the purchase of Tor Vale was completed:

I couldn't resist writing to congratulate you on the splendid book As Much As I Dare.

We got it a long while ago but I had to wait my turn until Mrs MacSween and Lily both got through it, and I started my read undisturbed. I am now finished reading it after enjoying every sentence in it, and especially the living picture you make of Mr Mackenzie. I don't mean his photo which is really very good, but your description of him is exactly what I would imagine him to be. . . . You should write something on the Western Islands.

The visit to Oxford and Burford and now to Somerset, where once upon a time Ruth Daniel and I had climbed to the top of Glastonbury Tor and wondered how long a time must pass before we were married, had made me determined to revisit one more glimpse of the moon and see what 'Holiday Haunt' was like today. I had originally planned to revisit Cornwall but we had spent longer in Wells than I had intended, and Cornwall had to be left out of this pilgrimage. So from Somerset we drove to Hampshire.

I had not visited for thirty-two years that garden I had planned with my mother in the two-roomed bungalow she had bought in 1896 and I wanted to see what the trees I had planted looked like now. I have written at length in Octave Two of the Beech Farm Estate and the fantastic figures that were scattered about it in response to the advertisement LAND FOR THE PEOPLE. As I write these words I have just heard that our bungalow is to be pulled down. Well, it has lasted for seventy years through six reigns. I hope when a new house is built they will not cut down that American oak I planted in 1896. I was impressed by its size when I saw it last in 1938.

It was we who first gave Beech near Alton as our address instead of the Beech Farm Estate; the inhabitants of Beech today would find it hard to believe what it was like seventy years ago.

I found it hard to believe even in that August of 1938. We had been warned in 1896 that the road would presently be widened and in planting the garden we had allowed for that. When I went to Beech in 1938 the road had not been widened. I wonder if it has been widened yet.

As I looked at the wide path of the old right of way past Wyard's Farm I saw with my mind's eye that narrow winding right of way through a hop-garden. I saw my young brother and myself resentfully trudging a quarter of a mile with pails to fetch water from the brick-kiln when our own well ran dry in the baking summer of the Diamond Jubilee.

We drove on from Beech to Wield. Again I was walking along the six miles of green lanes every Thursday morning in the summer holidays to serve the Vicar of Wield at eight o'clock Mass in what is the most beautiful small Norman church I have known. There were still ducks on the village pond. The signpost still pointed to the Candovers, Wield was still untroubled by the plague of cars; I can hardly hope that it is not infected by the plague of them today.

That pilgrimage to youth was all too brief an interlude. Back in London after escaping from it for five days I was booked all day for the rest of the month. To look back at those Augusts of once upon a time when London was as quiet all day as Sunday morning was to wish that Satan had never given the internal combustion engine to humanity. By 1938 London was as full and noisy and busy in August as in any other month. Yet when I reflect that I knew Rome when it was the quietest city in Europe what use to repine for London Augusts of the past? When I look through the few pages of my engagement book which have survived from this year I am tempted to write about the many people and the various occasions with which they were connected. Nevertheless, I have set myself the task of including nothing in these Octaves the remembrance of which was due to an odd letter or pages from an engagement book. I feel that the lunch or the dinner or the public meeting or the broadcast one had forgotten will never come to life again in writing about them.

I was glad in the middle of that crowded time to get a letter from

Father Neil MacKellaig which made me feel that the pilgrimage had been fruitful. It was written from Bishop's House, Oban:

I am back again to normal Oban existence but not without magnificent memories to relieve the dull monotony of life here—as many pictures to which I can revert when I remember that I am not allowed to go to the cinema. Ever since my return here I have been trying to think what I enjoyed best but I cannot make up my mind.

I was really thrilled with our visit to Oxford. I will long remember the fascination of wandering with a ghost through Magdalen, seeing the sites of famous bonfires and the scenes of amusing escapades in a combined setting of architecture and horticulture unrivalled. Nor can I forget what we saw and experienced in the West Country. Wells as a sight, a storm in the Mendips, as an experience what better could we have had!

But then the memory of the charm of Wield, of Burford and Bibury, refuses to be dimmed, and I wonder what I enjoyed best.

Anyhow, I can spend a lot of time musing over all this myself but I must not waste more of yours. I should like just to say thanks for all you gave me and did for me. . . .

I hope you are keeping well and that you are not being harassed by lawyers, publishers and the rest as you were when we were at Hampstead. . . .

It was good to get that letter. It was an assurance that self-indulgence can sometimes be shared with others.

Today the newly ordained Neil MacKellaig of 1938 is Monsignor Neil MacKellaig, Dean of the Isles, at Daliburgh, South Uist. Alas, our much loved Dominic died in 1960 just after he became a Canon. John MacQueen and Sydney MacEwan were already Canons. I rang up Dominic from Edinburgh to congratulate him.

"Canons to right of me, Canons to left of me, someone has blundered," I said.

I heard his gay laugh in Roy Bridge at the other end of the telephone. He was no longer with us to laugh twenty-four hours later.

I suppose it was wishful thinking by somebody who loved Italy which made me support so eagerly Neville Chamberlain's effort to detach Mussolini from Hitler. At the same time, I could not help being deeply moved by the way that man on the edge of seventy set out to fly to Germany in the hope of staving off another world war. It may have been true that he was in the words of Churchill "a town councillor looking at Europe through the wrong end of a municipal drainpipe". Nevertheless, he had inherited the present European situation from the disastrous government of Bonar Law followed by the even more disastrous government of Baldwin.

When the panic preparations for immediate war were carried through in that September, with millions of gas-masks being distributed, hardly four dozen anti-aircraft guns in the whole country and ludicrous trenches being dug all over the London parks and Hampstead Heath, I felt, as so many other people felt, that it was vital to obtain a postponement of immediate war even at the expense of Czechoslovakia. It is easy now for historians with hindsight to argue that Germany was no more ready for war than we were and dust their pages with 'ifs'. If 'ifs' were horses beggars would ride.

One incident during that panic remains with me unforgettably. In Tottenham Court Road I saw men painting out the 'Gentlemen' and 'Ladies' of a public lavatory because the white plates would help German bombers to hit their mark. That incident symbolizes for me the mental state of London in September 1938.

To my friends of the Left who at the time of Munich were talking as if they had taken a bold stand against Hitler from the moment he became Chancellor I used to show a passage in *The Windsor Tapestry*:

"If the Government had defied the omen of the East Fulham election and had been defeated at the polls in asking for a mandate for rearmament those well informed about the situation in Europe could have been accused of taking an unpatriotic risk; but it did not seem to occur to Mr Baldwin that if he and his friends, with far better opportunities of knowing the facts, were so uneasy over what was happening in Europe the right course was to take the electorate fully into their confidence and abide by the result. Instead they sat mumbling like rheumatic old women whose twinges were warning them of a change in the weather, but who were afraid to ask for warmer clothes lest they should be turned out of the almshouse.

"There was only one outstanding problem in international politics in 1933 and that was the determination and ability of Germany to rearm with sufficient rapidity and effect to become once again a menace to the peace of the world. In pre-Hitler days the Labour Party had tried to raise every obstacle in the way of a cast-iron agreement between Great Britain and France or between Great Britain and Italy, and although by 1936 Labour had become comparatively bellicose we have noted earlier in this chapter the fatuity of its attitude at the Edinburgh Conference. The Labour Party was indeed no more than a great wobbly blancmange streaked here and there with cochineal. In 1935 the wave of pacificism came up with a splash against the menacing fact of the German re-occupation of the Rhine territory, and this direct violation of the Versailles Treaty by Germany was followed by another cynical breach of it in the shape of the Anglo-German Naval agreement of 1935, which not merely convinced France of the duplicity of British foreign policy but drove Mussolini into his desperate Abyssinian adventure, he being equally convinced that Great Britain meant to come to terms with Germany and override the rest of Europe.

"We in Great Britain who were aware what little blood and iron there was in that National Government found it hard to understand why it should have been credited with such a doughty ambition; but we had to wait until November 1936 to be told by the leader of that Government that our foreign policy was built of ballot-boxes. And for consolation the country was to be assured that it was in the nature of a democracy to be a couple of years behind dictatorship in the maturity of its plans. Mr Baldwin might as usefully have observed that it was in the nature of an elephant to spend two years in gestation, of a rabbit to spend six weeks. Yet when democracy did begin, he boasted, it could act with at least equal vigour. At least equal vigour in preparation is not enough to overtake an inertia of two years. However, the country was under Mr Baldwin's spell. He had succeeded in giving constipation as bright an aureole of romance as the poets of the 1830's gave consumption. Moreover, any apprehension of the Government's moral courage was completely tranquillized on November 10th when the Public Order Bill was read and the country heard that Sir Oswald Mosley was no longer to be allowed to wear a black shirt in public."

My friends on the Left used to maintain that if Chamberlain and Daladier had held out at Munich the Soviet Union would have aligned itself with Great Britain and France. I agreed that the less than half-hearted attempts by Chamberlain to ascertain Stalin's real intentions had been feeble. I agreed that at the back of his mind and of the minds, if minds they could be called, of most of the members of the Government, was a hope that Hitler instead of seeking to dominate the West would go to war with the Soviet Union. At the same time, I was convinced that the Soviet Union would do nothing.

"Willie Gallacher was right to remain seated when the news from Hitler was read to the House by Chamberlain, but do not forget that Duff Cooper resigned as First Lord of the Admiralty. That means he may have thrown away his political career. I think myself he may be too optimistic about the Navy's belief that the submarine is no longer a threat and that with a strong Navy we were ready to go to war with Germany. Never mind. This was a genuine resignation because he felt that Munich was an ignominious surrender. Eden resigned out of wounded vanity because Chamberlain insisted on publishing the news of the Foreign Office from Downing Street. And do not forget that if Willie Gallacher remained seated Jimmie Maxton of the I.L.P. was on his feet cheering the news from Hitler as loudly as the Tory back-benchers."

There will be more to say in my next Octave about Chamberlain. In September 1938 I was as grateful to him as the vast majority of the country. But I never thought for a moment that it would be peace in our time as Chamberlain, that tragic figure, really did believe. Listening over the radio to the voice of that damnable revivalist and hearing the answering chant of "Sieg heil" from a nation in the hysterical state of the converted under that influence, I knew it would inevitably be war again in our time.

I was glad to hear that a translation of *The Windsor Tapestry* had been banned by the Nazis. I knew then that what I had written in it about Germany had struck home.

I was surprised one morning to receive a note from somebody in Jermyn Street who signed himself Haäs-Heye to ask if he could come and see me about a confidential matter.

In due course a tall distinguished man of about my own age came to Woodbine Cottage. He told me he was a son of the late proprietor of the *Münchener Tageblatt*, a paper which once had the status in Germany enjoyed by the *Manchester Guardian* in Great Britain. It was now in the hands of the Nazis. He had avoided fighting in the war by getting himself into a mental home in Switzerland. With his fine profile, his carefully brushed hair and moustaches, and his delicate hands Haäs-Heye was a Bavarian aristocrat of the past, speaking perfect English. I felt at once that we had been friends for a long time.

"I have come to tell you that the Princess Hermina, the second wife of the Kaiser, is a great friend of mine, and she has told me that the Kaiser has read your book *The Windsor Tapestry* and that he feels you might write a book about him and present him fairly to the world. He was a little hurt by one or two things you said about him in *The Windsor Tapestry* but he feels that if he put all his private papers at your disposal you would understand his motives better. What do you think of this very important suggestion?"

I was used to so many callers and correspondents with very important suggestions as fragile as soap-bubbles that I told this charming envoy I should be greatly interested by such a suggestion without supposing for a moment that it had any more substance than a soap-bubble.

"I will write and tell the Princess that you are interested, and I hope we shall be able to arrange for you to meet the Kaiser in the spring."

A week or two later Haäs-Heye came along to say that the Princess was hoping the Kaiser would receive me at Doorn where the project could be discussed with him personally. There was only one thing which had worried her. The Kaiser had said he hoped I was no relation of the Morell Mackenzie who had defied the opinion of the German doctors and written that book about his father.

"Well, as a matter of fact, Morell Mackenzie was my first cousin once removed—a rather near relation."

Haäs-Heye was so shaken by this news that he took out the comb he always carried and combed back his hair, which he evidently felt must have been ruffled by the shock.

"Yes, yes, that is certainly a difficulty," he said with a sigh, "but Morell Mackenzie is no longer alive."

"He's been dead for over forty years."

"But I think I will say nothing of the relationship. It would be more prudent. And we must move prudently. The Kaiser must not think you are so eager for this task. He has always been very suspicious since the Eulenberg scandal and on top of that Krupp."

I have had at the back of my mind for a long time a third novel about Capri. I knew most of the people who were involved in that scandal which ended in Krupp's shooting himself. It is an astonishing story but I doubt if I shall ever tell it.

In May next year I should go to Doorn with Haäs-Heye but the tale of that visit will not be told until my next Octave.

By coincidence about the time Haäs-Heye came to Woodbine Cottage Emil Ludwig who had written a brilliant life of the Kaiser called there to see me. I had never met him but I had chased him out of Athens in April 1916. He had turned up as correspondent of the *Berliner Tageblatt* and an interview with King Constantine had been published in the pro-German Greek paper *Embros*. I looked up that interview in a copy of my suppressed *Greek Memories*.

Here is an extract:

"His Majesty then went on to speak of Germany in the warmest terms.

" 'Ask my peasants,' he said, 'if they know the Kaiser. Tell them it was Germany who gave them Cavalla and they will tell you, "No, it was the Kaiser." ' "

Emil Ludwig and I became great friends, but much as I should have liked to talk over with him that suggestion about the Kaiser, I decided it might be indiscreet. Ludwig had been planning to write a life of the Duke Windsor but he gave up that idea.

That autumn the Council for Civil Liberties in conjunction with the National Union of Journalists held a conference in the Beaver Hall to discuss the threat of the Official Secrets Act to the freedom of the press. The Beaver Hall was the headquarters of the Hudson Bay Company in the City, a circular affair with rows of seats rising in tiers and a platform from which I suppose the auctioneer offered the furs for bidding.

Gwilym Lloyd George[1] was in the chair; and there were several speakers, among them myself as one who had practical experience of the workings of the Official Secrets Act. I said that prosecution under that Act was in effect a Star Chamber business, and that the danger of such an Act to liberty if it ever were administered by an unscrupulous government was clear.

"At this moment we are making a parade of our freedom, and certainly for the moment we have at any rate an illusion of more freedom than the victims of totalitarianism. We have been given gas-bags to protect us

---

[1] The late Lord Tenby.

against the poison gas which we are told the enemy will shower on us if war comes. If war does come let us use those gas-masks to protect ourselves not only against the poison-gas being exhaled by Hitler but also against the hot air of some of our own politicians. The tendency of our democratic rulers is moving steadily towards repression, and the Official Secrets Act is a convenient weapon for tyranny. Two members of the Labour Shadow Cabinet in 1932 were approached with a view to asking a question in the House of Commons about my case; their reply was that they might want to use the Official Secrets Act themselves when they were next in power. They, the avowed guardians of liberty, knew too well the value of that threat to liberty. Even Cabinet Ministers are protected by this Act, and there is no clearer sign of the decay of statesmanship in this country than this eagerness of second-rate politicians to preserve the secrets of their own place-hunting and time-serving.

"The ease with which public servants protected by the Official Secrets Act can now hide the proofs of their incompetence is completely destructive of true democracy, and until bills of impeachment have become once more a feature of our political life true democracy will not revive."

By far the best speech at that Conference was made by W. J. Brown, who at that date was no longer Labour Member for West Wolverhampton and not yet Independent Member for Rugby. What a loss he was to Rugby when they foolishly failed to re-elect him! What a loss, indeed, to the whip-directed herds of M.P.'s are the Independent Members of other days. Now we have a herd of sheep when in power and a herd of goats when in opposition.

About the best series there has ever been on television was that Sunday afternoon of free speech with Bob Boothby, W. J. Brown, Alan Taylor and Michael Foot.

The Conference at the Beaver Hall in the autumn of 1938 was just a waste of breath.

Scottish literature had suffered a heavy loss when James Leslie Mitchell died in February 1935 before he was able to read my book *Catholicism in Scotland* which he had been instrumental in my writing for the Routledge series—the *Voice of Scotland*. He had been generous enough to dedicate to me his life of *Mungo Park* in the previous year.

In this November I received a letter from Leslie Mitchell's widow.

Because of the good reviews you have given my late husband's books—"Lewis Grassic Gibbon"—and because of a very kind letter you sent me after his death, I am presuming that you will be kind enough to help me now.

I am contemplating, or rather attempting, to get my daughter Rhea admitted to Christ's Hospital where I think she will receive a really good education. So that you need not wade through explanations I'm enclosing the particulars of eligibility for admission. . . . If you feel you can let me have a testimonial to my late husband's standing in literature . . . with a view to helping Rhea's claim I shall be deeply indebted to you. I am thinking of writing to Mr Linklater to ask his favour.

I replied:

It gives me much pleasure to testify to the distinguished position your late husband occupied in letters, and I regard his premature death as having cut off the career of a young writer who was expected by myself and many other writers to rise to genuine eminence. Not only was he a novelist of unusual fertility and variety, but he was also a good archaeologist and historian, and the body of work he had produced both under his own name and under the pseudonym Lewis Grassic Gibbon was remarkable as an achievement for one so young, and not less remarkable for the steady growth it made toward the fulfilment of the highest expectations.

I sincerely hope that the Council of Almoners will give favourable attention to your application on behalf of your little daughter Rhea, and I have no hesitation in declaring her to be the child of a person distinguished in literature in the strictest meaning of the phrase.

The quality of the trilogy Mitchell wrote as Lewis Grassic Gibbon is becoming increasingly recognized in his own country, but I regret that a work of prehistoric fantasy called *Three Go Back* seems to have been forgotten. In my opinion the books he wrote as J. Leslie Mitchell were just as good as those he wrote under the pseudonym and deserve more attention than they have received from contemporary critics.

A few days after this I received a letter from a young man of nineteen:

I have for some time been preparing an anthology in biography from D. H. Lawrence. I have been selecting passages from his own works and given his books by his friends with the object of giving, as far as possible, a complete portrait of him, not principally as an artist, nor as a psychologist, but as a man. . . . Would you contribute something to this book? . . .

I wrote back:

I am afraid it is out of the question for me to contribute to your proposed book, partly because I have no time to spare and partly because it would be a mistake from your point of view to include character studies which might easily conflict with your own theories.

I know of only one study of Lawrence to which I attach the slightest importance and that was the anonymous portrait of him by the girl to whom he was once engaged. All these books by female devotees are so much bunkum, and the portrait by Middleton Murry is just as bad. However, I wish you well in your difficult task.

That turgid stream of books about D. H. Lawrence still flows on both sides of the Atlantic.

Throughout that summer and autumn I was getting letters about *The Windsor Tapestry*. Over six hundred were friendly; about a hundred were hostile. What interested me was that practically all the hostile letters were anonymous.

Many of them asked me to come and speak to various clubs and societies, but of these I accepted only one.

Mr Sheridan-Bickers, the Chairman of the South Devon Literary and Debating Society, wrote:

The intense and widespread interest you have aroused by The Windsor Tapestry *(vindicating the heroic self-sacrifice and unique national service of our beloved former King and expressing the sickening hypocrisy and Vicar of Bray-like intrigues of Earl Baldwin) has impelled me to ask if you will do our Society the honour of coming to Torquay this autumn or winter to open a Public Discussion I am arranging under this Society's auspices on* The Windsor Tapestry. . . . *It may interest you to know that Richard Brinsley Sheridan was my great-great-grandfather.*

In accepting the invitation I wrote:

It is an interesting coincidence that you are the third Sheridan to express your warm approval of this book. A Sheridan was one of the Seven Men of Moidart and the greatest Sheridan of all was the most loyal friend of George IV.

The meeting was held in the ballroom of the Torbay Hotel. My father used to say that *The School for Scandal* played twenty minutes longer north of the Trent than it did south of the Thames. It was difficult to stir English audiences in the south; they were nearly always permeated by an atmosphere of anxious gentility. Within my experience that is equally true today, but the anxious gentility has been replaced by an equally anxious effort to keep up with the neighbours whether with the right car or the right book. The critics of the Sunday Press today are the equivalent of the etiquette writers of a hundred years ago for the *nouveaux riches*. They tell Mrs Smith what is the right book to have in her "lounge" so that Mrs Brown will realize she is just as intellectual as herself. Once upon a time the hostess of a mid-Victorian drawing-room was given help with her etiquette; today the hostess knows that the right etiquette for a lounge is to laugh at such old-fashioned manners, and that the only thing that matters is to be 'with it' whether with pictures or books, with cars or swimming pool, or the right coast to visit in Spain.

A speaker should always be spontaneous but this spontaneity will flag unless he has a spontaneous audience. I can see now the members of that audience waiting for others to applaud first. I have seldom felt so tired after a long speech. Nevertheless, I was assured by my enthusiastic hosts that they had never known a Torquay audience so responsive. Well, well. . . .

Joyce Weiner had gone to America in September, where she felt she could be useful to Stokes who were going to publish *The Windsor Tapestry* in the States. I was writing to her on September 6th:

Thanks for your interesting letter which reached me at the end of the week in bed with the usual thing. I am tired out really. Instead of the money from Rich and Cowan I have been asked for an extension of time. However, they did pay £500 on account which I immediately had to pay out. They have promised to pay now by the end of October but who knows? . . .

Letters about the book continue to swarm. . . . I had a charming letter from Roger Fulford who pointed out that the Liverpool Cabinet in 1820 tried to avoid the scandal of a Royal Divorce by getting the marriage made morganatic and giving Caroline the rank of Duchess of Cornwall. We missed that one, but Fulford has given me the reference and you can look them up when you come home.

Frederick Chamberlain, the keeper of the King's Library at the British Museum, wrote to congratulate me on the amount of research done in such a short time. . . .

The most astonishing thing that has happened was a magnificent notice in Punch *last week which I should think must have drawn howls from Blimpland!* . . .

The most interesting contacts I have had were Colonel and Mrs Scanlan. He is Air Attaché at the American Embassy and was with H.R.H. on the night that he left England. She, a devout Catholic, is the Duchess's best friend and was going to stay with them just after I met her at lunch. She told me all the Duchess's letters to her were opened. She was reading the Tapestry *for the third time when I met her.*

On October 4th I was writing:

I have every confidence you will be able to demonstrate that literary judgment was corrupted by political prejudice over here. It is significant that Punch *which was never friendly to Edward had the courage to print a fair review, because it was not a paper making one in a group. You might also let it be known in New York that the only book in London unaffected by this last week of crisis was the* Tapestry. *I shudder to think what we might have been doing tonight had Baldwin remained at the head of affairs.*

Macartney has been trying to persuade me to take out my complimentary allusion to Chamberlain on the ground that American opinion is against him. If that be so I am sorry for American opinion. . . . I have been driven nearly mad by the illogicality of the Left.

On October 13th Joyce Weiner was writing:

I am glad to be able to tell you that Stokes hope to get the book out on Armistice Day. . . .

The luncheons with the critics have so far been entirely successful and their reviews should, at least, be accurate and informed. . . . The point you mentioned was my biggest argument—I called it "unofficial censorship" and as they think all our press is muzzled anyway they found that quite credible. . . .

I'm afraid English stock is very low here at the moment. I find it very hard to bear in spite of the objectivity I have learnt from you. It's different attacking one's own from hearing it attacked by other people whose ignorance of the situation is really colossal. I have tried to laugh off the criticism and I have tried to ignore it, but they force it down your throat and it has turned social life into a bear-garden.

My "objectivity" coupled with my being half American has always enabled me to take a particularly objective attitude about my two countries. I felt that American criticism of Chamberlain was as illogical as the criticism of him by the British Left. What had either done any more than Baldwin and that wretched National Government to deal with Hitler before it was too late? I found that desperate effort by an old gentleman with an umbrella to avert war much more heroic than that of the young volunteers who went off to fight for the Spanish Republic. What neither America nor Left Book Club opinion realized was that the Germans were as much in the power of that evil genius as Faust was in the power of Mephistopheles. Alan Taylor in the volume which brings the Oxford University Press *History of England* to a close considers such a view melodramatic. If the folly of uniting East and West Germany is accomplished that United Germany will in due course bring about the Third World War. There is a profound belief in the German heart that Germany is more capable of running the world than any other nation. People fail to realize that a nation which calls itself the Fatherland and even makes the moon masculine is a menace to the future of a world which is at long last beginning to wonder whether the influence of women may not be more important for the future of humanity than that of men. I am tempted to think that when the cradle of civilization allowed itself to be rocked by patriarchs instead of matriarchs humanity made the world safe for millenniums of intolerable boyhood. Whatever I may have achieved in my life has been achieved because throughout that life women have been more important to me than men, but I did not fully realize their importance until those months at Gallipoli which left me exclusively at the mercy of male conversation and, paradoxically if you like, it is this which makes me hope that the Savile will not go the way of the Garrick or the Arts; I occasionally need a rest from the stimulation of feminine company.

To my immense pleasure the reviews of *The Windsor Tapestry* in the United States were not merely favourable but unanimously enthusiastic. Joyce Weiner could congratulate herself upon the way she had been able to present my case to the critics.

By the end of that October I knew that if I wanted to complete *The Four Winds of Love* as I dreamt of it I should have to find new publishers. I had been warned repeatedly that Rich and Cowan were soon liable to exist no longer as a firm of publishers. I knew also that the firm of J. B. Pinker and Son was in danger of dissolution, but I could not bring myself to leave a sinking ship. I have always been handicapped by what I suppose must be called the feebleness of leaving my business affairs in the hands of people when I knew they were no longer capable of handling them properly. It is nothing to do with sentiment; it is due to my always putting myself in the other person's place and feeling his mortification instead of my own position. To be Protean is a great advantage for the kind of novelist I am but it is a handicap to practical affairs.

In the conviction that I must look for new publishers I attended the Saintsbury Dinner on October 26th at the Vintners' Hall. The Saintsbury Club dined twice a year—in April as near as possible to the birthday of Shakespeare and in October as near as possible to the birthday of George Saintsbury. I never had the good fortune to meet one of the most inspiring Professors of English Literature that Edinburgh University has ever had, but he wrote me an encouraging letter about my *Poems* in 1907 and in 1913 as a footnote to his *History of the English Novel* he said that 1913 had opened as auspiciously with *Sinister Street* as 1813 with *Waverley*. This coming from a man who must have read more novels than anybody else in the world was like a glass of his own wine. *Notes from a Cellar Book* was a classic for the lover of wine and the Saintsbury Club was founded to do that man reverence. He was seventy-three when he gave up his Edinburgh professorship in 1915 and he lived on for another eighteen years.

There were fifty-one sitting round that great table. Baron de Cartier de Marchienne, the Belgian Ambassador, was in the chair at the rounded end; A. J. Symons, the Secretary, at the head of the other end. On his left was Ian Parsons, a guest. Between him and me was Dick Wyndham. I did not know who Ian Parsons was and talked to Dick Wyndham about my need to find another publisher. Just beyond me on the other side was Desmond Flower, and I half hoped he would hear what I was saying and ask if I would like to return to Cassell's.

After dinner I told Desmond I was leaving Rich and Cowan and he suggested that Ralph Pinker should get in touch with him. Presently Ian Parsons came up to me and said he could not help hearing what I had been saying to Dick Wyndham and that Chatto and Windus, of which he was a partner, would welcome the idea of publishing my future books. I took a great fancy to Ian Parsons and asked him back to the Savile where he says I went on talking until after two o'clock. This is not incredible to me, I fear.

I told Ralph Pinker about Chatto's and Cassell's and a few days later he let me know that he had fixed up a very good contract with Chatto and Windus to give them a novel a year and another book. I signed the contract and was invited to lunch at the Écu de France in Jermyn Street with Ian Parsons and Harold Raymond. The latter joined Charles Prentice immediately after the war in the old-established business of Chatto and Windus, then in St Martin's Lane. Later they moved to new premises in Chandos Street, presently to be foolishly re-named by the London County Council William the Fourth Street. Pinker told me that Cassell's had not been interested in my return to them and I was surprised to get a letter from Desmond Flower in the middle of December:

Dear Monty

We have recently received a note from Ralph asking if we are willing to part with our stock and rights in those of your books which we have published.

In the light of the conversation which we had after the Saintsbury Club Dinner, I was surprised to receive this request. Although I expected it to take time, I was hoping to have a call from Ralph one day to talk business.

Of course if there is no possibility of your returning to La Belle Sauvage, there is no particular point in our holding on to the rights which we have, and if we can sell to advantage we might as well do so. But I think you know that all of us here would very much rather see you back on the Cassell list.

We are getting out the figures which Ralph asked for as a matter of course. But I would not like you to construe our supplying the information as a lack of interest in your work or a desire to be freed from it. The actual position is very much the reverse.

Yours always
Desmond

I was rather upset by this letter because I had supposed that Ralph Pinker had given Cassell's the opportunity to have me back and that they had turned it down.

I do not remember the details, but I know that Chatto's bought *Gallipoli Memories* and *Athenian Memories*. What I also know is that Cassell's behaved with their usual generosity and that the novels were bought back by me for small sums.

Destiny ruled that I was to go to Chatto's and nearly thirty years later I am still with them.

Faith with Chrissie and Colin Summerford to help her had made the move from Connaught Street to Peace Close.

Faith wrote in *Always Afternoon*:

"Colin took some hours off from the racket to be received into the Catholic Church at Haverstock Hill, and next day we were all three following the furniture down the West."

That December 16th was a halcyon day, but it was followed that night by a killing frost and it was still freezing when I got down to Peace Close for Christmas.

Faith wrote:

For Christmas dinner we had a duck perfectly cooked by Chrissie. We sat in the big bungalow room, with a tremendous fire and two electric heaters; after champagne and crackers we dozed over the fire with our paper caps still on our heads. M. was exhausted by a year in London. Besides the pains and anxieties of The Windsor Tapestry *he had been lost in a maze of cinematographic propositions all ending in blind alleys, from which he had at last emerged exactly where he entered, except for the loss of an immense amount of time and energy.*

I have not bored myself or my readers with trying to relate those cinematographic proposals. It is a merciful thing that television proposals are conducted more rationally. If television had fallen into the hands of the film it would never have reached the status it deservedly occupies today.

I was delighted to find when I got back to Woodbine Cottage after the New Year a letter waiting for me which said

WITH LORD SAMUEL'S COMPLIMENTS

FROM THE DAILY EXPRESS

From a car advertisement:

"£119 ! ! ! A car that has literally been wrapped up in cotton wool since originally put on the road. . . ."

1939 had started with a good laugh. How would it end?

APPENDICES

T

APPENDIX A

GLASGOW UNIVERSITY

RECTORIAL ELECTION

OCTOBER 1931

On 24th October 1931 Mr Compton Mackenzie was elected Lord Rector of Glasgow University by 849 votes against 762 votes polled by Sir Robert Horne, 581 votes for Professor Gilbert Murray, 110 votes for Mr Tom Johnston and 21 votes for Sir Oswald Mosely. In thus electing the first Scottish Nationalist Lord Rector, the students of Glasgow University have broken away from the tradition of honouring prominent leaders of the Conservative and Liberal Parties, a tradition which was only once before broken during the war years when Monsieur Raymond Poincaré was elected. Since 1919 the Rectorial chair has been the monopoly of the Conservatives, and Mr Compton Mackenzie, as a Nationalist, succeeds Rt. Hon. A. Bonar Law, the Rt. Hon. Earl of Birkenhead, the Rt. Hon. Sir Austen Chamberlain and the Rt. Hon. Stanley Baldwin, whilst the pre-war list of distinguished men who have held the office includes such names as the Rt. Hon. Arthur James Balfour, the Rt. Hon. Joseph Chamberlain, the Earl of Rosebery, the Rt. Hon. Herbert H. Asquith, the Rt. Hon. Baron Curzon and the Rt. Hon. Augustine Birrell.

The Rector who is elected by the Matriculated Students of the University is the President of the University Court, the governing and directing body of the University. The Rector has the power to nominate to the Court an assessor. Previous rectors have not usually attended the meetings of the University Court, delegating their duties to the assessor but Mr Compton Mackenzie has broken this precedent.

It must be remembered that in the election of 1925 there were only 3 candidates, Conservative, Liberal, and Labour. In the election of 1928 there were 4, the addition being the Nationalist nominee, Mr R. B. Cunninghame Graham, whilst in this year's election there were 5 candidates, the New Party having entered the field.

In the election of 1928 the Nationalist campaign had been hampered by the fact that the Nationalist Association had only been in existence three or four months. On this occasion, the Nationalist Association backed by 3 years' experience, had considerably improved its organization and it was organization which won the day. Packed meetings, an open-air demonstration, a 'victory march' through the streets of the City, pipers and the Scottish Standard (hoisted over the University) were instruments in raising enthusiasm where before there was apathy, no doubt in consequence of the near proximity of the General Election. The enthusiasm reached such a pitch that in the traditional battle on the morning of the election, no one could stand up against the furious onslaught of the Nationalist Fighting Squad, who used their 'ammunition' of soot, flour, peasmeal and ochre to deadly effect and achieved a minor victory which augured well for the greater one to follow later in the day.

The election of Mr Compton Mackenzie came as a complete surprise to everyone and naturally attempts were immediately made to explain away the epochmarking defeat of Sir Robert Horne. In this connection it is to be regretted that the question of Religion has been introduced.

It is a matter of interest that before the campaign opened it was the general opinion in the University that Compton Mackenzie had little chance of success in view of his religion, yet during the campaign the question of religion was never openly raised. There were, however, one or two Nationalists who intimated privately that their religious principles would prevent them from voting for Mr Mackenzie. They would not however (being Nationalists), vote for any of the other candidates. Whether Mr Mackenzie's religion lost him many votes is uncertain but it is interesting to note that he polled 129 votes *fewer* than did Mr R. B. Cunninghame Graham in 1928, whereas Prof. Gilbert Murray polled 200 votes *more* than did the Liberal candidate, Sir Herbert Samuel, in 1928.

The suggestion that the election was influenced by the organized vote of Irish and Catholics is perfectly ridiculous and entirely without foundation. One might as well say that election was influenced by the votes of English and Episcopalians, or by the votes of Indians and Hindus.

At no time during the election campaign was there the slightest sign of any attempt to enlist the support of the small number of Catholic students for Mr Mackenzie. The speakers addressing the propaganda meetings in the Nationalist campaign included no Roman Catholic.

Certainly, Catholic students took a prominent part in the Rectorial Campaign. There were three Roman Catholics on the Liberal Committee organizing support for Prof. Gilbert Murray, one Roman Catholic on the Tory Committee supporting Sir Robert Horne, three on the New Party Committee, and one on the Nationalist Rectorial Committee. The greatest thorn in the side of the Nationalists was the R.C. Leader of the Liberals.

The Roman Catholic officials of other clubs were no less active in the campaign, furthering the interests of their respective candidates and opposing Mr Mackenzie's candidature. Following the election the Roman Catholic vice-president of the Unionist club, moving a vote of thanks to Sir Robert Horne at a political meeting in Hillhead, said that he hoped the electors would not follow the deplorable example of the students of the University (or used words to that effect).

It must be remembered that for purposes of voting, the students are divided into 4 nations, viz.:—

1. *Natio Glottiana* consisting of all students born within the County of Lanark.

2. *Natio Transforthana*. Students born within any of the counties of Orkney and Shetland, Caithness, Sutherland, Inverness, Ross and Cromarty, Nairn, Moray, Banff, Aberdeen, Perth, Angus, Kincardine, Clackmannan, Fife, Kinross, Argyll, Stirling and Dumbarton.

3. *Natio Rothseiana.* Students born in Bute, Renfrew or Ayr.

4. *Natio Loudoniana.* Students not included in other nations.

Compton Mackenzie not only had a majority over the other candidates amongst all the votes polled but also had a majority in 3 nations, viz., Glottiana, Transforthana, Rothseiana. We may say that most Catholic students belong to Nation Glottiana and Loudoniana.

The voting in the respective nations was as follows:—

	Compton Mackenzie	*Sir Robert Horne*
Natio Glottiana . . .	445	403
Natio Transforthana . . .	143	120
Natio Rothseiana . . .	168	130
Natio Loudoniana . . .	93	109
	849	762

It is significant that the "Nation" which Compton Mackenzie did not win was Loudoniana which includes English and Irish students.

(In the election of 1928 Mr R. B. Cunninghame Graham gained a majority in one nation only, viz. Transforthana.)

Mr Mackenzie's success is due mainly to the better organization of the women students who were the main cause of the defeat of Mr R. B. Cunninghame Graham. The Nationalist Association at the 1928 election had 12 women members. The present women membership is over 200.

Certainly a candidate's religion will always be a factor in elections and, knowing human nature, it would be absurd to deny that some Catholics voted for Compton Mackenzie because he is Catholic, as it would be absurd to deny that some Protestants did not vote for Compton Mackenzie because he is a Catholic.

It is denied, however, by students of all creeds and none, who voted for Compton Mackenzie that an organized Irish Roman Catholic vote influenced the election.

FACTORS INFLUENCING THE RECTORIAL ELECTION

(1) Apathy, due probably to General Election over-shadowing.

(2) Influential women's Committee, organizing women's vote.

(3) Compton Mackenzie, candidate with greatest appeal to average student with no strong political convictions.

APPENDIX B

ADDRESS

Address by Compton Mackenzie, O.B.E., B.A., LL.D., delivered in the St. Andrew's Hall on January 29th 1932, on the occasion of his Installation as Rector.

LADIES AND GENTLEMEN,

Nobody in this hall is better aware than myself how slight are my pretensions to enjoy the privilege of addressing you on this occasion, since neither fame of eloquence, nor force of action, nor weight of civic achievement offers any evidence of my fitness to deserve so remarkable an honour. Yet with that truism I must repudiate in the same breath a ruse to win your indulgence by an assumed modesty, for, however profoundly conscious I may be feeling of my own inadequacy to the Rectorial office, I have no qualms about the adequacy of the cause with which my name is linked. In that long line of greater predecessors none has stood for a greater cause, and by the greatness of that cause being myself completely overshadowed I shall confront this ordeal without further excuses.

Some of my listeners may be apprehensive that I am steering this address toward the contending streams of political argument. That is not my plan, and I shall use every endeavour to keep clear of such rough water. The political aspect of nationalism is not the only one that offers itself for discussion, and at a time when the various impulses stirring in the mind of man to set the course of the future were never more clearly discernible. I hope you will not find it unseemly for a believer in the ethics of nationalism to look beyond politics for the inspirations of a creed which is regarded by such a preponderant body of intellectual opinion with suspicion, nay with hostility, as one obstructive, retrograde, and mischievous.

Three years and three months ago to this very day I was waiting in the lounge of an Edinburgh hotel to hear the result of the previous Rectorial. I had allowed myself to hope for a vote sufficiently conspicuous to impress itself upon what was seeming at that time—three years and three months ago—the scepticism or apathy of the country. When that old cavalier, the defeated candidate, came into the lounge, holding between his fingers like a lace handkerchief the telegram from Glasgow which told how high he stood, a pale regretful dream of mine haunting the lost battlefields of our race was in that moment by a single gesture of contemporary youth magically endowed with pulsating life. If you will stop to consider the acute condition of self-consciousness to which the Scottish nation has been reduced by that experiment and adventure of yours, three years and three months ago today, I believe you will acquit that last sentence of rhetorical inflation.

And now may I say that I regard my own tenure of office as a renewed experiment and a repeated adventure? Many comments have been written about the break with tradition that your election of myself betokens, so many indeed that I hope I may be forgiven if I take advantage of the prevailing self-consciousness, which now surrounds Scotland like a mirror, to look at the Rectorial status. We can dismiss from that status, so long as I hold office, any suggestion that it denotes an honourable reward for public service. Do not misunderstand me. Election to be your Rector can never be anything except a great honour; but by so many of my predecessors the honour was already earned, whereas for myself it included the task of earning it. That was the experiment you made, the experiment of testing the practical academic value of one not too deeply involved with the larger affairs of state to devote himself to the University which he cannot indeed salute as *alma mater*, but which he hopes he may salute as foster-mother, a hallowed relationship in the long history of our race. Beyond this duty of service to which you have called me there lies another aspect of the Rectorial status. Shall I dare too greatly in claiming for it a symbolic status as the incarnate expression of the spirit of youth? Grant me this status, and, albeit with a severely chastened sense of responsibility, I shall go on to claim that you have warmed a cool experiment with the heart of adventure.

It would be presumptuous for a man of middle-age to suppose that in a single address he could touch upon all the multitudinous problems of future career, behaviour, and belief which are perplexing those who are about to impinge on the world with their own personalities. Of recent years so much stress has been laid upon the comparative simplicity and clarity of the future as it presented itself to the eyes of youth thirty years ago that I shall invite you to turn back for a few moments to the prospect before a young man or a young woman when most of you present this morning did not yet exist in the 'dark backward and abysm of time.' I venture to think that you will find many of your own problems already adumbrated. We had suffered in boyhood the shock of the South African war. The legend of British invincibility had been shattered in a week. To be sure, it had been assailed before; but there had always been Mr Gladstone to blame for any muddle overseas. That black week of defeat occurred after a long period of Unionist administration, and scarcely two and a half years after we had been dazzled by the Imperial grandeurs of the Diamond Jubliee. It would have been an exceptional boy who just before the South African war would have ventured to express a doubt of the permanency of the British Empire. It would have been an exceptional young man who after that war would not have believed that the permanency of the British Empire must depend on some radical readjustment of its component parts. The failure of British youth to respond unanimously to the attempt by Joseph Chamberlain to weld the British Empire together with tariffs may have expressed an instinctive distrust of its future, There was a rapid increase among young people of what was called 'little Englandism.' It was, perhaps, significant that the Imperialists should reproach a man who opposed the idea of Imperial expansion and development with being a 'little Englander.' The Empire might be British, but it was clear that Britain itself was England. It was certainly significant that not one of the leading 'little Englanders' was a pure-blooded Englishman. In every case he showed a Celtic predominance in his blood. Let me say in parenthesis that I am using the word Celtic in its conventional sense: there is no time for ethnical niceties. Now, why should a Celtic origin predispose a man toward 'little Englandism' when the British Empire owed as much to the Celtic as to the Saxon element in that fusion of races we call British? The explanation I have given to myself is that the Celt has always divined that the Empire was wrongly centred. Although it might be reasonable to maintain that if the capital of the British Empire had been Glasgow instead of London, the British Empire would be a more homogeneous whole today than it is, it would be absurd to pretend that the Celt has always been fully conscious of the Empire's wrong centre. His discontent, in the psychological jargon of the moment, was repressed. He either convinced himself that his race was still dominant by winning a ruling position against the Anglo-Saxon background, or he asserted himself by voting Liberal. In Scotland and in Wales liberalism took the place of nationalism, and it is noteworthy that in the more Celtic parts of England like Cornwall, Lancashire, and Cumberland liberalism was the most constant political attachment. Ireland, for reasons which it would introduce too much controversy to discuss, preferred to fight suppression from without than repression from within. When the great Liberal revival of 1906 flamed across the whole of Britain, we who were then young believed that the country had learnt its lesson from the South African war. We imagined that January election twenty-six years ago to be the real opening of the new age in succession to that age with which the death of Queen Victoria on a January evening five years earlier had come to an end. It would be unprofitable, and indeed inappropriate, on such an occasion as this to discuss the vicissitudes of liberalism since 1906. Another war lies between now and then, a war which has roughhewn a new world regardless of the most adroit political masons, a world whose ends you, under God, are called upon to shape.

There was perhaps in the 'little Englandism' of the Celt another factor, and that was the feminine instinct to make the hearth secure first. You will many of you have noticed the possibility of attributing masculinity or femininity to nations as wholes, and even within nations you will have noticed the masculine and feminine characteristics that reveal the mixture of races from which they have been evolved. It could be maintained that in this island the Celtic part provides the more feminine characteristics, the Anglo-Saxon what is pre-eminently masculine. Now France is pre-eminently a feminine nation, and the failure of England and France to understand one another is comparable to the inclination of man usually to misunderstand woman and of woman almost always to misunderstand man, as soon as either of them develops a life beyond the sphere of sexual attraction. Hence, as it seems to me, the greater ease with which Scotland has understood France. Granted that the 'auld alliance' was primarily an alliance of self-interest against a common foe, it could hardly have been maintained so long without a sympathy and mutual appreciation, the absence of which has always destroyed the possibility of a genuine and lasting alliance between France and England. You will expect me to define more particularly what I mean by feminine and masculine characteristics. To be frank, I should have to find different characteristics for different nations; but one expression of Celtic femininity may be found in an adaptableness, which is due partly to a quicker emotional response, partly to the more pliable nature that enables the Celt to resist the disintegration of a new environment, paradox though that may sound. The Scot is a greater colonist than the Englishman, because he adapts himself more readily to fresh conditions; but he and his descendants preserve their racial characteristics for generations after the Englishman has lost his. Another feminine characteristic of the Celt is a capacity for facing facts. He will decorate his realism and allow the masculine Saxon, who like man himself is much more easily deceived, to suppose him a romantic. The Celt does indeed possess the precious gift of making hard facts romantic, and in doing this he can face them when a Saxon faced by the same hard facts will sentimentalize over them and run away. To an Englishman something is what it is called: to a Scotsman something is what it is. Let me illustrate my contention with a single example. The Germans, a masculine nation, call their country the fatherland. Why do the English, another masculine nation, call theirs the motherland? As a matter of fact Britain was first called the motherland by a Scotsman, Thomas Carlyle, and in the different sense of their responsibility and in the different interpretation of their duty toward that mother can be measured the profound difference between the Englishman and the Scot.

This divagation allows me to remind you that in my youth we had to contemplate the effect of recognizing the political status of women. We had to contemplate it, moreover, through the distorting lens of militant suffragism, which was not favourable to sanity of judgment. We were confused by the ever-increasing extension of mechanical development, foreseeing the problems of unemployment it must inevitably produce sooner or later. We were beginning to feel the bad effects of popular education, and we were wondering how long must elapse before we should feel its benefit. We were bewildered by the continuously growing power of the Press. And, worst of all, we saw the immediate future darkening under the shadow of ineluctable war. To many of us the prospect of war offered an escape from what was coming to seem the vile humdrum of slavery to the machines we had created to be our servants. We desired to delete Germany not because Germany was an Imperial rival, but because a prepotent Germany seemed to us the chief menace to what was left of individual freedom. To us the triumph of Germany meant the triumph of bureacracy. Do not accept that current lie of pacificism which relates that the young men of Britain were deluded by the old into fighting. The disillusionment that succeeded was caused by the realization that war like everything else was at the mercy of the uncontrollable machinery of modern existence. Much that was good in that existence was better through the war: all that was bad was worse. And since in the present state of human evolution the bad far outweighs the good, war presents itself to our imagination as an unmitigated evil. A renewed attack upon man's freewill by a determinism based now upon the theories of science and mathematics instead of upon the speculation of a pessimistic theology coincides with a general attack upon man's liberty. In such an atmosphere the rights of small nations appear as much out of place as the rights of the individual, and although the war was nominally fought for the preservation of those rights the survival of small nations is now regarded as the prime cause of war. The dream of a United States of Europe cannot but beguile the fancy. Yet if such a federation were to offer a contribution to human progress similar to that of the United States of America, it might be considered a premature experiment by those unwilling to accept the proposition that the security of material comfort at the expense of spiritual freedom is the be-all and end-all of human existence.[1] Even if in truth our life be nothing more than a lighted candle flickering unaccountably for a few moments amid the blackness of an eternal oblivion, it is difficult to be greatly concerned about the length of the wick or the quality of the grease in which it burns. In the reaction against the last war we are at present enjoying a mood of tolerance; but the indifference of exhaustion is not real tolerance, neither is a state of peace sustained by common fear a competent substitute for a state of peace nurtured by mutual love. Those of my listeners who hope to see the towers of a new Jerusalem reflected in the heavenly blue waters of Geneva's lake must not be too readily disillusioned by the occasional failure of the League of Nations to function. The League of Nations is subject like everything else in this world to the theory that might is right, and so long as it remains ultimately subject to the will of great Powers the strength of it is the strongest link, which is not the strength of an effective chain. It is difficult, however, for one who believes in the vital importance of Celtic culture to the future of mundane civilization to believe with equal fervour in a League of Nations that does not include representatives from Scotland, Wales, or Brittany. The assembly at Geneva is not called an association of States or Governments, and that being so I cannot be accused of political prejudice in claiming the exclusion of Scotland as a grievance, though, let me quickly add, I do not believe that this resurgence of national consciousness apparent throughout contemporary Scotland is due to a series of major or minor grievances. Many of the critics of that form of nationalism called Scottish argue, and perhaps justifiably, that what some consider the injuries of Scotland are actually no more than superficial pin-pricks. Yet, when a body begins to be more than usually aware of its own existence the lightest pin-prick will be felt more sharply than the deepest stab by the flesh of a cataleptic, and even Lilliputian pin-pricks can in quantity make the most insensitive Gulliver strain to loose himself at last. However, I do not propose to take up your time with a tale of pin-pricks. I venture to suggest that you should probe your own selves more deeply than can be done by any pin-prick from without, and then decide whether the source of nationalism may not be a spiritual discontent rather than a political grievance . . . whether indeed the purest manifestation of it may not be the impulse of the individual to save his own soul.

This year we celebrate the centenary of Goethe, of the last human being great enough to live with the world for his background, yet one who was never under the necessity of moving farther away than Italy from the small German principality where he spent most of his life. Is there anybody here who believes that a universal man like Goethe could exist today? Why, a genius of ten times the demonic force of Goethe would evaporate in the conditions of modern life. Complaints about the paucity of great contemporary figures are the stock in trade of journalistic philosophers; but if progress pursues the path it is now taking before another century shall pass the greatest personality then alive will think the poorest creature alive today a richer figure than himself. It might be argued by those who desire to speed up international communication and who perceive

[1] I am glad to read that as early as 1932 I should have been in sympathy with President de Gaulle in 1967.

in geographical frontiers an impediment to the free expansion of the human mind that the potential life of man is richer today than it has ever been. Rapidity of transport, the prospect of longer life, a higher standard of comfort, a decrease in contagious diseases, extended opportunity for education and entertainment, these, they would urge, are the lavish gifts of progress, for the benefits of which a diminution of individual personality to mass standards and an obliteration of national characteristics are a small price to pay. To some the resultant standardization will render worthless all the material gains of such a progress. The task of the reactionary thinker is always more difficult than that of the progressive. He knows the evils that lie behind him, and the boldest reactionary is apt to quail at the prospect of persuading his fellows to turn back and face them again. That steady evasion of the ultimate implications of reaction was the ruin of true conservatism as a political theory. It may be that when woman begins to exert the full force of her political influence we shall see once more a genuine conservatism, so genuine indeed as to embarrass and perhaps to thwart the justifiable and necessary empiricism of man. Nationalism in its political aspect is essentially a reactionary theory of government. It is the admission by the part of an inability to adjust itself to the whole. It is reactionary too in its opposition to centralization, the upholders of which can claim that man's ascent in evolution is the result of centralizing his nervous system. Reaction, however, should be only temporary, hardly more than the ebb of the tide before it flows again. Nationalism desires to perfect the parts before it allows progress to move forward to achieve the perfect whole. The present threat to ultimate perfection is the too ready sacrifice of backward or imperfect parts to achieve a premature centralization which when achieved will diffuse not life but death. Nationalism is a demand by the soul of man to afford him leisure for the contemplation of his own destiny, to restore to him a richer personal life, and by narrowing his background to enable him to recover a measure of trust in his own significance in time and space. Such nationalism by exalting the importance of the individual might seem to promote the aggressive individualism of a nation and thus to indicate nationalism as being in very fact the chief cause of war.

But I had in mind such an enrichment of the individual through the responsibility of his personal contribution to the national life that any kind of hungry assertiveness could no longer exist. The ethical trend of the time is to bring into prominence the aspect of man as a social creature, and though I should never dream of inviting you to regard him as an anti-social creature I am prepared to argue that man's fitness to be a valuable social creature at this stage of human development is greatly exaggerated. Let me put it another way. I believe fervidly that a perfect democracy is attainable in the far future. I believe fervidly that by the Divine Will mankind will always be advancing toward that perfect democracy. What I disbelieve with equal fervour is that legal enactments can hasten the inexorable laws of human growth. The apparent success of much of our social legislation is undeniable; but the threat to free will from such interference with moral liberty, unless it can be checked, may end in the destruction of our civilization. The sordid horrors conjured into being by American prohibition are but an earnest of what we may expect universally if we surrender to the benevolent intentions of humanitarian materialists. The greatest evil of the war was its demonstration to governments that men and women will tolerate slavery.

Even education is being made an implement of servitude. The life of every human embryo performs in the womb the drama of evolution. The life of every human creature performs after birth the drama of social development; but the point capable of being reached varies with every individual, and the object of education is to ensure that every individual shall be given a chance to develop himself to that point. This if anything may be postulated as a birthright, and it may strike you as a truism not worth enunciating. Yet, at the back of every contemporary system of education lies the intention to educate a man to be of service not to himself but to others. And is not that the best intention? Not if at any stage in the process of achieving a working average crystallization is imposed. Many of you are being educated at this moment in order to educate others to be educated as you are being educated in order to educate others to be educated as you are being educated . . . and so on in a recurring decimal of futility. You and your future pupils are involved through the conditions of our culture in a common confusion of purpose. Is there one among you prospective teachers who could declare that you have sounded the gamut of human experience in the education provided for you to educate others? Is not every one of you the prisoner of a system designed to provide as much good as possible for the greatest number?

But take your education for granted and examine the various facets of our modern life that flash upon your attention. Never before was the world apparently so full of opportunities. Never before, if individual happiness and complete self-expression matter, has it been so empty. Do you plan to be a politician? Statesmanship is now a profession. You need no longer trouble to stimulate a detached and disinterested patriotism. You will not be expected to rise above place-hunting. Your career will depend on the skill with which you can mingle impudence on the hustings with modesty on the back benches. If you should be fortunate enough to represent a Scottish constituency you will be able to give up to party what was meant for country, and you will call the sacrifice a realization of larger issues. But I must not single out the profession of politics for what will be seeming a calculated sneer without making haste to present the profession of letters as an equally soulless affair. The necessity of pleasing the many is become as urgent for the man of study as for the man of state, and, when a poet's music demands as much economic consideration as his wife, the divine fire is too often regulated by the price of fuel. It was never so easy as it is nowadays to earn a living by the pen: it was never so difficult to win a life. The freedom of the artist is an illusion. Failure and success are alike synonyms of bondage. Some of you will be thinking I have chosen for a peg on which to hang the dark cloak of pessimism two professions which are essentially self-indulgent and for the choice of which a man or woman must pay the penalty of disillusionment. I chose them as more likely examples of your hearts' desire than the many professions into which you will drift because they seem to offer the most obvious way of fitting yourselves into the huge economic jigsaw of modern life. For every one of you that becomes a teacher, a physician, a lawyer, a civil servant, or what is called a man of business, because he wants to be that above everything else, there will be ten who become one or the other because it will solve a parental problem or provide a quick independence. Malicious word! Even among the technical professions, where a more deliberate choice may be presumed, the future will always be at the mercy of "rationalization", that latest poison-gas of a cynical industrialism, to which I shall apply the searing phrase of Tacitus for an earlier manifestation of barbarous expediency. *Solitudinem faciunt: pacem appellant.* They make a desert: they call it peace.

But set on one side the problem of your livelihood and contemplate the world you will presently enter, not as competitors in the struggle for existence, but as cool observers. As each year goes by that world becomes a little smaller. New achievements in rapid flight make it possible to suppose that before you die you may go round the world in eighty hours with more ease than Jules Verne's hero went round it in eighty days. Long before that, however, wireless and television will have made even such a brief voyage tiresome, for you will have already heard and seen the whole world from your own armchairs. There will be so much to titillate your attention when you are not slaving at a desk in the service of some machine invented to serve mankind that you may lose the habit of reading, and perhaps the ability to read anything except the jargon of commercial exchange. Even illustrated newspapers with a few headlines may be extinct before any of you have reached the century of years which with the perfection of hygiene most of you may reasonably expect to reach. Art in any sense in which we use the word today will be confined to the efforts of architects to pack people into their huge concrete hives, of dramatists to stimulate with coloured stereoscopic films the appetites of a satiated and incurious public, and of musicians to translate industry into rhythm by volumes of electrical sound.

The task of education will be to create various group-minds and to take care that the group-mind thus created shall never advance beyond a fixed condition, so that it may not interfere with other group-minds. Recreation will still be provided by various forms of ball games, and as members of the British group of commercial interests you will recall, not without pride, that Britons taught the rest of the world to play association football. The relentless onset of knowledge will have finally disposed of the myth of immortality; but by offering artificial rejuvenation together with a normal expectancy of a century of life, or even longer, it will justify the old proverb that a bird in the hand is worth two in the bush, I might add that there will be few actual birds left in the air, few fish left in the sea, and though by the enclosure of municipal parks a certain amount of wild life will be preserved for the amusement of those who on holidays cannot find room at the football matches, there will be few animals elsewhere except rats.

Perhaps in offering to you the prospect of attaining such an earthly paradise I am being optimistic; but be not down-hearted, your children will live to enjoy it. And if some of you cherishing a few shreds of what is scornfully known as romance resent such a future for posterity, if some of you still believe that after death you will wake to the truth of life's object on this mathematically insignificant green planet, you must weigh your private regrets against the benefits of material progress. There will be no poverty. There will be no disease. Physical pain will not be allowed. Mental agony will not be able to exist in that rich ennui. The commodities of the world will be equitably distributed; and there will be hot and cold water laid on in every room. To be sure, nobody in posterity will be able to call his soul his own; but that will not greatly matter, because by then it will have been definitely established that nobody possesses such an exclusively personal piece of property.

This picture of a new humanitarian world freed from the shackles of nationalism and individualism may seem a caricature of the ideals of those who now in an intellectual majority condemn people like myself as the romantic exponents of discredited social, political and religious theories; but it is not more unkindly distorted than the picture of a parochial nationalism which it amuses the fancy of international idealists to draw. If nationalism be something more than a sentimental emotion it must be able to fight for itself in the arena of mundane tendencies. I have too infrangible a faith in the spiritual destiny of man to propose that Scotland should retire from the struggle in order to preserve an ignominious unimportance as a small nation on the edge of the great Eurasian continent. If I suggest that she should step back it is because I believe that by stepping back and living upon herself she can leap forward to the spiritual and intellectual leadership of mankind. It is not because I believe that Scotland is dying, but because I believe that Scotland is about to live with a fullness of life undreamed of yet, that I count it the proudest moment of my career to be standing here today.

I would have wished to avoid the intrusion of personal history; but I know not how to express my belief in the value of that idea which has finally brought me to where I stand at this moment without any allusion to my own experience. I have reminded you that this year we are celebrating the centenary of the poet Goethe. We are celebrating at the same time the centenary of one nearer and dearer to ourselves, the centenary of the greatest man of letters our country has produced. Although against the universal mind of Goethe the mind of Walter Scott may seem somewhat provincial, let us remember that even Goethe was proud to acknowledge its influence upon himself. Indeed, except Byron, Scott was the only writer in English at that date to exercise a widespread influence upon continental thought. While night after night I have been struggling to put into words these reflections, of the inadequacy of which to such an occasion I am bitterly conscious, there has lain upon my table a volume whose pages are spongy and thumbed with the hard reading of careless boyhood. That volume is Scott's *Tales of a Grandfather*, presented to me in January on my seventh birthday. To the hours of youth spent in reading and re-reading those pages I owe the honour of standing here almost exactly forty-two years later, for I was born again in that book, never a page of which reminded me that a hundred and fifty sundering years lay between myself and my natural background.

It happened that soon after I became possessed of this talisman to live in the past of that race from which I sprung I travelled northward alone. It was near dusk on an evening of earliest Spring. Somebody in the railway-carriage announced that we were crossing the border, and I craned my head out of the window to enjoy the magical sensation. Down the long train came a faint sound of cheering, and from windows far ahead I could see hats being waved. An austere landscape in the fast-fading dusk, a stream of flamy smoke from an engine, a few cheers ringing thinly above the roar of a train, a waving of hats: not much perhaps, but enough for a child of eight to sit back again in a dim railway-carriage and dream over, his heart blazoned like a herald's tabard with the bright symbols of his country's life, his heart draped like a hatchment with the sombre memories of defeat upon defeat. Thence onward I lived secretly in the past of my country: but because through the closing years of the nineteenth century and through the opening years of the twentieth the future of which I was dreaming seemed as improbable as a Jacobite hope, as fruitless as a white rose reverie, I did what so many sons of Scotland were doing and abandoned myself to the pursuit of material success in that larger world which seemed to be submerging one by one all the smaller nations. Yet, some intuition of the future must have prevented my squandering any of those most intimate aspirations on the merely literary expression of them. I shall not weary you with a map of the devious paths by which through a quarter of a century of what I think I may without presumption call an existence of unusual variety and fullness I reached the point at which by other paths enough of my countrymen had already arrived to give me the assurance that I was not an isolated eccentric. The vision of Scotland which as a boy I had beheld in the *Tales of a Grandfather* was no longer a dream that faded when the book was closed; it was omnipresent in the daily round of life.

You are luckier than I am, my constituents. You have not to return to Scotland: you are there. And you have not had to maintain your faith through the shifting and deceptive colours of a dream, waking from it only in middle-age to behold the white and clear and steadfast dawn. You are young at that awakening. There is at this moment sitting in one or other of these halls a student who when ten trienniums shall have passed will stand where I stand now, and he triumphant in the golden noon of his country's new life. But that country can live only by the fullness with which every individual man and woman begins now to live with it, and for it, and by it. The measure of such a fullness will be the ruthlessness with which you expel the incomplete group-selves that are being formed by the spirit of the time and replace them at whatever the cost to your material comfort with the true and perfectible selves of the individual man and woman. We now alive in Scotland, though not necessarily therefore living, are offered the grace of sharing in the rebirth of a nation. That mysterious gift of Divine life which is continually being granted to individuals has hitherto eluded the analysis of any psychologist. We are familiar with, and with familiarity often contemptuous of, the phenomenon of religious conversion. We know that in many cases it is an hysterical phase of adolescent growth. Yet when we have disposed of a hundred cases there will be found one of which we cannot deny the permanence and fruitfulness. Among the constant characteristics of all genuine conversions is the subject's suddenly heightened sense of ordinary life and an immensely wider perception of its richness. In a single instant of revelation he is made aware of the immortal substance of things; but his secret remains incommunicable. The phenomenon of conversion, though usually accorded a religious significance, is not peculiar to religion. An artist may pass through a mental state analogous to conversion in the first moment of an imaginative conception, and when he does we call it 'inspiration'. I have seen the phenomenon of conversion among those who have been wakened to a sudden comprehension of what true nationalism is. They are changed by some mystical experience, and in loving their country they love their fellow-countrymen. It is such a love which alone can justify the reformer. Too many attempts at reformation have been made either in a spirit of hate and destructiveness or, what is ultimately more deadly, in a spirit of constructive utility. Desire the good of your fellow men, but desire it because you love them, not because a well-fed, well-clad, well-housed creature will be an economic asset to the state. Many of you present are filled with ambition to re-create a nation; but your immediate and predominant duty is to re-create yourselves, for only in re-creating yourselves will you re-create that nation.

The richness of your heritage as Scots is nowhere surpassed, and if action has taken precedence of thought, and thought itself too often turned to disputation through our history, we are perhaps for that very reason still the most virile stock in the British fusion of races. In a book recently written by a Frenchman this remark occurs: 'The English think themselves superior to every other nation in the world. And the Scots think themselves superior to the English.' If we do, it is because we believe in our greater capacity for action. Even our literature usually exhibits men of letters who seem to be thwarted men of action; but for that very reason our literature holds more promise of a golden age in the future, because in a virile race action is always apt to precede thought until such a moment comes as came once in the England of Elizabeth when action and thought were perfectly attuned. The capacity for action seems to be diminishing in England. Beware lest we too succumb to the fatigue of a long imperium and incapable of enduring the travail of re-birth, bring forth a nation stillborn. I speak to youth. Spend the richness of your heritage. Circulate its wealth all round the world. You have two languages. Use them. Gaelic is not a mixture of philology and sentiment. It is still a vital tongue and express a fundamental habit of thought. Through Gaelic you can reach Spanish and French by the same road as the Spaniard and the Frenchman trod. Add to your English the strength and savour of the Doric. It is ludicrous that Dutchmen and Russians should have so far outrun Scotsmen as linguists. It was not so before Scots copied the arrogant laziness of the English by sitting down to wait for English to become the universal language. Scotsmen have long been taking their hands round the world; but they have made a habit of leaving their tongues behind them. You have something more than two languages: you have two attitudes towards life. Use them. Do not allow both to be submerged in an attitude which whatever may be its virtues, represents neither. You have a tradition of imperial worth. Revive it effectively, or let it die, and turn back to preserve all the elements of national worth which are being threatened by the spirit of the time. I must repeat at the risk of being tiresome that no special case for the practical expression of Scottish nationalism can be presented adequately until it is grasped that the movement in Scotland is part of an impulse everywhere perceptible to obstruct the contrary tendency, which would substitute for the diversified individual standardized groups. The mighty contending forces in evolution that will sway the future of mankind for centuries are gathering to fight an Armageddon of the mind. I look at the bees and the ants and the termites, and I ask if in some hideous nightmare of a far future mankind shall be as they are.

When the Roman Empire broke up and Europe was ravaged by horde upon horde of barbarians from the East, almost the only light that shone forth into the bloodstained darkness shone from Erin and from the holy Western Isles of Alba. It may be that once again beside the Atlantic the souls of men will save themselves, and in saving themselves save the soul of man. It may be that this task is the supreme destiny of the Celtic race. I cannot but think that the rise of nationalism primarily in Glasgow is of tremendous significance to the potential force and endurance of the movement, for, though we must acclaim Edinburgh as the capital, the stern and masculine parent, Glasgow is the metropolis—the mother city. No other city is so representative of the whole country, and what is true of Glasgow is true of Glasgow University. Every criticism which is levelled against it may be levelled against Scotland itself. The virtues, faults, hopes, fears, ambitions, and dreams of the country as a whole are more completely expressed in this University than anywhere. Its very position in the midst of a crashing industrial turmoil and yet always within sound of the two voices of liberty, the voice of the sea and the voice of the hills, is a prefigurative symbol of our country's future.

A few weeks ago upon the Campsie Fells I gazed down at Glasgow. From a mass of dark cloud the sun, himself obscured from where I stood, sloped his golden ladders into that rain-washed city, which lay with all her spires and chimneys, with all her towers and tenements and sparkling roofs, like a vision of heavenly habitations. I have looked down over Athens. I have looked down over Rome. With beauty unparagoned the glory and the grandeur of the past have been spread before my eyes; but in that sight of Glasgow something was added which neither Rome nor Athens could give—the glory and the grandeur of the future, and the beating heart of a nation.

In reading through that Rectorial Address, which will be exactly 35 years old when this Octave is published in January 1968, I cannot help feeling faintly depressed by the way my apprehensions about the future are coming true. At the same time I am consoled by the hope that now at last Scotland is beginning to grasp that she must rouse herself from the sedative drugs administered by Tories and Socialists, or wither.

C.M.

APPENDIX C

REX V. COMPTON MACKENZIE

STATEMENT OF DEFENDANT

Lewis & Lewis
Ely Place,
Holborn, E.C.1.

EDWARD MONTAGU COMPTON MACKENZIE states:—

I reside at Eilean Aegas, Beauly, Inverness-shire.
I am forty-nine years of age.
I am Rector of Glasgow University.
For the last twenty-one years I have been a writer of novels and plays.
In April 1915 I was gazetted lieutenant in the Royal Marines, Royal Naval Division, and joined the staff of Sir Ian Hamilton in Gallipoli in May 1915.

In September 1915 I was invalided out of active service and was seconded for service with an Intelligence Department in Athens which was known as 'M.I.1(c)'.

In June 1916 I was appointed Military Control Officer attached to the British Legation in Athens, and on July 28th 1916 I was promoted Captain, Royal Marines.

In the spring of 1917 I was appointed Director of the Aegean Intelligence Service, with headquarters in the Island of Syra in the Cyclades.

At the end of August 1917 I was recalled to London when the organization was broken up and given long leave for reasons of health.

I subsequently went to the Island of Capri in Italy on sick leave and in July 1918 I underwent a medical examination in Italy and was pronounced still unfit for active service.

On December 31st 1918 I was demobilized.

I was decorated by the British, French, Serbian, and Greek Governments.

It was my original intention to write a long novel based on my experiences in the Near East, but owing to the publication of various works purporting to give a true history of events in Greece and matters connected with the British and French intelligence services during the War I finally in the year 1929 came to the conclusion that I should serve the cause of historical truth better by writing a straightforward narrative. This in its original plan was to be a work of

U

four volumes. The idea was then temporarily changed to make it a work of five volumes, but finally it was settled by me to be a series of four volumes.

My first volume, entitled *Gallipoli Memories*, was published by Cassell and Company in November 1929. *Gallipoli Memories* consisted chiefly of personal memories, and since I had not occupied a prominent position during the period of time covered by this book I presumed that any so-called "revelations" would lack importance. At the same time I did quote from various official documents which had come into my possession as Intelligence Officer.

For instance, on page 194 I quoted a telegram from the intelligence organization in Athens to which I was afterwards attached to "G.H.Q.I." denouncing five alleged spies supposed to be working on the Island of Tenedos.

On page 251 of the same book I quoted a letter from G.H.Q. referring to Mr Heathcote-Smith's scheme to land irregulars at Aivali in Asia Minor. Mr Heathcote-Smith was at the time referred to H.B.M. Consul at Mitylene and is at the present time H.B.M. Consul General at Alexandria, Egypt.

On page 274 I quoted a report made by me to G.H.Q. on camping grounds for troops in the Island of Mitylene.

On page 280 I quoted the whole of a memorandum I wrote on the possible methods of eliminating enemy agents from the islands off the coast of Asia Minor.

In Chapter 16 of this book, from pages 298 to 327, I gave the whole account of the action taken in regard to the alleged spies on the Island of Tenedos alluded to above, in the course of which I quoted the actual examination of the alleged agent on board H.M.S. *Canopus*. I should mention, of course, that in my references to the agents the actual name was not given, but on the other hand the name of the British Agent who dealt with the case was given.

On page 389 I quoted the telegram of a Brigade-Major from Suvla to G.H.Q.

When that book was published no comment of any sort or kind was passed upon or objection taken by the authorities to any of the intimate details I gave in *Gallipoli Memories*, on the subject of my intelligence work.

My second volume, entitled *First Athenian Memories*, was published in or about March 1931.

In the preface to this book I stated that under circumstances over which I had no control nearly every document connected with my work in the autumn of 1915 was destroyed. I intended to convey by this that I had had documents and had intended to quote them.

At the end of this preface I pointed out that "Every indiscretion and extravagance is my own, and that I have carefully avoided consulting anybody about facts or theories".

I said this in order to make it clear from the beginning that it had never been my intention to submit my volumes for the consideration of the authorities, and I expected that by this plain statement in the preface I should receive from the authorities a warning if they saw any danger in what I was proposing to do in any future volumes.

On page 79 of this volume I quoted a letter from Sir Wyndham Deedes, who was at the time referred to in charge of what was an Intelligence Branch at G.H.Q., Imbros, proposing that I should do counter-espionage work in Athens.

On page 222 I quoted the draft of a telegram sent by the Military Attaché in Athens to the Foreign Office.

On page 243 I quoted a letter from one of my agents on a matter connected with the discipline of the organization, and on page 274 I quoted an agent's report.

On page 349 I made the following announcement:—

"I instituted at 3 Visarionos a large question-book in which section chiefs were set puzzles for the sub-agents under them to solve. At the same time another large book for the answers was started, in which Tucker had to enter up the solutions. Later the answers were all incorporated in our files, and the answer book was destroyed; but the question book I still have and it may serve to give some idea of our work at this date if I reproduce some of the questions that occupied us during the last fortnight of 1915."

and I then go on to set out forty-four questions from this question-book.

On page 387 I quote from a confidential letter of mine to Sir Wyndham Deedes containing criticisms of the behaviour of Army Headquarters at Salonika and an allusion to a Foreign Office telegram.

After the publication of this volume again no objection was taken or comment passed by the authorities.

I have alluded above to various works by other authors purporting to give a history of events in Greece during the War, and more particularly of the British and French Intelligence Services. The first to which I would now call attention is *Tales of Aegean Intrigue* by J. C. Lawson, a Fellow and tutor of Pembroke College, Cambridge, published by Chatto & Windus in the year 1920.

Mr Lawson served as Intelligence Officer on the staff of the Senior Naval Officer at Suda Bay, Crete. Mr Lawson in this book published intimate details both of the counter-espionage work under my direction in Athens and an account of the way in which the Provisional Government of M. Venizelos was set up in Crete. Mr Lawson in this book made several inaccurate statements about the service under my direction, and his statements were quoted in a book *Greece and the Allies, 1914-1922* by Mr G. F. Abbott, with a preface by Admiral Mark Kerr, C.B. This book was published by Methuen in 1922, and was written with the deliberate intention of discrediting M. Venizelos and both the British and French Intelligence Services. The book was full of inaccuracies but it too has been quoted extensively, and has come to be accepted as authoritative.

It was obviously impossible for me in 1920 or 1922 to put forward my case for the British and French Intelligence Services, or the case for M. Venizelos, because I hesitated doing so owing to the shifting political situation in Greece.

It is not possible to complain that the authorities took no action in regard to Mr Abbott's book, because he was not employed in a confidential position, but with regard to Mr Lawson, he was an Intelligence Officer who obtained his funds from the organization which I directed and his statements in his book were most damaging to that organization.

I have no grievance for that reason, because I intended one day to present the simple truth, and I am not in the least suggesting that Mr Lawson was actuated by any but the best motives in trying to state the truth from his point of view, and with whatever materials might be in his possession. At the same time I must emphasize that for such intimate details to have been allowed publication so early as 1920 was actually to expose certain people to the possibility of legal action and financial loss, in addition to providing a peg for innumerable propagandist lies to be hung on in the future.

Another book I would refer to is *Souvenirs de Guerre d'un Amiral* by Vice-Amiral Dartige du Fournet. This, of course, was a French publication, but at the same time it has been widely quoted and used as a first-class authority by English propagandist writers, and it made many false statements about the Intelligence Service.

Another book I would refer to was a most scurrilous work by an American, *Constantine I. and the Greek People*. The writer was an American journalist named Paxton Hibben. This book was published in America, but freely sold in London.

I should here again point out, with regard to Mr Abbot's book, that Admiral Kerr in his preface makes use of the following expression: "Many documents which have not hitherto been before the public are quoted by him from the official originals to prove the case." Admiral Kerr, of course, is not here referring to British official documents.

The next book I wish to call attention to is *Political Memoirs 1914-17* by His Royal Highness Prince Nicholas of Greece, published by Hutchinson in 1928. Prince Nicholas's account of the Allied secret services is a complete travesty of the truth, and the following footnotes on page 99 indicate the kind of statements made:—

"1: The fact that the individuals who formed the personnel of the Franco-British Police were mostly recruited from Constantinople, Smyrna, Alexandria and Crete, rendered them still more hateful to the inhabitants of Athens. Mr Abbott gives the following analysis of the official list signed by the Prefect of the Greek Police, by the end of 1916 (when the force was disbanded):

" 'Of the 162 individuals who composed the Franco-British Police only about 60 were natives of old Greece. The list revealed among the rest: 7 pick-pockets, 8 murderers, 9 ex-brigands, 10 smugglers, 11 thieves, 21 gamblers, 20 white slave traffickers. The balance is made up of men with no visible means of subsistence.'

"2: Mr Abbott remarks: 'Unfortunately or fortunately, no authoritative record has been published of its British counterpart. Mr Lawson's account (J. C. Lawson: *Tales of Aegean Intrigue*) deals only with a provincial branch of the establishment.'

"I have personally heard many Englishmen in Greece give a very sad narrative of the doings of the Chief of the British Section of the British Secret Police. I must abstain, however, from repeating them here, as they do not constitute substantial proof."

The climax, however, in the way of misrepresentation, was reached only last year (1931) by Sir Basil Thomson, whose book *Allied Secret Service in Greece* was published by Messrs. Hutchinson a week after the publication of my book *First Athenian Memories*. The publishers claimed for Sir Basil Thomson that in his position as Director of Intelligence, 1919 to 1921, he had had access to many unpublished documents and that in one or two cases he had actually printed reproductions of secret documents. The official position which Sir Basil Thomson had occupied gave to his work a certain fictitious importance, for though in actual fact he does not quote any British official documents his book does suggest that he had opportunity of access to documents at the Quai d'Orsay.

To give an idea of the effect of Sir Basil Thomson's book on the public mind I may quote a review by Mr Cecil Roberts in the *Sphere* of April 4th 1931 in which he says "Again and again these two authors (meaning myself and Sir Basil Thomson) are thus ranged against each other, and it must be said for Sir Basil that his facts are documented and not mere expressions of opinion".

I may further quote from a review in *The Times* of March 31st, 1931, in which appeared a composite review of my book *First Athenian Memories* and Sir Basil Thomson's book, in which it is stated "it will probably be possible for him (meaning myself) to review in a series of footnotes if not in the text of his next volume some of the assertions accepted by Sir Basil as authentic accounts of events actually witnessed by Mr Mackenzie".

When I read Sir Basil Thomson's book I realized that if the truth about the diplomatic and intelligence history of Greece during 1915 was to be told with any authority it would have to be considerably documented.

Greek Memories, the third volume of my war history, was written during the spring and summer of this year, and the complete manuscript was delivered to Messrs. Cassell in July.

In the early autumn the following announcement appeared in Messrs. Cassell's list of forthcoming books, the contents of which was communicated to the Press:—

"*Greek Memories*, by Compton Mackenzie. This is the third volume of Compton Mackenzie's war memories. His original intention was to devote two volumes to the history of the year 1916, but by making this volume longer than *Gallipoli Memories* and *Athenian Memories* he has been able to include the whole of 1916 in one volume. Much of the diplomatic history of Greece during 1916 is here recorded for the first time. The volume is fully documented throughout, and is a complete answer to much untrustworthy and ill-informed propagandist and apologetic writing which has been published during the last twelve years. The scene of this volume is mainly Athens, but there are pictures of Malta, Taranto, Rome, Paris and London, and it ends in the Island of Syra in the middle of the Cyclades, which will be the setting for the final volume entitled *Aegean Memories*.

"The book contains enough incident for a dozen novels, and enough for a dozen plays. It tells for the first time the true story of the tragic events of the 1st and 2nd of December 1916; of the expulsion of the enemy Legations in November; of the expulsion of Baron Schenck and the German agents in September; of the capture of the German mail bag in August; the secret history of the Note of June 21st. The author describes this volume as a book of verbs, not adjectives.

SYNOPSIS OF CHAPTERS

This announcement was followed by a circular letter by the publishers again pointing out, *inter alia*, that the book was fully documented. This circular was quoted in numerous papers, including *The Times Literary Supplement*.

I make it clear in the preface to *Greek Memories* that many of the documents printed in the book are printed for no other reason than to give an accurate account of our dull administrative work and I actually say that they can be skipped by the reader who desires only entertainment.

In the opening chapter the report on the intelligence organization is only reprinted because it provides a convenient summary of what has already been related in detail in my preceding volume *First Athenian Memories*, which by this time was twenty months old.

On page 41 the account of work done is merely a parallel of the account already referred to on pages 349 et seq. of *First Athenian Memories*.

The dispatch from Sir Edward Grey set out on page 100 was, of course, attached to the letter which I was told by Sir Francis Elliot, the British Minister, to write in answer.

The publication of Appendix A did not seem to me to provide any information of the slightest importance sixteen years after the events, and it may be pointed out that the only part of the original document which might have had some importance, that is to say, the instructions about secret marking of passports, was destroyed before I left Syra in 1917.

In case it should be thought that the retention of my personal papers for so many years was running a risk of allowing them to fall into other hands, I may add that they have never been exposed to the slightest danger of being tampered with, and that I had given orders to my two private secretaries, in the event of anything happening to me, to destroy them immediately. Furthermore I may add that as soon as the necessary excerpts had been typed out from my private papers for the manuscript of this volume the original letters and memoranda were destroyed, so that the other material in them which I thought should not be published never can be published. I must here again reiterate that my sole object in writing these Memories was simply to tell the truth with regard to a state of affairs about which hardly any truth had been told. I have impugned nobody's honour or personal motives. Any criticism I have made is intended as criticism of people playing a part in what seemed to me a drama that was long since over.

Wherever the publication of a private individual's name might hurt even his self-esteem I have substituted a fictitious name.

The only names of agents mentioned are those whose names were handed in officially to the Greek Government by the British Legation in 1916.

Finally I would observe that for these three volumes hitherto published I have received a sum total of £1,500 in full purchase of all English rights.

The sum total of the pages of the books is 1,386. When I say that for a novel of 300 much shorter pages I should receive for Great Britain and the Colonies £1,500, and from the United States £750, it will be seen that so far from publication of my war memories being profitable they represent a contingent loss to me of not less than £7,000 which I might have earned by writing novels instead. Actually a long biography of Prince Charlie published on the same day as Greek Memories and occupying a quarter of the time in writing was paid for at the same rate—£500. It is a sixth of the length of Greek Memories.

I should add that only Gallipoli Memories was published in America, and that I received for that American publication £125.

Neither First Athenian Memories nor Greek Memories has been published in America, and it is not proposed that the fourth volume should be published there either.

There is one matter which I should mention in conclusion on the question of the Appendix to Greek Memories, that so far as any names are printed in that Appendix I had understood that the office of Military Control Officer was a public one and I have described myself in Who's Who as "Military Control Officer, 1916".

APPENDIX D

The Petition of the Fishermen and Crofter-Fishermen of the Islands of Vatersay, Barra, Eriskay, South Uist, Benbecula, and North Uist, relative to the Prohibition of Ring-Net Fishing within the Lochs and Bays of this District and within the Adjacent Area of the Minch.

We, as members of the fishing communities of the Islands of Vatersay, Barra, Eriskay, South Uist, Benbecula, and North Uist, are unanimously of the opinion that the practice of ring-net fishing should be entirely prohibited in all the lochs and bays of our district, and in all that part of the Minch adjacent to our coasts. We therefore crave that the necessary steps be taken, without any delay, in this connection.

The main grounds on which this petition is based are as follows:—

(1) The fact that all the local fishermen favour, and always have favoured, the drift-net method of fishing.

(2) Since the ring-net began to be used here by fishermen from across the Minch, the earnings of the local fishermen have fallen very considerably, owing to the increasing scarcity of the herrings. The local fishermen are agreed that this deterioration, which began soon after the ring-net was first used, here, is due almost entirely to this method of fishing.

(3) Fishermen from other districts commenced to come here after they had ruined the fishing in their own districts by using the ring-nets there. It is a fact well-known to fishermen, which any fishery officer can verify, that no herrings worthwhile have been caught in the lochs of Skye since the ring-net boats began to frequent them immediately after the end of the War.

(4) The ring-net fishermen, and indeed all who take an interest in the matter, know that the herrings round our shores are very much more difficult to catch in the ring-net than those of places such as Loch Fyne and the Firth of Clyde; where, of course, the ring-net is almost always used, to the great deterioration of the quality of the fish caught there. Since the herrings here are difficult to catch in the ring-nets, the use of ring-nets is bound to be ever so much more destructive in breaking up the herring shoals hereabouts.

(5) It is impossible for ring-net fishing and drift-net fishing to be carried on at the same time and place, without great damage arising to the drift-nets, caused by the crossing of the ring-net boats when trying to locate shoals. The ring-net fishermen often thus cut off buoys, and have been known often to destroy the nets themselves.

(6) The ring-net fishermen, and indeed all seine-net and otter-trawl fisher-

men, by their methods of fishing, break up the herring shoals. They thus prejudice the drift-net fishermen's catches, and also destroy the spawning beds.

(7) The ring-net fishermen can only work in comparatively calm weather. Thus they cannot supply the market regularly, as the drift-net fishermen can, since the latter can operate in all but the most severe weather.

(8) As all the herring fishermen of these islands use the drift-net method, it is obviously very unfair if the fishing here is going to be ruined by ring-net boats; for then the drift-net fishermen will be entirely deprived of their means of livelihood.

(9) The ring-net fishermen are so greedy to catch the herrings that they very often take within the net two or three times the amount of herrings their boats can carry. After they have taken aboard what they can manage, the rest is dumped and left to rot on the bottom, polluting the waters of the area in which the catch was made; other shoals will avoid the spot, and experience shows that the herring will not return there for many years.

Examples of such Dumping in this District:—

(a) About 6th December 1933 outside Castlebay, Barra, the motor boat *Letitia* (INS) dumped something like a hundred crans of herrings, according to various estimates including that of her own crew.

(b) In the beginning of December 1932, at Poll Choire Bhig, Loch Skipport, South Uist, the motor boat *Maggie MacLean* (CY, Bernera, Harris) dumped what her skipper estimated to be about two hundred crans of herrings; and would not even give them to the local fishermen who would have done something with them in order to prevent such an enormous waste. This case is well known, as the local fishermen, and some Lochboisdale and Eriskay boats were there at the time. The result is of course that no herrings have been found in Poll Choire Bhig since that time.

(c) There was good fishing in Loch Eynort, South Uist, inside the narrow channel known as Sruth Beag in the winter season of 1925-1926. Again in the winter of 1926-1927 the same place was full of herrings, and there were many local boats and herring drifters from East Coast there. But the ring-net boats were also there in force that winter, and dumped so many herrings that the whole place was polluted with putrid fish so that the people could not come out of their houses owing to the smell of decaying herrings. No herrings have been caught there since that time. The local people petitioned the Fishery Board twice, and were finally told that they could prohibit the use of the ring-net in that place altogether for reasons of sanitation.

The drift-net fishermen of this district have no objection whatever to stranger fishermen coming here provided that they use the same gear as the local fishermen use, and do not interfere with the drift-net fishing or damage the nets or gear of the drift-net boats. But it is essential that the fishermen of these islands should be protected from the destructive methods of the ring-net boats immediately, or they will soon be forced to give up fishing entirely. Ring-net fishing has been a constant source of trouble here, especially during the winter fishing, and in the early summer as well. Your Petitioners accordingly crave that immediate steps should be taken to make ring-netting illegal in this district so as to protect the interests of the local drift-net fishermen and give them a reasonable chance of making a living.

15 February 1934.

1967. Of course nothing was done to keep the ring-netters out of the Minch, and the drift-net fishing was ruined. However, the ring-netters must now face the prospect of devastating competition from new boats employing purse-nets. Their turn has come to petition the authorities with no more likelihood of being helped than the drift-netters of thirty years ago.

APPENDIX E

1938

re THE WINDSOR TAPESTRY

JOINT OPINION

METCALFE COPEMAN & PETTEFAR
3 & 4 Clements Inn, W.C.2.

rc THE WINDSOR TAPESTRY

OPINION

We are asked to advise whether those responsible for the writing and publication of a book to be called *The Windsor Tapestry* are in danger of prosecution for criminal libel. Generally speaking, as pointed out by the late Professor Kenny in his *Outlines of Criminal Law*, "Judges of the present day desire to see Indictments for defamation restricted to those cases in which the libel is aggravated either by its intrinsic gravity or by its obstinate repetition". It is therefore necessary to look in the manuscript for passages which may be considered (*a*) libellous, and (*b*) libellous to the degree of such intrinsic gravity that the Government, through the Director of Public Prosecution, would think it necessary to prosecute those responsible.

Assuming that the alterations suggested by us in consultation with the author, Mr Compton Mackenzie, and those instructing us, are carried out, we are of opinion that there is negligible likelihood of such a prosecution.

Such a work as this must necessarily be partly fact and partly comment. To the extent that it is fact, in our view the truth of those facts would constitute the fullest defence to any prosecution for libel, on the ground that though they are true, it is obviously pro bono publico that they should be made known. To the extent that the book consists of comment, in our view, the comments made are always sufficiently justified by the facts to be described as fair, thereby escaping the category of 'intrinsic gravity'.

From the point of view of the prosecution it would, in our view be disastrous to prosecute and fail, and we think that the Director of Public Prosecutions would be unlikely to institute criminal proceedings unless he felt reasonably sure of success.

In view of these considerations, we are of opinion that so far as criminal libel is concerned, although it is impossible to say with certainty what view the authorities may take, those responsible for the publication of this book have little to fear.

G. B. McCLURE
X—— Y——

22nd June 1938
Temple

APPENDIX F

UNE FÉTE D'AMITIÉ FRANCO-BRITANNIQUE

Le

Club des Cent
reçoit le
SAINTSBURY CLUB

PARIS
18-19 JUIN
1938

LE PRÉ CATALAN

Sous la présidence de
Son Excellence Sir ERIC PHIPPS
Ambassadeur de Grande Bretagne

DINER

Cantaloup frappé
Consommé de Volaille double en tasse
Timbale de Homard Newburg
Selle de veau Orloff
Mousseline Soubise
Velouté de Champignons
Chaufroid de Caneton à la Voisin
Cœur de Romaine en salade
Fromages
Fraises au granité d'Ananas
Tous les Fruits

VINS

Vieux Porto
Riquewishr Pinot 1934
Château Palmer Blanc 1927
Château Mouton-Rothschild 1928
Beaune 1923
Heidsieck Monopole 1928 (en jéroboam)
Perrier Jouet 1928 (en double-magnum)
Grande Fine Champagne

18 Juin 1938

LE PAVILLON ROYALE

Avant le Grand Steeple d'Auteuil

DÉJEUNER

Saumon de la Loire froid
à la Parisienne
Ortolans des Landes en cassolettes
Fonds d'artichauts Mornay
Selle d'agneau de pré salé Venaison
Salade de laitues
Glace aux fruits d'or
Mignardises
Fraises des bois à la crême
Café

VINS

Blanc de Blanc 1934
Clos de Tart 1919
Veuve Clicquot brut 1928
Grande Fine Champagne

19 Juin 1938

LE YACHT MOTEUR CLUB

Réception offerte par
Monsieur LAURENS-FRINGS

Président

du   du
Club des Cent   *Y. M. C. F.*

Les Harnois de gueule
Champagne Perrier-Jouet 1926

DINER

Tortue claire
Homard à l'Ecossaise
Poularde de Bresse rôtie
Pommes nouvelles au beurre
Asperges d'Argenteuil
Fromages
Fruits de Saison
Café
Liqueurs

VINS

Traminer 1932
Veuve Clicquot 1926
G. H. Mumm 1926—Pommery-Greno 1926

19 Juin 1938

TO OUR BRITISH GUESTS

It affords us great pleasure, to greet in you the distinguished representatives of the illustrious Saintsbury Club on your short visit, much too short to really comply with our heart's desire.

We still have present to our memory the spontaneous and charming hospitality which you extended to us when a few months ago, we answered your kind invitation.

We sincerely hope that, under the leadership of your estimeed Counsel in well-eating and drinking, Monsieur André Simon, you will follow your natural inclination for good fellowship, and very soon again and often let us enjoy your company, and thus co-operate in cimenting the ties that bind us together as brothers in gastronomy, in a most satisfying 'entente cordiale'.

And now, Gentleman,
　　If you run, run for your life!
　　If you swear, swear for your Country.
　　If you lie, lie for a pretty woman.
　　AND IF YOU DRINK,
　　　　DRINK WITH US!

LE CLUB DES CENT